A PLUME BOOK

EMOTIONAL FIRST AID

GUY WINCH, PH.D., has a private practice in Manhattan, where he helps patients learn to apply emotional first aid to their own lives. His books, including *Emotional First Aid* and *The Squeaky Wheel*, have been translated into fifteen languages. A member of the American Psychological Association, Dr. Winch is also an in-demand keynote speaker. Occasionally, he can also be seen practicing stand-up comedy at clubs in and around New York.

Praise for *Emotional First Aid*

"Dr. Guy Winch's practical, clever, and clearheaded book offers proven remedies for the myriad pains of daily life. Timely application will prevent small- and medium-size emotional ills from becoming bigger ones—and that's just what the psychotherapist ordered."
—Jeanne Safer, Ph.D., author of *Cain's Legacy: Liberating Siblings from a Lifetime of Rage, Shame, Secrecy, and Regret*

"The advice Winch offers in this refreshingly useful book is both practical and practicable—down-to-earth techniques that really can bring relief when things feel like they're falling apart."
—Anneli Rufus, author of *The Big Book of Low Self-Esteem*

"[An] outstanding work . . . This smart tome is a valuable addition to the self-help oeuvre." —*Publishers Weekly*

"Excellent for all disgruntled souls out there." —*Library Journal*

"Imagine . . . after a day filled with hassles, setbacks, and hurt feelings (a typical day, in other words), you open your psychological medicine cabinet and take out some soothing and healthy emotional first aid. . . . This is what we are all seeking, and this is what 'self-help' should mean—effective and healing self-care."

—Meg Selig, author of *Changepower!*
37 Secrets to Habit Change Success

"Insightful and practical . . . a book with depth and relevance."

—*New York Journal of Books*

"Reading Guy Winch's excellent new book proved to be a surprisingly powerful experience."

—Dr. Susan Heitler, PowerofTwoMarriage.com

"Many of the ordinary emotional lows people experience can be treated with one or more simple do-it-yourself strategies. Once you figure out which treatment to apply, the results can build your immunity and your psychological health for years to come."

—Susan Krauss Whitbourne, Ph.D., author of
The Search for Fulfillment

Emotional First Aid

||||||||||||||||||||||||||||||||

HEALING REJECTION, GUILT, FAILURE, AND OTHER EVERYDAY HURTS

Guy Winch, Ph.D.

A PLUME BOOK

PLUME
Published by the Penguin Group
Penguin Group (USA) LLC
375 Hudson Street
New York, New York 10014

USA | Canada | UK | Ireland | Australia | New Zealand | India | South Africa |China
penguin.com
A Penguin Random House Company

First published in the United States of America by Hudson Street Press, a member of
Penguin Group (USA) LLC, 2013
First Plume Printing 2014

REGISTERED TRADEMARK—MARCA REGISTRADA

THE LIBRARY OF CONGRESS HAS CATALOGED THE HUDSON STREET PRESS EDITION
AS FOLLOWS:
Winch, Guy.
    Emotional first aid : practical strategies for treating failure, rejection, guilt, and
other everyday psychological injuries / Guy Winch, Ph.D.
      pages cm
    Includes bibliographical references and index.
    ISBN 978-1-59463-120-7 (hc.)
    ISBN 978-0-14-218107-2 (pbk.)
    1. Self-help techniques. 2. Emotions. 3. Mental health. 1. Title.
    BF632.W556 2013
    158.1—dc23   2013005852

Printed in the United States of America
10 9 8 7 6 5

Set in Minion Pro

Contents

Introduction

Ask a ten-year-old what you should do if you catch a cold and the child would immediately recommend getting into bed and drinking chicken soup. Ask what you should do if you get a cut on your knee and the child would advocate cleaning it (or using antibacterial ointment) and bandaging it. Children also know that if you break a bone in your leg you need to get a cast on it so it mends correctly. If you then asked why these steps were necessary they would tell you that treating such injuries helps them heal and prevents them from getting worse, that colds can turn into pneumonia, that cuts can become infected, and that if broken bones heal incorrectly you'll have trouble walking once the cast comes off. We teach our children how to take care of their bodies from a very young age and they usually learn such lessons well.

But ask an adult what you should do to ease the sharp pain of rejection, the devastating ache of loneliness, or the bitter disappointment of failure and the person would know little about how to treat these common psychological injuries. Ask what you should do to recover from low self-esteem or loss and trauma and adults would be equally challenged. Ask how you might deal with intrusive ruminations or nagging guilt and you are likely to be met with sheepish looks, feet shuffling, and a pointed effort to change the subject.

Some might confidently suggest the best remedy is to talk about our feelings with friends or family members, certain that no mental health professional in his or her right mind would object to talking about feelings. But while discussing our feelings might offer relief in some situations, it can actually be damaging in others. Pointing out these dangers usually causes another round of sheepish looks, feet shuffling, and a pointed effort to change the subject.

The reason we take little to no purposeful action to treat the psychological wounds we sustain in daily life is because we lack the tools with which to manage such experiences. True, we could seek the counsel of a mental health professional in such situations, but doing so is often impractical, as most of the psychological wounds we sustain in life are not serious enough to warrant professional intervention. Just as we wouldn't pitch a tent outside our family doctor's waiting room at the first sign of a cough or sniffle, we can't run to a therapist every time we get rejected by a romantic prospect or whenever our boss yells at us.

But while every household has a medicine cabinet full of bandages, ointments, and pain relievers for treating basic *physical* maladies, we have no such medicine cabinet for the minor *psychological* injuries we sustain in daily life. And sustain them we do, just as frequently as we do physical ones. Each of the psychological wounds covered in this book is extremely common and each of them is emotionally painful and potentially psychologically damaging. Yet, until now, we've had no conventional means to ease the pains, soothe the aches, and relieve the distresses of these events despite the regularity with which they occur in our lives.

Applying emotional first aid to such injuries can prevent many of them from affecting our mental health and emotional well-being going forward. Indeed, many of the diagnosable psychological conditions for which we seek professional treatment could be prevented if we applied emotional first aid to our wounds when we first sustained them. For example, a ruminative tendency can quickly grow into anxiety and depression, and experiences of failure and rejection can easily lead to erosions in our self-esteem. Treating such injuries not only accelerates their healing but also helps prevent complications from developing and mitigates the severity of any that do arise.

Of course, when the psychological injury is serious, emotional first aid treatments should not replace seeing a mental health professional any more than having a well-stocked medicine cabinet abolishes the need for physicians and hospitals. But while we know our limitations when it comes to our physical health, the same is not true of our mental health. Most of us can recognize when a cut is deep enough to require stitches, we can usually tell the difference between a swollen bruise and a broken bone, and we tend to know when we're dehydrated to the point of needing an infusion of plasma. But when it comes to our psychological wounds, we lack not only the wherewithal to do anything about them but also the ability to identify when they require professional intervention. As a result, we often neglect our psychological wounds until they become severe enough to impair our functioning. We would never leave a cut on our knee unattended until it compromised our ability to walk, but we leave psychological wounds unattended all the time, often until they literally prevent us from moving forward in life.

This discrepancy between our general competence in treating assaults to our physical health and our complete incompetence where our mental health is concerned is extremely unfortunate. If no such emotional first aid techniques existed, if it were impossible to treat these psychological wounds, this state of affairs might be tolerable. But such is not the case. Recent progress in numerous areas of psychological research has unveiled many treatment options for exactly the kinds of psychological injuries we sustain most often.

Each chapter in this book describes a common and everyday psychological injury and the various emotional first aid techniques we can apply to ease our emotional pain and prevent the problem from becoming worse. These science-based techniques can all be self-administered, much as we self-administer first aid for our physical ailments, and they can also be introduced to our children. The techniques in this book represent the future staples of our psychological medicine cabinets, the mental health medical kits we can carry with us as we go through life.

During my years studying clinical psychology in graduate school I was frequently criticized for giving my patients specific and concrete suggestions for how they might alleviate their emotional pains. "We're here to do deep psychological work," one supervisor used to admonish me, "not to dispense psychological aspirin—it doesn't exist!"

But offering immediate relief and doing deep psychological work are not mutually exclusive. I believe everyone should have access to emotional first aid treatments, just as they should any other treatments for dressing emotional wounds. Over the years, I've made it a practice to distill innovative research findings into practical suggestions, treatments my patients can apply to the emotional hurts of daily living. I've done so for one main reason— they work. For some years now, my patients, friends, and family members have been urging me to collect these emotional first aid treatments into a book. I decided to do so because it's time we took our mental health more seriously. It's time we practiced mental health hygiene just as we do dental and physical hygiene. It's time we all owned a psychological medicine cabinet with the emotional equivalents of bandages, antibacterial ointments, ice packs, and fever suppressants.

After all, once we know psychological aspirins do exist, we'd be foolish not to use them.

How to Use This Book

The chapters in this book cover seven common psychological injuries we sustain in daily life: rejection, loneliness, loss, guilt, rumination, failure, and low self-esteem. Although they were written as stand-alone chapters I advise reading the book in its entirety. Even if some of the chapters have no immediate relevance, knowing the kinds of psychological injuries we might sustain in various situations will help us recognize them when we or our friends and family members encounter them in the future.

Each chapter in this book is divided into two sections. The first describes the specific psychological wounds each injury inflicts—including those we often fail to recognize. For example, we might think it obvious that loneliness causes emotional pain, but we might not be aware that untreated loneliness has such serious implications for our physical health that it can shorten our life expectancy. Also less apparent is the fact that lonely people often develop self-defeating behaviors that lead them to unconsciously push away the very people who could alleviate their suffering.

The second section of each chapter presents the treatments readers can apply to each of the wounds discussed in the first section. I provide general treatment guidelines to clarify how and when each of the recommended techniques should be administered as well as treatment summaries and "dosage" recommendations. Because this book represents a psychological medicine cabinet and is by no means intended to function as a substitute for medical or psychological care by a trained professional, I end each chapter with guidelines for when readers should consult a trained mental health specialist.

The suggestions in this book are based on top-notch scientific studies that have been subjected to peer review procedures and published in first-rate academic journals. References for each of the studies and treatments can be found in the endnotes.

Emotional First Aid

||||||||||||||||||

CHAPTER 1

REJECTION

The Emotional Cuts and Scrapes of Daily Life

O f all the emotional wounds we suffer in life, rejection is perhaps the most common. By the time we reach middle school we've already been turned down for play dates, picked last for teams, not invited to birthday parties, dropped by old friends who joined new cliques, and teased or bullied by classmates. We finally get through the gauntlet of childhood rejections only to discover that an entirely new array of rejection experiences awaits us as adults. We get turned down by potential dates, refused by potential employers, and snubbed by potential friends. Our spouses rebuff our sexual advances, our neighbors give us the cold shoulder, and family members shut us out of their lives.

Rejections are the psychological cuts and scrapes that tear our emotional skin and penetrate our flesh. Some rejections are so severe they create deep psychological gashes that "bleed" profusely and require urgent attention. Others are like emotional paper cuts that sting quite a bit but bleed only a little. One might expect that, given the frequency with which we encounter rejection in one form or another, we'd have a clear understanding and appreciation of its impact on our emotions, thoughts, and behaviors. But such is not the case. We drastically underestimate the pain rejections elicit and the psychological wounds they create.

The Psychological Wounds Rejection Inflicts

Rejections can cause four distinct psychological wounds, the severity of which depends on the situation and our emotional health at the time. Specifically, rejections elicit emotional pain so sharp it affects our thinking, floods us with anger, erodes our confidence and self-esteem, and destabilizes our fundamental feeling of belonging.

Many of the rejections we experience are comparatively mild and our injuries heal with time. But when left untreated, even the wounds created by mild rejections can become "infected" and cause psychological complications that seriously impact our mental well-being. When the rejections we experience are substantial, the urgency of treating our wounds with emotional first aid is far greater. This not only minimizes the risk of "infections" or complications but also accelerates our emotional healing process. In order to administer emotional first aid and successfully treat the four wounds rejection causes, we need a clear understanding of each of them and a full appreciation of how our emotions, thought processes, and behaviors are damaged when we experience rejections.

1. Emotional Pain: Why Even Stupid Rejections Smart a Lot

Imagine you're sitting in a waiting room with two other strangers. One of them spots a ball on the table, picks it up, and tosses it to the other. That person then smiles, looks over, and tosses the ball to you. Let's assume your tossing and catching abilities are up to the task. You toss the ball back to the first person, who quickly tosses it to the second. But then instead of tossing the ball to you, the second person tosses it back to the first person, cutting you out of the game. How would you feel in that situation? Would your feelings be hurt? Would it affect your mood? What about your self-esteem?

Most of us would scoff at the idea. *Two strangers didn't pass me a stupid ball in a waiting room, big deal! Who cares?* But when psychologists investigated this very situation, they found something quite remarkable. We do care, far more than we realize. The ball-tossing scenario is a well-researched psychology experiment in which the two "strangers" are actually research confederates. The "subject" (who thinks they are all waiting to be called for an entirely different experiment) always gets excluded after the first or second round of ball tossing. Dozens of studies have demonstrated that people consistently report feeling *significant emotional pain* as a result of being excluded from the ball-tossing game.

What makes these findings remarkable is that compared to most of the rejections we experience in life, being excluded by two strangers tossing a ball is about as mild as rejection gets. If such a trivial experience can elicit sharp emotional pain (as well as drops in mood and even self-esteem) we can begin to appreciate how painful truly meaningful rejections often are. That is why getting dumped by someone we're dating, getting fired from our job, or discovering that our friends have been meeting up without us can have such a huge impact on our emotional well-being.

Indeed, what separates rejection from almost every other negative emotion we encounter in life is the magnitude of the pain it elicits. We often describe the emotional pain we experience after a significant rejection as analogous to being punched in the stomach or stabbed in the chest. True, few of us have actually been stabbed in the chest, but when psychologists asked people to compare the pain of rejection to physical pains they had experienced, they rated their emotional pain as equal in severity to that associated with natural childbirth and cancer treatments! As a counterpoint, consider that other emotionally painful experiences, such as intense disappointment, frustration, or fear, while highly unpleasant, pale in comparison to rejection when it comes to the sheer visceral pain they cause.

But why do rejections hurt so much more than other emotional wounds?

The answer lies in our evolutionary past. Humans are social animals; being rejected from our tribe or social group in our pre-civilized past would have meant losing access to food, protection, and mating partners, making it extremely difficult to survive. Being ostracized would have been akin to receiving a death sentence. Because the consequences of ostracism were so extreme, our brains developed an early-warning system to alert us when we were at risk for being "voted off the island" by triggering sharp pain whenever we experienced even a hint of social rejection.

In fact, brain scans show that the very same brain regions get activated when we experience rejection as when we experience physical pain. Remarkably, the two systems are so tightly linked that when scientists gave people acetaminophen (Tylenol) before putting them through the dastardly ball-tossing rejection experiment, they reported significantly less emotional pain than people who were not given a pain reliever. Sadly, other negative emotions like embarrassment do not share these characteristics, rendering Tylenol ineffective when we get the date wrong for our office Halloween party and show up to work dressed like Marge Simpson.

Rejection Rejects Reason

Martha and Angelo came to couples therapy to deal with frequent arguments about Angelo's inability to seek new employment after he had been downsized by his company six months earlier. "I'd been with that shipping company twenty years," Angelo explained. The hurt was still apparent on his face. "Those people were my friends! How could they do this to me?"

While Martha had been sympathetic initially, she was becoming increasingly frustrated about Angelo's inability to recover from the emotional blow and start looking for a new job. It quickly became apparent that Angelo was as frustrated with himself as Martha was. He tried to motivate himself and talk himself into making efforts, but he simply felt too consumed by emotional pain. He tried reasoning with himself to let go of the hurt and "get over it," but nothing worked.

Many of us find it difficult to talk ourselves out of the hurt we feel when we experience rejection. One of the reasons rejection is often so devastating is that our reason, logic, and common sense are usually ineffective when it comes to mitigating the pain we feel. For example, when scientists told participants who had been excluded in a computerized version of the ball-tossing experiment (called Cyberball) that their exclusion had been rigged, finding out the rejection wasn't even "real" did little to ease the pain they felt. Scientists are a tenacious bunch, so they told a different set of participants that the people who'd excluded them were members of the Ku Klux Klan. Surely rejection would hurt less if we despised the people who rejected us. But nope, it still hurt just as much. They even tried replacing the cyber*ball* with an animated cyber-*bomb* that was programmed to explode at random, "killing" whoever had possession of it at the time. But subjects felt just as much rejection pain when they were not passed a cyberbomb as they were when they were not passed a cyberball.

Rejections impact our ability to use sound logic and think clearly in other ways as well. For example, merely being asked to recall episodes of acute rejection was sufficient for people to score substantially lower on subsequent IQ tests, tests of short-term memory, and measures of reasoning ability and decision making.

Romantic rejections are especially potent when it comes to scrambling our brains and tampering with our good judgment, even when they occur extremely early in a relationship or, indeed, before a "relationship" even exists (breakups after long or serious relationships are covered in chapter 3). One young man I worked with flew to Europe to "surprise" a woman he had met on a week-long summer vacation despite her clearly telling him she was not interested in pursuing a relationship. Still smarting from that rejection, the young man convinced himself that his impromptu "romantic gesture" would "melt her heart and change her mind for sure!" The woman was so startled when he showed up at her front door at an indecent hour of the morning the only thing she changed was the locks. The desperation we feel in the wake of certain rejections can drive many of us to confuse a romantic gesture with a creepy one.

2. Anger and Aggression: Why Doors Get Broken and Walls Get Punched

Rejections often trigger anger and aggressive impulses that cause us to feel a powerful urge to lash out, especially at those who rejected us, but in a pinch, innocent bystanders will do. One group of innocent bystanders that know this all too well are the countless doors and walls that have had fists punched through them by freshly rejected men, and at times women (although those made of brick and solid wood usually get the last laugh). Keeping such dangers in mind is equally important when we're the ones doing the rejecting. Even if the person we plan to reject is a model of kindheartedness, our Hummel figurine collection might still be in grave danger.

Lest we judge the wall punchers and figurine breakers too harshly, we should consider that even the most inconsequential rejections stir up highly aggressive tendencies in the best of us. For example, after a game of Cyberball, people were given the option to blast an *innocent* participant with unpleasant white noise (someone they were explicitly told had not been part of the ball-tossing situation). Rejected subjects blasted innocent participants with much louder and much lengthier durations of noise than nonrejected subjects did. In different series of studies, rejected subjects forced innocent participants to eat four times as much hot sauce as nonrejected subjects did, to consume terrible-tasting beverages, and to listen to extremely aversive audiotapes. In case you're wondering how often the scientists behind such experiments get recruited by reality TV executives to devise disgusting challenges for their game show contestants, your guess is as good as mine.

Unfortunately, our tendency to respond to rejection with anger has far darker and more serious manifestations as well. Severe and repeated experiences of rejection can elicit the kind of aggression that goes far beyond the realm of white noise or hot sauce. When psychological wounds of this nature are left untreated they quickly become "infected" and threaten serious damage to a person's mental health. Stories of injurious and self-injurious aggressive behaviors following rejections are frequently in the news. Jilted lovers who seek revenge, fired postal workers who . . . "go postal," and the terrible epidemic of bullied children who take their own lives are just a few such examples of what happens when the psychological wounds caused by chronic and severe rejections remain untreated.

In 2001 the office of the surgeon general of the United States issued a report that found social rejection to be a greater risk factor for adolescent violence than gang membership, poverty, or drug use. Feelings of rejection also play a huge role in violence between romantic partners. Many incidents of violence are triggered by jealousy and suspicions of infidelity, which are tightly related to feelings of rejection. When scientists examined 551 cases in which men killed their wives, they found that almost half occurred in response to real or imminent separations. Indeed, men who murder their wives often later admit to being unable to deal with the rejection they felt.

Studies of school shootings, including the 1999 Columbine tragedy, found that thirteen of fifteen incidents involved perpetrators who had experienced significant interpersonal rejection and ostracism from schoolmates. In many cases, shooters specifically targeted students who had bullied, teased, or rejected them in the past, often seeking them out first.

We all experience rejection to some degree and thankfully only a tiny minority of us end up in the headlines as a result. However, the link between rejection and aggression is strong, and it is extremely important to recognize that the pain rejections cause can spur some of us to behave in ways we never would otherwise.

3. Damaged Self-Esteem: Kicking Ourselves When We're Already Down

Experiencing profound or repeated rejection is extremely harmful to our self-esteem. In fact, the mere act of recalling a previous rejection is sufficient to cause a temporary drop in feelings of self-worth. Unfortunately, the pounding our self-esteem takes rarely stops there. We often compound our rejection experiences by becoming extremely self-critical—essentially kicking ourselves when we're already down. Responding this way is common but it can easily cause the psychological cuts and scrapes of the original rejection to become "infected" and consequently to have a truly debilitating effect on our mental health.

Angelo lost his job at the shipping company because his entire department got eliminated in a cost-cutting measure, yet he perceived the rejection as highly personal ("Those people were my friends! How could they do this to me?"). Personalizing the rejection made Angelo feel as though he was unwanted by his friends and abandoned by his long-time colleagues. He avoided contact with anyone from his former company, as he was convinced that communicating with them would only expose him to the disapproval, disappointment, or disrespect they felt toward him, despite such fears being utterly unfounded. When friends and coworkers did reach out to him (which of course they did), he avoided responding to their e-mails and voice messages even when they contained leads for other jobs. After several months, his friends stopped reaching out entirely. In Angelo's mind, their eventual silence only justified his fear that they'd never cared for him in the first place.

Angelo is not alone. We all have a tendency to take rejections too personally and to draw conclusions about our shortcomings when there is little evidence that such assumptions are warranted. Think back (even if way back) to when you were rejected by someone romantically. Did you find yourself listing everything that might be wrong with you? Did you fault yourself for not being attractive enough or sophisticated enough or smart enough or rich enough or young enough, or all of the above? Did you think, "This always happens to me!" or "No one will ever love me!" or "I'm never going to find someone!" Personal rejections are rarely as personal as we experience them to be, and even when they are, they rarely involve such a sweeping indictment of our flaws.

In addition to unnecessarily personalizing rejection, we also tend to overgeneralize it even when we have no grounds to do so (for example, by thinking, "This always happens to me" or "I'm never going to find someone") or to engage in needless self-criticism by assuming we could have prevented the rejection had we done something differently. Self-criticism is especially problematic following romantic rejections, as many of us spend hours analyzing everything we said or did in a desperate search for our elusive "critical wrong move" (e.g., "Why did I wait so long before calling her?" "I should never have had that last drink!" or "Maybe it was too soon to show her my Elmer Fudd underwear collection").

In reality, critical wrong moves are exceedingly rare (although, granted, there's probably never a *right* time to show a woman one's Elmer Fudd underwear collection). The most frequent reasons we get turned down as romantic prospects (or as job applicants) are because of a lack of general chemistry, because we don't match the person's or company's specific needs at that time, or because we don't fit the narrow definition of who they're looking for—not because of any critical missteps we might have made nor because we have any fatal character flaws.

These errors in thinking serve little useful purpose and they only deepen the pain we already feel by adding unnecessary and highly inaccurate self-recriminations that further damage our already battered self-esteem. Rejections hurt enough—we certainly don't need to add salt to our own wounds or kick ourselves once we're already down.

4. Threatening Our Need to Belong: People Who Need People Are *Not* the Luckiest People

One of the reasons our self-esteem is so vulnerable to rejection is that we are wired with a fundamental need to feel accepted by others. When our need to belong remains unsatisfied for extended periods of time, either because of the rejections we've experienced or because we lack opportunities to create supportive relationships, it can have a powerful and detrimental effect on our physical and psychological health.

Some of us have such challenging life circumstances that satisfying our need to belong can present a real challenge. David, a young man I worked with some years ago, faced far greater hurdles than most in this regard. His story taught me that once we've suffered profound and repeated rejection over our lifetimes, finding our place in the world and feeling as though we belong can be the hardest struggle of all.

David was born with a rare genetic illness that typically affects multiple bodily systems and causes a significantly shortened life span (at the time, most children born with the illness died before reaching the age of twenty). Although David had a relatively mild form of the disorder, he still required numerous surgeries and hospitalizations throughout his childhood. David's illness affected not just his health but his appearance as well. Musculoskeletal problems made his gait unsteady and he had noticeable irregular facial characteristics, such as a flattened upper lip, a prominent lower jaw, and significant dental trauma. Further, problems regulating saliva meant he was prone to drooling.

Children born with more severe forms of David's illness often have significant physical disabilities and life-threatening medical problems that prevent them from attending regular schools. David's milder condition (and the fact that intelligence is not affected) meant he was one of the few children with the disorder who was able to attend a local elementary and high school. But for David, this "blessing" came at a terrible price. His appearance, his lack of coordination, and his tendency to drool when he concentrated led him to experience cruel and daily rejections from his peers throughout his school years.

David was never invited to parties, he had virtually no friends, and he spent every lunch hour and recess sitting alone. His lack of coordination and muscle weakness prevented him from participating in after-school or extracurricular sport activities with the other neighborhood boys. His few attempts to explore after-school activities for children with disabilities ended poorly because his comparative "health" made him stand out (at times, literally) and rendered him a poor fit for such programs as well. As a result, David's basic need to belong remained entirely unmet throughout his childhood and teen years and the regular (and often harsh) rejections he suffered caused him tremendous emotional pain.

I met David soon after he graduated from high school and a few months before he was to start classes at a local community college. Although David was excited to attend college he was terrified at the prospect of facing a novel round of painful rejections from a new cadre of peers. His well-meaning parents assured David that college students were more "mature" and more accepting than high school kids were and that he would have a far easier time "fitting in" than he did in high school. But a lifetime of rejection had devastated David's self-esteem and he feared otherwise. "They're going to take one look at me and turn away," he said in our first session. "And those will be the nice ones. The mean ones will turn away and laugh behind my back."

I agreed with David that first impressions might be problematic for him (I saw no point in denying what a lifetime of experience had already demonstrated), so I asked him whether he had a plan to correct those first impressions when opportunities arose to do so. We started discussing how he might handle potential social interactions and it quickly became clear that David's social skills were severely underdeveloped. Years of alienation and a dearth of social experiences meant David often struggled to come up with the right thing to say or do in common situations, something he readily acknowledged.

We decided to spend the summer working on his social skills. We identified potential social situations and role-played how he might handle them. David was also willing to accept that any initial harsh or rejecting reactions he received from college classmates would likely not be strictly personal, but rather a result of their unfamiliarity with his medical problems and their own feelings of discomfort around people with disabilities. Consequently, we decided to brainstorm possible ways for him to relieve any awkwardness or tension his unsteady gait and his drooling might evoke in his classmates (for example, by joking about them when it was appropriate to do so). By the time September rolled around, David felt ready to begin his college career. He was still apprehensive about the prospect of being rejected, but he also felt as though he had much better tools with which he could approach social situations. We scheduled his next session for after his first week of classes.

The anguish on David's face was evident from the second he walked into my office. He dropped onto the couch and sighed deeply. "I arrived early for my first class and sat in the front row," he said. "No one else sat there. So when I arrived early for my second class I sat in a middle row. The row in front of me filled up, as did the row behind me, but no one sat in my row. I arrived early to my third class as well but this time I waited until class was about to begin and went and sat between two people. I said hello. They nodded. One of them moved two seats away from me a few minutes into the class. The other never glanced at me again and bolted as soon as the class was over. As for everyone else, it was the same story. People stared if they thought I couldn't see them or they looked away. No one talked to me. No one made eye contact, not even the professors."

I was extremely disappointed to hear David's news. After dealing with so much physical and emotional hardship and after suffering such extreme social rejection, I truly wanted for him to have a positive experience. My hopes had not been unreasonably high, as I believed that even a small taste of social acceptance would have done so much for his self-esteem and his quality of life. We had spent months working on how David might correct any negative first impressions he evoked, but if his classmates continued to avoid him, if no one would sit next to him or meet his eye, if no one was willing to talk with him, it would be extremely difficult for him to do so.

David's morale was at a low point and I was afraid he might slip into despair. The psychological wounds inflicted by lifelong rejection ran deep and David had already been exposed to more emotional pain than most people experience in their lifetime. I was determined to help David turn things around. Disappointing as his first week had been, I believed it was too soon for him to lose hope. But if he was to have any chance of succeeding, he would first need to treat the fresh wounds inflicted by the rejections he had just suffered.

How to Treat the Psychological Wounds Rejection Inflicts

Many of the rejections we face are significant (like Angelo's), reoc-curring (like school or workplace bullying), or both (like David's repeated rejections by his peers and classmates). In such situa-tions, the risk of leaving our emotional wounds unattended can be profound. But not all rejections require emotional first aid. For example, the "survivors" of the ball-tossing experiments would probably have recovered fully from their experiences even if they hadn't been thoroughly debriefed about the real purpose of the studies (which they all were). Let's open our psychological medi-cine cabinet and review our treatment options.

General Treatment Guidelines

Rejections can inflict four distinct emotional wounds, each of which might require some form of emotional first aid: lingering visceral pain, anger and aggressive urges, harm to our self-esteem, and damage to our feeling that we belong. As with any kind of wound, it is best to treat the emotional wounds of rejection as soon as possible to avoid the risk of "infection" and psychological com-plications. Remember, these are first aid treatments only and might be inappropriate or insufficient for more profound rejection expe-riences or ones that have a substantial impact on our mental health. At the end of the chapter I present guidelines for when one should consult a mental health professional.

Some of the treatments that follow are effective for soothing more than one type of wound while others are more specialized. The treatments are listed in the order in which they should be administered. Treatments A (managing self-criticism) and B (reviving self-worth) primarily target emotional pain and damaged self-esteem, while Treatment C (replenishing social connections) targets threatened feelings of belonging. Each of these three treatments is also beneficial for reducing anger and aggressive impulses. Treatment D (lowering sensitivity) is optional as it can have uncomfortable emotional side effects.

Treatment A: Argue with Self-Criticism

Although it is important to question our part in a rejection so we might rectify any obvious mistakes we made and avoid such experiences in the future, doing so requires a delicate touch. Too often our quest to understand "what went wrong" leads to overpersonalizing or overgeneralizing the rejection or becoming too self-critical in its wake. Needlessly finding all kinds of faults in our character, our physical appearance, or our behavior will only deepen the pain we feel in the moment, provoke further emotional bleeding, and significantly delay our healing. Therefore, it is far more useful to err on the side of self-kindness when evaluating our role in a rejection experience than it is to criticize ourselves for any mistakes or shortcomings.

Nonetheless, the urge to be self-critical in such situations can be extremely powerful. In order to avoid kicking ourselves when we're down, we have to be able to "argue" with our self-critical voice and adopt a kinder perspective. To win this internal debate we need talking points, arguments we can use to formulate a more balanced understanding of why the rejection occurred.

EXERCISE FOR ARGUING WITH SELF-CRITICISM

1. List (in writing) any negative or self-critical thoughts you have about the rejection.

2. Use the following self-criticism "counterarguments" from a variety of rejection scenarios to formulate personalized rebuttals to each of the self-criticisms you listed. Feel free to list more than one counterargument per self-critical thought when it is relevant to do so.

3. Whenever you have a self-critical thought, make sure to immediately articulate the relevant counterargument(s) fully and clearly in your mind.

Counterarguments for Romantic Rejections

After twenty years as a psychologist in private practice, I've heard countless tales of romantic rejection both from those doing the rejecting and those getting the heave-ho. People reject romantic partners and prospects for many different reasons, most of which have nothing to do with anyone's shortcomings. Most often it is a simple matter of chemistry—either there is a spark or there isn't. Rather than reaching unnecessary and inaccurate conclusions about your faults, consider these alternative explanations: Perhaps the person prefers a specific type that you do not fit (e.g., she's into blonds and you have brown hair or she has a thing for guys with shaved heads and you have an unruly mop). It's also possible the person's ex reentered the picture, or she might be going through a crisis at home or in her personal life. Or you might simply be a poor lifestyle match (e.g., she's a creature-comfort homebody and you love camping and urinating in the woods).

It's also possible you're "too good" for the person in some way. You take a hard line on vices and unbeknownst to you he parties so hard he has regular blackouts, or your professional success might shine a spotlight on his floundering career, or you're a police officer and his best friend is the neighborhood pot dealer, or you're a talented pastry chef and he's struggling with weight loss and a weakness for Bavarian strudel. The person might have commitment issues and tend to run the moment he feels another person getting too close, he might have self-esteem issues and worry that if you're that interested in him there must be something wrong with you, or he might not be an especially nice, kind, or sensitive person to begin with.

Timing can be a crucial issue as well. You might be looking to settle down and the other person is not, or vice versa, one of you likes to proceed slowly and the other prefers intense courtships and more "instant" relationships, or you're just out of a long-term partnership and the person you're interested in had a bad experience with being someone's rebound romance.

In each of the above situations the person getting rejected did nothing wrong and the rejection had nothing to do with any inadequacies on his or her part. The bottom line is, if people give you the "It's not you, it's me" speech—believe them! And when they don't, assume it's them anyway. The rejection will still hurt, but much less so than if you insist on spreading the salt of self-blame on an already painful wound.

Counterarguments for Workplace Rejections

Similarly to dating, getting rejected by prospective employers has usually much less to do with any mistakes or inadequacies you displayed and more to do with your fit with the company or the job description. Some jobs listings are required to be publicized but were always meant to be filled internally, other times employers are looking for a specific skill set or background, and yet others might be required to come up with several candidates even though they already know who they plan to hire. I've heard some employers confess to rejecting candidates solely because they've had bad experiences with other graduates of their academic institutions, their former companies, or their home states.

One aspect receiving increased attention from scientists is the impact of being rejected in the workplace by members of our workgroup, our superiors, or both (e.g., you're never informed of group lunches or after-work get-togethers, you don't get e-mails about certain meetings, or you repeatedly get criticized and singled out by your colleagues and/or your boss). In most situations, the rejection or exclusion is motivated by dynamics related to the organization and its culture, not to your character or job performance. For example, whistle-blowers are frequently given the silent treatment and shunned by their fellow employees (shunning is an extremely painful form of social rejection) even when the whistle-blower's actions were beneficial to them.

One young man I worked with was extremely outspoken about how poor the work conditions and compensation were in his company (which they were) and he quickly became the target of mistreatment by his supervisor as a result. Even though his colleagues cheered his efforts at first, the culture of bullying in the company soon led them to treat him just as poorly in hopes that doing so would curry favor with their supervisor. Fortunately he was able to recognize that the rejections he suffered at work were not a reflection on his performance (he was an outstanding employee) or his character. Indeed, his initiative and courage were admirable.

When we encounter rejection in the workplace we should

consider the extent to which it is motivated by conforming to a negative or bullying corporate culture, acting out of ambition and rivalry, or making efforts to appeal to higher-ups and superiors. Doing so will help us avoid unfounded assumptions about our abilities or character and prevent us from making the experience even more painful and damaging than it already is.

Counterarguments for Social Rejections

Our friendships and social circles usually nourish our belonging needs but they can also be the source of extremely painful rejections. One of the situations I hear about most is when individuals discover their friends have been meeting up without them. Although it might seem impossible not to take such exclusions personally, these things often happen for entirely other reasons. For example, an established group of friends might have an unspoken requirement of exclusivity of the kind you are not willing to give. Sure, you hang out with them but you also want to be able to hang out with other groups and they do not (a trend that is extremely common in middle school and high school but also occurs among adults).

The same situation might be true of individual friends. Someone might be looking for a best friend scenario that requires the kind of time and emotional commitment you are unable or unwilling to give (because of family, work, or other constraints or because it would take away from other friendships you value). This friend then intensifies his relationship with a different friend who is willing to give him the time and attention you were not, and your friendship with each of them gets marginalized as a result. Hurtful as it is to discover two of your friends are now spending more time with one another than they are with you, it is usually not your fault, nor in essence is it theirs. Certainly it says nothing about your desirability as a friend.

In other instances, you might find yourself being excluded from a group that shares a passion you feel less fanatical about than they do. Some social groups love to get together and discuss the same issues over and over again, whether sports, politics, parenting, or celebrities. In one case, a mother of a toddler was "dropped" by her "mommy group" because she had made repeated efforts to expand the topics of conversation beyond diaper changing, breastfeeding, and developmental milestones. Doing so threatened the integrity of the group and so she was slowly marginalized. Once she understood why this occurred she was actually relieved. She told me, "If I had to listen to one more story about cleaning vomit out of car seats I would have screamed."

Sometimes our social groups recognize we've outgrown them even before we do.

TREATMENT SUMMARY: ARGUE WITH SELF-CRITICISM

Dosage: Administer whenever you experience a rejection and repeat as necessary whenever you have self-critical thoughts related to the rejection experience.

Effective for: Soothing hurt feelings and emotional pain and minimizing damage to self-esteem.

Secondary benefits: Reduces anger and aggressive impulses.

Treatment B: Revive Your Self-Worth

One of the best ways to mitigate the hurt rejection causes and replenish our confidence and self-worth is to remind ourselves of important aspects of our character that others find valuable and desirable (even if those who rejected us did not). As an example, one attractive young woman I worked with dealt with any rejections from men by examining herself in a full-length mirror and saying aloud to her reflection, "Nope, it's not you. You look great!"

A similar albeit more complex process of self-validation played a critical role for David, the young man with a rare genetic illness, when it came to his recovery from the rejections he experienced during his first week in college. David's classmates seemed to reject him outright, much as his high school peers had, and David's self-esteem suffered accordingly. I knew that unless David's sense of self-worth recovered, even a little, he would lack the strength to make any efforts to connect with his classmates and correct their first impressions of him. Fortunately, there was one area in which David excelled and although it had nothing to do with academia, I was certain it could bridge the gulf that separated him from his fellow students.

David had the habit of arriving early both to his appointments with me and to his classes. Armed with several local newspapers, he would then proceed to scour each of their sports sections, reading every word and examining every statistic. He also spent hours listening to sports radio. As a result, David was extremely knowledgeable about sports, none more so than baseball. David was a huge Yankees fan and discussing them always caused a huge shift in his demeanor. He would sit up straighter, state his opinions fluidly and with confidence, and come across as enthusiastic, smart, and insightful about his team, the league, and the sport at large.

After his second week of college, David observed that he was not the only person who tended to arrive early to class. Several male classmates also came early and they too read the sports sections while waiting for class to begin. Given their attire and paraphernalia, David concluded that most of them were Yankees fans as well. I suggested that David choose one of them and start a conversation about the Yankees. David's first reaction was to refuse. He was convinced any such move on his part would be rebuffed or ignored. But a few days later the Yankees secured their place in the playoffs and David discussed the team's prospects in our session. His analysis was impressive.

"I feel like taking notes," I joked, "so I could pass off some of your opinions as my own."

"Feel free," he said. "Trust me! That's exactly what's going to happen in the playoffs."

"You're that certain?"

"No one knows the Yankees like me!" he said proudly.

"Not even those other guys who come to class early?" I challenged him.

"No way!" David insisted.

"That would make for an interesting discussion then," I pointed out. David didn't answer. His fear of rejection was still too strong to allow him to commit to a course of action. But after the Yankees won their first playoff game, his excitement got the better of him and he found himself throwing out a comment to a classmate about the team's prospects of winning the World Series. Much to his surprise, the young man responded by agreeing heartily and raising his hand for a high-five. David was stunned. He offered another comment and was soon shocked to find himself in the midst of a three-way discussion with two of his classmates.

This one preclass interaction had a huge impact on David's feelings of self-worth and he agreed to instigate further discussions about the Yankees. He was thrilled to discover that his classmates were just as eager to discuss their team's success as David was. The more David spoke up, the more interest his classmates took in his opinions. Their preclass discussions soon became a ritual. David and several other classmates gathered before each class to dissect the Yankees' latest game and discuss the team's prospects for winning the World Series.

The impact these unofficial gatherings had on David's demeanor and mood was profound. For the first time in his life, he felt respected by his peers. The more the Yankees succeeded, the more eager David was to get to class and discuss the games with his classmates. And the more he exhibited his knowledge and insights, the more acceptance and validation he received from them.

A key moment occurred when during one of their discussions, David was so focused on what he was saying he forgot to swallow and drool dripped down his chin. Despite a moment of panic, David was able to keep his composure well enough to use one of the lines we had come up with to address exactly such a situation. He wiped his chin and said, "You're not a real Yankees fan unless their success makes you drool." His classmates laughed and continued their discussion as though nothing had happened. David's ability to avert a potentially awkward moment served to fuel his confidence even further.

Fortunately, the Yankees had a great postseason that year and they provided ample opportunity for David and his classmates to get to know each other. His proudest moment came when he arrived later than usual and just in time to hear one student ask another, "Where's David, the Yankees guy?" He walked in a second later and was received with warm hellos.

"I've overheard people talking about me all my life," David confessed in our next session. "I was always *the weirdo*, *the retard*, *the spaz*." He paused, a big smile breaking onto his face. "Now I'm *David, the Yankees guy*!" David beamed with pride. "It feels like I finally found a way in, like I'm one of them. They look at me and see me as a real person. I can't tell you how good that feels!"

Connecting to a sense of self-worth played a vital role in David's recovery from the wounds inflicted by the rejections he suffered. Although he still had a long path of emotional healing ahead of him, David's first semester at college allowed him to experience social acceptance, and for the first time in his life, he felt like he belonged.

EXERCISE FOR REVIVING YOUR SELF-WORTH

The following exercise will help you get in touch with meaningful aspects of your character and revitalize feelings of self-worth.

1. Make a written list of five characteristics, attributes, or traits you value highly that you possess within yourself. Try to keep your list relevant to the domain in which the rejection occurred. It is important to take the time to think about qualities that really matter to you (for example, if you've been rejected by a romantic partner and you know the following qualities to be true you might list items such as caring, loyal, good listener, considerate, and emotionally available).

2. Rank your list of characteristics according to their order of importance to you.

3. Choose two of the top three attributes you listed and write a short essay (one or two paragraphs) about each one, covering the following points:

    • Why the specific quality is important to you

    • How this attribute influences your life

    • Why this attribute is an important part of your self-image

TREATMENT SUMMARY: REVIVE YOUR SELF-WORTH

Dosage: Administer whenever you experience a rejection and repeat as necessary.

Effective for: Soothing hurt feelings and emotional pain and rebuilding damaged self-esteem.

Treatment C: Replenish Feelings of Social Connection

Although the sting of rejection can make us hesitant to engage others, we should make efforts to overcome these fears and turn to our social networks for support or find other ways to refuel our feelings of social connection. Social support mitigates stress of all kinds but it is especially valuable in the wake of rejection. It creates an immediate reminder of our significant relationships, which in turn can help restore depleted feelings of belonging. In one study, even a brief exchange with a friendly experimenter was sufficient to reduce subjects' aggression following a social rejection. In another, instant messaging online with an unfamiliar peer after a rejection restored adolescents' and young adults' self-esteem.

Getting social support from our close friends and confidants following a rejection can sometimes be challenging because they are likely to underestimate the pain the rejection in question caused us. Estimating visceral and physical pain, whether our own or that of others, is something we're all bad at (unless we happen to be experiencing the same kind of pain in the moment). For example, the majority of women who plan to forgo pain medication during childbirth reverse their decision once they go into labor.

Family members, friends, and teachers of bullied students

who've resorted to desperate measures (such as suicide) are often stunned because they had not appreciated the magnitude of the distress the person was feeling. A recent and compelling study found that teachers who were first put through the ball-tossing exclusion experiment had a far greater appreciation for the emotional pain a bullied student felt than teachers who were not made to feel rejected. They also recommended the bully get a more severe punishment as a result.

Social support can be even more crucial when the rejection we experience involves discrimination. Much as we would like to believe we are an enlightened society, our track record when it comes to accepting those who are different from ourselves argues otherwise. Race, nationality, sexual orientation, religious beliefs, disability, gender, and age are all factors that cause millions of people to face extremely painful rejections by their friends, family, employers, neighbors, and strangers. Seeking support from members of our group after being the target of discrimination has been shown to reduce feelings of anger and depression, strengthen our group identity, and counterbalance the harmful effects of being devalued by a dominant culture.

Find New Affiliations with a Better Fit

Our need to belong has some *substitutability*, meaning that new relationships and memberships can psychologically replace those that have ended, especially if they provide a better fit for our personality and interests. Painful as rejections are, we can always view them as opportunities to evaluate whether the romantic partner, social circle, friend, or employer in question was a good fit for our personalities, interests, lifestyles, or careers.

Our choice of social group is often motivated by circumstance.

We get close to randomly assigned college roommates, colleagues we meet at work, or the parents of our children's playmates. While many such friendships succeed, others dissolve when we or they outgrow them. This is especially common when the circumstances that brought us together change: when we graduate from college, move to new jobs, or our children stop playing with theirs. Despite the initial sting of rejection we feel, we might later realize we're far less upset about losing the relationship or friendship than we initially thought.

Sometimes merely spending time with a group with whom we feel a strong connection can help replenish feelings of social connectedness even if few words are spoken (such as shooting hoops with our buddies or seeing a show or a movie with friends). When seeking one-on-one social support we should be thoughtful about our choices, especially if we're still hurting from the wounds of a fresh rejection. Dear friends might care for us deeply, but if they are limited in their capacity to express empathy and support they might not be our best choice.

Anyone who has suffered a serious illness or physical injury or struggled with a disability (like David) has probably experienced people feeling uncomfortable and looking away, avoiding contact, "forgetting" to call or visit, and even losing touch entirely. Cancer patients and those with other illnesses often join support groups to help manage the stress of the illness and their treatments while gaining support from others who've faced similar struggles and rejections.

Have a "Social Snack"

Although it is best to connect with those who can provide social support and feelings of connection it might not always be possible for us to do so. In the film *Cast Away*, Chuck Noland (Tom Hanks) is stranded alone on an island for four years, during which he copes with social starvation by looking at a photograph of his girl-friend, Kelly, and by talking aloud to a volleyball he names "Wil-son" and who becomes his much-beloved companion. Much like having a snack eases our hunger when we don't have the opportunity to eat a full meal, "snacking" on reminders of our significant emotional connections eases our "social hunger" when we feel rejected, excluded, or alone.

Social snacking can take many forms, but scientists have found that photographs of loved ones are one of the most emotionally nutritious snacks we can consume after being rejected. In one study, subjects placed photographs on their desks of either loved ones or celebrities and were asked to vividly relive a significant rejection experience from their own past. Subjects with pictures of celebrities on their desks suffered a large drop in mood as a result of recalling the rejection while those with pictures of loved ones registered almost no change in mood at all. Such findings imply that teens and tweens entering the gauntlet of middle school might be well advised to replace posters of musicians and actors with glossy eight-by-tens of Grandpa Dwight and beloved Aunt Flossie.

Photographs are not the only social snacks with nutritional value. Other experiments found that merely recalling positive relationships or warm interactions we've had with our nearest and dearest was sufficient to reduce the amount of aggression people felt after being rejected. Reading meaningful e-mails or letters, watching videos of loved ones, or using valued mementos of those to whom we feel most connected also have nutritional value as social snacks. Mementos and inanimate objects can also have significant "caloric value," especially when a rejection is compounded by general loneliness, as was the case for Chuck Noland with "Wilson." The next time we ask someone on a date or apply for a new job we might want to have pictures of our friends and loved ones available in our pocket just in case, or, if we must, a volleyball.

Treatment Summary: Replenish Feelings of Social Connection

Dosage: Make sure to administer whenever you experience a rejection. Since there are numerous ways in which you might be able to replenish feelings of social connection, you may wish to apply several forms of this treatment as necessary (e.g., spending an afternoon with family members who appreciate and love you and social snacking on pictures of them later on).

Effective for: Replenishing your need to belong and reducing anger and aggressive urges.

Secondary benefits: Soothing hurt feelings and emotional pain and rebuilding damaged self-esteem.

Treatment D: Desensitize Yourself

Anyone who has ever made cold calls (for example, to prospective employers or to ask people to donate to a charity) knows how difficult it is to make the first few calls. It's extremely unpleasant to hear "No, thanks" and have the phone slammed in your ear. But something interesting happens around the fifth or sixth call—we begin to take "no" much less personally. We shrug it off, strike a line through the entry, and move on to the next person on our list. Actors, musicians, and performers have the same experience. If an actor rarely auditions, getting rejected is likely to feel painful, but those who audition several times a week find it much easier to let such rejections go.

The reason this happens is because of a psychological process called *desensitization*. The more we're exposed to situations we find uncomfortable or unpleasant, the more used to them we become and the less they disturb us. Of course, this isn't true for all situations and it certainly isn't true for some of the more significant or profound rejections we might encounter. Some life experiences are acutely painful and emotionally damaging no matter how repetitive they become. But when it comes to situations such as asking people out on dates, calling prospective employers for jobs, applying to internships or other educational programs, or initiating new friendships, trying to desensitize ourselves can be beneficial.

I once had a male patient in his twenties whose fear of rejection made him hesitant to approach women, and I gave him the task of asking out nine women in one weekend. He had plans to attend three different social events, and I promised him that if he approached three women per event, by the time he got to the third (a birthday party for a work colleague) he would feel very differently about the prospect of getting turned down. Interestingly, merely agreeing to the challenge had an immediate impact on him. "The thought of approaching so many women made me feel kind of confident before I even began. Once I accepted that I'd be getting rejected *a lot*, it made the idea of any one woman rejecting me seem more manageable for some strange reason."

As we now know, that "strange reason" is actually desensitization. My patient never made it to the third social event. He struck out three times at the first event of the weekend, but was shocked when two women gave him their number at the second, "and one of them wasn't even fake!" he reported happily. The young man ended up skipping the third event in order to go on a date with the woman who had given him her nonfake number.

Desensitization can be an effective technique for reducing the emotional impact of rejections but it should be used both sparingly and wisely. It is one of those treatments that should come with clear warning signs on the label. Readers should be advised to treat themselves with desensitization only if they feel their self-esteem is up for the challenge and only after giving careful thought to how they could implement the treatment in ways they would find beneficial. The most important aspect is to concentrate our efforts into a limited time frame, as spreading out the task over time dilutes it and renders it ineffective. For example, if my patient hadn't had several social events planned, it would have been harder for him to find the right circumstances in which to ask out nine women within three days.

TREATMENT SUMMARY: DESENSITIZE YOURSELF

Dosage: Administer for specific tasks only: when seeking to initiate dates or friendships, when applying to jobs, internships, or other programs, or when making cold calls.

Caution: Use sparingly and wisely, as this treatment involves significant discomfort. Use only if you feel your self-esteem can tolerate being exposed to numerous "minor" rejections.

Effective for: Creating a layer of resilience to future rejections so as to reduce the hurt feelings and emotional pain they evoke and the damage to self-esteem they cause.

When to Consult a Mental
Health Professional

Applying emotional first aid following rejections should soothe each of the four wounds we typically suffer as a result of such experiences and reduce our risk of long-term psychological complications. Treating older rejections might also be beneficial as it can help nudge us toward a path of healing and recovery. However, some rejections are so painful and the wounds they create are so deep, emotional first aid alone is not sufficient to correct the psychological damage they cause.

If the rejection you've experienced is profound (e.g., you've been rejected by your entire family or community because of your sexual orientation or religious beliefs) or if you've experienced chronic rejection over a period of time, you might benefit from seeking the advice of a mental health professional. If you've applied the treatments in this chapter and your emotional pain did not subside, your self-esteem remains too damaged, and engaging with people feels too risky, you should consult a mental health professional. If your anger and aggressive impulses have become too powerful for you to control, or if you have any thoughts of harming yourself or others, seek the immediate help of a mental health professional or go to your nearest emergency room.

CHAPTER 2

||||||||||||||||||||

LONELINESS

Relationship Muscle Weakness

Our world is shrinking. Social media platforms allow us to stay in touch with dozens if not hundreds of friends at once, dating websites offer us lavish smorgasbords of potential mates we can peruse from the comfort of our homes, and a simple click of a computer key allows us to forge new connections with strangers from across the globe who share our interests and passions. Yet, despite this era of unprecedented global human connection, more people than ever are suffering from severe loneliness.

The 2010 U.S. Census found that 27 percent of households in America are single-person households, now outnumbering all other groups (such as one- or two-parent households with children). Of course, not everyone who lives alone is lonely and not everyone who is lonely lives alone. Many of us suffer from loneliness despite living with a spouse or being in a committed relationship. In fact, cohabitating with someone with whom we share a physical proximity but little else often highlights the immense emotional distance and profound disconnection we feel, leading to powerful feelings of isolation.

What determines our loneliness is not the quantity of our relationships but rather their subjective quality, the extent to which we perceive ourselves to be socially or emotionally isolated. Indeed, many of us have address books full of casual acquaintances yet still ache from a lack of deep friendships. Some of us have a tight network of supportive friends yet feel the acute absence of a romantic partner. We might spend our days surrounded by work colleagues yet feel removed and isolated from all of them. We might be blessed with strong familial relationships but find ourselves geographically distant from those who care for us most. Those of us who are fortunate enough to grow into old age with our health and faculties intact might experience a rising tide of loneliness as we witness friends and partners succumb to illness and die one after the other.

What Loneliness and Cigarette Smoking Have in Common

Having meaningful relationships is essential for leading a happy and self-fulfilled life, but chronic loneliness can damage us in ways that go far beyond limiting our basic happiness. In addition to the emotional pain and longing loneliness causes, it is also associated with clinical depression, suicidal thoughts and behaviors, hostility, and sleep disturbances.

More important, loneliness has an alarming effect on our general health. It alters the functioning of our cardiovascular systems (leading to high blood pressure, increased body mass index, and higher cholesterol), our endocrine systems (increasing stress hormones), and even our immune systems. As an illustration of how directly loneliness impacts our physical health, one study found that in otherwise healthy college students, lonely students had a significantly poorer response to flu shots than nonlonely students did. Loneliness also causes a decline in our mental abilities, including poor decision making, decreased attention and concentration, impaired judgment, and a more rapid progression of Alzheimer's disease.

Shocking as it may seem, loneliness poses just as large a risk factor for our long-term physical health as cigarette smoking does, as it literally shaves years off our life expectancy. While cigarette packs come with health advisories, few of us are aware of the dangers of inhaling two packs a day of social isolation. As a result, feeling lonely rarely triggers a sense of urgency and we rarely prioritize the need to break free of its clutches and treat our psychological wounds.

Loneliness Is Contagious

Another factor that adds urgency to our need to treat the psychological wounds loneliness inflicts is that recent studies have demonstrated something rather stunning—loneliness is contagious! One study tracked the spread of loneliness within social networks over time and found that loneliness spreads through a clear contagion process: individuals who had contact with lonely people at the start of the study were more likely to become lonely themselves by the end of it. Further, the virulence of the contagion depended on the degree of closeness between the lonely and nonlonely person. The closer nonlonely individuals were to a lonely person the more virulent the effect of the contagion and the lonelier they became later on.

Specifically, scientists found that lonely individuals were continually pushed toward the periphery of their social networks and into positions that were increasingly more isolated. Once people were in close contact with lonely people they became affected and were pushed toward the periphery as well. Alarmingly, this contagion was "transmitted" from one person to another even beyond the immediate circle of the lonely person, such that it spread throughout the entire social network. Such studies help demonstrate both why and how loneliness is at epidemic proportions in today's society.

Unfortunately, despite its contagiousness and despite the severity of the health risks it poses, loneliness remains one of the most neglected psychological injuries we sustain in daily life. Few of us realize how crucial it is to treat the psychological wounds loneliness inflicts and fewer still know how to do so effectively.

The Psychological Wounds Loneliness Inflicts

Given the severity of the risk loneliness poses to our physical and mental health, we should make every effort to escape its impact as soon as possible. However, two factors are likely to make it challenging for us to do so. First, loneliness causes us to become overly critical about ourselves and those around us, and it makes us judge our existing relationships too negatively, all of which impact our interactions with others. Second, one of the more insidious effects of loneliness is that it leads us to behave in self-defeating ways that diminish the quality and quantity of our social connections even further. As a result, the very fibers that comprise our "relationship muscles"—our social and communication skills, our ability to see things from another person's perspective, and our ability to empathize and understand how others feel—become weak and are likely to function poorly when we need them most.

To be clear, it is not our fault that we are lonely, nor is it usually a reflection on our social desirability. But regardless of the circumstances that cause it, once loneliness sets in, it triggers a set of psychological reactions that can lead us to inadvertently perpetuate our situation and even to make it worse. Because such dynamics usually operate outside our awareness, the most important tool we can carry with us going forward is an open mind. We might strongly believe we've done everything in our power to change our situation and that we're certainly doing nothing to make matters worse. But by being open to the possibility that our behaviors might be contributing to our predicament, we can be open to discovering ways to change them. Difficult as it is to open our hearts and minds, to challenge our established perspectives, and to take emotional risks, we must be brave enough to do so if we wish to treat our loneliness.

1. Painful Misperceptions: Why We Feel Invisible but Our Loneliness Isn't

People confide many negative things about themselves to their therapists, but one of the things people rarely have the courage to admit is how lonely they feel. Loneliness carries a stigma of shame and self-blame that operates in all our minds to some extent. Over 40 percent of adults will suffer from loneliness in their lifetime and virtually all of them will think poorly of themselves because of it. Indeed, one of the more significant emotional wounds loneliness creates is that it leads us to develop inaccurate perceptions of ourselves as well as of others and to take too harsh a view of our existing relationships and social interactions.

Lionel, a former World War II officer who received numerous medals for valor, was referred to me for psychotherapy some years ago by his daughter, a social worker who lived out of town and was concerned about her father's increasing social isolation. Lionel lived alone (his wife had died some years before), and although his daughter called him every day, their conversations were usually quite brief as Lionel believed that "phones are for making appointments, not for idle chitchat!" I quickly learned that Lionel was not a fan of any kind of chitchat, idle or otherwise, something that made our sessions somewhat challenging at first. For example, my efforts to assess the extent of Lionel's social isolation went something like this.

"Who else do you speak with regularly other than your daughter?"

"Housekeeper. Comes twice a week. Cooks and cleans."

"Tell me about the conversations you have with her."

"She tells me what she made. I leave her money on the counter."

"What about other family members?"

"No relatives other than my daughter."

"What about friends from the service or even former colleagues, are you in touch with any of them?"

"No."

"Why do you think that is?"

"Because they're dead."

I resisted the urge to sigh and gave Lionel a sympathetic nod. I kept probing and eventually discovered that Lionel did engage in one regular social activity—he belonged to a chess club. Every Tuesday Lionel would put on a jacket and tie and go down to the seniors' center to play a couple of games. Unfortunately, as far as games go, chess is about as conducive to social interaction as solitaire is, if not less so. True, chess does require two people to play, but any talking during the game is strictly discouraged as it can interfere with the concentration of the other player.

"Do you play with the same people?" I inquired. I was curious about whether any of the regulars tended to meet outside of chess club hours.

"Mostly."

"Have you ever socialized with any of them?"

"They're not interested."

"How do you know?"

"Why would they want to socialize with me? I'm eighty!" I doubted that age was the real issue. The club was for seniors, after all; how much younger could the other players be?

"You're eighty and they are . . . ?"

"Not interested."

"Do they socialize with one another?"

"Sometimes."

"And they've never invited you to join them?"

"They're not interested!"

Lionel was convinced the other, "younger" members of the chess club would rebuff any attempt he made to forge friendships with them, despite the fact that he had no evidence whatsoever that his age or anything about him would cause them to snub him. But he was determined to avoid disappointment and rejection at all costs. He arrived right before game time and left immediately following the last round. He approached no one and spent coffee breaks sitting in a corner reading a book. In other words, he gave the other chess club members no opportunity whatsoever to get to know him.

Lionel had already been suffering from loneliness for some years when we first met and his self-defeating strategies were already well entrenched. However, the damage loneliness inflicts on our perceptions of social situations can happen extremely quickly. For example, scientists found that simply asking college students to recall a time in their life when they felt lonely or socially isolated was sufficient to elicit from them a more negative assessment of their current social support systems as well as to boost their shyness, increase their social anxiety, cause a drop in their mood and self-esteem, and impair their optimism.

Loneliness also causes us to evaluate others more harshly and to perceive our interactions with friends and loved ones more negatively than we would if we were not lonely. Another study videotaped students as they interacted with a friend and then asked them to rate the quality of the interaction and that of the friendship. Lonely individuals rated both their interactions and their friendships far more negatively than nonlonely people did. The participants were then shown the videotapes again one week later. While there was no change in the assessments of nonlonely people, lonely people rated their friendships even more negatively the second time around.

Lionel believed the members of the chess club ignored him and marginalized him because he was essentially invisible to them. However, the tragic irony of loneliness is that while we often feel invisible to others, our loneliness is usually very visible to them indeed. Numerous studies have found that lonely people are easily recognizable to others and that once we're judged as being lonely we're likely to be viewed negatively as a result. Lonely people are often seen as less attractive and even less intelligent than nonlonely people (physical attractiveness provides no immunity from loneliness whatsoever; attractive individuals might draw a greater quantity of people initially but the quality of their relationships are no different and they are just as likely to experience loneliness).

The bottom line is that loneliness affects perceptions in numerous ways. It impacts how we perceive ourselves and others, as well as how we perceive the quality of our interactions and our relationships. Loneliness also impacts how others perceive us, making us appear less interesting and less appealing as social prospects. The combination of these factors makes it extremely difficult to shed our cloaks of invisibility and engage in successful efforts to forge new social connections or deepen existing ones.

2. Self-Defeating Prophecies: Why Trying Harder Leads to Failure

Many journeys into loneliness begin during periods of transition and change. College freshmen often feel extremely lonely when they first arrive at college, surrounded by unfamiliar faces, far from home, and removed from the comfort of their friendships. Divorce, separation, and bereavement, especially when they befall us unexpectedly, can leave us entirely unprepared for the palpable loneliness that accompanies such losses. When work and colleagues provide our primary source of social interaction and engagement, losing our job can mean losing our entire social support system when we most need it. Relocations and emigrations are often characterized by extended periods of loneliness as we labor to build new social and support networks from scratch.

In each of these cases, we typically emerge from loneliness once we adjust to our new realities and rebuild our social infrastructures. Most college freshmen eventually make new friends, divorced people typically begin to date within a year following their separation (although it takes longer in cases of bereavement), looking for a new job often requires us to network and to contact people with whom we lost touch, and most of us eventually forge social and intimate connections in our new towns and communities.

Yet, at times, the cold grip of loneliness extends far beyond the normative adjustment period. We become trapped in it, paralyzed by waves of emotional pain, defeated by feelings of worthlessness and hopelessness, and overcome by the devastating emptiness of our profound social and emotional isolation.

Why does this happen? What is it that prevents some of us from breaking free of the bonds of loneliness and getting our lives back on track?

The answer is that in addition to painful misperceptions, loneliness also drives us into cycles of self-protection and avoidance that cause us to create self-fulfilling prophecies and to inadvertently push away the very people we hope to engage.

Serena, a high school teacher I worked with recently, found herself in exactly such a vicious cycle and she too was entirely unaware of it. What brought her to psychotherapy was her "nonexistent dating life." At first I was at a loss to understand why she had never been in a serious relationship. She was in her midthirties and, furthermore, she was simply stunning. I had no doubt that she received plenty of attention from men. I soon learned that Serena's appearance had gone through a radical transformation four years earlier, when she lost eighty pounds.

"I was heavy my whole life. Men would look right past me as if I wasn't even in the room. And trust me," Serena added with a wistful smile, "I was hard to miss. Now they stare, they smile, they wink, and somehow it still feels the same. Like they're responding to my appearance, but when it comes to who I am as a person, they're still looking right past me."

Serena was desperate to find a husband, but she was equally desperate to avoid getting hurt. While her hesitancy and mistrust were certainly justified after the years of rejection and loneliness she'd experienced, her fears caused her to come across as withdrawn, defensive, and suspicious. As a result, her dates with men were often tense and awkward, and few of the men expressed an interest in seeing her again. Their failure to follow up only confirmed Serena's suspicions that they were never interested in the "real her" to begin with. The fact that the "real Serena" spent every moment of her dates hiding behind a psychological wall and was never truly present in the first place was something she never considered.

The reason we get trapped in such cycles is that loneliness tips the balance of our social motivations. Once we feel vulnerable and socially disconnected we become intensely self-protective and we seek to minimize any potential negative responses or rejection from others. As a result we approach people with distrust, suspicion, cynicism, and anxiety or we make efforts to avoid them altogether. Because we don't expect our social interactions to be positive, we make fewer efforts to seek them out and we are less responsive to them when they occur.

Unfortunately, the longer our loneliness lasts, the harder it can become to change our perceptions and behaviors and to break the cycle of self-defeating thoughts and behaviors that perpetuate it. We end up behaving in ways that push away the very people who could alleviate our loneliness and we then view their distance as further evidence of our basic undesirability. As a result we feel like passive victims in a harsh world and fail to realize the extent to which we are active contributors to our own predicament.

3. Atrophied Relationship Muscles: We Use Them or We Lose Them

Alban, a successful sales executive, came to couples therapy with his wife, Blanca, after months of urging on her part. "Blanca accuses me of being married to my job and I guess I am. It's not that

I want to be, but my job demands it. Blanca gets frustrated that I have to work even when I'm home and I totally understand how she feels." Alban put his arm around his wife and gave her a wink. "I keep telling her it's natural for the 'other woman' to feel jealous."

Blanca quickly pulled away. "You know I don't think that's funny!" Blanca turned to me and said, "He keeps telling people that joke and I hate it." She turned back to Alban and her eyes welled with tears. "It's not that you're away so much that bothers me, it's that there's a real disconnect between us when you are home. There's no affection, no romance, no intimacy. I'm lonely and miserable . . . and you don't care."

Alban's eyes also welled up. "Of course I care! And I feel lonely too. But it's hard to connect when you're angry all the time. Last week I brought you flowers and a card for Valentine's Day and all you did was yell at me."

"Because you never even gave them to me! You were in such a rush to check e-mails from work you just left them on the kitchen counter. I only discovered them two hours later and by then you were already asleep!"

"But I got them for you! You keep telling me it's the thought that counts, except it doesn't!"

"You got them *for* me but you didn't think to give them *to* me. Your *thought* was to leave them on the kitchen counter in the same spot you leave money for the cleaning lady!"

As their discussion progressed it became evident that leaving the flowers on the kitchen counter was not the only instance of Alban's good intentions going awry. He clearly cared about Blanca, but something went consistently wrong when it came to translating his feelings into actions. Given how angry Blanca felt and the level of disconnection between them, it had clearly been going wrong for some time.

When we lack meaningful and deep connections with others or when we fail to invest in the relationships we have, we stop exercising the skill sets required to maintain such relationships. Our "relationship muscles" function in much the same way regular muscles do. When we fail to use relationship muscles regularly (such as our ability to empathize or see things from the other person's perspective) or when we use them incorrectly, they atrophy and become less functional.

The problem is we're often unaware of just how weak our relationship muscles have already become. Alban believed his relationship muscles were functioning properly, but they were not. True, he'd invested thought and effort in getting Blanca flowers and a card, but leaving his gifts on the kitchen counter and forgetting about them undid any positive impact his efforts might have had.

When we try to walk after spending a week in bed with the flu we are often surprised by how our legs buckle under us and leave us in a heap on the floor. While we are quick to realize our muscles have weakened in such situations, we rarely have the same insight when it comes to poorly functioning relationship muscles, no matter how many times we find ourselves in a metaphorical "heap on the floor." Indeed, rather than concluding that his relationship muscles were faulty, Alban was convinced Blanca was simply being unappreciative.

As another example, when we falter in our first dating efforts after a long dry spell of being alone, we rarely attribute the result to our having rusty dating skills and weak relationship muscles. Instead we take the rejection extremely personally and assume it is merely a reflection of our fundamental undesirability.

Even once we're aware of the need to strengthen our relationship muscles, we often fail to anticipate how uneven our efforts are likely to be. For example, once I made Serena aware that she might be contributing to her lackluster dating experiences, she was determined to change how she was coming across to her dates. However, her first few efforts were just as unsuccessful, this time because she was trying too hard and appearing too desperate.

While improving our social skills is certainly doable, many who experience loneliness face the far more daunting task of developing relationship muscles we've never used before. Serena had no experience with serious dating and Lionel had little to no experience and a very limited tolerance for casual socializing and small talk. Alban, on the other hand, lacked the ability to empathize, to understand Blanca's needs and feelings well enough to make his efforts meaningful to her. In all of these cases, they needed to learn new skills and find the courage to practice them, despite the emotional risks involved.

Lionel was a good example of someone who regularly overlooked vital information of this sort. I was eventually able to persuade him to approach Stanley, the chess club member whom he enjoyed playing against most, and suggest they grab coffee. We discussed how important it was to precede the actual request with a comment or two about the game, so as not to come across as too abrupt. Lionel came into our next session and immediately informed me that he had taken the plunge and asked Stanley to have coffee with him.

"Great!" I responded. "So he said yes?"

"He declined."

I tried to hide my disappointment. "I'm sorry to hear that. Did he say why?"

"He didn't have to. It's because he's a sore loser." Lionel went on to explain that Stanley used to be the best player in the club until Lionel joined and that he'd lost to Lionel regularly ever since. I was dismayed that Lionel had not thought this information important enough to mention earlier. Had he considered things from Stanley's perspective, he might have realized that winning all his games, refusing to interact with the other members, and reading in the corner during breaks made Lionel appear aloof if not actually disdainful of the others, Stanley most of all.

Understanding a person's needs and feelings from his or her perspective is vital for creating and sustaining close friendships and emotional intimacy. When these relationship muscles are weak, we overlook crucial information about how the other person thinks and feels and our efforts often fail.

How to Treat the Psychological Wounds Loneliness Inflicts

Many of the circumstances that lead to being lonely are temporary and allow us to recover in a relatively short amount of time. For example, kids usually forge new friendships within hours or days of starting summer camp, and people whose relationships make them feel lonely might actually feel relieved after a separation if they take steps to reconnect with friends and loved ones with whom they had lost touch. Treating the wounds of loneliness becomes much more urgent when we've been in its grips for extended durations and when we feel discouraged about being able to change our social and emotional isolation. Let's open our psychological medicine cabinet and review our treatment options.

General Treatment Guidelines

In addition to the pain and suffering loneliness causes, three other psychological wounds require emotional first aid. First, we must identify and change the misperceptions that lead to self-defeating behaviors. Although we might struggle to see such patterns, if we've been lonely for some time, they are definitely there. Second, we need to strengthen and enhance our relationship muscles so that our efforts to forge new connections and deepen existing relationships will be more successful, meaningful, and satisfying. Third, we need to minimize the ongoing emotional distress loneliness causes, especially in cases in which the options for improving existing social connections and creating new ones are limited.

The treatments that follow are listed in the order in which they should be administered. Treatments A (challenging negative perceptions) and B (identifying self-defeating behaviors) are effective primarily for correcting the misperceptions loneliness causes and the self-defeating behaviors that result. Treatments C (taking the other person's perspective) and D (deepening emotional bonds) will help strengthen relationship muscles crucial for forming new connections or deepening existing ones. Treatment E (creating opportunities for social connection) will help identify new avenues for social engagement; and Treatment F (adopting animals) discusses ways to reduce the emotional suffering loneliness inflicts and is especially suited for people with limited options to expand or improve the quality of their social connections (because of geographic isolation, health or mobility limitations, or other special circumstances).

As with all emotional injuries, it is best to treat the wounds loneliness inflicts as soon as possible. The longer we go without exercising the full range of our relationship muscles, the more they will atrophy and the longer it will take for us to regain their full functionality. Further, rehabilitating muscles of any kind requires repetition, practice, and patience. If we try to rush our recovery we are likely to reinjure ourselves and encounter setbacks and disappointment. And remember, not all forms of loneliness can be remedied by first aid techniques alone. At the end of the chapter, I discuss when it is recommended to consult a mental health professional.

Treatment A: Remove Your Negatively Tinted Glasses

Loneliness makes us constantly on guard, prepared for the disappointment and rejection we are sure will come. As a result, we miss opportunities to make social connections and we behave in ways that push others away. In order to challenge these distorted perceptions and avoid acting in self-defeating ways we need to do three things.

1. Fight the Pessimism!

Loneliness makes our minds generate instant negative thoughts as soon as we contemplate engaging in social interaction. We get invited to a party and vivid scenes of awkwardness, rejection, and disappointment pop into our heads entirely unbidden. We become convinced we won't know anyone there. We envision ourselves standing alone by the hummus and vegetable dip, feeling conspicuous and embarrassed. The thought of approaching a stranger or, worse, a group of strangers, and initiating a conversation is enough to cause a sense of panic, and we anticipate any such efforts ending disastrously.

Although we are unlikely to prevent pessimistic scenarios from elbowing their way into our thoughts, the best way to fight our fears and pessimism is to purposefully visualize scenarios of success that are both reasonable and realistic. By picturing successful outcomes in our minds we are more likely to recognize such opportunities when they arise and to take advantage of them. For example, we could acknowledge that it is just as likely for people at the party to be friendly, welcoming, and happy to meet and chat with us. Even if we don't meet new people, it's just as possible we'd have a perfectly nice time catching up with the one or two folks we do know. We might even end the night by making plans to see them again in the near future.

Lionel had to overcome the belief that none of the other players in the chess club were interested in socializing with him ("Why would they want to socialize with me? I'm eighty!"). Once Stanley turned him down he was extremely reluctant to approach anyone else. The first order of business was to help Lionel see his part in creating the situation.

"You've been seeing things too negatively, Lionel," I explained. "True, they haven't asked you to hang out but you also haven't given them any reason to do so. They know nothing about you, nothing about your life, and nothing about your thoughts or feelings."

"So you also think it's pointless." Lionel nodded.

"No, I'm saying the opposite. I'm saying it's not as bleak as it seems and that you can do something about it. Let them get to know you. Chat a little, exchange pleasantries, kvetch about the weather, or ask about their weekend. Make the effort for a couple of weeks and I assure you they will be far more open to hanging out, even Stanley."

Lionel was extremely hesitant to initiate conversation with the

chess club members, but when I appealed to his military experience and presented the challenge as a mission he had yet to accom-
plish, he finally agreed. After a few weeks of occasional chatting, he
mustered the courage to ask another member to coffee. They met
at a diner several weeks later. I told Lionel how impressed I was
with his efforts. "I know it was difficult to open up and start chatting but I'm so glad you did. I'm sure it made a difference with
other club members as well. Who knows," I added, "maybe you
and Stanley will have coffee one day after all."

"That'll never happen," Lionel said immediately.

"Here's that negativity again," I cautioned him.

"It just won't happen," Lionel insisted.

"Really?" I demanded. "Why not?"

"Because Stanley's dead."

Lionel told me Stanley had died two weeks earlier. His death
led to the other members talking more among themselves and getting closer. They decided to attend Stanley's memorial service later
in the month and when they did, Lionel went with them.

2. Give the Benefit of the Doubt!

Another misperception loneliness burdens us with is that we tend
to assume the worst about how others feel about us. Toby, a young
man who had recently lost his job, was devastated when the holiday season approached and he failed to receive an invitation to his
good friend's annual Christmas party (the friend still worked for
the same company). Toby was convinced his friend no longer
wanted to be associated with him because he had been fired. Since
I knew Toby's e-mail had recently changed (he had used his work
e-mail for personal communications) I suggested he check his
spam folder. Lo and behold, there was the invitation, where it had

been all along. Toby had spent the better part of two weeks feeling betrayed and mourning the loss of a friendship that was still perfectly intact (although, if he had missed his friend's party with no explanation, it might not have been intact for long).

Loneliness might make us question how our friends feel about us, but we should always balance our doubts with reminders of our mutual history and the shared experiences that created and sustained the friendship over time. Doing so will help reassure us that our friendships are probably a lot more stable than our loneliness-fueled fears might lead us to believe.

Serena, the high school teacher who had gone from heavy to bombshell, was also quick to judge others and their intentions toward her. She was certain any man who expressed an interest in her did so solely because of her appearance and had no intention of getting to know the "real" her. Although men were unquestionably drawn to her appearance, they definitely cared about her personality. Indeed, it was her closed and guarded behavior that made most of them reluctant to ask her out again.

A couple of years later, at a social event, Serena bumped into one of the men she thought had rejected her. She was extremely surprised when he introduced her to his friends as "Serena, the beauty who dumped me after one date." Clearly, he had mistaken her guardedness for disinterest. Had Serena given him the benefit of the doubt and expressed interest he would have happily initiated a second date.

Understandable as our fears are when we already feel lonely and leery of rejection, indulging them will only bring about the very thing we seek to avoid. Instead, we must battle the internal tide of skepticism we feel and give the new people in our lives and the ones with whom we have existing relationships the benefit of the doubt.

3. Take Action!

Chronic loneliness causes us to perceive ourselves as passive victims of our harsh circumstances and we feel helpless to change our social, emotional, or intimate isolation. Such feelings, powerful as they might be, are nonetheless founded on perceptions that are too negative and pessimistic. There are always steps we can take to improve our situation. It is important to do so because taking action of any kind will make us feel better about ourselves as well as about our prospects. Lionel had a room full of chess players from which to choose when it came to making new friends, Serena had numerous men clamoring for her attention, and Toby had plenty of people from his former job who were interested in continuing a friendship with him. Yet loneliness made all of them perceive their situation as one in which their options were severely limited.

Exercise for Identifying Avenues for Social Connection

The following writing exercise will help identify potential actions you can take to expand and deepen your social connections and, by doing so, counter feelings of helplessness.

1. Go through your phone numbers, e-mail addresses, and social media contacts and make a list of people you consider friends or good acquaintances.

2. For each person, note when you last saw or communicated with him or her and create a master list of people you haven't been in touch with for a while.

3. Prioritize your list by ranking all the people on it according to who in the past has made you feel best about being

you. Your final ranking represents the order in which you should contact the people on your list. Reach out to at least one or two people a week and, when possible, initiate plans to meet.

4.   Go to websites that list meetings or activities and scroll through their categories. For example, Meetup (meetup .com) is a website that lists meetings for people with mutual interests, hobbies, passions, or careers. Even if you don't find a specific meet-up that fits your interests, such sites are good places to get ideas for activities or hobbies that might intrigue you.

5.   Identify at least three activities or topics you might want to pursue (e.g., book clubs, adult education classes, hiking or biking groups). Search online for meetings in your area.

Use your lists to recharge your old friendships and to explore venues for creating new ones.

TREATMENT SUMMARY: REMOVE YOUR NEGATIVELY TINTED GLASSES

Dosage: Administer full treatment and repeat as necessary until you've revitalized your social or dating life.

Effective for: Correcting painful misperceptions and avoiding self-fulfilling prophecies.

Secondary benefits: Reduces emotional suffering.

Treatment B: Identify Your Self-Defeating Behaviors

Loneliness makes us approach people with caution and suspicion, and our hesitancy usually comes across loud and clear to others, prompting them to retreat from our bad vibe. We then feel crushed and conclude we were right to be suspicious and cautious in the first place. The fact that our own actions created a self-fulfilling prophecy often eludes us entirely. As is often true in life, when we act out of fear we risk inviting the very thing we hope to avoid.

But if our self-defeating judgments and behaviors seem completely justified in our own minds, how are we to identify those that are self-sabotaging?

The truth is that while we're often blind to our self-defeating behaviors in the moment, we're much better at identifying them in hindsight. For example, we might feel justified in keeping to ourselves at a social event if the few people we know are already engaged in other conversations. But once our social anxiety has diminished the next day, we would probably recognize that we could have simply joined their conversations or introduced ourselves to at least one or two people we didn't know.

More important, we tend to repeat the same self-defeating behaviors in a variety of situations, which should make identifying them easier once we're alerted to their existence. Once we recognize what these tendencies are we can become more mindful of them and catch them in action going forward.

So consider yourself alerted.

While the notion of analyzing our own behavior accurately might seem daunting at first, when I ask patients to reflect on their social encounters and identify their errors, they typically do so quite successfully. Once we accept the basic premise that at least some of our actions are not serving us well, we should be able to start identifying things we've said and done that might have had unintended consequences. For example, Serena was quick to recognize that she asked her dates very few questions about themselves and that such omissions probably led her dates to conclude she had little interest in them. In addition, her anxiety was such that she rarely smiled when she was on a date and she was certainly too tense to laugh. Once she realized this, she thought back on her dates with dismay but with insight.

"They must have thought I really wasn't enjoying their company. Geez, I'm one heck of a lousy date!"

"Lousy!" I agreed, which made Serena laugh. "But whether you continue to be is up to you."

Serena's self-sabotaging behaviors are by no means unusual. Other common forms of self-defeating behaviors are finding poor excuses to turn down invitations to social events, skipping spontaneous get-togethers because you're "unprepared" either emotionally or otherwise, neglecting to convey birthday wishes or other celebratory messages to friends and colleagues, taking friendly ribbings too personally, using defensive body language (e.g., folding your arms over your chest, standing with your hands in your pockets, exaggerated rummaging through your purse, or faking intense interest in nonexistent text messages), responding with curt or monosyllabic sentences or overtalking and hogging the conversation, neglecting to ask others about their lives and opinions, and confessing your faults and insecurities to people you've just met.

EXERCISE TO IDENTIFY SELF-DEFEATING BEHAVIORS

Take time to reflect on how you might come across to your friends, colleagues, and loved ones or when you are on a date or any other type of social engagement. Try to identify at least three behaviors (including omissions, such as not conveying interest), even if they seem entirely justified and even if they seem relatively minor, that might be pushing other people away.

1. My self-defeating behaviors are:

2. Once you've identified what you might be doing incorrectly, be extremely mindful of avoiding such behaviors in the future. Keep your list handy and read it before you attend social engagements. Self-defeating mechanisms can be changed once you've identified them correctly but don't expect to eliminate them all at once. As we will see in the next section, all social skills require practice.

Treatment Summary: Identify Behaviors That Work Against You

Dosage: Administer full treatment as soon as possible after unsuccessful social interactions. Make sure to go over your list before attending any forthcoming social interactions so you can be as mindful as possible to minimize self-defeating behaviors.

Effective for: Improving social and romantic interactions, avoiding self-defeating behaviors, and correcting painful misperceptions.

Secondary benefits: Reduces emotional suffering.

Treatment C: Take the Other Person's Perspective

Relationships of any kind are always about give-and-take. But to "give" successfully we have to be able to "take" the other person's point of view. Known as *perspective taking*, accurately reading another person's point of view is a vital relationship muscle. It allows us to understand their priorities and their motivations, to anticipate their behavior, and even to predict their reactions. It enhances our ability to negotiate and cooperate successfully, to strategize and problem-solve, to communicate effectively, and to access our compassion, altruism, and empathy.

Loneliness and social isolation weaken our perspective-taking muscles and make us far more likely to commit social gaffes or to come across as inappropriate, too eager, or too detached. The fastest way to rehabilitate this relationship muscle is to identify our perspective-taking blunders and to correct them. The following three errors are the most important to keep in mind, as they represent our most frequent oversights.

1. Failing to Engage Our Perspective- Taking Muscles When We Should

As simplistic as it may sound, the reason we usually don't understand the other person's perspective is we never tried to in the first place. Perspective taking is a mental exercise, not a mind-reading trick. If we don't make the effort to think through how other people might see things, how they might react, or how their agenda might be different from our own, we are unlikely to take such considerations into account when interacting with them. One common manifestation of this omission involves our use of humor. When we're considering whether to tell a joke, we typically give almost exclusive priority to whether *we* find the joke funny and fail to consider whether it will be funny to others. Alban thought referring to his wife as "the other woman" (relative to his job) was hilarious, while Blanca obviously did not. Had Alban given even a moment's thought to how she reacted to the joke in the past, her feelings about it would have been immediately obvious to him.

2. We Favor Our Own Point of View

Our own perspective is so apparent to us that we often fail to give the other person's point of view sufficient weight. For example, scientists studied how people interpret sincere versus sarcastic phone messages (where tone of voice is helpful in detecting sarcasm) and those communicated by e-mail. We are all aware that written messages lack tonal cues that help the recipient understand our intended meaning. Yet time and again we anticipate readers will be able to distinguish between our sincere and sarcastic e-mail messages with the same accuracy as they would a phone message. And time and again we are surprised to discover that our messages are taken the wrong way.

The reason this happens is that although we're aware electronic communications can easily be misinterpreted, we tend to assume such errors are the reader's fault; but research clearly demonstrates it is the person who sends the message whose assumptions are faulty. To correct this specific error we must give sufficient weight to how the other person might interpret our electronic communications (and, no—emoticons are not the answer).

3. We Consider the Wrong Information

We often fail to consider *accurate* information that could potentially provide insight into another person's point of view (such as his or her facial expressions) but happily consider *inaccurate* information (such as broad stereotypes or gossip). For example, when evaluating the preferences of people we perceive as similar to us, we tend to use ourselves as reference points. But when we perceive others as being less similar, we are more likely to resort to stereotypes to assess their preferences. Once we consider how this dynamic might play out in gift-giving scenarios, it becomes clear why Grandpa ended up with twenty-three pairs of woolen socks for Christmas but without the Kindle he'd been hinting at since Thanksgiving.

Perspective-Taking Errors in Intimate Relationships

The more familiar we are with another person, the more accurate our efforts to understand their point of view should be. As such, we might assume that the longer a couple has been together, the fewer perspective-taking errors they make with one another. But, as most couple therapists can attest, couples who've been together longest are often those who exhibit the most perspective-taking flubs.

Why does this happen?

Unfortunately, it is the couple's very familiarity with one another that trips them up. The more time we've spent with our partner the more confident we feel in our ability to assess his or her point of view without giving it much thought (perspective-taking error #1 in action). However, since familiarity with a person rarely bestows the ability to read the person's mind, such confidence is likely to land us in the doghouse more often than not.

This blind spot can be extremely troublesome for intimate relationships. For example, partners often dread birthdays and Valentine's Day for this exact reason. One thinks, "Why can't my spouse ever get it right?" and the other, "No matter how much trouble I go to, nothing is ever good enough." In reality, neither person is taking the time to examine things from the partner's point of view. If they did they would communicate with one another and clarify their expectations ahead of time, rather than just playing out the same gift-giving debacle year after year.

Of course, having such "relationship discussions" is not always easy. One of the reasons Blanca initiated couples therapy with Alban was that he tended to clam up whenever she tried discussing relationship issues with him. Indeed, women are often more proficient than their husbands at discussing their feelings and expectations, which can make men feel they're fighting a losing battle. Rather than saying the wrong thing, they prefer to say nothing and get their "inevitable defeat" over with as soon as possible. The best way for women to fight this tendency is to avoid outtalking their partners. Women should give men the space and leeway to express their thoughts and even to restate them (without incurring a "penalty") if their words do not reflect their true intent. When men are more proficient at emotional expression than their partners, they should take similar precautions.

In short, we should always ask ourselves how the other person's point of view might differ from our own. We should give weight to what we know about their priorities and preferences, to the history of the relationship between us, and to the context of the current situation. Taking a few minutes to answer such questions can save hours of relationship talks to smooth over a situation that could have been prevented had we made the effort to think through the other person's perspective ahead of time.

TREATMENT SUMMARY: TAKE THE OTHER PERSON'S PERSPECTIVE

Dosage: Administer full treatment and practice frequently. Do not get discouraged by initial failures, as building and improving these skills takes both time and practice.

Effective for: Rebuilding and strengthening weak relationship muscles, improving social interactions, and enhancing relationships.

Secondary benefits: Reduces emotional suffering.

Treatment D: Deepen Your Emotional Bonds

Empathy involves stepping into another person's shoes in order to gain an understanding of their emotional experience and then conveying our insights to them convincingly. Rather than merely acquiring their point of view as we do when perspective taking, we seek a deeper understanding so we can glimpse how they actually feel. Much as we do with perspective taking, we regularly overestimate our capacity to employ empathy successfully. One of the reasons this happens is that empathy is not necessarily an easy skill. It requires a Jedi mind trick of sorts, albeit one we do to our own minds. Specifically, we have to direct our awareness to a place it does not automatically go—to what it actually feels like to be another person—linger there for a moment until we register the other person's emotional landscape, and then return to our own reality.

Surveys of college students have found that their empathy skills have decreased significantly over the past thirty years, which probably reflects a larger societal trend. Most of us could use a tune-up when it comes to both our empathy and perspective-taking skills. For example, Alban had trouble understanding why his wife, Blanca, was so angry with him for leaving the flowers and card he got her for Valentine's Day on the kitchen counter. After all, he'd not only remembered Valentine's Day (as opposed to previous years in which he had forgotten it entirely), but despite the huge amount of work waiting for him when he got home he'd taken the time to stop and get his wife tokens of his affection. When I asked Alban to consider things from Blanca's point of view, he quickly conceded he'd screwed up, but he just didn't understand why his good intentions counted for so little.

How to Access Our Empathy

The only way to gain insight as to how other people feel is to imagine ourselves in their situation, not just for a second or two, but until we can use our own emotional compass to point to how they might be feeling. To do so accurately, we need a good sense of their emotional landscape—the context leading up to the situation in question. For example, I asked Alban to consider Blanca's expectations, how she might have experienced the two hours between the time he arrived home and when she discovered the card and flowers on the kitchen counter.

"She saw me working in the study," Alban said, thinking aloud, "but she didn't see the flowers because they were in the kitchen." Alban's eyebrows shot up and he turned to Blanca. "You thought

I'd forgotten Valentine's Day again! That's why you didn't respond when I said good night."

Blanca nodded. I asked Alban to continue the exercise. "Now, taking that into consideration, how did Blanca react when she saw you in the study?"

"She didn't," Alban said. "She must have been upset, but she didn't say anything because I was working."

"So she was being considerate," I said. Alban nodded. "So how was she feeling right before she discovered the flowers in the kitchen?"

"She was upset and disappointed; but she decided to be considerate and not discuss it with me until I finished working."

"For two whole hours," I pointed out. "She sat on her feelings for two hours. You go to bed and only then does she pass by the kitchen."

"And sees the flowers and cards on the counter," Alban continued. "And . . . damn!" He turned to Blanca. "You must have thought I don't even care enough to hand them to you in person." Blanca nodded. "You made efforts to contain your disappointment all evening and I couldn't even take a moment to hand you the flowers in person." Blanca nodded, exhaling deeply. Alban put his arms around her. Slowly, she softened into his embrace. "I'm such an ass," Alban whispered. "How do you stand me?"

"You do make it difficult," Blanca responded with a brief smile. Alban quickly promised to take Blanca out for a belated Valentine's dinner to make it up to her.

I continued to work with Blanca and Alban for several months. Alban had done a good job exercising his empathy muscles in the session, but it takes more than a single empathy workout to build up relationship muscles to their full strength. Alban continued to practice using empathy, and the more he persisted, the happier he and Blanca became. Over time, and with lots of work, their strained and distant marriage changed to one in which they both felt trusted, supported, and cared for by the other.

Improving our empathy skills will do wonders for our most important relationships. The caring and consideration that empathy conveys can spark a cycle of goodwill, affection, and generosity of spirit that radically deepens bonds of marriage, family, or friendship. Obviously this works best when both people are strengthening their empathy muscles with one another at the same time, but even unilateral efforts can bear significant fruit.

Because of the practice this skill requires, we should endeavor to practice our empathy muscles in a variety of situations and with numerous people. In doing so, we should seek opportunities to anticipate how people might feel about future situations as well as past ones. Keep the following in mind:

Visualize yourself in their situation. The best way to assess another person's emotional experience is to visualize yourself in his or her situation in as immersive a manner as possible. Take notice of the surrounding environment, of who else is there, the time of day, the person's mood, and any physical pains or ills the person may be suffering from. Imagine how you come across to him or her, not how you actually feel but what you actually convey to the other person. Keep in mind that in many situations we experience feelings that are contradictory. For example, when Blanca found the flowers on the kitchen counter she probably felt pleased that Alban had made the effort even though she also felt hurt, disappointed, and angry that he'd executed it so poorly.

Context is key. Understanding someone's feelings involves having at least a rough sense of his or her frame of mind at the time. The following questions are ones you might want to consider: What are the person's previous experiences with similar situations? What fears, doubts, hopes, or expectations might he or she have about the situation? What else is happening in his or her life at the time? What has his or her day been like up to this point? How might other relationships be impacting his or her responses?

Convey your insights thoughtfully. Having insight into another person's feelings only matters if we can convey our understanding convincingly and compassionately. Knowing how someone feels but communicating it poorly is akin to buying him or her flowers and then leaving them on the kitchen counter. Be as descriptive as possible. The more the other person realizes you've put thought and effort into appreciating his or her point of view, the more impact your empathy-informed communications will have.

Treatment Summary: Deepen Your Emotional Bonds

Dosage: Administer full treatment and practice frequently. Do not get discouraged by initial failures, as building and improving these skills takes both time and practice.

Effective for: Rebuilding and strengthening weak relationship muscles, improving social interactions, and enhancing relationships.

Secondary benefits: Reduces emotional suffering.

Treatment E: Create Opportunities for Social Connection

Loneliness makes us extremely hesitant to create new opportunities for social engagement or to take advantage of existing ones. We feel uncomfortable attending social events (especially those with too many unfamiliar faces), we hate traveling by ourselves, and we are reluctant to sign up for new activities or social groups because we dread showing up alone. We might see options for social activities around us, but we fear coming across as "losers" or "loners" and inviting the very stigma of loneliness we are desperate to escape.

The best way to overcome feelings of vulnerability, reduce our hesitancy, and avoid being labeled as lonely is to approach situations with a larger goal in mind. For example, participating in a speed-dating event would feel far less uncomfortable if we were doing so as research for an article on our blog or college newspaper. We would be far less apprehensive about signing up for a tour with other singles if we were amateur photographers or artists and planned to paint, sketch, or photograph the sites we visited for our portfolios. And we would find it easier to join a swimming, biking, or running group if we were training for a triathlon.

By having an additional agenda, we come across not as someone who is lonely, but as someone who is passionate about our hobby, devoted to our goals, or serious about our creative endeavors. Having a larger goal also helps reduce insecurity and self-consciousness because our attention is focused on the task at hand; documenting our speed dates, creating art for our portfolios, or making it through the triathlon.

Go Online

The Internet allows us to connect to people with whom we might share common interests and experiences without leaving our homes. It also allows us to adopt identities through which we can interact with others and express ourselves in ways that might not be possible in our regular lives. For example, Second Life (secondlife.com) is a three-dimensional virtual world where users interact with one another using a digital representation of their own choosing. Users can switch genders, make themselves older or younger, choose how attractive they would like to be, and give themselves various other characteristics and abilities. The interactions in Second Life cover the gamut from chatting to virtual mating, from conducting business to constructing homes, and participants report having meaningful friendships and relationships with one another.

Relationships and friendships that start online can be substantial and they often translate into in-person interactions. For example, a recent study found that online dating is now the second most common way couples meet (being introduced by mutual friends is the most common), surpassing previous romantic venues, such as bars, clubs, and the vegetable aisle in the local supermarket on Sunday afternoons.

Volunteer to Help Others

Another option for creating new social bonds is to volunteer. Helping others reduces feelings of loneliness, increases feelings of self-worth, and makes us feel more socially desirable to others. Helping others contributes to more happiness and greater life satisfaction, and it can also reduce our fear and hesitancy about engaging with new people (or indeed with people in general). By setting out to give rather than get, we can focus on the person in need instead of on ourselves, which in turn makes us feel less self-conscious, less insecure, and less vulnerable.

Treatment Summary: Create Opportunities for Social Connection

Dosage: Administer full treatment as needed and repeat as necessary.

Effective for: Reducing emotional suffering and increasing opportunities for social interaction.

Secondary benefits: Strengthens weak relationship muscles.

Treatment F: Adopt a Best Friend

In some cases, circumstances may prevent us from creating new social bonds or enhancing existing ones. People with limited mobility, who are isolated geographically, or who cannot reach out to others for various reasons frequently adopt pets to soothe feelings of loneliness. Dogs are great at soothing feelings of loneliness in people who are isolated, elderly, or dealing with a significant illness or psychological injury such as post-traumatic stress disorder. Dogs are also great people magnets, and many friendships and relationships have started with the sentence, "Oh, your dog is so cute! What's its name?"

Attesting to the singular therapeutic powers of our canine friends, one study had lonely people spend time alone with a dog or with another person and a dog together. Those who spent time alone with a dog reported feeling significantly less lonely than those who shared the company of the dog with another person. Whether the "other persons" in the study were informed they came in second to animals that drink out of the toilet and lick themselves is unknown.

Despite the many advantages of dog therapy, adopting any pet, especially a dog, is a huge responsibility and one that some of us cannot undertake for practical reasons. Cats have been studied less frequently than dogs, but they too can provide significant companionship and they are easier to care for than dogs, especially by people who are homebound.

Treatment Summary: Adopt a Best Friend

Dosage: Administer as needed and to the extent circumstances allow.

Effective for: Reducing emotional suffering.

When to Consult a Mental Health Professional

Treating loneliness with the emotional first aid techniques discussed in this chapter should help soothe the emotional suffering loneliness creates, correct the perceptions and behaviors that sabotage our efforts to deepen and expand our emotional and social connections, and provide new opportunities for social interaction.

However, if your emotional pain is so great you have thoughts of harming yourself or others, or if you find yourself thinking about what it would be like if you were no longer around, you should seek the immediate help of a mental health professional or go to your nearest emergency room. If you have not had self-injurious thoughts but nonetheless feel too hopeless or discouraged to apply these first aid treatments, or if you've tried to do so but were unsuccessful, a mental health professional could help you assess factors that might be holding you back and provide the emotional support necessary for you to move forward.

CHAPTER 3

IIIIIIIIIIIIIIIIII

LOSS AND TRAUMA

Walking on Broken Bones

Loss and trauma are an inevitable part of life, and their effects are often devastating. Losing a loved one, being victims of violence or crime, becoming disabled, developing a chronic or life-threatening illness, being exposed to terrorism or war, or living through other life-threatening and traumatic experiences can derail our lives and leave deep psychological wounds. Healing such wounds usually involves an extended process of readjustment and recovery that can be different for each of us. Much like broken bones that need to be set correctly, how we go about putting the pieces of our lives back together after loss or trauma makes a huge difference in how fully we recover from such events.

Some of the losses and traumas we experience are so deeply scarring they require the skills of expert mental health professionals and probably extended psychotherapy. As such, this chapter is not intended for those who've suffered extremely adverse impacts, and such readers are strongly advised to seek help from a trained mental health professional if they have not already done so.

However, many of the losses and traumatic experiences we

sustain in life are not severe enough to cause long-term psychological or emotional damage. For example, when we lose our job, when our best friend drops us after a bad argument, or when an elderly grandparent dies, we go through a period of sadness and adjustment but we usually return to our previous level of psychological and emotional health. However, the same loss can have different subjective meanings to different people. For example, if losing our job caused our family to become homeless, if our best friend was also our only friend, or if our grandparent raised us and had been in good health, the loss we experience and the impact it has on our lives can be far more substantial.

Whatever differences we might exhibit in how we cope with loss and trauma, we all face similar challenges when it comes to rebuilding our lives and achieving a full emotional and psychological recovery. We have to reset our broken psychological bones—reassemble the pieces of our lives back into a well-integrated and fully functional whole. Treating the psychological wounds loss and trauma inflict can not only accelerate our recovery but in some cases make it possible to emerge from such experiences with meaningful changes in our priorities, a deeper appreciation of our existing relationships, an enhanced sense of purpose, and greater life satisfaction—a phenomenon known as *post-traumatic growth.*

While many of the variables that determine whether we emerge from loss and trauma with diminished or enhanced emotional well-being are not in our control (such as the severity of the events, our basic psychological makeup, and our previous exposure to hardships), some are. In order to best utilize the emotional first aid treatments in this chapter we will need a clear understanding of the psychological wounds loss and trauma inflict and the challenges they present to our mental health and emotional well-being.

The Psychological Wounds
Loss and Trauma Inflict

In addition to the severe emotional distress they cause and the real-world changes we have to contend with in their aftermath, loss and trauma inflict three psychological wounds, each of which represents a different set of bones that need to be reset. First, loss and trauma can create such havoc in our lives that they threaten our self-perceptions, our roles, and our very sense of identity. Second, tragic events often challenge our fundamental assumptions about the world and our place in it, such that we struggle to make sense of the events or to integrate them into the larger framework of our belief systems. Third, many of us find it difficult to remain connected to the people and activities we used to find meaningful and we might even feel as if reengaging in our lives would represent a betrayal to those we've lost or a discounting of the suffering we've experienced.

Emotional pain engulfs all who experience loss and trauma but the extent to which we encounter these three psychological wounds can vary dramatically. Some of us might experience them only in mild form while others might find their lives profoundly impacted by them for years and even decades. Let's examine each of them in greater detail.

1. Life Interrupted: Overwhelming
Emotional Distress

The emotional distress we experience in the first torturous days following loss or trauma can be utterly paralyzing. We might lose the ability to think straight or to perform even the most basic functions of self-care, such as eating or bathing. Engulfed in emotional pain, we often experience every detail of our lives anew as we are forced to live through a wrenching series of "firsts." Our first meal without the person we lost, our first night alone after being victims of violent crime, our first look in the mirror after the events that altered the course of our lives. This endless array of "firsts" can keep coming at us for weeks and months: our first trip to the supermarket after separating from our spouse without buying his or her favorite foods, our first Christmas after losing our job without money to buy gifts for our children, or our first Thanksgiving without our recently deceased parent.

Every "first" evokes memories, painful longings, and deep yearnings for that which we've lost, and we might find it hard to care about anyone or anything else. Plunged into the depths of despair, our feelings might be darker even than those experienced by people suffering from the most severe clinical depression. However, grief is a normal psychological response to extreme circumstances, not a mental disorder. Regardless of how searing our initial emotional pain, it almost always subsides with time. As we begin to absorb the reality of our loss or trauma, the visceral pain begins to dull, even if by the most minute of measures.

Indeed, time is a hugely important factor in our recovery. We often move past the most acute stages of grief and adjustment after six months—although such timetables are obviously dependent on the nature of the loss or trauma and its tangible as well as its subjective impacts on our lives. But when we do not, whether because the loss or trauma we suffered was too significant or because circumstances prevented us from moving through the healing and recovery process as we should, we risk allowing ourselves to become defined by our experiences. The most unique aspects that made us who we are can become lost, subsumed by our grief, hidden from view such that even we no longer glimpse them. Our interests, our creativity, our joy and enthusiasm can all become obscured by sadness, pain, and endless rumination about the past, and our lives become truly interrupted in every sense of the word.

2. Identity Interrupted: How Loss and Trauma Challenge Our Roles and Self-Definition

Grant was a sales rep with a promising career and a love for shooting hoops with his friends when he wasn't on the road. One winter evening, Grant and two colleagues were driving to the airport after a long business trip when snow and icy conditions contributed to their driver losing control of the car. Grant was dozing off in the middle backseat when it happened.

"I went straight through the windshield, landed in the road, and lost consciousness. I came to a few minutes later. I opened my eyes and saw one of my colleagues lying right in front of me, dead. I tried to get up but I couldn't. I looked down and saw I was covered in blood. And my legs . . . my legs were missing." Grant swallowed hard. This was our first session and, judging by the emotions on his face, these were not events Grant spoke of often.

"Next thing I remember is the hospital and the surgeries, many, many surgeries." Grant spent over a year in various hospitals, where doctors treated his massive injuries and started him on a long road of intense physical rehabilitation. He also attended psychological counseling sessions. Grant's broken body slowly began to heal but his mind did not.

"I can't tell you how many times I wished I had died that night. It would have been easier. People wanted to visit, but I couldn't stand the thought of seeing anyone. I couldn't stand the thought of seeing myself either. Six years later and I still can't look in a mirror. When I do catch a glimpse of myself, all I see is a stranger. The person I used to be died that night. This new person, this broken-bodied cripple, is not me!"

My heart ached for Grant, not just for the horrible injuries he sustained but because six years later he was still in such terrible emotional distress. The psychological wounds inflicted by the loss and trauma he experienced were as raw as ever. His broken psychological bones had never been reset correctly and as a result, he never adapted to the new realities of his life.

Loss and trauma often force a new reality on our lives that, depending on the severity of the events we've experienced, can completely redefine our identities as well as the narrative of our life stories. Before the accident Grant had defined himself by his career, by his outgoing personality, and by his athleticism. But those three pillars of his identity were now completely absent and played no role in his life at all. Grant desperately needed to redefine his identity, to reconnect with the aspects of his personality and character that remained buried beneath his grief, to decide what his life could be about.

The challenge of redefining ourselves and our identities accompanies many experiences of trauma and loss. We might have defined ourselves by our careers and lost our jobs, we might have defined ourselves by our couplehood and lost our partner, we might have defined ourselves by our athletic ability and lost our health, or we might have defined ourselves by our parenthood and seen our last child leave home. In each of these situations we need to take the time to rediscover who we are, to search within for things we find meaningful, and to find new ways of expressing aspects of ourselves that lay dormant, buried under an avalanche of sorrow. When we fail to do so we are left with a terrible void that only amplifies the extent of our loss, fragments our basic sense of self, and sets us adrift in the stormy seas of self-doubt and self-loathing.

3. Beliefs Interrupted: Why Loss and Trauma Challenge Our Perceptions of the World

One of our most compelling human drives is the need to make sense of our experiences in life. We each have our own way of understanding how the world works (even if we've never articulated it to ourselves explicitly), and we filter most of our experiences through that lens. Our beliefs and assumptions about the world guide our actions and our decisions and they often provide us with a sense of meaning and purpose. One person might view everything that happens in life as "God's will," another might believe "We reap what we sow," some might believe "Everything happens for a reason," and others believe "Things happen for no reason at all." Some of us feel the world is generally fair while others are convinced the opposite is true, and some of us believe life is largely predictable while others revel in their belief that events are entirely arbitrary.

Whatever thoughts and perceptions we have about such things, loss and trauma can challenge our basic assumptions about the world and how it operates and cause us significant additional emotional distress as a result. Our struggle to make sense of what happened often compounds our initial shock and sends us on a desperate quest to integrate our new realities into a framework of fundamental beliefs that no longer provide us with the security they once did. Indeed, such "crises of faith" are common. We become flooded with questions and doubts and we often embark on a search for answers.

This intense need to make sense of things can leave us ruminating incessantly about how the events occurred, why they happened the way they did, and what we could have done to prevent them. We might analyze each of a thousand small decisions and moments that, if altered, might have spared us the painful realities we now face. As a psychologist working in New York City during and after the events of September 11, 2001, I heard many such questions expressed by my patients. "If only she had left a few minutes later she would have missed her train and not been at her desk when the plane hit the building," "If he hadn't moved to Boston he would not have been on that plane," and "If I hadn't stopped to look up, the falling debris would have missed me," are all examples of the thoughts and ruminations shared by many people on and after that horrific day.

We often spend months dwelling on such questions as we search for ways to make sense of the events. While many of us begin making sense of tragedy within six months of it occurring, many others fail to do so even years later. Yet, the sooner we reconstruct our worldviews in ways that integrate our experiences of the loss or trauma, the quicker the intensity and frequency of our ruminations will diminish, the better our psychological adjustment will be, and the less likely we will be to exhibit poor emotional well-being and symptoms of post-traumatic stress disorder.

4. Relationships Interrupted: Why We Struggle to Connect to Those Who Remain

Maxine came to psychotherapy to deal with her looming fiftieth birthday. Ten years earlier she had promised her husband, Kurt, she would celebrate the milestone with him by flying to Africa and going on a safari. Maxine had never left the country before, despite Kurt's many pleas for her to do so over the years. "It was ten years in the future, but it still wasn't a vow I made lightly," she explained. "I fully intended to keep it."

A few months after she turned forty, Kurt began to get severe headaches. "They gave him one test after another, but they couldn't figure it out," Maxine explained. "Then they did a brain scan. The doctor told us he had a tumor. They would try to remove as much of it as they could, but basically, they gave him three years at most. We cried each other to sleep for nights. Kurt was terrified of the surgery. He knew there was a lot that could go wrong. Right before they wheeled him into the operating room I promised him that as soon as he recovered from the operation we would go on the safari and that we would travel as much as we could in whatever time we had left together. He smiled for the first time in weeks."

Maxine paused to wipe tears from her eyes. "He died in surgery two hours later," she said, her hands trembling, tears now streaking down her face. "I miss him . . . so much! I still talk to him every day: when I get home from work, when I get up in the morning. I know this sounds crazy, but I even make his favorite dinner once a week. It comforts me, makes me feel less alone." Maxine gathered herself and continued. "I'm here because my fiftieth birthday is coming up in six months . . . and I don't know what to do. A part of me feels as though I have to keep my promise and go on the safari. But to do that without Kurt, to go without him, I'm not sure I could stand it."

Maxine and Kurt had no children, but they had enjoyed a thriving social life organized primarily around their love for camping and the outdoors. However, in the years since Kurt died, Maxine had lost touch with most of their old friends and she had given up camping and even hiking altogether. Her social network consisted of a sister who lived on the west coast and a few casual friends from work with whom she had dinner every few months. When I asked her if she ever considered dating again she dismissed the notion immediately and explained that doing so would feel as though she were betraying Kurt.

Many of us respond to profound loss by withdrawing into ourselves, obsessing about the person who died, talking to the person in our heads, and imagining his or her thoughts and reactions to our experiences. However, such phases are usually temporary. In time, we begin to let go of the person we've lost and move on, either by reengaging with the people and activities that populated our lives previously or by finding new people or experiences in which to invest our emotions and energies. But some of us become stuck. We maintain vivid representations of the person we lost, we hang on to the person's memory, and we keep investing our emotional resources in the dead instead of the living.

As another example, Sean, a young man I worked with in the summer and fall of 2001, lost his first cousin and best friend, a firefighter who died when the North Tower collapsed. In the months that followed, Sean became obsessed with the Twin Towers themselves. He spent all his free time watching hours of documentaries and films about their construction, reading everything he could find about their history, and researching various aspects of the buildings' maintenance and operations. Meanwhile, he withdrew from his large family. He refused to attend family gatherings and generally avoided the very people who shared his loss and grief the most.

While such coping mechanisms are reasonable in the aftermath of tragic events, when they continue too long we risk getting stuck in the past as Sean and Maxine did. In many cases, such habits represent a breakdown in our grieving process. Instead of resetting our broken bones, healing, and redefining ourselves and our lives anew, we end up adrift in our memories, relating more to what no longer exists than to what does. When left untreated, such patterns can persist for years and even decades, putting our lives on hold and keeping our futures tethered to the loss and trauma that have come to define us.

How to Treat the Psychological Wounds Loss and Trauma Inflict

Loss and trauma can shatter the pieces of our lives, ravage our relationships, and subvert our very identities. To put the pieces back together—to reset our broken bones—we first need to recover from the overwhelming emotional distress we feel in the immediate aftermath of loss or trauma. While the treatments in this chapter can help, if the tragedy you've suffered is profound, if years have passed and you have yet to recover from the events, or if you experience symptoms of post-traumatic stress disorder, such as intrusive flashbacks, nightmares, emotional numbness, or jumpiness and agitation, you should seek the counsel of a trained mental health professional. Let's open our psychological medicine cabinet and review our treatment options.

General Treatment Guidelines

Loss and trauma create four psychological wounds. They cause overwhelming emotional pain, they undermine our basic sense of identity and the roles we play in life, they destabilize our belief systems and our understanding of the world, and they challenge our ability to remain present and engaged in our most important relationships.

The treatments in this section are presented in an order that roughly mirrors the sequence of psychological adjustment and recovery we go through as we heal from loss and trauma. Treatment A (soothing emotional pain) suggests guidelines for how to manage emotional pain and discusses common fallacies that can delay our recovery. Treatment B (recovering lost aspects of "self") is focused on reconnecting to aspects of life that might have gotten lost and reestablishing a sense of identity, and should be administered only once we've returned to normal functioning within the home, at work, or in school. Treatment C (finding meaning in tragedy) is focused on making sense of the events and moving closer to finding meaning and even benefit in them. Treatment C should be reviewed first and then completed only after enough time has passed for our initial emotional pain to subside and we feel emotionally strong enough to do so.

If you feel as though any of the exercises and treatments in this chapter would be too painful to complete, please review the section at the end of the chapter that discusses when to seek help from a mental health professional.

Treatment A: Soothe Your Emotional Pain Your Way

Working in New York City during and after the events of September 11, 2001, I found that the majority of my patients, as well as those of most mental health professionals, were personally affected by the tragedy in some way. One of my patients was killed when the plane struck the South Tower, some were injured in the attacks, others' homes were destroyed when the buildings collapsed, and several lost close friends or family members. While many of my patients spent weeks processing their loss and trauma, some of those who were most affected by the attacks chose not to discuss their experiences in therapy at all. For example, one young man who was injured by falling debris clearly stated he preferred not to think about what happened to him that day ever again.

Although many of us believe it is essential to talk about traumatic events after they occur in order to minimize the risk of psychological complications, such is not the case. Indeed, a wave of recent research has demonstrated that many of our most cherished notions about coping with loss and trauma—well-known theories such as the five stages of grief (denial, anger, bargaining, depression, and acceptance) and common wisdoms such as the importance of expressing our feelings and the danger of keeping them bottled up—are largely incorrect.

For example, a technique called critical incident stress debriefing (CISD) is used by both the military and the Federal Emergency Management Agency (FEMA). The technique requires people who experience traumatic events to discuss them in great detail as soon after the events as possible, under the assumption that expressing what happened and how they feel about it should minimize the incidence of post-traumatic stress disorder. However, we now know much more about how memories (including traumatic ones) are actually formed in our brain. Specifically, the mere act of recalling an event changes our actual memory of it in minor ways. When we recall traumatic experiences while we're still flooded with intense emotion, we are inadvertently cementing the link between the memory and our intense emotional reactions to it. By doing so we are making it even more likely the memory will continue to evoke intense emotions going forward. As a result, we risk getting vivid flashbacks and making the traumatic memories themselves even more psychologically central and emotionally impactful than they otherwise would be.

However, that is not to say we should try to repress such memories or that we should refuse to discuss them. Indeed, most experts now believe there is no "right" way to cope with the aftermath of loss and trauma. The best each of us can do is to deal with such experiences exactly as our proclivities, personality, and worldview dictate. If we feel the need to talk, we should, and if we don't feel the need to share our thoughts and feelings with others we should not push ourselves to do so. For example, because my patient who was hit by falling debris on September 11 felt such a strong reluctance to think about the events, choosing not to discuss them was the correct course of action for him. Indeed, there is evidence to suggest that those who find it less pressing to discuss traumatic experiences might benefit from their natural tendency to avoid talking about their thoughts and feelings.

One online study began following over two thousand people in, as it happened, August 2001. Once the tragedies of September 11 occurred, the researchers realized they had a huge subject pool at their disposal. They decided to give the study participants the option of posting their feelings and thoughts about the events on the study website should they wish to do so. Three-quarters of the subjects chose to share their thoughts and feelings and one-quarter did not. The researchers continued to follow the subjects for two years and were able to examine their emotional well-being over time. For people geographically closest to the attacks, those who chose not to express their emotions had fewer symptoms of post-traumatic stress disorder two years later than people who had shared their thoughts and feelings online. Furthermore, the more people wrote (i.e., the longer their posts), the poorer they fared two years later.

These results by no means suggest we should avoid discussing our feelings if we feel the need to do so. The best course of action we can take in the aftermath of tragic events is to do exactly as our feelings dictate. Those who feel the need to share their thoughts and feelings with others should do so, and those who feel the need to remove themselves from such discussions should avoid them as best they can.

Following our natural inclinations might be advisable, but it can also be challenging at times. Those of us who prefer to discuss our feelings and experiences might find it difficult to do so if we lack sources of social support, while those who prefer not to discuss their feelings might find it equally difficult if they find themselves surrounded by vivid reminders. It was practically impossible for those affected by the events of September 11 to avoid thinking about their experiences, as reminders of the tragedy were everywhere. For months one could not step into the streets of Manhattan without seeing evidence of the attacks: the ruined buildings, the dust, the stench of burning materials, and the pictures of missing loved ones that were plastered on every wall, bus stop, and street sign along with heart-wrenching pleas for information about their whereabouts.

My patient avoided these reminders as best he could at the time, by burying his head in a magazine when he was on the subway, stepping away from water-cooler conversations when he was at work, and letting his close friends and family members know they should refrain from discussing the topic in his presence. Indeed, it is always best to let those around us know whether we wish to discuss tragic events or avoid such conversations so they know how best to conduct themselves around us.

For those who feel inclined to share thoughts and feelings with others, doing so can help us come to terms with the realities of our loss or trauma. Indeed, many religious rituals around grieving have exactly such a purpose in mind. For example, both Jewish shivahs and Irish wakes involve the gathering of friends and family to provide an outlet for the bereaved to express their feelings, thoughts, and memories while surrounded by sources of social and emotional support (not to mention copious quantities of food and alcohol).

When sources of social support are lacking or if we prefer to do so, we can also write about our experiences or compose letters to the people we've lost. Expressing thoughts and feelings we had not been able to share with the person before they died can give us comfort and even provide a measure of closure.

Regardless of how we choose to soothe our emotional pain in the immediate aftermath of loss or trauma, the most effective treatment—and one that is available to all of us—is time.

TREATMENT SUMMARY: SOOTHE YOUR EMOTIONAL PAIN YOUR WAY

Dosage: Administer as soon after the events as possible. Make sure to communicate your preferences with regard to discussing your feelings and experiences to those around you.

Effective for: Managing and reducing emotional pain.

Treatment B: Recover Lost Aspects of Your "Self"

When Maxine lost her beloved husband, Kurt, to brain cancer, she lost substantial parts of herself as well. Her life after Kurt died was completely different from what it had been when he was alive. She and Kurt had been extremely active and enjoyed a thriving social circle, frequent camping and hiking trips, and countless evenings spent with good friends. But Maxine stopped participating in all such events after Kurt died and, as a result, she lost touch with the friends and the activities that had been a substantial part of her life.

Many of us are inclined to avoid people, places, or activities associated with the person we lost or with the traumatic events we faced in the first weeks and months after such events occur. But maintaining such avoidance for extended periods of time is problematic when doing so involves cutting out significant aspects of our lives. Maxine lost touch with many of the very experiences and relationships that had defined her, and consequently lost touch with important parts of herself. Relinquishing so many meaningful roles and functions altered her very sense of identity and these losses were never replaced. She found no new interests and passions to fulfill her and she made few new friends. The void her husband's death left in her life was still as large as it had been almost ten years earlier.

Maxine desperately needed to fill these gaps either by going back to previous activities or relationships or by finding new ones. Many of us face similar challenges. We go through our lives feeling empty and incomplete even years after the tragic experiences that changed us.

Exercise to Recover Lost Aspects of Your "Self"

The following writing exercise will help you identify aspects of yourself you might have lost by finding new ways to express these missing parts of your identity and identifying new ways to recover meaningful roles you might have forsaken. I've included Maxine's responses to each of the questions for illustration purposes.

Caution: If the events are still fresh and the emotional distress you feel is still extreme, do not push yourself to complete this exercise unless you feel psychologically ready to do so.

1. List your qualities, characteristics, and abilities that you valued in yourself or that others valued about you before the events occurred (aim for at least ten items).

Maxine's list included the following: loyal, passionate, adventurous, curious, intelligent, leader, outdoors lover, expert camper, bonfire storyteller, compassionate, considerate, supportive, enthusiastic, loving, caring, and communicative.

2. Which of the above items feel most disconnected from your life today or tend to be expressed less today than they had been previously?

    Maxine indicated the following: adventurous, leader, outdoors lover, expert camper, storyteller, considerate, enthusiastic, loving, and caring. (Note that Maxine's list clustered around two aspects that had been central to her life before her husband died: her love of camping and the outdoors, and her close bond with the circle of friends who shared her passions.)

3. For each quality you listed, write a brief paragraph describing why you feel disconnected from the attribute in question or why the quality is no longer expressed as extensively as it had been previously.

    For example, Maxine wrote the following about why she rarely felt "adventurous": "I never thought of myself as a lone adventurer. For me, adventure was always about sharing new experiences with Kurt. What made it exciting was having the adventure together. Having them without him doesn't seem worthwhile and it even seems sad."

4. For each quality you listed, write a brief paragraph describing possible people, activities, or outlets you could pursue that would allow you to express the quality in a more substantial way than you are able to do currently.

When I asked Maxine to do this she struggled. She simply couldn't figure out how she might express her adventurous spirit without Kurt there to share the experience. "You think I should reconnect to my spirit of adventure by going on the safari, don't you?" she said, quickly adding, "But I can't, I really can't!"

"Actually, that's not what I was thinking at all," I responded. "I believe in taking small steps and a safari is hardly a small step. Actually, what caught my attention about your lists was that you stated adventures were experiences to be shared with Kurt. But it wasn't just Kurt. You were both part of a larger group of people who shared the same interests and passions, people with whom you might still share adventures, even if small ones. So here's what I was thinking," I said. "Which of your old camping friends would be someone you could see yourself going on a short hike with?" Maxine exhaled noticeably. She had been so convinced I was going to press her to go on a safari, she was happily willing to discuss taking a short hike with one of her old friends.

As another example, Grant had been very athletic and loved basketball before losing both his legs in a car accident. I pointed out that basketball was an extremely popular wheelchair sport and suggested he get information about local amateur leagues he could join.

5. Rank the items from the previous question according to which of them seem both doable and emotionally manageable.

6. Set yourself the goal of working through the list as best you can and at whatever pace seems most comfortable

(taking into account that taking action on each of the items is likely to cause at least some emotional discomfort at first). By working through the items on your list you will begin to reconnect to meaningful and valuable aspects of yourself and your personality, and by doing so, move forward.

Treatment Summary: Recover Lost Aspects of Your Self

Dosage: Administer once you have returned to normal functioning (e.g., within the home, at work, or in school).

Effective for: Restoring important aspects of one's identity and rebuilding disrupted relationships.

Secondary benefits: Reduces emotional pain.

Treatment C: Find Meaning in Tragedy

Since Viktor Frankl wrote *Man's Search for Meaning*, it has been accepted that finding meaning in loss and trauma is essential for coping effectively with such experiences, and thousands of studies have confirmed these assumptions. Finding meaning was a crucial factor in recovery from every kind of loss and trauma studied, from those with spinal cord injuries to bereaved parents of young children, from victims of violence and abuse to frontline veterans of wars. To recover from our tragic experience we need to set our bones correctly and put the pieces of our lives back together in ways that lend meaning and significance to the events by weaving our experiences into the larger fabric of our life stories.

But the question that arises for many of us is *how* to do so. We might be aware that people with similar experiences reached conclusions such as "I came to accept that it was God's will," "I realized I could help others who went through what I went through," or "I figured out what mattered to me and made big changes," but that doesn't tell us how these people reached their insights or how we might go about attaining our own epiphanies.

Scientists who examined how people go about finding meaning in loss and trauma realized the process includes two distinct phases, *sense making* and *benefit finding*. Sense making refers to our ability to fit the events into our existing framework of assumptions and beliefs about the world so they become more comprehensible to us. We are usually able to begin making sense of tragic events within six months of experiencing them (although completing the process of sense making can sometimes take months and even years). Once we do, we are likely to have far better emotional and psychological recoveries.

Benefit finding refers to our ability to wrestle whatever silver linings we can from our experiences. We might gain a greater appreciation of life and of our own strength and resilience, we might realign our priorities and identify new purpose, and we might recognize new paths that have opened before us as a result of our new realities. Benefit finding occurs only in later stages of our recovery, as it is not something most of us can or should do when still in the grips of severe emotional pain. That said, once sufficient time has passed, people who are able to identify benefits in their loss or trauma tend to display greater emotional and psychological well-being than those who are unable to do so.

How to Find Meaning in Tragedy

Once of the most common ways in which people derive meaning from tragic events is by taking action in ways that are directly related to the loss or trauma they sustained. Family members of someone who died of a rare disease might start a foundation to increase awareness of the illness that took their loved one. A survivor of sexual or physical assault might decide to speak out and educate others about how to avoid such experiences or how to cope with them if they occur. Veterans who've lost a limb in war often volunteer to help recently wounded soldiers adjust to their injuries and support them through their long process of rehabilitation. Many people who lost loved ones in the attacks of September 11, 2001, became involved in planning memorial sites in New York; Washington, DC; and Pennsylvania. Of course, not every loss affords us these options, nor are they appropriate for everyone.

The following exercises will help us identify new avenues of thinking that could make our individual explorations more productive. Two exercises facilitate sense making. The first should be completed only once we've begun to recover from the initial assault of emotional pain. The second should be applied slightly later, when we are emotionally able to contemplate potentially painful "what-if" scenarios. The third exercise facilitates benefit finding and should only be considered once we feel substantially recovered and stronger emotionally. If any of the following exercises are too painful to complete, please refer to the section at the end of the chapter that discusses when to seek the advice of a mental health professional.

Make Sense of Tragic Events by Asking *Why*, Not *How*

We often struggle to accept the basic reality of tragic events when they first occur and we replay *how* things happened over and over again in our minds. For example, Maxine frequently replayed memories of her last conversation with Kurt. Natural as it is to do so, when such ruminations persist, they become unproductive and serve only to reactivate our emotional pain. Going over how things happened and replaying similar scenes tends to add no new insights and does not help us make sense of the events. But tweaking one important aspect of these ruminative thoughts could make them more conducive to attaining new insights and to fostering sense making.

Specifically, numerous studies demonstrate that asking ourselves *why* events happened as opposed to *how* they happened is sufficient to trigger a qualitatively different and more productive thought process. Difficult as it is to answer such questions, by asking why instead of how we widen the scope of our thinking and of our associations and are forced to consider the larger existential, spiritual, or philosophical implications of the events. Such bigger-picture thought processes are more likely to help us find meaning in the events in time, and to reach a greater measure of internal peace as a result.

Almost ten years after losing her husband, Maxine never asked herself the big questions about why Kurt died and whether she could derive any meaning or purpose from losing him. In fact, such questions were so foreign to Maxine's way of thinking that she seemed momentarily confused and disoriented when I first asked them. However, once she was able to begin giving thought to the question of why Kurt died she found that she spent much less time replaying the events of his last weeks and months. For Maxine, asking why opened the door to fresh and meaningful thought processes that helped her move forward in her mourning after being stalled for many years.

Make Sense of Tragic Events by Asking *What Might Have Been*

Another feature of the obsessive thoughts we experience in early stages of loss or trauma is they are often characterized by fantasies about alternate outcomes. We ponder such questions as "What if the person who died in an accident had taken a different route?" "What if the cancer had been found earlier?" or "What if our attacker had chosen a different victim?" Some of us might feel that pursuing thoughts of "what might have been" can only focus us on the randomness of the events and thus make it more difficult for us to accept what *is*. But studies have found the opposite. Rather than eliciting a sense of randomness, thoughts that consider alternatives to the factual realities we've experienced (known as *counterfactuals*) can help us feel like the events were predestined and meant to be, thereby lending them greater meaning.

Much like asking why instead of how, counterfactual thoughts force us to think more abstractly, to make connections between different parts of our lives, to utilize our analytic abilities, and to see the bigger picture. All of these are essential aspects of the meaning-making process. Such exercises can help us break out of rigid perspectives that limit our ability to consider the larger context of our lives so we can arrive at fresh comprehensions and new perspectives.

Our natural tendency is to employ counterfactual thoughts to explore how we might have avoided the loss or trauma, but we can also direct our thoughts to how things could have been worse.

Some experts believe the best way to extract meaning from tragic events (again, once we've recovered sufficiently) is to combine both types of counterfactual thinking and consider both what our lives would have been like had the events not happened and the ways in which things could have been worse.

Thought Exercise: "What Might Have Been"

Caution: Readers should be advised that counterfactual thought experiments can be emotionally painful. *Review the exercise and complete it only if you feel emotionally ready to do so.* Further, those who do not believe in fate or predestination might not benefit from this exercise as much as those who do, and therefore they should not complete it if they feel that doing so will be either unhelpful or too emotionally distressing. For those who feel ready, it is best to complete this exercise in one sitting. Written responses are strongly recommended.

1. How would your life be different today if the events had not happened?

2. In what ways could the outcome of the events have been even worse than they were?

3. What factors prevented these worse outcomes from occurring?

4. How grateful are you that these worse outcomes did not occur?

Once you've completed this exercise, give yourself time to recover and to absorb any thoughts, insights, or fresh perspectives it might have evoked (at least a day or more) before moving on to the benefit-finding exercise. You may also choose to wait weeks or months or to skip the benefit-finding exercise entirely if you feel unready or unable to complete it.

How to Identify Benefits in Loss

Finding benefit in loss and trauma once enough time has passed is an important way to ascribe meaning and significance to the events so we can put them in their place and move on with our lives. Although it can take time to identify any such "silver linings," doing so can open doors to paths and opportunities that can become sources of both meaning and life satisfaction later on. Helping others who've had similar experiences; creating awareness about diseases, societal problems, or other dangers; starting foundations in memory of those we've lost; writing about the events and creating art and performances about them; and becoming para-athletes are all examples of ways in which people have extracted benefit and purpose from tragic events.

While identifying potential pathways for deriving benefit from tragedy can have a positive impact on our recovery it is the real-world application of these benefits that does our emotional and psychological recovery most good. Therefore, we need to find ways to put any benefits we identify into action. For example, we might come away from a tragedy with a greater appreciation of our family, but if we don't take action based on these insights, the benefit we derive from our new perspective will be limited. However, if we make changes that allow us to spend more time with family members or increase the quality of the time we already do spend with them, we are much more likely to have truly gained from our loss and reap the psychological blessings of doing so.

Exercise to Identify Possible Benefits

When completing the following exercise, make sure you have the time and space to relax and let your thoughts explore various possibilities without feeling rushed or pressured.

Imagine yourself ten years in the future. You have been able to achieve something meaningful and significant (not necessarily "Nobel Prize worthy" but meaningful to you). You have a quiet moment to look back and reflect about your journey and how it has led you to this current moment in (future) time. Complete the following sentences.

1. I never imagined back then that such tragic events would lead me to:

2. What I did was significant and very meaningful to me because:

3. The first step of my journey toward the achievement was when I:

4. My achievement was possible because I changed my priorities such that:

5. Changing my priorities led me to make the following changes in my life:

6. Along the way I realized my purpose in life is:

Treatment Summary: Find Meaning in Tragedy

Dosage: Review the treatment and administer it only when you feel you can manage the emotional pain or discomfort it might evoke.

Effective for: Reducing emotional pain, recovering lost aspects of our identity, and reconstructing damaged belief systems.

Secondary benefits: Restores and rebuilds damaged or neglected relationships.

When to Consult a Mental Health Professional

When the loss or trauma we've sustained is significant or when it impacts our lives in extreme or fundamental ways, we should always seek the counsel of a mental health professional. If you think you might be experiencing symptoms of post-traumatic stress disorder, such as intrusive flashbacks, nightmares, emotional numbness, or jumpiness and agitation, seek the counsel of a trained mental health professional who specializes in trauma. Further, if you've applied the treatments in this chapter but doing so has not helped your emotional or mental state or you have not been able to make changes to better your situation or resume your life fully and productively, you should also seek the help of an experienced mental health professional, preferably one who specializes in loss, trauma, or bereavement.

If at any point after tragic events occur you feel as though you are in too much emotional pain and have thoughts of harming yourself or another person in any way, you should seek immediate help from a mental health professional or go to the nearest emergency room.

CHAPTER 4

||||||||||||||||||||

GUILT

The Poison in Our System

Guilt is an extremely common feeling of emotional distress caused by the belief that we've done something wrong or caused harm to another person. We all fail to live up to our own standards from time to time and even the best of us can act in ways that offend, insult, or hurt someone, inadvertently or otherwise. How common are guilty feelings? Studies estimate that people experience roughly two hours a day of mild guilt, five hours a week of moderate guilt, and three and a half hours a month of severe guilt. In some cases guilty feelings persist for years and even for decades.

The reason we don't walk around feeling incapacitated by guilty feelings is that we usually experience them for only short durations. Indeed, guilt's primary function is to signal to us we've done or are about to do something that violates our personal standards (such as when we cheat on our diets, buy something that wasn't in our budget, or play video games instead of doing work) or that causes direct or indirect harm to another person. We respond to this signal by reevaluating our plan of action or apologizing to those we've harmed and mending the situation as best we can, and our guilt typically dissipates rather quickly thereafter.

Unpleasant as it is, guilt serves a crucial function in maintaining our individual standards of behavior and in protecting our personal, familial, and community relationships. When our spouse tears up in the middle of a heated argument, guilt makes us soften and reach out. When we're extremely busy and stressed at work and realize we forgot our mother's birthday, guilt swoops in to nag at us until we drop what we're doing and shoot her a highly apologetic e-mail or phone call. And when our friend discovers we revealed something he or she told us in confidence, guilt motivates us to offer a heartfelt apology, a promise of future discretion, and maybe even a nice dinner as compensation.

Guilt does so much to protect our most cherished relationships it practically deserves its own superhero costume and cape. But before we break out the spandex, we should consider that not everything guilt does is psychologically beneficial. In the above examples, the harm we caused the other person was mild and our efforts to apologize or atone for our errors were successful. Therefore our guilty feelings ceased immediately or at least decreased significantly as a result. Similarly, when we fail to live up to our own standards, compensating for our wrongdoing and correcting our behavior is usually sufficient to eliminate our guilt substantially if not entirely.

But there are times when our guilty feelings outstay their welcome and become literal squatters in our minds. While guilt can be heroic in small doses, in larger ones, it becomes a psychological villain, poisoning both our peace of mind and our most cherished relationships. And once the toxins of unhealthy guilt are circulating in our systems, extracting the venom is no easy task.

Unhealthy Guilt and Relationships

Although we feel guilty when we violate our personal standards, such guilt rarely lingers. When we cheat on our diet, when we spend too much money, or when we neglect our duties in some way, we might make efforts to compensate for our actions, but we are rarely traumatized by them. No one wakes up screaming in the middle of the night consumed with guilt about the chocolate cheesecake they wolfed down last Christmas. When emotional distress about violating our personal standards does linger, it usually engenders feelings of regret rather than guilt.

Rather, unhealthy guilt occurs primarily in situations involving our relationships—when there are implications for the welfare of others. Unhealthy relational guilt typically manifests in three primary forms, all of which inflict similar psychological wounds: *unresolved guilt*, which is the most common and often the most damaging, *survivor guilt*, and *separation guilt* (or the closely related *disloyalty guilt*).

Although there are innumerable offenses that can elicit relational guilt, one of the main reasons our guilt might remain unresolved is that we're much less skilled at rendering effective apologies than we tend to realize. Another is that even when our apologies are on point, the harm we caused the other person might simply be too great for that person to forgive us for or the person might want to forgive us but simply feels unable to do so (often a sign our apology was ineffective after all). In some situations circumstances might prevent us from being able to communicate an apology to the person at all. In each of these scenarios, our guilt remains unresolved and unremitting and can quickly become toxic.

Some forms of guilt occur without clear wrongdoing on our part. Survivors of wars, accidents, illnesses, or other tragedies often find it impossible to engage in their lives fully because doing so evokes images or memories of those who perished. They might be consumed by questions about why they survived while others did not. Or they might feel responsible in some way even though there was nothing they could have done to prevent the events from occurring. Many of those with severe cases of survivor guilt also suffer from post-traumatic stress disorder (PTSD). As such, their survivor guilt is merely a symptom of a more complex psychological disorder and the treatments in this chapter would not be appropriate for them. When survivor guilt is related to wars, accidents, and other traumatic events, it is best to consult a mental health professional who is specifically trained in treating PTSD.

Survivor guilt is often made worse by circumstance. We might have argued with a sibling just before he was killed in a driving accident, forgotten to call back a friend just before she committed suicide, or insulted a colleague moments before he was fired. One of the most unfortunate examples of how circumstances can induce survivor guilt involves Waylon Jennings, who was a guitarist for Buddy Holly. Jennings had a seat on Holly's plane the day it crashed, killing all aboard, but he gave up his seat to J. P. Richardson ("the Big Bopper") and took the bus because Richardson was sick. If that wasn't enough to induce survivor guilt, the last exchange Jennings had with Holly was when Holly teased Jennings for having to take the bus by saying, "Well, I hope your ol' bus freezes up!" Jennings retorted, "Well, I hope your ol' plane crashes!" Jennings later became a star in his own right, but he was forever haunted by incredible survivor guilt both by Richardson's death and even more so because of his parting words to Buddy Holly.

Fortunately, many of the situations that cause survivor guilt are far less dramatic or tragic than Jennings's. When we find ourselves more fortunate than others, either because we're doing exceptionally well or because they are faring unusually poorly by comparison, our empathy and conscience can combine to elicit an exaggerated sense of guilt. As a result we might experience psychological disruptions in our lives despite no wrongdoing on our part. For example, we might find it difficult to enjoy a promotion because our friend and colleague had competed for the same position. We might feel unable to celebrate our engagement to the person of our dreams because our older sibling is still single and unhappy. Or we might have trouble celebrating getting into our first choice of colleges because our best friend did not.

What makes survivor guilt especially hard to purge is that there are no actions for which we must atone, no relationship ruptures to mend, and no outstanding apologies to be rendered. As such, our guilt serves no relational purpose and its warning signals constitute nothing more than a deafening false alarm that poisons our quality of life.

Separation guilt involves feeling guilty about moving forward and pursuing our own life when doing so involves leaving others behind. We might find it impossible to enjoy a night out with our spouse because we feel guilty about leaving our children with a babysitter, even one with whom they are familiar and comfortable. We might feel guilty about living far from our aging parents, even when they are well cared for. Or we might feel guilty about taking a job or studying overseas when we know how much our families will miss us.

Disloyalty guilt arises when we feel such binding ties of loyalty to close family members or friends that pursuing our own goals or making choices that deviate from their norms and expectations makes us feel bad. We worry that our families will perceive our choices as hurtful condemnations of their own values and as betrayals of family loyalty. Such guilt is especially common around themes of religious practices and sexual orientation. One mother I worked with turned to her lesbian daughter who had just come out (and had agreed to join her for the session) and cried, "How could you do this to me?!" Her daughter responded by saying, "I'm not doing anything to you! I just want to be happy!" and promptly burst into tears while mouthing to her mother, "I'm so sorry. I'm so sorry."

Family members often feel betrayed in such situations and, unfortunately, they often convey their feelings to us in no uncertain terms. Of course, many adult children feel just as betrayed by their parents' lack of support and empathy, but guilt usually falls far more heavily on their shoulders than it does on those of their parents or other family and community members.

While the consequences to our relationships should obviously be addressed in such situations, what makes our guilt maladaptive is that it arises in response to an otherwise healthy desire to express our autonomy, to live our own lives, to make our own choices and tend to our own emotional and psychological needs.

Regardless of whether our unhealthy guilt results from wrongdoing on our part or not, the more excessive it is or the longer it lingers, the more toxic its effects become and the greater the wounds it can inflict on our mental health.

The Psychological Wounds Guilt Inflicts

Excessive unhealthy guilt causes two types of psychological wounds, each of which can be poisonous to our quality of life. The first involves the impact guilt has on our individual functioning and happiness. In addition to creating paralyzing emotional distress, guilt seriously hampers our ability to focus adequate attention on our own needs and obligations, and it often causes us to resort to blatant self-punishment. The second is that it wreaks havoc on our relationships. The effects of excessive or unresolved guilt impair our communication with the person we've harmed and limit our ability to relate to him or her in an authentic manner; in addition, its toxic effects often ripple outward and create tensions and allegiances that ensnare entire families, social circles, and even communities.

The reason it is urgent to treat unresolved or excessive guilt is that such feelings often intensify and devolve into remorse and shame. Once that happens, we begin to condemn not just our actions but our entire selves, leading to self-loathing, low self-esteem, and depression. In order to treat these two wounds successfully we will need a clear understanding of the impact they have on our lives and the damage they inflict on our relationships. Let's examine them in greater detail.

1. Self-Condemnation: How Guilt Plays Whac-A-Mole with Our Joy and Happiness

Guilty feelings come in a range of severities. On the lighter side, our guilt can manifest as an annoying pest that constantly nags at us and tugs at our shirtsleeves. It can distract us as we labor to attend to our obligations and slow us down as we go about the daily business of our lives. In its more severe form guilt can consume us, paralyze us, and become the central organizing theme of our very existence.

Yoshi, a college student, was only months away from graduating when he came to see me for psychotherapy during his spring break. His parents, both physicians, had immigrated to the United States from Japan in their early thirties, then struggled to find jobs as clinicians and took research positions instead. "My father says the happiest day of his life was when I was accepted into an Ivy League school with one of the best premed programs in the country," Yoshi explained. "They expected me to go straight to Harvard Medical School and eventually open a successful medical practice, so I could fulfill the dream they were denied."

The pressure his parents' expectations were putting on Yoshi was enormous, but as he continued his story I realized he was far beyond stressed—he looked absolutely haunted.

"I hated premed from the first class I took," he continued. "I kept at it for the entire first year and I did well, but I was miserable. Premed wasn't for me. Medical school isn't for me. So I switched majors. Only I didn't know how to tell them without breaking their hearts. They've sacrificed so much for me, for my education, I just couldn't . . . I've been lying to them ever since. But I graduate in a few months and then . . . they'll know!" Yoshi covered his face with his hands. "I feel so guilty I could throw up. I keep imagining their faces when they find out." Yoshi began sobbing. He was unable to speak for several minutes. "They've worked so hard to pay for my schooling. I could have gone to a state school and saved them so much money. They think I'll be hearing from Harvard any day now. They're going to be crushed, just crushed!" Yoshi broke into a fresh round of sobs. "I don't know what to do! I can't concentrate, I can't focus, I can't study . . . it's all I can think about!"

After managing his guilt for three years, Yoshi could no longer keep it at bay. His guilty feelings now consumed him, screamed at him, nagged at him, and made it impossible for him to ignore their presence any longer. They hampered his ability to concentrate, to focus, to think clearly, and to move forward in his studies.

Guilt makes many of us experience mental and intellectual disruptions that are so significant we might struggle to meet our basic obligations and to function at work or in school. Until we take steps to address the cause of our guilt or minimize its impact, we will continue to remain at its mercy.

Unfortunately, unhealthy guilt doesn't only make us feel bad, it prevents us from feeling good as well. In one study involving regular college students (i.e., not ones preselected for guilt issues), scientists flashed words associated with guilt, such as "blameworthy," "culpable," and "guilt-ridden," on a screen at high speed such that the participants did not perceive the words consciously but were impacted by them nonetheless—a process called "priming." A second group of people was primed with words associated with sadness, and a third (control) group was primed with neutral words. Participants were then asked to indicate how they might spend a fifty-dollar coupon. While subjects in the neutral and sadness groups allocated most of their funds to things such as music and movies, subjects who were primed with guilt-related words chose far less indulgent items such as school supplies.

This experiment and others like it serve as testaments to guilt's significant party-pooping powers, as even subliminal exposure to guilt-related words was sufficient to function as a killjoy for people who weren't even feeling guilty at the time. Certainly when we are in the throes of unrelenting or excessive guilt it is extremely difficult for us to enjoy our lives in any substantial way. Things that used to bring us pleasure, joy, or excitement lose their appeal, not because we no longer enjoy them, but because we no longer permit ourselves to do so.

This is especially problematic for people who suffer from various forms of survivor guilt. For example, parents whose children are victims of accidents or chronic illness, children (and even grandchildren) of Holocaust survivors, survivors of other atrocities, and spouses who lose their partners often feel guilty at the very thought of having fun or indulging themselves in any way. Such extended and severe guilt serves no productive purpose other than to unnecessarily diminish our own quality of life.

A Fight Club of One

Another toxic effect of excessive guilt is that we might try to relieve our emotional distress by punishing ourselves for our wrongdoings (consciously or unconsciously) with self-sabotaging or self-destructive behavior. Some of us even resort to punishing ourselves physically. Self-flagellation has a long and particularly stomach-turning history as a form of atonement and was especially popular during outbreaks of bubonic plague in thirteenth- and fourteenth-century Europe. People believed that publically whipping themselves with irons or flaying their own flesh would cleanse them from sins and ward off the Black Death. As civilization advanced, so have our methods of self-punishment, as evidenced by the dearth of people who whip themselves into a bloody mess in public and the abundance of folks who bang their heads against a wall in private.

Head bangers aside, far more of us resort to self-punishment than we might realize. In one study, people who were made to feel guilty by depriving a fellow subject of lottery tickets were willing to give themselves highly uncomfortable electrical shocks, especially when they found themselves in the presence of their "victim." In other studies, subjects who were made to feel guilty were willing to keep their hands submerged in freezing water for painful periods of time (and much longer ones than nonguilty subjects). What makes such findings remarkable is that the participants weren't warding off the plague—they just felt bad about a fellow student missing out on a few lottery tickets!

Seeking self-punishment when we feel responsible for harming someone whom we are unable to compensate for our actions is known as the *Dobby effect* (so named after the self-punishing house-elf in the Harry Potter series). The reason we nonmagical creatures resort to such measures, and the reason we might even do so publicly, is that such actions represent a clear signal of remorse. By making others aware of our emotional distress, we redistribute the emotional (or physical) pain our "victims" felt, even the score with them, and hopefully restore our standing in our social circle, family, or community.

2. Blocked Relationships: How Guilt Poisons Arteries of Healthy Communication

Significant guilt poisons the arteries of authentic communication and connection between us and those we've harmed (or, in the case of guilt trips, those who perceive themselves to have been harmed by us whether they were or not). Even if we don't realize it, unresolved guilt impacts our behavior around the other person, and it usually affects how that person behaves around us as well. In many cases, it also embroils others in our social or family circles, such that the natural flow of authentic communication between all the affected people quickly becomes poisoned and our relationships become extremely strained. The ongoing toxicity of our unresolved guilt in such situations can damage our relationships even more substantially than our original offense did.

We often experience guilt in waves and when it comes to our relationships, the waves are at their highest when we interact with the offended person. In such moments, our guilt can spike so dramatically that it feels like being hit in the face in dodgeball. Understandably, our natural inclination is often to duck these painful encounters whenever we can. In order to minimize any chances of injuring the person further, we avoid any mention of the guilt-inducing incident itself, when interacting with that person and with other family members. We steer clear of any related topics that might segue into the incident, a list that tends to grow as time goes on. We might also avoid people or places that remind us of our wrongdoing, and eventually we begin making efforts to avoid the person altogether.

While such strategies represent ineffective solutions at best, they are all but impossible when the person we've harmed is our spouse. Blake, a stay-at-home dad, and Judy, a pharmaceuticals sales representative, initially came to couples therapy to deal with parenting issues. They had three children, two of whom were diagnosed with attention deficit and hyperactivity disorder and all three of whom failed to respond to any efforts the parents made to set limits. However, their parenting differences were swiftly pushed aside when Blake discovered a text message indicating Judy might have had an affair with a coworker the previous year. He confronted her about it in our next session. Judy was stunned by Blake's ambush but she confessed to the affair right away. "It was a one-time thing and I've regretted it ever since," she said. "We had a drink after work and it just happened. But it didn't mean anything! It was just a stupid mistake, a terribly stupid mistake."

Blake, who had hoped Judy would be able to offer a compelling explanation for the text message, was absolutely shattered. "You slept with another man," he mumbled, shaking his head in disbelief. "You slept with another man. . . ."

Judy's face was a mask of guilt and anguish. "I'm sorry, Blake! I truly am! But I promise you it meant nothing. It was a mistake, that's all. You have to believe me!"

Judy was incredibly relieved when Blake informed her that

he'd decided to stay in the marriage. However, that did not mean he forgave her. In fact, Blake continued to feel so wounded he struggled to think of anything else. Every time Judy looked at him, she saw the terrible hurt in his eyes and she felt incredibly guilty because of it. As the weeks went by, they began to fall back into their normal patterns and routines, but Blake's pain lingered on and so did Judy's guilt. Judy's job in sales required her to be energetic and positive and she was able to adopt that mind-set when she was at work. But at home she felt oppressed by her guilt. She began working longer hours (making sure to call Blake every thirty minutes to reassure him she was legitimately in her office). She found excuses to avoid family engagements, both with his and with her own family, and she became less involved in the kids' extracurricular activities.

I decided to meet with Judy privately to discuss her increasing disengagement. "It's not just your guilt that you're avoiding," I pointed out, "it's your entire marriage." Judy nodded silently. But her guilt had become so overwhelming she simply wasn't sure whether she could tolerate it much longer. She was desperate to receive forgiveness from Blake and he in turn was desperate to forgive her and move on—but he simply couldn't. The cycle of hurt, guilt, and avoidance that played out between them devastated their ability to communicate authentically with one another and presented an even greater threat to their marriage than her affair had. When we play dodgeball with our guilt, we rarely win.

Tripping on Guilt Trips

Guilt trips almost always take place in close relationships and their most common theme is one of interpersonal neglect. "I could be lying here dead and you'd never know it because you never call," "If you get that tattoo it'll break your mother's heart!" and "Your father's been a wreck since your argument with him last week!" are common yet benign examples of everyday guilt trips that are the bread and butter of many family communications. The main reason we seek to induce guilt in others is to influence their decisions and behavior. But guilt trips have a boomerang effect we rarely consider in that, along with guilt, they also induce resentment.

In one survey, 33 percent of people indicated they felt resentful toward those who make them feel guilty while only 2 percent of guilt inducers mentioned resentment as a potential consequence of their guilt-inducing efforts. Indeed, few guilt trippers are aware of the self-defeating consequences of their actions. When we are the recipients of guilt trips we might respond to a person's charges of neglect by engaging with them, but the resentment we typically feel by doing so is likely to motivate us to avoid them even more going forward. Mild as the poisonous effects of most guilt trips are, over the long term, their toxicity can build and cause our interactions and communication to become superficial and perfunctory, and the quality of our relationships to diminish.

How Guilt Poisons Entire Families

When our transgression is significant or when the person we harmed remains unforgiving, it doesn't take much for the poisonous effects of our guilt and the condemnation of the person we hurt to spread to other members of our family or social circle. All it takes is for one person to take sides and invoke unspoken expectations of loyalty in doing so, and a divide is quickly established. Other family members then quickly line up on either side of the rift, poisoning arteries of healthy communication even further and affecting everyone to one degree or another. Many a multigenerational family feud was birthed in just this way.

The most fertile grounds upon which these toxic family dynamics play out are family events and religious holidays. Large gatherings create perfect stages upon which to revive a family's "greatest hits" of past wrongdoings. Of course, aside from inducing powerful guilt in those who committed the transgressions it creates tensions and divisiveness that can mar even the best-planned and most festive events.

Antonia, a twenty-year-old college student, was the third oldest of twelve siblings, ten of whom were girls. By Antonia's own admission, she, of all the siblings, had the most tumultuous relationship with their mother. "I'm from an Italian family," she explained in our first session. "Very Italian, you know? I always give my mother respect but I argue with her too. Anyway, things are really bad between us now and I have to do something." I nodded sympathetically, encouraging Antonia to continue. "I know this sounds terrible and everything," she said, "but the reason everyone is so upset is . . . I mean, what happened was I . . . ran her over with the car."

My eyebrows shot up so hard I thought my forehead would "ding."

"I mean her foot!" Antonia hastily clarified. "I ran over her foot with the car! And it was a mistake. A mistake!"

Antonia had been visiting her parents when she and her mother had one of their "scream-fests." Antonia decided to leave. She was about to pull out of the driveway when her mother ran out because, in Antonia's words, she "still had more scream left in her." Apparently Antonia's mother proceeded to deplete her reserves of "scream" by yelling at Antonia for disrespecting her and walking away in the middle of an argument. It seems her mother delivered her tirade so loudly and with such profanity, neighbors came out-side to watch. "I've never seen her so furious," Antonia recalled. "There was spit all over the car window. I mean saliva!"

Antonia, no slouch in the yelling department herself, yelled at her mother to move away from the car. "My mom stood back but she looked scary mad. It really shook me up. She made me so crazy, I forgot to straighten the wheel and didn't realize it was turned." Antonia swallowed hard. "I pressed on the gas and before I could hit the brake, I drove right over her foot." Her lower lip began to tremble. "I thought I would die. Die! I jumped out and saw my mother clutching her left foot and screaming. I almost had a heart attack when I realized I must have driven over it. She had bunion surgery on that same foot just last year! I was, like, 'Ma, I'm sorry! I didn't realize the wheel was turned! I'm sorry!' But she didn't even look at me. She just moaned in pain."

Antonia wanted to drive her mother straight to the emergency room, but her mother refused and insisted Antonia's older sister drive her instead. "I waited for them at home all night," Antonia continued. "I felt so guilty I could vomit. Vomit! Then my sister Maria comes up to me and tells me my mother says I ran over her on purpose! Can you believe that? How could she think that?!"

By the time Antonia's mother got home, her sisters had already divided into camps: those who believed she had run over her mother's foot on purpose and those who were horrified by the mere suggestion. Unfortunately, her mother's foot took months to heal, during which members of the extended family were slowly recruited to one side or the other. All the while, Antonia continued to visit her parents and communicate with her mother, albeit somewhat minimally, such that on the surface things appeared normal. But below the surface, the unspoken accusations and re-sentiments and Antonia's guilty feelings were snowballing. By the time the family gathered for Thanksgiving the tension was so thick, it ruined the holiday for everyone. Antonia decided to seek my advice before their Christmas was ruined as well.

Similar tensions and tests of loyalty are common in workplaces, among friends, and in other social circles such as recreational sport teams. When our guilt is substantial and unresolved, the poison that impairs healthy communication and creates stress between ourselves and another person can easily expand and become toxic for the entire group.

How to Treat the Psychological Wounds Guilt Inflicts

Guilt usually serves an important function by alerting us to when we might have harmed another person or when any actions we're considering might do so. Once we modify our plan of action or atone for our transgressions, either by apologizing or in some other way, our guilt subsides. Therefore, we do not need to apply emotional first aid treatments in every situation. However, if our offense is serious or if we've already made significant efforts to apologize to the person we harmed or to atone for our actions in other ways and our guilt remains excessive, or if we suffer from substantial survivor guilt, or separation and disloyalty guilt, emotional first aid is indeed necessary. Let's open our medical cabinet and review our treatment options.

General Treatment Guidelines

The most effective way to treat unresolved guilt is to eliminate it at the source by repairing our relationship with the person we've harmed. Mending the rupture and garnering the person's authentic forgiveness will cause our guilt to diminish significantly, and most likely dissolve completely, soon thereafter. Treatment A (rendering effective apologies) focuses on how to repair damaged relationships by crafting psychologically effective apologies that can detoxify any ill will the other person still harbors and promote relationship repair.

Treatment B (self-forgiveness) focuses on situations in which the circumstances prevent a direct apology to be issued or ones in which it is impossible to repair the relationship for other reasons, and provides other ways to alleviate guilt, and reduce self-condemnation and self-punishment. Treatment B is not as effective as Treatment A in removing the venom that is at the root of excessive guilt but it does provide a form of "psychological antitoxin" that can deliver much-needed emotional relief. Treatment C (reengaging in life) is focused on survivor and separation and disloyalty guilt (in which there are no relationship ruptures to mend). At the end of the chapter I discuss guidelines for when one should consult a mental health professional.

Treatment A: Learn the Recipe for an Effective Apology

In theory, the solution to toxic relational guilt is simple—you render an authentic apology to the person you've harmed and, assuming your sincerity shines through and your transgression was not too monumental, all will be forgiven, especially with time. However, research demonstrates that in practice, this simple transaction of apology and forgiveness goes awry far more often than we might expect, regardless of the area of our lives in which it occurs. Further complicating matters, both psychologically and communication-wise, when our apologies are perceived as insincere they can actually backfire and make a situation worse, spreading even more poison into an already toxic interpersonal dynamic.

The reason this happens so often is that crafting apologies that are effective enough to garner authentic forgiveness is far more complicated than we realize. In fact, until recently, it was far more complicated than most psychologists realized as well.

How is it possible that something as basic as an apology befuddles so many of us? After all, most of us are taught to say "I'm sorry" as soon as we can talk. Surely as adults we should be at least somewhat proficient at offering effective apologies. Alas, we're not. Although we're taught *when* to say "I'm sorry," we're never really taught *how* to say it, or at least how to voice it effectively. This exact issue eluded psychologists for many years. Hundreds of studies have investigated apologies and forgiveness but the vast majority of them have examined only if and when an apology was rendered, not how it was articulated nor what distinguished a successful apology from an unsuccessful one. Fortunately, relationship experts and researchers have finally begun to investigate the specific ingredients that make apologies effective and more likely to elicit authentic forgiveness from the offended party.

The Recipe for Communicating
Effective Apologies

Most of us conceive of apologies as including three basic ingredients: (1) a statement of regret for what happened; (2) a clear "I'm sorry" statement; and (3) a request for forgiveness—all of which must be delivered with sincerity (e.g., "Wow, I completely forgot about our date night! I feel really bad about it and hope you can forgive me!" as opposed to "Oops! Was that tonight?"). Although each of these ingredients might seem obvious, it is remarkable how often we end up omitting one of them. When I point out such omissions to my patients, they often respond as if I'm being petty by calling them on a mere "technicality." "Aw, come on!" they often say, "I'm apologizing, aren't I? The 'I'm sorry' part is implied!"

My response is usually to point out that flour is an implied ingredient when we're baking a cake, but if we forget to put it in, what we end up with won't look like cake and it won't taste like cake either. The analogy is important because if we want our apologies to be effective, we have to follow a clear recipe, and the three items above are not the only ingredients we need to include. Scientists have discovered three additional components that also play a vital role in an apology's effectiveness: validating the other person's feelings, offering atonement, and acknowledging we violated expectations. Let's look at these additional ingredients and then examine which of the total of six apology components were present or lacking in the apologies offered by Antonia, Judy, and Yoshi, and how their apologies fared as a result.

Validate Their Feelings

We generally find it hard to forgive people who hurt, angered, or disappointed us unless we believe they really "get" how they made us feel. But if their apology demonstrates a clear understanding of the emotional pain they caused us and if they take full responsibility for doing so, we feel substantial emotional relief and have a much easier time letting go of our resentment because we feel like our feelings have been validated.

Emotional validation is a powerful tool when used correctly, and a great toxin remover when used in apologies. Consequently, we need to put ourselves in the other person's shoes and understand the specific consequences of our actions, how the person was affected by them, and the feelings they caused. Validating the person's emotions by conveying we "get" how he or she feels does not imply we meant for the person to feel that way. Doing so merely acknowledges the person felt wronged, regardless of our intentions.

The reason this ingredient is so often omitted from apologies is because when we've caused someone harm, acknowledging how upset he or she seems strikes us as a risky proposition. The idea of telling someone who's angry, frustrated, or horribly disappointed in us that he or she indeed should feel angry, frustrated, or horribly disappointed seems akin to pouring fuel on the fire. Consequently, our instinct is to avoid addressing the individual's emotional state entirely. Yet, counterintuitive as it might seem, when we validate someone's feelings *accurately*, something quite magical happens. Rather than inciting further fury and pouring fuel on the fire, our message of emotional validation actually douses the flame.

Emotional validation is something we all seek and crave far more than we realize. One of the reasons so many of us feel compelled to discuss our feelings with others when we feel upset, angry, frustrated, disappointed, or hurt is that we hope to *get things off our chest* and ease our internal distress by doing so. However, in order to feel true relief, we need them to "get it," to understand what happened to us and why we feel the way we do. We need them to validate our feelings by conveying that understanding along with a generous dollop of empathy. When we spill our guts to our friends we hope they'll say "Wow," "Gosh," and "That's terrible!" We would find it incredibly unsatisfying if their only response to our heart-wrenching tale was to shrug and say, "Bummer."

How to Offer Authentic Emotional Validation

There are five steps to offering authentic emotional validation. The most important factor is accuracy. The more accurate we are when conveying our understanding of the wronged person's feelings, the more relationship poison we remove by doing so.

1. Let the other person complete his or her narrative about what happened so you have all the facts.

2. Convey your understanding of what happened to this person from his or her perspective (whether you agree with that perspective or not and even if that perspective is obviously skewed).

3. Convey your understanding of how the person felt as a result of what happened (from his or her perspective).

4. Acknowledge that his or her feelings are reasonable (which, given that person's perspective, they are).

5. Convey empathy and remorse for the person's emotional state.

For more detailed instructions on how to access our empathy and accurately assess how another person feels, see the sections on *perspective taking* and *empathy* in chapter 2.

Offer Compensation or Atonement

Although it might not always be relevant, necessary, or possible to do so, making offers to compensate or atone for our actions in some way can be extremely meaningful to the offended party, even if he or she turns down the offers we make. By conveying our recognition that there is an imbalance in the relationship and suggesting actions that can restore a sense of equity and fairness, we communicate a much deeper level of regret and remorse, as well as a strong motivation to repair the imbalance and make things right (e.g., "I'm so sorry I got drunk and ruined your birthday party. I know how much work you put into planning it. Perhaps I could throw a get-together in your honor to make it up to you.")

Acknowledge You Violated Social Norms or Expectations

One huge factor that prevents us from garnering authentic forgiveness from people we've harmed is they don't know whether we've learned our lesson. Are we changed people or are we just as likely to commit the same wrongdoing again? Therefore, we have to clearly acknowledge that our actions violated certain expectations, rules, or social norms and offer reasonable assurances that those will not be violated again in the future. Further, when possible, we should be specific and explicit about the steps we plan to take in order to make sure we avoid repeating our "offense" (e.g., "I've entered your birthday in my electronic calendar so I'll get a reminder every year.")

Effective Apologies in Action

Once I described these six components to Judy, Antonia, and Yoshi they were each able to identify numerous ways in which their initial apologies fell short. For example, Antonia's apology covered the three basics in that she expressed ample regret for running over her mother's foot, she made numerous "I'm sorry" statements, and she repeatedly begged her mother for forgiveness. Further, Antonia made efforts to atone for her actions (by offering to drive her mother to the hospital and offering to help out around the house), and she even expressed empathy for her mother's physical pain. But she did not do the one thing her mother needed most—Antonia failed to acknowledge that she violated the family norm of never turning her back on her parents and walking away (or in this case, turning the wheel and driving away) and conveying disrespect to them by doing so. Until Antonia offered her mother assurances that she would avoid violating this family rule in the future, her mother would not be able to forgive her.

When Yoshi finally confessed to his parents that he would not be going to Harvard Medical School and that he had not taken premed courses since his freshman year, they were every bit as devastated as he feared they would be. "My mom gasped and burst into tears and my dad just stood there stoically, trying not to break down, saying nothing. I told them how sorry I was, that I knew how much anguish, disappointment, and heartbreak I was causing them. And still he said nothing. I told them I knew how wrong it was to deceive them and to disrespect them by lying and I begged for their forgiveness, but he didn't utter a word. He couldn't even look at me. Every moment of his silence was like a dagger of guilt thrusting deeper into my heart. Eventually there was nothing more

I could say. He just turned, put his arm around my mom, and walked out. They haven't spoken to me since."

Yoshi's apology was extremely sincere and heartfelt and it had a lot going for it in other ways as well. He was extremely sensitive to his parents' feelings and he voiced repeated expressions of empathy. He also acknowledged the many social and family norms he violated. However, the one ingredient he omitted was that he made no offers to compensate his parents for the huge sums of money they would have saved had Yoshi been honest about his aspirations and attended a much less expensive school. Doing so would have impressed upon them how sincere he was about atoning for his transgression and doing the honorable thing. In addition, it would also have allowed them to save face with friends and other family members. They could explain that their son had a change of heart about medical school and that he planned to take full responsibility for his decision and repay the tuition they had invested in his education.

Obviously, even had he done so, the rupture in the relationship with his parents was profound and it would take time for them to reestablish their bond and mend things fully. But garnering even provisional forgiveness and feeling as though he was at least on the path of relational repair would have been sufficient for Yoshi's guilt to begin to diminish.

Judy, who cheated on her husband, Blake, expressed a clear "I'm sorry" statement as well as a statement of remorse ("It was a one-time thing and I've regretted it ever since"). But she kept asking Blake to "believe" her, rather than to "forgive" her. As simplistic as it might sound, if we never ask the other person for forgiveness, we are not likely to receive it. Judy's apology was deficient in other regards as well. Although she acknowledged her actions were wrong ("It was a stupid mistake!"), she did not explicitly address the fact that she broke their marital vows of fidelity.

When I pointed this out to her, she insisted it wasn't necessary to acknowledge something that Blake already knew full well, as it would just upset him further. But the real reason she failed to acknowledge she'd violated their marital contract was that doing so would expose her to an emotional "dodgeball in the face"—a surge in guilt and psychological distress. While her reluctance was understandable, by not making such an admission, Judy failed to come across as taking full responsibility for her actions. Most important, Judy made various offers of atonement (for example, by agreeing to call Blake every thirty minutes when she worked late), but she failed to express sufficient empathy for what Blake was feeling and she demonstrated no insight into his emotional state. As a result, she was unable to validate Blake's emotions in any way. For example, she said nothing to acknowledge how difficult it would be for him to trust her going forward or how challenging it would be for him to recapture his previous feelings for the marriage, even if it were possible for him to do so.

TREATMENT SUMMARY: EFFECTIVE APOLOGIES

Dosage: Apply the principles in this treatment fully and thoughtfully to the person(s) you have wronged. Make sure to craft your apology carefully and give thought to the best time and place to deliver it.

Effective for: Reducing guilt and self-condemnation and repairing damaged relationships.

Treatment B: Forgive Yourself

Apologizing to the person we harmed and receiving authentic forgiveness in return can dramatically alleviate our guilt and make it unnecessary for us to continue our avoidant behavior. However, forgiveness is sometimes impossible to secure, either because circumstances do not allow it (such as when the person we harmed is unavailable to us) or because our best efforts to elicit forgiveness have already failed. In such situations our guilt continues to poison our quality of life and our self-condemnation persists.

Although it is always preferable to receive forgiveness from the person we've harmed, when we are unable to do so, the only way to ease our torment is to forgive ourselves. Self-forgiveness is a process, not a decision (granted, it is a process that starts with a decision). We first have to recognize that we've beaten ourselves up enough and that our excessive guilt is serving no productive purpose in our lives and then we have to make the emotional effort necessary to work through it.

Self-forgiveness can be emotionally challenging but the results are definitely worthwhile. Studies have demonstrated that self-forgiveness reduces feelings of guilt and can eliminate our need to avoid the person we harmed. It also increases our ability to enjoy life and decreases our tendency to self-punish or act in ways that are self-destructive. Case in point, people who forgave themselves for procrastinating when they should have been studying were found to procrastinate significantly less than procrastinators who did not explicitly forgive themselves.

The Steps for Attaining Self-Forgiveness

Self-forgiveness by no means implies our behavior was acceptable or that it should be condoned or forgotten. Rather, self-forgiveness should be the outcome of a conscious process, an effort to come to peace with our wrongdoing. The danger of self-forgiveness is that we might forgive ourselves too easily or too readily or that we might fail to implement the changes, mindfulness, and caution necessary to prevent us from repeating our transgressions. Therefore, self-forgiveness requires us first to take full responsibility for our actions and give ourselves an honest and accurate accounting of the events causing our guilt. We must be able to explicitly acknowledge both our wrongdoings and their impact on the person we harmed, both practically and emotionally.

Coming to terms with our actions and their consequences can be emotionally uncomfortable if not painful but unless we go through such self-examination any self-forgiveness we grant ourselves will not be authentic. In cases in which our wrongdoing caused significant harm (e.g., we drove under the influence and caused an accident that resulted in people dying or suffering grave bodily harm) and we are unsure of whether we can or indeed if we should find self-forgiveness, we should seek the counsel of a mental health professional.

Once we take full responsibility for our actions and their consequences, we will be ready to take the second step and work on forgiving ourselves. In order to come to peace with our actions we will need to make some form of amends or reparations for the harm we've caused and find ways to minimize the likelihood of committing a similar transgression in the future.

EXERCISE FOR SELF-FORGIVENESS, PART 1: ACCOUNTABILITY

To create a clear divide between accountability and atonement the following writing exercise is presented in two parts. The first will help you accurately assess your part in the events so you can find ways to forgive yourself for your wrongdoings in part 2 of the exercise. You may complete both parts of the exercise as a single unit.

1. Describe your actions or inactions that led to the other person feeling harmed.

2. Go through your description and take out any qualifiers or excuses. For example, "She claimed she was insulted" should read, "She felt insulted." Items such as "He did the same thing to me once" or "She made it into a bigger deal than it was" should be omitted entirely.

3. Summarize the harm the other person sustained both tangibly and emotionally. For example, if you criticized a fellow employee unfairly and that person was fired as a result, you should mention aspects such as his or her economic hardship, the time and effort the person will need to invest in order to find another job, the blow to the individual's self-esteem, and his or her feelings of embarrassment, resentment, and demoralization.

4. Go through your above description of harm and make sure it is as realistic and as accurate as possible. It is important not to give yourself too much of a pass, but you should not beat yourself into a pulp either. Counterintuitive as it may seem, while some of us minimize the consequences of our transgressions, plenty of us exaggerate

them. For example, when Antonia first told me about the incident with her mother she didn't say, "I ran over her foot," she said, "I know this sounds terrible . . . I ran her over with the car," which made me immediately envision Antonia mowing down her mother while white-knuckling the wheel and doing sixty. Yes, she caused her mother serious pain, emotional distress, and a frustrating healing process—but that's still vastly different from what most of us envision when we hear someone was run over.

One way to make sure your descriptions are realistic is to imagine that an objective stranger will film the description you write as if it were a script. Would the film depict an identical rendition of the actual events? If not, make whatever corrections are necessary.

5.   Now that you have an accurate and realistic description of the events and your responsibility in them, it is fair to consider extenuating circumstances. Did you intend for events to unfold as they did? If so, why? If not, what were your original intentions? For example, Antonia never intended to run over her mother's foot, and Yoshi's original intent was not to wait three years before telling his parents he was not going to medical school. He just avoided the confrontation until his impending graduation prevented him from keeping up the pretense. If your intention was to harm, it is important to explain what drove you to do so and you will need to work on any character flaws in part 2 of the exercise. If your intentions were benign, what went wrong?

6.   What extenuating circumstances, if any, contributed to your actions or to their consequences? For example, Judy

had met her colleague for drinks during a particularly stressful period at work, and at a time she and Blake were struggling with their three children. She proceeded to have too much to drink and thus was more receptive than she might have otherwise been to her colleague's advances. The idea is not to excuse your actions, but to understand the context in which they occurred so you can ultimately find ways to forgive yourself for them.

EXERCISE FOR SELF-FORGIVENESS, PART 2: ATONEMENT

Now that you have a fair formulation of your actions, their consequences, and their causes, you can focus on self-forgiveness. When you cannot make amends to the person you've harmed, the best way to purge excessive guilt is to "even the score," first by making sure you don't repeat your transgression and then by atoning for your actions in some way. Studies have found that both atonement and reparations are effective mechanisms for purging excessive guilt, as long as you feel as though the actions you take represent a fair way to "balance the scales."

7. What changes do you need to make in your thinking, your habits, your behavior, or your lifestyle that would minimize the likelihood of you repeating the transgression in the future? For example, a parent who feels guilty for disappointing his or her child by missing a basketball game or school concert for the fifth time might decide to re-evaluate his or her work priorities and make changes that allow for fuller participation in the children's lives (i.e., switching jobs, taking a different role, or just rearranging their work schedule).

8. Once we've minimized the likelihood of committing the same transgression in the future, we need to purge our remaining guilt by atoning for our actions or making meaningful reparations. One way to do this is to strike a deal with ourselves and identify significant tasks, contributions, or commitments that would make our self-forgiveness feel well earned. For example, one fifteen-year-old girl I worked with who felt guilty about repeatedly stealing money from her parents' wallets decided to make reparations when she discovered they had been struggling financially. She was convinced that simply admitting to the theft would shatter her parents' image of her as a "good girl" and cause them significant emotional distress during an already difficult time. Since they never realized she had stolen any money to begin with, her solution was to increase her babysitting shifts and sneak the cash back into her mother's wallet as she earned it. Keep in mind that most teens who steal money from their parents' wallets feel no guilt whatsoever, let alone put themselves on a work detail reparations program.

As another example, a young man I worked with was driving through a "bad neighborhood" late at night when he scratched and dented two parked cars while making a tight turn. He panicked and fled the scene without leaving a note. He felt extremely guilty about his wrongdoing later on, especially when he realized it was likely the owners of the two vehicles might not be able to afford to repair the damage he had caused. He decided to atone for his actions by donating money (an amount significantly larger than what he estimated would have been the cost of the repairs) to a community center in the area, as well as to a local youth program.

What atonement or reparations could you make so that, once completed, your efforts would feel substantial enough to earn self-forgiveness?

9. Create a short ritual to mark the completion of your atonement. For example, once the teenage girl who'd stolen money from her parents snuck the last ten-dollar bill into her mother's wallet, she planned to surprise her parents by making dinner so she could enjoy her first guilt-free evening with them. You might remove a photograph of the person you harmed from an album and return it only once your task is complete and then literally close the book on your guilt. Or if you decide to donate time or money to a charity, find a way to note the completion of the task in some way, so as to signal to yourself that your penance is now complete.

Treatment Summary: Forgive Yourself

Dosage: Administer this treatment fully if you are unable to administer Treatment A for whatever reason or if you've administered Treatment A but were not successful in eliciting authentic forgiveness.

Effective for: Reducing guilt and self-condemnation.

Treatment C: Reengage in Life

Treating survivor or separation or disloyalty guilt is challenging because there is nothing for which we need to take responsibility or atone. Ironic as it may sound, it is easier to induce self-forgiveness when we've done something wrong than it is when our hands are clean and there is nothing for which we actually need to forgive ourselves. Nonetheless, while we cannot undo the suffering and loss of others, we can take steps to end our own.

The best way to move past our guilt when we didn't do anything wrong is to remind ourselves of the many reasons it is crucial we do so. The following three exercises are composed of sentiments my patients expressed over the years that allowed them to shed survivor, separation, and disloyalty guilt. Taken together, they represent powerful rationales for reengaging in life and they offer various avenues through which we can each seek to do so.

EXERCISE FOR SUFFERERS OF SURVIVOR GUILT

The following writing exercise includes sentiments expressed by people who suffered from survivor guilt but found ways to manage and overcome it. Write a brief paragraph about how relevant sentiments might apply to your own circumstance.

1. Morris was seventy-two when he lost his wife of fifty-one years to a heart attack. "I realized it was unfair of me to mourn for so long. She would have wanted me to enjoy the life I had left."

2. Sylvia, a breast cancer survivor, lost her best friend to the disease. "If I don't live my life to the fullest it would be as if the cancer claimed another victim. I decided it would be wrong to let cancer claim another victim."

3. Joey was a father of three who lost his wife in a car accident when she was running an errand he was supposed to

do himself. "I felt dead inside for many months. But I realized I had to get out of it. Otherwise my kids would feel as though they had lost both parents."

4. Jeremiah was the only member of his high school football team to get a full scholarship to a top university. He felt guilty about it for months and then spoke with his pastor. "He made me realize it would be ungrateful of me to deny the gifts and chances I was given. The best way for me to show gratitude is to take full advantage of them."

5. Shandra was the sole member of her department to survive a brutal round of layoffs. "I decided I'm going to excel, advance, and get to a position of authority so I can make sure good employees don't get fired."

EXERCISE FOR SUFFERERS OF SEPARATION GUILT

The following writing exercise includes sentiments expressed by people who overcame or learned to manage the separation guilt that arose when focusing on their own lives meant being less focused on the needs of a loved one. Write a brief paragraph describing how relevant sentiments might apply to your own circumstance.

1. Billy is the father of a severely disabled child. "Caregiving is emotionally stressful and extremely depleting. I figured out that when I make time to do things that bring me satisfaction and, yeah, even joy, I have much more to give."

2. Wanda looks after an elderly parent. "I always keep the airplane demonstrations in mind. In case of emergency, first put on your own oxygen mask and then tend to the

other person. You can't take care of others if you don't take care of yourself."

3. Marsha's severely depressed husband would break down in tears whenever she went out with friends. "I stayed home for months until I realized that by going out and enjoying life I'm not projecting callousness, I'm modeling optimism."

4. Cam and Bev felt guilty about leaving their twin toddlers with a babysitter. "They cried like they were being slaughtered the first time we left. But we realized that the more we coddled them the less resilient and the less independent they would be. Even if it hurts sometimes, we have to be able to have date nights both for our sakes and for theirs."

Exercise for Sufferers of Disloyalty Guilt

The following writing exercise includes sentiments expressed by people who overcame or learned to manage their disloyalty guilt. Write a brief paragraph describing how relevant sentiments might apply to your own circumstance.

1. Levi, an accountant, was an orthodox Jew who fell in love with and married a non-Jewish woman. His entire family felt betrayed but none more so than his father. "His feelings are understandable. But if I let him dictate how I should live my life he'd be basically leading two lives and I'd be leading none—and that isn't fair either."

2. Juan's Catholic father refused to accept his homosexuality. "I supported my dad when he got fired from his job even

though I was a kid and it made it hard on me too. Remembering that made me realize I deserve the same support from him. So instead of apologizing, I started demanding he show me respect for having the honesty to live the life I believe in."

3. Lucas came from a long line of home-schooled children. When he enrolled his daughter in first grade at a private school, his mother, a home-schooling advocate, took it as a personal rejection. "It didn't matter how much I tried to explain, she simply couldn't get over it. But I realized I was not willing to sacrifice doing what I know is right for my child because it might hurt someone's feelings."

Treatment Summary: Reengage in Life

Dosage: Administer this treatment fully and repeat as necessary whenever you feel surges of guilt about moving on or living your own life.

Effective for: Reducing guilt and self-condemnation.

When to Consult a Mental Health Professional

If you have applied the treatments in this chapter and you still feel overwhelming guilt, if you are unable to apply them for whatever reason, or if your guilt still impairs your quality of life and your relationships, consult a mental health professional to assess whether there might be other psychological factors at play, such as depression, anxiety, or post-traumatic stress disorder.

If you find the exercises in Treatment B too difficult to complete, or if you're concerned about your ability to come up with accurate assessments of your responsibility, you might benefit from discussing the events and your feelings about them with a trained mental health professional. If your guilt is so severe you have thoughts of hurting yourself or another person, consult a mental health professional immediately or go to the nearest emergency room.

CHAPTER 5

||||||||||||||||||||

RUMINATION

Picking at Emotional Scabs

W hen we encounter painful experiences we typically reflect on them, hoping to reach the kinds of insights and epiphanies that reduce our distress and allow us to move on. Yet for many of us who engage in this process of self-reflection, things go awry. Instead of attaining an emotional release we get caught in a vicious cycle of rumination in which we replay the same distressing scenes, memories, and feelings over and over again, feeling worse every time we do. We become like hamsters trapped in a wheel of emotional pain, running endlessly but going nowhere. What makes rumination a form of psychological injury is that it provides no new understandings that could heal our wounds and instead serves only to pick at our scabs and infect them anew.

Unfortunately, our tendency to ruminate is set off almost solely by painful feelings and experiences and rarely by positive or joyful ones. Few of us stay up nights on end replaying how we had everyone in stitches at a dinner party. Nor do we feel the need to go over every nuance of how our boss complimented our latest efforts at work. But if everyone at the dinner party was laughing at us rather than with us, or if our boss criticized our performance and yelled at us in front of our colleagues, we can stew over it for weeks.

The danger of rumination is not only that it deepens whatever emotional distress we already feel about the events, but that it is linked to a wide range of threats to our psychological and physical health. Specifically, rumination increases our likelihood of becoming depressed and prolongs the duration of depressive episodes when we have them; it is associated with greater risk of alcohol abuse and eating disorders, it fosters negative thinking and impaired problem solving, and it increases our psychological and physiological stress responses and puts us at greater risk for cardiovascular disease.

Despite being aware of these dangers for decades, many psychotherapists struggle when it comes to treating rumination in their patients because their approaches are based on the assumption that the best way to purge ourselves of our preoccupations is to talk them through. But when we have ruminative tendencies, revisiting the same feelings and problems over and over again, even with a therapist, only increases our drive to ruminate and makes matters worse.

To be clear, not every attempt to analyze emotionally painful experiences is doomed to cause us more harm than good. Certainly there are many forms of self-reflection that are perfectly useful and adaptive. The question is, what distinguishes these adaptive forms of self-reflection from the maladaptive ones? Further, can those of us with ruminative tendencies find ways to think about our feelings and problems more productively so that we don't end up picking at our emotional scabs and preventing them from healing?

These questions have been occupying and preoccupying the

thoughts of a new generation of researchers. Fortunately, their ruminations about rumination have yielded fascinating studies and promising new approaches. As a result, we've finally begun to pull back the veil on the mechanisms that underlie both maladaptive rumination and helpful self-reflection and we've begun to learn how we can modify our ruminative tendencies to make them less damaging and more psychologically beneficial. In order to utilize these new discoveries we first need a better understanding of the psychological wounds rumination inflicts.

The Psychological Wounds Rumination Inflicts

Ruminating on our problems and feelings scratches at our emotional scabs and causes four primary psychological wounds: it intensifies our sadness and allows it to persist for far longer than it might have otherwise; likewise, it intensifies and prolongs our anger; it hogs substantial amounts of emotional and intellectual resources, inhibiting motivation, initiative, and our ability to focus and think productively; and our need to discuss the same events or feelings repeatedly for weeks, months, and sometimes years on end taxes the patience and compassion of our social support systems and puts our relationships at risk. Let's examine each of these wounds in greater detail.

1. Supersizing Our Misery: Why Rumination and Sadness Are Best Friends Forever

One of the reasons rumination is so difficult to treat is its self-reinforcing nature. Ruminating about problems tends to make us even more upset about them, and the more upset we are the stronger the urge to ruminate becomes. This dynamic represents the primary reason rumination puts us at risk for developing clinical depression: hyperfocusing on painful emotions and experiences can damage our mood, distort our perceptions so we view our lives more negatively, and make us feel helpless and hopeless as a result. Further, once we have a tendency to ruminate, it becomes easy to trigger a ruminative cycle whenever we self-reflect, even if there is nothing necessarily distressing going on in our lives at that moment.

A simple experiment demonstrates this dynamic beautifully. Scientists asked regular people on a regular day to reflect on their feelings for eight minutes. Many of us can do this without it having any impact on our mood whatsoever, and indeed, we might struggle to fathom why it should. But people who were a little sad to begin with, and those with a tendency to ruminate, reported feeling significantly sadder after this eight-minute exercise than they had been previously. Again, people's emotions were not manipulated in any way in these experiments, they were simply asked to think about their feelings.

My work with Linda, a corporate attorney, provides a good illustration of how persistent ruminations can be. Linda graduated at the top of her class at an excellent law school and was quickly snatched up by one of the best law firms in New York City. A few years later, one of the firm's senior partners requested she transfer to his department and join his team. It was the most exciting moment of Linda's professional career to date. It was also the start of her downfall. Her new boss turned out to be a nightmare. He was critical, dismissive, patronizing, passive-aggressive, and condescending while at the same time incredibly demanding of her time and efforts. He was also a screamer, something to which Linda had not been exposed previously.

A year passed and Linda was utterly despondent. She considered transferring back to her old department, but her new boss made sure to dangle the carrot of partnership in front of her, hinting that if she improved her efforts and worked harder, he would nominate her for the promotion within a few years. He did give Linda above-average yearly reviews, but at the same time he also continually put her down, diminished her contributions, and embarrassed her by publicly belittling her efforts and yelling at her in meetings. Linda found herself regularly crying in the bathroom. With the encouragement of her husband, she decided to confront her boss about when she would be nominated for partnership. He promised that if she continued to perform as she had, he would nominate her by the end of the following year. Linda asked him to put his promise in writing and, much to her delight, he did.

Linda doubled her efforts. When her boss finally invited her to his office to discuss her future she could barely contain her anticipation. But instead of announcing her promotion, he handed her a terrible yearly review, chastised her for "slacking off" (despite her having worked harder than ever before), and told her she had no chance of making partner at the firm. Linda was devastated. She transferred to another firm soon thereafter, taking a large pay cut in the process.

Linda came to see me a full year after starting her new job because although she liked her new boss, she simply could not stop ruminating about her experiences with her old one. "I'm just miserable all the time," she explained. "I keep thinking about how he rolled his eyes whenever I spoke in meetings, the expression of disgust he had when he criticized my work, how angry he looked when he yelled at me in front of my colleagues." The emotional pain these and other experiences evoked was etched plainly on

Linda's face. Linda had sought out psychotherapy previously, but doing so had done little to reduce her ruminations and sadness.

Many traditional therapies involve patients examining their experiences in great detail and from every angle, something that can actually increase ruminative tendencies. Other approaches, such as cognitive therapy, involve less heavy pondering and instead teach people to identify negative thoughts so they can dispute them. However, this approach can also be problematic where rumination is concerned because in order to practice refuting such thoughts one has to keep bringing them to mind.

Illustrating this problem, in a recent study, researchers gave college students at risk for depression either a cognitive therapy workbook or an academic skills workbook. The participants' levels of depression were measured immediately after they completed the workbook and again four months later. Subjects with high ruminative tendencies felt significantly more depressed after completing the cognitive therapy workbook than those who completed the academic skills workbook. Asking people with ruminative tendencies to identify their negative thoughts and feelings, even if for the purpose of learning to refute them, caused them to ruminate about their feelings even more and to become sadder as a result. That their sad feelings persisted even four months later is a testament to the tenacity of ruminative urges once they become entrenched.

2. Anger Inflation: How Rumination and Venting Fan the Flames of Fury

Another emotion that tends to elicit powerful ruminative urges is anger. Many of us replay experiences that elicit our ire over and over in our heads. As with the self-reinforcing cycle that gets triggered with sadness, the more we ruminate about our anger and the more we discuss anger-provoking thoughts and experiences with others, the angrier we feel as a result and the stronger our urge to ruminate about these feelings and problems becomes.

Carlton, a young man I worked with a few years ago, fell prey to this very dynamic. Carlton's father had come from modest means, but after making a fortune in the stock market he insisted his son want for nothing. For example, after graduating from college, Carlton expressed an interest in moving to New York. His father promptly put him up in a newly purchased penthouse apartment and gave him a generous monthly allowance because, as he told Carlton many times over the years, "Nothing but the best for my son!"

Carlton tried his hand at several careers, landing one plum job after another with the aid of his father's connections. However, since he had neither the experience nor the qualifications to succeed in these positions, Carlton usually spent less than a year in each of them before being gently advised by his superiors to "try something else" or to "move on." The suggestion that he wasn't performing adequately caught him by surprise more than once.

"I kept assuming these companies would never offer me a job I was unqualified for. But they were just doing my dad a favor," Carlton explained when we first met. "Since they figured I wouldn't be there for long, they never told me what I wasn't doing well or what I could do to improve. They'd just ask me to leave. You have no idea how humiliating it was each time it happened!" Carlton's nostrils flared at the memory. "I didn't ask my dad for the apartment, I didn't ask for the allowance, and I never asked for help getting a job, not once. I'd just mention I was interested in something and the next thing I knew I'd get a call about a possible opening. No one told me these positions were over my head. Good ol'

Dad just kept setting me up for failure. *Nothing but the best for my son!*" Carlton added in a bitter imitation of what I assumed was his father's voice.

When Carlton was twenty-five he met Solana, a marketing professional. They married a year later. In the fall of 2008, a few months after their wedding, the world entered a global recession and Carlton's father was hit hard. He was forced to sell the apartment in which Carlton and Solana were living and to cut off every penny of his allowance. Carlton was between jobs at the time and he and Solana found themselves having to manage with Solana's salary and the small sum of money Carlton had left in the bank.

"I started looking for work like crazy," Carlton explained. "I applied to hundreds of jobs over the next six months and got rejected by all of them. No surprise there, my resume looked like one failed career choice after another. My dad was so into being the hero, he didn't care if it made me totally financially dependent. He didn't care if it screwed up my professional life. He didn't care that it could leave me with no chance of getting anywhere!" Carlton's face was red with anger. "I'm twenty-seven years old and I have no skills, no qualifications, and no prospects! He ruined my life! I'm angry all the time and poor Solana gets the brunt of it. She tells me to stop obsessing about my father, but each time I get rejected from a job I hear his voice in my head: *Nothing but the best for my son!* It's making me crazy! If I don't stop yelling at Solana she'll leave me. She's even said as much. And then I'll really have nothing!"

Getting stuck in an angry ruminative loop can leave us awash in fury and resentment and make us feel irritable and on edge much of the time. Angry feelings activate our stress responses and our cardiovascular systems such that over the long term, having consistent and intense anger ruminations can place us at greater risk for developing cardiovascular disease.

An even more insidious consequence of anger ruminations is that the general irritability they cause can make us overreact to the mildest provocations. As a result we often end up taking out our frustrations on our friends and family members. We snap at them, jump down their throats, and respond in exaggerated ways to minor and everyday irritations.

As an illustration of how easily we displace our anger onto innocent people, one study put people through a frustrating experience and then induced some of them to ruminate about it. Participants who ruminated after the frustrating experience were far more likely to display aggressive behavior toward an inept but innocent confederate compared to those who had been through the same frustrating experience but had not been induced to ruminate about it afterward. Even though the confederate had nothing to do with the situation that caused their frustration, the angry ruminators went as far as to sabotage the confederate's chances of getting a job they knew was hugely important to his livelihood and career.

Although it is no treat for our partners and family members when we get caught in a depressive ruminative loop, their quality of life (as well as ours) tends to take a much greater hit when the ruminative cycle holding us hostage is one of anger and irritability.

3. Cognitive Leakage: How Rumination Saps Our Intellectual Resources

Rumination involves such intense brooding it consumes huge amounts of our mental energies. By doing so it impairs our attention and concentration, our problem-solving abilities, and our motivation and initiative. Further, the faulty decision making we employ in its wake often proves incredibly costly to our physical and mental health. For example, women with strong ruminative tendencies were found to wait two months longer than women without ruminative tendencies to see a physician after discovering a lump in their breast—a potentially life-threatening difference. Other studies found that cancer and coronary patients with ruminative tendencies had poorer compliance with their medical regimens than people with similar disease profiles who were not ruminators.

Rumination causes us to stew in our negative feelings until we become so consumed with them that we begin to see our entire lives, histories, and futures more bleakly. Our negative outlook then causes us to view our problems as less manageable, to come up with fewer solutions to them, and to avoid implementing the solutions we do find. We might be able to recognize that certain mood-enhancing activities would be helpful to us but we are far less willing to pursue such activities nonetheless.

This leads some of us to soothe our pain with alcohol or other substances. Many of the ruminators I've worked with over the years claimed that drinking eases their irritability and makes life more manageable for those around them. While having a drink might take the edge off our irritability and make us more agreeable to others, the question is whether someone can stick with one drink or whether they tend to go for two, three, or more. When we use alcohol to manage our mood, our consumption is unlikely to remain at moderate levels for long. The more inebriated we get the less impulse control we have and the more likely we are to express our anger and aggression in destructive ways.

Our first steps onto the path toward alcohol abuse or dependence are often prompted by a misguided effort to manage the emotional distress and anger our ruminations cause. Some of us might turn to binge eating or purging instead. But whether we

turn to food or to alcohol or other substances to manage such feelings, the ruminations causing them remain unaddressed and we
only increase the risk of sustaining long-lasting psychological
damage.

4. Strained Relationships: How Our Loved Ones Pay a Price for Our Ruminations

Our ruminations are often so consuming, we fail to consider how
our need to constantly discuss them can impact our friends and
families and put a strain on our most important relationships. In
addition, we usually fail to spread our efforts evenly and prefer to
share our feelings with those who have been most supportive and
compassionate in the past, making them shoulder a dispropor-
tionate load of supportive duties. Even if these individuals care for
us tremendously, repeating the same discussions over and over
will eventually tax their patience and compassion and risk making
them feel resentful and angry toward us as well. When I point out
these risks to my patients they grudgingly acknowledge why someone might lose patience but not why that person might become
resentful or angry.

To understand why this might happen we need to consider
that lending emotional support and assistance to people who are
close to our hearts is one of the most rewarding aspects of close
friendships and relationships. Helping others we care about makes
us feel better about ourselves, it fosters stronger relationship bonds,
it increases trust and loyalty for both parties, and it allows us to
feel valuable and meaningful in the world.

Consider, then, that by bringing up the same thoughts and
feelings we've discussed many times before we cannot help but
communicate to those around us that their previous efforts to help

us were ultimately lacking because here we are asking them to do so all over again. At best they were able to provide us with a measure of relief but it clearly didn't last long if we're expecting them to repeat their efforts. Our supportive friends and family members might not pick up on this embedded "insult" consciously but they are likely to find themselves feeling vaguely angry and resentful nonetheless.

Further, we each have an internal statute of limitations when it comes to how long we feel it's fair for someone to be distressed about certain events. Once that period has expired and we're asked to listen and be supportive again nonetheless, we might offer our support and compassion out of duty, obligation, or guilt but we'll probably feel somewhat resentful and angry about having to do so.

I once worked with a young man whose fiancée had left him only weeks before their wedding, and he spoke about little else with his buddies for over a year. From what I gleaned, his friends were showing every sign of losing patience with his constant obsessions and soliloquies about his ex. They started changing the nature of their get-togethers with him so that instead of activities that fostered conversation, like golf, dinners, or meeting at bars, they suggested movies and activities such as basketball or football. Unfortunately, the young man did not heed any of his friends' hints nor my own warnings about their rising resentment. When he broached the subject for the umpteenth time during a game of basketball, one of his friends became so exasperated he stopped the game and yelled, "Come on, dude! Just man up already!" and punctuated his statement by throwing the basketball straight into my patient's face, breaking his nose in the process.

Clearly the friend's resentment had been building up over many months and had reached a boiling point. But he hadn't said a word about feeling burdened by my patient's incessant ruminations. Indeed, none of his friends had. The assaultive friend did receive his comeuppance, however, as he spent the next five hours in the emergency room, listening to my patient replay nasal renditions of the breakup while avoiding sprays of bloody gauze from his nose.

Of course, few of our friends throw things at us in exasperation when we chew their ears off, but that doesn't mean they don't feel like doing so. Intense ruminations can often make us so focused on our own emotional needs that we become blind to those of the people around us and our relationships often suffer as a result.

How to Treat the Psychological Wounds Rumination Inflicts

It is natural to reflect on upsetting events after they occur and to mull them over in our minds. The intensity and frequency of normative preoccupations should decrease with time and as such they do not usually require treatment. But when time has passed and the frequency and emotional intensity of our preoccupations continue unabated, we should make efforts to break the cycle of rumination and apply emotional first aid. Let's open our psychological medicine cabinet and examine the treatment options available to us.

General Treatment Guidelines

In order to break the self-reinforcing nature of ruminative thoughts and allow our wounds to heal we must interrupt the cycle of rumination once it gets triggered, and we should weaken the urge to ruminate at the source by diminishing the intensity of the feelings that fuel it. We must also make efforts to monitor our relationships and to ease the emotional burden we might be placing on our loved ones.

The following treatments are listed in the order in which they should be administered. Treatment A (changing perspective) is focused on reducing the intensity of the urge that compels us to ruminate, and Treatment B (distraction from emotional pain) is focused on reducing the frequency of ruminative thoughts (which is easier to do once the urge to ruminate is less intense). Treatment C (reframing anger) targets the anger and aggressive impulses ruminations can evoke, and Treatment D (managing friendships) is useful for monitoring our relationships with those who provide emotional support.

Treatment A: Change Your Perspective

When scientists began investigating the mechanics of how we self-reflect on painful feelings and experiences in an effort to understand what distinguishes adaptive from maladaptive forms of self-reflection, one factor emerged as hugely significant—the visual perspective we use when going over painful experiences in our minds.

Our natural tendency when analyzing painful experiences is to do so from a self-*immersed* perspective in which we see the scene through our own eyes (also known as a first-person perspective). Analyzing our feelings in such a way tends to allow our memories to unfold in a narrative form (i.e., the play-by-play of how things happened) and to elicit emotions at a level of intensity similar to when the events occurred.

But when the researchers asked people to analyze a painful experience from a self-*distanced* perspective (a third-person perspective) and actually see themselves within the scene from the point of view of an outside observer, they found something quite remarkable. Instead of merely recounting the events and how they felt about them at the time, people tended to reconstruct their understanding of their experience and to reinterpret it in ways that promoted new insights and feelings of closure. This result was amplified even further when they suggested people employ a self-distanced perspective while reflecting not on *how* things happened but on *why* they happened.

In numerous studies, subjects who were asked to analyze painful experiences this way experienced significantly less emotional pain than those using self-immersive perspectives. In addition, their blood pressure was less reactive (it rose less and it returned to normal baseline more quickly), indicating that using self-distanced perspectives lowers our stress responses and causes less activation of our cardiovascular systems. The good news didn't end there. Follow-ups one week later indicated that people using self-distanced perspectives reported thinking about their painful experiences significantly less often, and they felt less emotional pain when they did ruminate about them than people who used self-immersed perspectives. These findings held true for both depressive and anger ruminations.

When I first read about these findings I immediately thought of Linda, the lawyer who ruminated about her abusive ex-boss.

Linda's descriptions of how she saw her boss's face (e.g., "I keep thinking about how he rolled his eyes whenever I spoke in meetings") clearly indicated she reflected on her experiences using a self-immersed as opposed to a self-distanced perspective. I was curious as to whether changing her perspective would impact her ruminations. I told Linda how to tweak her ruminative thoughts so she was using a self-distanced perspective and suggested she be as judicious as possible in doing so until we met next two weeks later.

Linda walked into our next session with a huge smile on her face. "It worked!" she announced before she even got to the couch. Linda reported that for the week following our session she had been diligent about employing a self-distanced perspective whenever she thought about her ex-boss; then she added, "But soon after that something shifted. It took me a few days to realize it, but I was thinking about him far less than usual." Even better, when Linda did think about her ex-boss, she reported feeling much less upset than she had before and she was able to put such thoughts aside more easily. She also found it easier to use distraction (Treatment B) when the thoughts did persist. The combination of the two approaches, perspective change and distraction, helped significantly reduce her ruminations in a short amount of time.

EXERCISE FOR CHANGING PERSPECTIVES

Switching visual perspectives to ones that afford us greater psychological distance from the topics of our ruminations requires practice. Complete this exercise when you have the time and space to do so without interruption and practice the technique for each topic or experience that elicits unproductive ruminations.

Sit or lie comfortably, close your eyes, and recall the opening snapshot of the scene or the experience in question. Zoom out so you see yourself within the scene, or if the scene involved two locations (e.g., if you were on the phone) imagine a split screen so you see both yourself and the other person or locale. Once you see yourself within the scene, zoom out even further so you can watch the scene unfold from an even greater distance. Allow the scene to unfold as you observe it from afar, as if you were a stranger who happened to pass by as it occurred.

Make sure to use this same perspective every time you find yourself thinking about the events in question.

Treatment Summary: Change Your Perspective

Dosage: Practice the technique in this treatment when you can do so without interruption and then apply it consistently whenever you ruminate. Once the intensity of the feelings the rumination elicits and the urge to ruminate subsides, focus on using Treatment B to cut off any ruminative thoughts as soon as they appear.

Effective for: Reducing depressive and angry ruminations, and restoring impaired intellectual and mental functioning.

Secondary benefits: Reducing physiological stress responses.

Treatment B: Look at the Birdie! Distract Yourself from Emotional Pain

Even once our urge to ruminate is weaker, cutting off a ruminative train of thought once it begins is still quite challenging. The main reason we tend to indulge the urge to ruminate even once we're fully aware of how damaging it can be is that we often catch our-selves ruminating only once our emotions are already churning. Trying to simply suppress our ruminative thoughts is not only dif-ficult, it is inadvisable too. Decades of research on thought sup-pression demonstrates that nothing compels us to think of something more than trying desperately not to think of it.

In now-classic experiments, people were instructed to see if they could avoid thinking of a white bear for five minutes and to ring a bell if they caught themselves thinking of one (the choice of white bear had no significance other than it was assumed that white bears were not something the subjects thought about often—maybe because the study was done in Texas). Less than a few seconds passed before the average participant rang the bell, and it was usually rung repeatedly thereafter. The more interest-ing finding was that once the five minutes were over and the sub-jects were "permitted" to think of whatever they liked, they experienced a rebound effect and found themselves thinking about more white bears than the average Klondike ice-cream truck driver. Since the original white bear experiments, many studies have demonstrated that efforts to suppress unwanted thoughts are likely to cause similar rebound effects, such that the very thoughts we try to banish return with a vengeance the mo-ment our concentration wavers.

While suppression is a dud as far as our war on rumination goes, distraction has proven to be a far more effective weapon. Dozens of studies have demonstrated that distracting ourselves by engaging in tasks we find absorbing or ones that demand our con-centration, such as moderate to intense cardiovascular activity, so-cializing, doing puzzles, or playing computer games, will disrupt a ruminative thought process. Distraction has also been found to restore the quality of our thinking and of our problem-solving abilities because once we cease ruminating, we recover our ability to apply our intellectual skills effectively rather quickly.

While socializing or going to the movies can take our mind off our ruminations, it is not always practical to engage in such time-consuming activities. However, brief and less labor-intensive distractions can also be effective in cutting off ruminative thoughts. For example, spending a few minutes engaging in a brief mental exercise like completing a quick Sudoku puzzle on our phone or imagining the layout of our local supermarket (e.g., *aisle two—cleaning supplies and toiletries, aisle five—Klondike bars*) was found not only to interrupt people's ruminations but to improve their mood as well.

Identifying which distractions work best, given the specifics of our situation (i.e., whether we are at home or at work, trying to study or sitting on the subway) and the nature of our ruminations, can require trial and error, as our assessments of how absorbing various activities or thought exercises will be are not always accurate. Whenever possible, we should test out our arsenal of potential distractions ahead of time so we can identify which work best for the settings in which we tend to ruminate most. The more distractions we have from which to choose, the more effectively we will be able to derail the ruminative train of thoughts that plague us.

Exercise for Identifying Potential Distractions

Complete this writing exercise for each topic or experience about which you tend to ruminate unproductively.

1. List the places and situations in which you tend to ruminate most often.

2. For each place and situation, list as many distractions as possible of both short durations (e.g., a game of Sudoku or supermarket layouts) and longer ones (e.g., a cardiovascular workout or catching a movie).

Once your list is complete carry it with you so you can refer to it when the need arises even if you're convinced you won't have trouble recalling the distractions you chose. Remember, our thinking is not as clear as it could be when we're in the midst of an intense rumination.

Treatment Summary: Distraction

Dosage: Create a list of distractions that work for you and apply the treatment as soon as possible whenever you catch yourself entering a ruminative cycle.

Effective for: Minimizing the impact of depressive and/or angry ruminations, and restoring impaired intellectual and mental functioning.

Treatment C: Reframe the Anger

In the film *Analyze This* a psychiatrist (played by Billy Crystal) encourages a patient who has anger issues to "hit a pillow" in order to let off steam. The patient (Robert De Niro), who also happens to be a mobster, pulls out a gun and fires a round of bullets into the pillow. The alarmed psychiatrist recovers his composure enough to ask, "Feel better?" The mobster thinks for a moment and then replies, "Yeah, I do!"

The notion that venting our anger produces a cathartic experience that will reduce our rage and improve our psychological state is widespread even among mental health professionals. Decades ago, therapists like the one played by Billy Crystal began advocating we vent our anger by assaulting benign objects and nary a couch pillow has felt safe ever since.

Indeed, the "catharsis model" of venting anger has spawned entire product lines with numerous forms of "therapeutic" toys for both children and adults. For example, one line of lifelike plastic figures comes with firm plastic bats children can use to express their anger "productively"—*by smashing the humanlike figures in the face and head.* The last time I observed a session in which the therapist used one of these figures it featured a seven-year-old bruiser who pummeled the figure mercilessly while the therapist stood to the side, saying, "Yes, you're very angry at Daddy, aren't you?" Not exactly a recipe for domestic tranquility, if you ask me.

The effectiveness of venting anger by letting off steam has been studied extensively and the verdict of all such studies has been virtually unanimous—the catharsis model is not only wrong, it is actually harmful! In one recent study angered participants were placed into one of three groups. They were instructed either to hit a punching bag while thinking of the person who angered them, to hit the bag while thinking of a neutral subject, or to do nothing at all. Subjects who hit the punching bag while thinking of the person who angered them felt significantly angrier afterward and displayed significantly more aggressive and vengeful behavior than those in the other two groups (bad news indeed for the "daddy" of the bruiser). In fact, it was the participants in the group that took no action at all who felt least angry and who displayed the least aggressive behavior.

Venting our anger by assaulting benign objects only serves to reinforce our aggressive urges in response to anger. These issues should be of special concern for the innumerable parents whose children's aggressive impulses are unwittingly being strengthened with every swing of the bat and every pound of the pillow.

So how should we manage our anger?

The most effective strategy for regulating emotions such as anger involves reframing the event in our minds so that we change its meaning to one that is less infuriating. By formulating a new interpretation of the events to one that is more positive we change our underlying feeling about the situation to one that is less enraging. For example, Michael Phelps, the most decorated swimmer in history, was often subjected to his competitors' taunts in the press before major competitions. Phelps gave several interviews in which he discussed how he dealt with the anger he felt in those situations. Rather than pounding the lane divider in the pool while his coach whispered, "Yes, you're very angry at that German swimmer, aren't you?" Phelps would reframe the situation as one in which he envisioned his rivals' taunts as motivational fuel that spurred him to train harder and to focus even more intently in his actual races.

Despite the effectiveness of reframing, many of us struggle to use the technique because it is not always easy to reinterpret upsetting events in benign ways. For example, Carlton, the man whose father went bankrupt and left him without financial support, was so angry at his father's previous meddling in his career that it was all he could think about. His constant ruminations exacerbated his anger to such a point that he had trouble tolerating even minor frustrations, leaving his wife, Solana, to bear the brunt of his irritability and aggression. Carlton needed to find a less enraging way of thinking about his situation, but even after I explained why it was crucial he do so, he struggled to reframe his situation in positive or more benign terms. I tried pointing him in the right direction.

"Carlton, you have a college degree from a great university and you spent the last five years working in every field in which you expressed an interest. Even if you did so for only brief periods of time, you did get a taste of these fields. Surely those experiences helped you figure out which of those directions holds the most appeal as a career choice."

"Sure. But what's the point? I'll never get the kind of job I really want without my father pulling strings."

"No, you won't. But that's exactly why you're angry with your father. He got you jobs you weren't qualified for instead of allowing you to get the kind of experience you needed. In the real world people don't start where you did, they start at the bottom and work their way up."

"But then these past five years were entirely wasted! That's what kills me!"

"Well, not exactly. They helped you identify what you want to pursue. If you thought of your previous experiences as internships that helped you figure that out, you might be able to see them as time well spent. Now that you know what you want you can start at the bottom and work your way up."

"Don't you get it?" Carlton snapped. "I don't want to start at the bottom!"

"I know," I responded softly, "and your dad didn't want you to either. Was it so terrible of him to want to spare you what you now wish you could spare yourself?"

The color drained from Carlton's face. He looked as if he had been struck. He had never considered that his father's hopes and intentions mirrored his own so closely. But once he was able to re-frame his father's meddling as well-intentioned as opposed to controlling, and his professional experiences as instructive as opposed to wasteful, it had a huge impact on him. His ruminations diminished rapidly, as did his anger and irritability. He began searching for positions more suited to his training and lack of experience, and within a few months he landed his first job entirely on his own merit—it was an entry-level position at the bottom rung of the ladder, and Carlton could not have been happier about it.

Reframing requires us to switch our perspective and to perceive the situation in ways that change its meaning and, consequently, how we feel about it. Although the focus here is on reducing anger, reframing can also help us feel less sad, less disappointed, or less victimized. For example, had Linda been promoted in her old law firm she would still be working for her abusive boss. Distraught as she was about taking a step back professionally, doing so did wonders for her quality of life. Reframing her boss's behavior as "useful" rather than as "destructive" allowed her to feel less victimized by her experience.

Exercise for Practicing Reframing

Although your ruminations are unique to your specific circumstance, certain themes and principles are common to many reframing situations. Use the following four suggestions to help identify ways to reframe your situation so that it elicits less anger (or sadness).

1. *Find the positive intention.* Much as Carlton's father had good intentions, most people who cause us to ruminate in anger have some redeeming qualities and might mean well regardless of how their words or actions impact us. Identifying these kernels of good can help us view the situation differently and modify the intensity of our emotions as a result.

2. *Identify the opportunities.* Today, many companies insist their managers reframe areas of weakness as "opportunities" when giving employees feedback. Doing so makes negative feedback easier for the employee to absorb without becoming demoralized. What makes this technique so successful is the universal truth it embodies. Many distressing situations might also provide opportunities for us to improve ourselves, to reevaluate things, to change direction, or to address problems that needed fixing anyway.

3. *Embrace the learning moment.* There is usually much we can learn from the situations that elicit our ruminations. Identifying mistakes we've made and ones we wish to avoid in the future, viewing negative situations as strategic puzzles that require creative solutions, learning who we can count on and who we cannot, and discovering our strengths, weaknesses, and vulnerabilities can provide valuable lessons that will boost our confidence and spare us future heartache and emotional distress.

4. *View the offending person as needing spiritual help.* Those of us with strong religious beliefs can reframe many situations as ones in which the person who caused us emotional distress is in obvious need of spiritual help. As such they deserve not our anger but our prayers. A series of recent studies examined the power of prayer to alleviate anger (using sound scientific principles and blind peer-review processes) and found that it can be an effective way to regulate our emotions, *as long as the nature of our prayer is positive.* Tempting as it may be to do so, praying that the person who angered us gets hit by a Mack truck will not

make us less angry, as it is the spiritual equivalent of shooting a couch pillow.

A secular version of this approach (albeit an untested one scientifically) would be to view the offending person as someone who might be troubled and in need of psychological help or psychotherapy.

TREATMENT SUMMARY: REFRAME THE ANGER

Dosage: Apply to situations, memories, or events that elicit anger or sadness and are the subject of repeated ruminations. Write down the reframed formulations you construct so you can revisit them whenever the rumination occurs.

Effective for: Reducing anger and anger-focused ruminations (as well as the intensity of other emotionally painful ruminations), restoring impaired intellectual and mental functioning, and reducing physiological stress responses.

Treatment D: Go Easy on Your Friends

When we repeatedly discuss the same problems with friends and family members we risk taxing their patience and compassion and we also risk making them feel resentful. In order to preserve these relationships we have to assess whether we are overburdening those who provide us with emotional support.

EXERCISE TO EVALUATE RELATIONSHIP STRAIN

Answer the following questions for each person in your social support system and take the recommended actions when it is relevant to do so.

1. How much time has passed since the event in question?

    Obviously some life events are extremely traumatic and they might dominate our thoughts and feelings for months and years. However, most of our ruminations do not fall in this category and we should be aware that people expect us to recover within a certain time frame. For example, a general rule of thumb for breakups is that it takes one to two months for every year of a relationship to recover. If we were in a relationship for three years, we should begin to recover from the initial surge of intense ruminations about how and why the breakup happened within three to six months and we should think twice about continuing to discuss the how and why aspect of things with our friends if the topic still dominates our discussions a year later.

2. How many times have you discussed these issues with this person?

    We all have our go-to people when it comes to getting social support. However, they are also the ones most likely to encounter "fatigue" when we discuss the same ruminative thoughts, events, and feelings too often. It might be wise to spread things around and utilize other sources of social support as well so as to avoid overburdening the people we go to most.

3. Does this person feel comfortable bringing up his or her own issues and problems?

If your conversations with a friend are too one-sided and tend to be all about your problems and rarely about his or hers, you might be at risk of jeopardizing the friendship. To assure a balance, make time to ask your friends about their lives and to have entire conversations in which you focus solely on them. If they ask about you when you are trying to do this, respond briefly and refocus the conversation on them.

4. What percentage of your communications with this person is dominated by the subject of your ruminations?

It is often only in hindsight that we realize the extent to which our discussions with friends were dominated by the subject of our ruminations. Allowing our emotional distress to dominate our relationships and determine what our friendships are about is bad for our friendships, but defining ourselves as victims is damaging to our own mental health as well. Make sure you keep a balance of light conversation, enjoyable moments, and fun whenever possible.

Treatment Summary: Go Easy on Your Friends

Dosage: Apply periodically to evaluate the health of your supportive relationships. Take action to repair any relationship damage when necessary.

Effective for: Evaluating and repairing strained relationships.

When to Consult a Mental Health Professional

If you've applied the treatments in this chapter and your urge to ruminate is still strong, if you find yourself ruminating just as frequently as you had previously, or if your ruminations are so intense and distracting they interfere with your basic ability to function in your professional or personal life, seek the advice of a mental health professional. If your intrusive thoughts are not focused on emotionally painful experiences but on things like catching germs, forgetting to lock the front door, or whether you turned off the gas before you left the house, a mental health professional will be able to assess whether you're exhibiting symptoms of obsessive-compulsive disorder.

Rumination is also strongly tied to depression. If you think you might be depressed and have symptoms such as a persistent low mood, feelings of helplessness about changing your situation, feelings of hopelessness about things getting any better, or disturbances in your eating and sleeping patterns, consult a mental health professional to assess whether you require professional treatment. If at any point you feel so emotionally distressed, sad, or angry that you have the urge to harm yourself or another person, seek immediate professional help or go to the nearest emergency room.

CHAPTER 6

||||||||||||||||||

FAILURE

How Emotional Chest Colds Become Psychological Pneumonias

None of us reach adulthood without encountering failure thousands of times and many more such experiences await us in life going forward. Failure is so common a human experience that what distinguishes us from one another is not that we fail but rather how we respond when we do. Such differences are especially apparent when observing those who fail more regularly and more frequently than anyone else—toddlers. Trying, failing, and trying again is one of the main ways toddlers learn. Fortunately, toddlers are generally persistent and determined (otherwise we'd never learn to walk, talk, or do much of anything), but they can also display dramatically different responses to failure.

Imagine four toddlers playing with identical jack-in-the-box toys. To open the box and release the cute teddy bear within, they need to slide a big button on the side of the box to the left. They know the button is where the action is, but sliding is a complex skill. Toddler #1 pulls the button. It doesn't move. She pushes the button hard. The box rolls out of reach. She extends her hand toward it but it's still out of reach. She turns away and starts playing with her diaper. Toddler #2 fusses with the button for a few moments without success. He sits back and stares at the box, his lower lip trembling, but makes no further efforts to open it. Toddler #3 tries to pry open the top of the box by force. Then she pulls the button. Undeterred, she keeps experimenting until ten minutes later—success! She slides the button, the top springs open, and Teddy pops out with a squeak. She squeals with delight, stuffs Teddy back into the box, and tries all over again. Toddler #4 sees toddler #3 open her box. He gets red in the face, smacks his own box with his fist, and bursts into tears.

When we encounter failure as adults, we tend to respond in very similar ways (albeit few of us resort to playing with our diapers). Failure can make us perceive our goals as being out of reach, causing us to give up too quickly (like toddler #1, whose box rolled away). Some of us feel so demoralized by failure that we become frozen, passive, and helpless (like toddler #2, who gave up). Some of us fail but keep trying until we succeed (like toddler #3), and some of us become so stressed and self-conscious that we can't think straight (like toddler #4, who burst into tears).

How we deal with failure is crucial to our success in life as well as to our general happiness and well-being. While some of us respond well to failure, many of us do not. Failure always hurts and disappoints but it can also be an informative, educational, and growth experience, as long as we take the failure in stride, figure out what we need to do differently next time, and persist in pursuing our goals. However, as with many of the psychological wounds we sustain in daily life, ignoring the injuries failure inflicts can make a bad situation worse, and at times, far worse.

Although our various ways of coping with failure are established early in our lives, we are by no means doomed to follow in the footsteps of our toddlerhood. Even those who respond to failures in the most unproductive and damaging ways can learn to employ more favorable and psychologically healthy coping styles. However, to do so, we must first understand the impact failure has on us, the psychological wounds it causes, and the emotional challenges we face if we wish to heal them.

The Psychological Wounds Failure Inflicts

Failures are the emotional equivalent of chest colds in that we all get them and we all feel terrible when we do. We usually recover from chest colds because we modify our activities accordingly once we get them—we rest, drink warm fluids, and dress warmly. If we were to ignore a cold entirely it would probably get worse and, in some cases, develop into pneumonia. We face similar dangers to our mental health when we encounter failure, yet few of us are aware of the need to employ the psychological equivalents of resting, drinking warm fluids, and dressing warmly. As a result, many of our failures cause unnecessary psychological damage, the implications of which can harm our emotional well-being far beyond the impact of the original incident.

Failure inflicts three specific psychological wounds that require emotional first aid. It damages our self-esteem by inducing us to draw conclusions about our skills, abilities, and capacities that are highly inaccurate and distorted. It saps our confidence, motivation, and optimism, making us feel helpless and trapped. And it can trigger unconscious stresses and fears that lead us to inadvertently sabotage our future efforts.

One of the reasons so many of us sustain psychological damage from failure is that it often takes only one or two incidents to set the entire vicious cycle into play. Further, when a failure is especially significant or meaningful to us (which it often is), leaving it untreated puts us at risk for developing psychological complications such as shame, crippling helplessness, and even clinical depression. Thus, what starts as a single episode of failure—a small emotional cold—can develop into psychological pneumonia that impacts our general functioning and mental health for the worse.

1. Honey, I Shrunk My Self-Esteem: Why Our Goals Seem Bigger and We Feel Smaller

Baseball players have long claimed that when they're on a hitting streak the ball literally seems bigger to them (and therefore easier to hit). Not surprisingly, when they're in a slump they report the baseball as appearing smaller and more difficult to hit. Most psychologists never took such claims seriously, perhaps because baseball players are a notoriously superstitious lot. Some players refuse to wash their underwear after a win so they don't "jinx" it and others sleep with their bats in bed to break out of hitting slumps. Which of those practices leads to more baseball wives sleeping on the sofa is anyone's guess.

When psychologists finally decided to investigate the players' claims scientifically they ran into a problem. It turns out major league umpires frown at the notion of pausing baseball games to allow players to complete psychological questionnaires. Consequently, scientists decided to test this phenomenon using regular people . . . and football.

Participants were asked to kick an American football through an adjusted field goal from the ten-yard line. They each had ten kicks. Before making any kicks, all subjects estimated the width and height of the goal similarly. But after their attempts, subjects who failed at the task (by scoring two or fewer successful kicks) estimated the goal as being 10 percent narrower and higher, and those who succeeded estimated it as being 10 percent wider and lower. It seems baseball players were right all along. Failure can make our goal seem literally more difficult and more imposing than it had appeared previously.

Failure not only makes our goal loom larger, it makes us feel "smaller" as well. Failing can induce us to feel less intelligent, less attractive, less capable, less skillful, and less competent—all of which have a hugely negative impact on our confidence and on the outcome of our future efforts. For example, if a college student fails a midterm exam, she might view herself as less capable and view the class as more difficult, making her more worried and less confident about doing well on the final. While some students might knuckle down and work harder as a result, others might become so intimidated they begin to question whether they can pass the class at all.

But what if that failed midterm also happened to be the first exam they ever took in college? What if they perceive not just the class but college as a whole as being a greater challenge than they're able to meet? Since they're unaware that failing the midterm has distorted their perceptions (such that the class and college appear harder than they actually are), they might reach premature and inappropriate decisions as a result. Indeed, many students drop out early in their freshman year for this exact reason (and toddler #1 is at risk for doing so as well).

Failure has an even greater impact on our self-esteem. Many of us respond to failures by drawing damaging conclusions about our character and abilities that seem incredibly compelling to us at the time even when they have no merit whatsoever. Many of us react to failure by thinking or voicing incredibly damaging thoughts such as: "I'm such a loser," "I can't do anything right," "I'm just not smart enough," "I'm such an idiot," "I'm a total embarrassment," "I deserve to lose," "People like me never get anywhere," "Why would anyone want to hire/date me?" or similar character assassinations.

Few people would argue that such demoralizing and unproductive thoughts have any redeeming value. Yet too often we allow ourselves to indulge in them, utter them aloud, and give them validity. If our six-year-old failed a spelling test in school and announced, "I'm a stupid loser who can't do anything right," most of us would swoop in, refute every word, and forbid him to say such terrible things about himself ever again. We would have no doubt that such negative thoughts would only make him feel worse in the moment and make it harder for him to succeed in the future. Yet we frequently fail to apply the very same logic and wisdom to our own situations.

The negative generalizations we often make after failing are not only inaccurate but they do more damage to our general self-worth and our future performance than the initial failure that spawned them. Criticizing our attributes so globally makes us hypersensitive to future failures, it can lead to deep feelings of shame, and it can threaten our entire well-being. Further, doing so prevents us from accurately assessing the causes of our failure so we can avoid similar miscalculations in the future. For example, if we blame our inability to attain personal improvement goals on our character shortcomings we are unlikely to identify and correct crucial errors in planning and strategic goal setting that are far more likely to be responsible for our failure.

Why New Year Resolutions Often Nudge Our Self-Esteem in the Wrong Direction

Every New Year we list our resolutions with hopes of improving our lives and feeling better about ourselves, only to abandon our efforts entirely by February (and often by January 2). As a result, instead of our self-esteem being strengthened by our accomplishments, we're left feeling weakened by failure and disappointment, which we quickly attribute to a lack of motivation or ability. We tell ourselves, "I guess I don't want to change," or "I'm just too lazy to do anything about my life," and feel even worse about ourselves than we did on December 31.

What makes such conclusions unfortunate as well as inaccurate is that the primary reason we complete so few of our resolutions is because we neglect to think through how we plan to achieve them. Without a carefully crafted plan in place our resolutions are unlikely to make it out of the starting gate no matter how motivated or capable we are. Indeed, one of the most common goal-planning errors we commit is neglecting to set a start date.

Another common New Year resolution error is goal bingeing. As a general rule, if your resolution list is longer than the one your child made for Santa, you might want to pare it down. Pauline, a recently divorced woman with two school-age children, marched into my office on the first Monday after the New Year and proudly thrust a sheet of paper into my hands. "My resolutions," she explained. "You've been encouraging me to take the wheel and steer my life in the right direction, so here, I'm taking it!" I glanced at Pauline's list and flinched. It had the following items: go to the gym four times a week and lose twenty-five pounds, try harder at work, organize the closets at home, paint the bedroom, make five new friends, post a profile on a dating website and go on at least two dates a month, join a book club, volunteer one afternoon a month, take a wine-tasting class, teach myself how to play the piano, and spend more time with the kids.

"What do you think?" she asked eagerly.

"I think that's what taking the wheel looks like—if you were a NASCAR driver," I said with a smile. "It might be a little much for a soccer mom with a minivan."

I explained that when we set too many goals for ourselves we are unlikely to complete any of them. Pauline's list included an entire smorgasbord of goal-setting errors. Some of the goals on her list conflicted with one another (e.g., getting to the gym four times a week and spending more time with the kids), others were too ambiguous (e.g., "try harder at work"), and others were too difficult (e.g., making five new friends, volunteering one afternoon a month, and going on two dates a month would be a challenging agenda for most single women, let alone a working mother of two).

Having multiple goals would be less of a problem if we took the time to prioritize them according to which were most urgent or most attainable given the circumstances of our lives at the time. We also neglect to break down long-term goals into smaller and more realistic subgoals. Without doing so, many of our goals can appear daunting and overwhelming. Last, we rarely take the time to develop action plans for dealing with the obstacles, hurdles, and setbacks that might arise along the way and we're then ill-equipped to deal with them when they do.

In short, we frequently fail to complete our New Year resolutions (as well as other goals) because we set the wrong goal(s) to begin with, and our self-esteem often suffers as a result.

2. Passivity and Helplessness: Why Not Only Mimes Get Trapped Inside Invisible Boxes

Failures sap our confidence, our motivation, and our hope. They can make us want to give up and forgo any future efforts and possibility of success. As a general rule, the more sweeping and negative our assumptions about our attributes and capacities are, the less motivated we'll be, as few of us make efforts to pursue goals we truly believe are out of reach. After all, if we're convinced we failed because we're not smart enough, capable enough, or fortunate enough, why would we persist?

What we neglect to take into consideration when the sting of failure is still fresh and our self-esteem is still bruised is that the very assumptions and perceptions that form the basis of our impulse to "surrender" are fundamentally incorrect.

Lenny, a thirty-year-old office manager at a sales company, came to psychotherapy after feeling increasingly depressed about his career. Although his day job provided basic financial support for his wife and new baby, Lenny's true passion was magic. He was a slender young man with angular features and a thick mustache (I've worked with numerous magicians over the years and why so many of them have mustaches remains a mystery to me). He wore oversized slacks and jackets, which I admit led me on more than one occasion to hope he would interrupt our session to pull out a stunning white dove, a cute rabbit, or even a string of colored handkerchiefs. Alas, the most exciting thing Lenny ever whipped out of his jacket was a throat lozenge.

Lenny had been performing as a magician since high school, but he never became successful enough to quit his job with the sales company. Although he was thrilled when his son was born, he also realized the added responsibility represented the death knell to his aspirations as a magician. Knowing little about the career path of magicians at that time, it wasn't immediately obvious to me why that would be so.

"There's no way to make a living as a magician without an agent," Lenny explained, "and I've never been able to get one. A couple of years ago I sent tapes to every agent out there, and nothing came of it. Yeah, I know," Lenny said, as if I was about to object, "you're wondering if my signature trick was good enough." Of course I wasn't wondering anything of the sort, but Lenny explained that agents only take on magicians whose signature trick— the one that serves as the magician's calling card—is a killer. Apparently, Lenny's was not.

"I spent the last two years working on my signature trick," Lenny continued. "But a couple of months ago, I turned thirty. Yeah, I know," he said in response to yet another imaginary objection on my part, "thirty isn't old. But I figured it was time to give up magic and focus on supporting my family. I stopped booking shows and I put away my stuff." Lenny took a deep breath. "But not doing magic anymore . . . it's killing me." Lenny swallowed hard. "Yeah, I know," he continued, "it doesn't matter how I feel because there's nothing I can do about it. I tried my best to make magic work, and I failed. I'll never be a professional magician: I have to accept that and move on. That's why I'm here, Doc. I need help. You have to help me accept that my life as a magician is over. Maybe once I do, it won't hurt so much."

Magic was Lenny's lifelong passion, but his failure to secure an agent or come up with a spectacular signature trick made him feel as though he'd exhausted all his options. In his mind, the only choice he had left was to give up his dream. Failure does that to us. It makes us feel hopeless and trapped, and it induces us to give up. We tend to fall prey to this kind of defeatist thinking far more than we realize. We get passed up for a promotion, so we cease making efforts because we believe our boss won't promote us no matter how well we perform. We skip the voting booth because we don't believe the candidate of our choice can win. We refuse to go back to the psychiatrist when our antidepressant medication fails because we assume if one of them didn't work, none of them will. We join a gym, sprain a muscle, and conclude we're too out of shape for physical activity. We break our diet and conclude we're one of those people who "just can't lose weight." When our intimate advances keep getting rebuffed by our spouse we conclude he or she no longer finds us attractive and we stop initiating sex.

In each of these scenarios failure convinces us that we have no chances of getting what we want and so we stop trying. Failure can be very persuasive.

Failure can also be very misleading.

Accurate as we feel our assessments are, in the vast majority of situations, ceasing our efforts only creates a self-fulfilling prophecy. By not taking action we guarantee we won't succeed, and we then view our eventual failure not as a lack of persistence on our part but as a confirmation that success was impossible all along. The fact that our own surrender has brought about the very outcome we feared eludes us, as does the fact that our pessimism has blinded us to the options and possibilities that do exist.

For example, we might have been second in line for the promotion at work and therefore next up for advancement had we continued to perform well. We could have campaigned for the political candidate we favored and by doing so increased that candidate's chances of getting elected. We could have tried another antidepressant, as it often takes trying several medications to find the one that works best for us (just as it does with over-the-counter pain relievers). Becoming more educated about exercise could have helped us avoid injury by planning workouts suited to our fitness level. If we found it too difficult to stay on a diet we could have taken steps to strengthen our motivation. And if our spouse rebuffed our advances we could have discussed things with him or her and resolved any larger issues that were at play.

Succumbing to feelings of pessimism, helplessness, and passivity is as damaging to our mental health as ignoring a worsening cold is to our physical health. Indeed, Lenny's "chest cold" took a rapid turn for the worse the moment he decided to give up magic. He became engulfed in feelings of hopelessness, helplessness, and despair, and he was at risk for developing full-blown depression, a "psychological pneumonia" that could threaten his mental well-being.

3. Performance Pressure: What to Expect When Expecting to Fail

When we fail at tasks in which our expectations for success are low, the psychological wounds failure inflicts are relatively minor. Failing to win a national lottery rarely sends people into a depression and the vast majority of untrained singers do not experience deep feelings of shame when they fail to get on a singing show (although they definitely feel disappointed). But when we possess the necessary skills and abilities to succeed and have expectations of doing so we are likely to feel much stronger pressure to perform well. Performance pressure can be useful in small doses but it becomes extremely unproductive in larger ones, as it can foster test anxiety, a fear of failure, and the risk of choking.

Many of us get anxious in test-taking situations regardless of our intelligence, preparation, or familiarity with the material. One of the reasons test anxiety is so common is that it is relatively easy to trigger. Even one episode of heightened anxiety is sufficient for us to feel intensely anxious when facing a similar situation in the future. Test anxiety is especially problematic because it causes massive disruptions to our concentration, our focus, and our ability to think clearly, all of which have a huge impact on our performance. As a rule, anxiety tends to be extremely greedy when it comes to our concentration and attention. The visceral discomfort it creates can be so distracting, and the intellectual resources it hogs so critical, that we might struggle to comprehend the nuances of questions, retrieve the relevant information from our memory, formulate answers coherently, or choose the best option from a multiple-choice list. As an illustration of how dramatic its effects are, anxiety can cause us to score fifteen points lower than we would otherwise on a basic IQ test—a hugely significant margin that can drop a score from the Superior to the Average range.

One of the more insidious but lesser-known manifestations of test anxiety occurs when we're reminded of negative stereotypes about our gender, race, ethnicity, or other group. Known as *stereotype threat*, such reminders often trigger subconscious worries and fears of conforming to stereotypes, even when entirely unwarranted and even when we believe the stereotype in question has no validity whatsoever. Such worries, even if they barely register in our awareness, can steal away just enough of our attention to hamper our performance on the task at hand.

As an illustration of stereotype threat, consider what happens when girls take math tests. When girls take math tests without boys present, they do substantially better than when taking the test with boys. Even in the twenty-first century, the presence of boys can subtly remind girls of the stereotypical yet false belief that men are innately better at math than women.

We Have Nothing to Fear
but Fear of Failing Itself

For some of us, failure is associated not just with disappointment and frustration but with far more damaging feelings, such as embarrassment and shame. As a result, the prospect of failing can be so intimidating that we make unconscious efforts to lower expectations for our success. While lowering expectations might seem like a reasonable approach, the way we go about doing so can result in our unwittingly sabotaging ourselves and bringing about the very outcome we fear.

Lydia, a woman in her late thirties I worked with some years ago, had taken a ten-year break from her career in marketing to raise three young children. When her youngest child started kindergarten, Lydia and her husband agreed it was time for her to resume working. Lydia quickly leveraged her connections to get job interviews at six different companies. But despite her inside track and impressive credentials, none of them called her back for a second interview. Lydia was horribly embarrassed by her failure, not to mention truly befuddled. Although she believed she had done the best she could, it quickly became apparent that a fear of failure had led her to unconsciously sabotage one opportunity after the other. Or rather, it quickly became apparent to me. Lydia, on the other hand, was convinced she had done all she could to succeed.

"Look, I understand why the first company turned me down," Lydia explained. "I didn't have time to read up on it before the interview because my daughter had an important basketball game and I promised I'd bake brownies for the team." Lydia's account of the second interview revealed an equally unconvincing imperative. "Ah, you see, my mother called the night before and I got stuck on the phone with her for three hours. She was upset about my cousin's wife feuding with her sister, and I felt bad about cutting her off." Lydia's take on what went wrong in the third interview was just as flimsy: "Well, what happened there was my nails were a mess and I thought I'd have time to do a quick mani-pedi before the interview, but I misjudged the time and got there half an hour late. Maybe forty-five minutes. Anyway, they refused to see me. Can you believe it?" I certainly could believe it, but I graciously refrained from nodding.

Lydia continued by explaining that a severe migraine headache kept her up the night before her fourth interview. "I was exhausted! Could you believe I even forgot to bring them a copy of my resume?" Lydia reported being afflicted with sudden "gastrointestinal distress" the morning of her fifth interview. "At some point my stomach was rumbling so loudly I just made a joke about it and apologized. But they hadn't heard a thing so it was kind of an awkward moment. I'm sure I'll laugh about it in the future." I doubted Lydia would ever find the situation chuckle-worthy, but again, I held my tongue.

Lydia claimed her sixth interview would have gone well, except—"My luck, I woke up on the wrong side of the bed, real irritable and impatient. My husband thought I should go to the interview anyway, but I should have listened to my gut and stayed home. The receptionist was so annoying I ended up getting into an argument with her. The interviewer came out to see what the ruckus was about and, whatever . . . it just went downhill from there. You know what they say, if it isn't meant to be, it isn't meant to be."

Most people hearing Lydia's account would immediately recognize an obvious pattern of excuses, avoidance, and self-sabotaging behavior that was sure to guarantee failure. But Lydia was truly oblivious to it. Her unconscious mind knew that by having obstacles to blame for any possible failures she could avoid the shame and embarrassment she feared. Fear of failure makes many of us engage in all manner of self-handicapping behaviors in which we exaggerate or create impediments to success without being aware we're doing so. Indeed, we are often extremely creative in the self-handicapping devices we construct in order to have something to blame for our failure.

Many of us procrastinate and "run out of time" to study before an important test. We might go out with friends and drink too much the night before an important presentation or get too little sleep. We might forget our study materials on the subway or at a friend's house. We might forget the cherries when packing our ingredients for the county fair cherry-pie-baking contest, or we might arrive at the marathon having packed only our left sneaker. And as Lydia demonstrates, there are endless physical ailments we can manufacture. If we do well despite these setbacks we have the added bonus of giving ourselves extra credit for succeeding when the odds were against us.

Of course, self-handicapping rarely leads to success. In addition, such strategies prevent us from examining our failures accurately and drawing useful conclusions about what we need to change or do differently in the future. For example, Lydia's resume might have needed changes or her job-interviewing skills might have needed sharpening, but it is impossible to assess such factors because they were obscured by the array of obstacles Lydia placed in her own way.

The unconscious nature of self-handicapping can blind us to its existence even when someone else points it out to us. Lydia was initially convinced that every one of her excuses was valid and that her failure was due to events over which she had absolutely no control. When I suggested otherwise, she responded with statements such as "You don't expect me to break a promise to my daughter, do you?" and "The problem was I didn't listen to my gut and stay home. My gut never leads me astray."

Fear of Failure in Families

Confronting Lydia's fear of failure was all the more urgent because studies show that parents who suffer from fear of failure often transmit such fears to their children. Most parents view their children as extensions of themselves as well as products of their parenting skills, so that when children fail, parents' own feelings of shame get triggered. They might then respond to their child's failure by withdrawing from them both subtly (e.g., with their tone of voice or body language) and overtly (e.g., expressing disapproval or anger). Children pick up on their parents' withdrawal, which triggers their own feelings of shame and teaches them that failures should be both feared and avoided.

To be clear, in the vast majority of situations, parents are entirely unaware they might be impacting their children so negatively. Lydia had three young children whom she loved dearly. However, the fact remains that unless she treated the psychological wounds failure inflicted and corrected her self-sabotaging habits, she was likely to perpetuate the cycle of fear of failure and pass it on to her children.

Choking Under the Influence

Bill Buckner had a stellar career as a Major League Baseball player, amassing over 2,700 hits, winning batting crowns, and playing as an All-Star. But he is most known for the error he made when playing for the Boston Red Sox in the 1986 World Series against the New York Mets. Buckner was on first when a ground ball that should have been simple to block went by him, costing the Red Sox the game and eventually the World Series. Buckner is hardly the only athlete to choke in a championship game when executing a simple skill they've performed perfectly thousands of times. Non-professional athletes choke in clutch moments just as frequently and choking is also common outside of sports.

Why do so many of us bowl a great game only to gutter the last ball? Why does a gifted vocalist sing flawlessly in a crucial audition only to deliver a cringe-worthy, off-key final note? Why does an advertising executive pitch the perfect presentation to every client, only to stammer incoherently and draw a blank when his company's president steps into the room?

Psychologists began researching why we tend to choke under pressure over two decades ago, but only recently have studies uncovered the psychological mechanisms responsible for these mental gaffes. Choking tends to happen because the stress we feel in high-pressure situations makes us overthink tasks and draw attention away from the part of our brain that executes the task automatically or fluidly. To illustrate this point try the following exercise. Fill a coffee mug with water, hold it by the handle, and walk it across the room. Easy, right? Now do it again, but this time, keep your eyes on the water as you walk and focus on making the adjustments necessary for the water not to spill. Most of us are far more likely to spill the water when we're trying not to than we are when we walk with the mug without thinking about it.

Choking is based on a similar dynamic. The greater the pressure of the situation, the more likely we are to overanalyze our actions and interfere with the smooth execution of a task we've performed or rehearsed hundreds of times. While we all make errors, choking usually occurs when the stakes are extremely high. The ramifications of choking and the self-recriminations that follow can be profound. Bill Buckner is still heckled for his gaffe even twenty-five years later, and many of us have trouble living down our own choking moments for years or even decades.

How to Treat the Psychological Wounds Failure Inflicts

Failures are often painful but not all of them warrant emotional first aid. Many of our failures are minor, and we shrug them off with relative ease, even if they do sting for a short while. Even substantial and meaningful failures might not require treatment if we are able to take them in stride, accurately assess what we should do differently next time, put in the necessary effort, and persist until we reach our goal.

But when we fail repeatedly or when we respond to failures in ways that set back our confidence, our self-esteem, and our chances of future success, we run the risk of allowing our emotional chest cold to turn into psychological pneumonia. Because much of the anxiety associated with failures can build upon itself, it is best to be prudent and apply psychological first aid treatments as soon as possible after meaningful or bothersome failures occur. Let's open our psychological medicine cabinet and review our treatment options.

General Treatment Guidelines

Failures inflict three kinds of psychological wounds. They damage our confidence and self-esteem and make our goals seem further out of reach. They distort our perceptions, make us feel hopeless about succeeding, and compel us to give up or stop trying. And they can create the kind of performance pressure that increases our anxiety and causes us to unconsciously sabotage our future efforts.

Treatments A (getting support) and B (regaining control) help minimize damage to confidence and self-esteem, they prevent the pessimistic and defeatist mind-sets that lead to loss of motivation and giving up, and they also boost our motivation, hope, and chances of success going forward. Treatment C (taking responsibility) is focused on owning the failure as well as the fears and feelings it elicits so as to minimize the likelihood of our self-sabotaging future efforts. Treatment D (managing performance pressure) helps reduce performance pressure, fear of failure, test anxiety (and stereotype threat), and choking.

Treatment A: Get Support and Get Real

Whenever a patient tells me about a disappointing and meaningful failure, my first response is to express sympathy and express warm emotional support—which often makes my patients reach for the tissue box. My second response is to point to some of the lessons they could learn from the failure that would help them going forward—which often makes them hurl the tissue box in my direction. Having silver linings pointed out to us when we're still getting rained on is always somewhat annoying.

Nonetheless, I respond this way for two reasons: First, because I'm really good at ducking. And second, because research has repeatedly demonstrated the most effective way to treat the psychological wounds failure inflicts is to find the positive lessons in what happened. Further, providing social and emotional support alone often makes people who experienced a failure feel *worse*.

But why is that so? Don't we always benefit from empathy when we're hurting?

Receiving concern and emotional support when we're still reeling from a failure can actually validate our (mis)perceptions about the deficits and shortcomings in our character and abilities. But if expressions of social support are quickly followed by realistic evaluations of the failure's implications, we could benefit from receiving emotional validation while still maintaining a realistic and grounded perspective that allows us to "get real."

This one-two combination of getting emotional support and assessing what we can gain or learn from the experience is the most effective strategy we can take in the immediate aftermath of a stinging failure. Most of us are proficient at getting emotional support, but figuring out the relevant takeaways when we still feel bad about ourselves can be challenging.

EXERCISE TO FACILITATE LEARNING FROM FAILURE

The following writing exercise will help you identify what you can gain from the failure. There are six general lessons that can be extracted from most failure experiences. Apply each of these lessons to your own situation.

1. *Failure is a great teacher*. Thomas Edison failed thousands of times before he invented the lightbulb and he viewed each failure as a learning experience. In his words, "I

haven't failed once. I've learned ten thousand things that don't work." Failure always tells us something about what we need to change in our preparation or execution of the task. What should you do differently next time?

2. *Failure provides new opportunities.* Henry Ford's first two car companies failed. Had they succeeded he might never have tried company number three, which was when he hit on the idea of assembly line manufacturing and became one of the richest men of his time. What opportunities might your failure possibly present?

3. *Failure can make us stronger.* Diana Nyad was sixty-two years old when in August 2011 she attempted to swim from Cuba to Florida, a distance of 103 miles. Unfortunately, asthma attacks forced her to give up her attempt after covering sixty miles of the distance. Remarkably she tried again less than two months later. This time she swam over eighty miles before painful Portuguese man-of-war stings forced her doctors to pull her from the water. Diana quickly announced she would not try the swim again. But once her exhaustion and initial disappointment wore off she realized that her two attempts had only made her stronger and more likely to succeed if she tried again. She made another attempt in August 2012 and although she swam farther than she had in her previous efforts, dangerous squalls forced her out of the water before completing her quest.

We all get demoralized when we fail. But bouncing back from our failure and learning from the experience will always make us stronger and more likely to succeed in the future. In what ways might your failure make you stronger?

4. *Some failures are also successes.* I've always wondered how the runner-up in the Miss Universe pageant feels once she's had some time to reflect and pick out the confetti from her hair. Does she feel proud to have represented her country so well, or does she feel devastated about coming so close and not winning? It's crushing when our amateur sports team loses the playoff game but does that nullify the accomplishment of getting to the playoffs in the first place? Sure, it's disappointing we didn't get the job offer after so many rounds of interviews but surely we should feel encouraged about being among the top applicants.

   Many of our failures are also successes in some way, except we tend to focus far more on aspects of failure than of success. No matter how disappointed we feel, we should always acknowledge the ways in which we were successful even if we ultimately failed. In what ways could you view your failure as a success?

5. *Failure makes future success more meaningful.* Studies show that the harder we work, the more failures and challenges we overcome, the greater the meaning, joy, and satisfaction we derive when we eventually succeed. Oscar Pistorius is a professional athlete from South Africa who in 2011 ran the four-hundred-meter sprints at the Track and Field World Championships in South Korea. However, unlike the other sprinters in the field, Pistorius is a double amputee; both his legs were amputated when he was a child. Running on metal "blades," he became the first disabled athlete ever to run in an able-bodied world championship meet. He then capped off his achievement by advancing to the individual semifinals and winning a

silver medal in the relay races (as well as setting a national record).

For Pistorius, just being on the track was a triumph. He had spent years fighting in court for the right to run in the world championships and the Olympics, eventually proving that his blades did not give him an "advantage" over the other athletes. Even after winning the legal battle, he struggled to make the minimum qualifying time for the event, failing to do so until the very last race before the deadline—one week before the championships began. When Pistorius took the track for his first race, every camera in the stadium was pointed at him. The sheer awe and joy on his face as his name was announced outshone that of every other athlete there and gave goose bumps to anyone watching. Pistorius then repeated his stunning performance and reached the semifinals of the four-hundred-meter sprints in the London 2012 Olympics. (Sadly, Pistorius gave fans goose bumps of an entirely different kind when he was arrested in February 2013 on charges of killing his girlfriend.)

The more we fail, the greater the impact our eventual success will have on our mood, self-esteem, and confidence. How much more will success mean to you now that you've encountered failure?

6. *Success is not always necessary.* Recent studies have begun to illuminate a surprising aspect about failure: many of the benefits we hope to reap by pursuing our goals are not necessarily dependent on our ability to complete them. In most situations, making steady progress toward our goals contributes more toward our sustained happiness and self-fulfillment than actually reaching them. The satisfac-

tion, excitement, sense of pride, and personal accomplishment we feel by inching ever closer to our target combine to create a heady mix of satisfaction and joy that does wonders for our mood, motivation, and psychological well-being. Can you identify ways in which you derived meaning and satisfaction as you pursued your goal?

Treatment Summary: Get Support, Then Get Real

Dosage: Apply the treatment as soon as possible every time you experience a meaningful failure.

Effective for: Minimizing damage to confidence, self-esteem, and motivation.

Secondary benefits: Reduces performance pressure.

Treatment B: Focus on Factors in Your Control

Failing can make us feel trapped and helpless, as though events are out of our control and we are doomed to fail. Once we believe nothing we do can bring about a different outcome, we tend to give up or make only feeble efforts. However, succumbing to such paralysis can turn an emotional cold into psychological pneumonia, as hopelessness and helplessness often lead to conditions such as clinical depression.

The tragedy of failure is that many of the assumptions and perceptions that lead us to draw incapacitating conclusions about our lack of control are actually false. Further, scientists have repeatedly demonstrated that changing our perspective and focusing on aspects of the situation that are in our control can have a hugely beneficial impact on our hope, motivation, and self-esteem. In some cases, merely acquiring information that refutes our incorrect assumptions of helplessness and lack of control is sufficient to cure our paralysis and prevent our "emotional cold" from getting worse.

One study illustrated this point with a group of seniors over the age of sixty-five. Seniors are often quite sedentary, which can seriously compromise their health (though being sedentary isn't a recipe for good health at any age). The problem is that seniors today often believe that being sedentary is a natural part of aging (which, of course, it isn't). Scientists taught the seniors to attribute their sedentary lifestyle not to age but to factors that were entirely in their control, such as how much walking they tended to do on a daily basis. One month later, this simple intervention led to the seniors increasing their walking by two and a half miles a week (which is hugely significant) and they reported equal improvements in their stamina and mental health.

The best way to regain a sense of control over the circumstances that led to our failure is to reexamine both our preparation (our goal planning) and our performance (how we executed our efforts) so we can identify elements that we perceived as being out of our control that could be in our control if we approached or perceived them differently.

Exercise for Gaining Control of Our Goal Planning

Since it is best to pursue one goal at a time, complete this exercise for each goal separately. I've included the responses of Pauline, the recently divorced woman with an abundance of New Year resolutions, for illustrative purposes. Pauline agreed to prioritize the item "make new friends," as her social circle had been severely reduced over the course of the divorce and she was eager to find new outlets for social engagements and new friends with whom she could enjoy them.

1.   Define your goal in as realistic and specific terms as possible.

   Keep in mind: Formulate clear and measurable objectives. For example, "get into shape for summer" is realistic but not specific. "Win the lottery" is specific but not realistic, and "write a best-selling novel" is neither specific (what is the novel about?) nor realistic (few novels become best sellers). Pauline defined her goal as "find three venues to meet people with similar interests."

   In addition, defining your goal in ways that are personally meaningful and that you find inherently interesting and enjoyable will help maximize your motivation over the long term. For example, you might define your weight loss and exercise goal as "develop a healthier lifestyle that gives me greater vitality and stamina so I can enjoy active pursuits with my children and grandchildren for many years to come." Give careful thought to the regimens you choose as well. For example, your motivation to exercise might be stronger and last longer if you joined a hiking group with friends than if you ran on a treadmill in your basement alone.

2.   Break down the goal into intermediate steps.

   Keep in mind: How we break down our long-term goals into smaller intermediate steps can have a huge and crucial impact on our motivation. Intermediate goals that require too little effort can cause us to lose interest and enthusiasm and become less engaged in pursuing our larger goal, and thus hamper our motivation. Intermediate goals that are too challenging tend to frustrate us and therefore also lead to a loss of motivation. Try to define intermediate milestones that provide a challenge but aren't too daunting. It is best to get some successes under our belt, so we should ramp up slowly by starting with easier challenges that become (incrementally) harder.

When defining our subgoals it is important to focus on variables within our control (e.g., our performance) rather than those outside our control (e.g., a specific outcome). For example, weight loss or fitness goals should focus on what we eat or how much exercise we get (as those are within our control) and not on how much weight we lose (as we cannot force our bodies to lose weight at a prede-termined rate). If we plan to start a blog we should deter-mine the allotments of time we plan to set aside to work on it, not the actual progress we hope to make (as it is difficult to foresee programming and design problems and other difficulties). It is better to feel we're making progress on our cheese lovers blog because we put in as many hours as we said we would than to feel as though we're failing because it took us half a day to resize a stunning picture of Swiss Flösserkäse.

Pauline broke her goal into the following subgoals: "Make a list of activities that interest me. Search online for possible venues. Explore one new venue a week."

3.   Set time frames for the overall and intermediate goals.
     Keep in mind: It is best to go through the intermediate goals on your list and indicate two time frames for each, a starting date/hour and a completion date/hour. Objective deadlines might make it necessary to create a time frame

for our larger goal first and then assign time frames to each of the intermediate goals accordingly (such as when we're training for a marathon or creating a portfolio for an upcoming job or school interview), but when possible we should set time frames for intermediate goals first, as doing so allows for more realistic and attainable schedules. Much as we did when forming our intermediate goals, making the time frames moderately challenging is the best way to maintain our interest, effort, and motivation. Pauline decided to start the next day and to explore one new venue a week until she found a suitable one, after which she would explore a new venue every two weeks.

4. List any potential detours, setbacks, or temptations that might arise.

   Keep in mind: We would be wise to adopt the Boy Scouts' motto and "be prepared" by troubleshooting not only what *might* go wrong but what *could* go wrong as well. For example, if our goal is to minimize our drinking and adopt moderation we might anticipate the need to strategize what to do during holiday parties at work but we should also consider what to do if we're asked to attend a last-minute business dinner with clients who are wine lovers. Pauline anticipated potential problems with her babysitter, who had a history of canceling at the last minute.

5. List the possible solutions for each of the above detours, setbacks, or temptations, including what you can do to avoid them and how you plan to implement these solutions. Phrase your implementation strategies as positive actions (e.g., "If I'm offered a cigarette I will say, *No, thanks,*

I quit," as opposed to, "If I'm offered a cigarette I won't take it").

Keep in mind: Anticipating problems and planning solutions to them ahead of time is crucial for avoiding discouragement and maintaining motivation and morale when difficulties arise. Any solution is only as good as our plan to implement it. For example, asking women intending to get a breast cancer exam to spend a few moments planning how and when they would do so made them twice as likely to follow through with the exam than women who did not make a plan. Pauline's solution was to find a spare babysitter she could call on if necessary.

Reexamining Our Execution of the Task

Not all our failures are due to faulty planning. We also need to identify ways for gaining control of how we execute the task. For example, Lenny abandoned his dreams of becoming a professional magician because he believed he had tried everything he could to develop a great signature trick yet still failed to do so. He spent hours going over lists of all the tricks he knew. He tried brainstorming new combinations and elaborations that could elevate them to a new level. But despite all these efforts, he failed to come up with a show-stopping trick.

After hearing about his efforts, I expressed sympathy for his feelings of disappointment (which made Lenny reach for the tissue box). I then told him I disagreed with his assessment entirely, and prepared to duck. Lenny was surprised by my comment but also extremely curious. I explained that there were still many brainstorming avenues he could explore and that by trying to generate ideas from his existing list of tricks he had actually limited his options and inadvertently rendered his brainstorming efforts ineffective.

I then gave him examples of other ways in which he could approach brainstorming, for example, from the top down, by first identifying conceptual themes he found compelling (family, nostalgia, love, culture, food, etc.) and only then considering how to evoke these concepts using magic. Or he could start with the emotional impact he was trying to elicit (awe, surprise, wonder, confusion, amazement, shock, etc.) as well as the sequence in which he wanted to evoke them. Or he could focus first on unconventional materials or approaches (such as reversals). For example, I suggested that it would be hilarious if instead of holding out cards, putting the chosen one in a hat, and pulling out a rabbit, he held out several rabbits for the audience member to choose from, put the rabbit in the hat, and pulled out a card (alas, Lenny did not share my vision).

Failure had caused Lenny to limit his options in other ways as well. He was convinced audiences were more interested in reality television stars and jokes about celebrities or politicians than they were in magic. However, he never considered integrating these concepts into his existing act and changing his patter accordingly. Lenny soon came to realize there were many more avenues to explore and that it was too soon to give up on his dream. His mood changed the instant he reached the decision and for the first time I saw a sparkle of hope in his eye.

EXERCISE FOR GAINING CONTROL OF OUR TASK EXECUTION

The goal in this writing exercise is to identify factors that contributed to the failure and that are in your control and to determine how to address these factors when making future efforts. I've included Lenny's responses for illustrative purposes.

1. Describe the failure in question. Make sure it is a single incident of failure. For example, if you failed a driver's test five times, list only the most recent attempt.

    Lenny wrote "I failed to become a professional magician."

2. List all the factors that contributed to your failure.

    Lenny listed "weak signature trick, no agent, lack of contacts, audiences don't care about magic."

3. Identify which of the factors on your list are in your control and which are not. For example, factors within your control might be "I failed to complete the marathon because I didn't give myself enough time to train," or "My marriage failed because we never learned to communicate with one another." Factors outside of your control might be "I failed the bar exam because I get nervous during important tests," or "I lost the customer because the product we delivered had too many problems."

    Lenny listed the factors outside his control as "No agent will take me on without a stronger signature trick," "I'm not a good enough magician to invent a great signature trick," "I don't have contacts that could help me get more bookings or secure an agent," and "Most audiences don't care about magic." The only factor he listed as within his control was "Giving up magic was my decision."

4. Go through each factor you listed as being outside your control and try to view it differently. See if you can replace the factor with one that is within your control. For exam-

ple, you might replace "I failed the bar exam because I get nervous during important tests" with "I didn't take steps to manage my test anxiety" (because we can always learn ways to do so), and you might replace "I failed to retain the customer because the product we delivered had too many problems" with "I lacked the necessary complaint-handling training to retain the customer" (because complaint-management training is something we can always get).

Lenny switched "I'm not a good enough magician to invent a great signature trick," with "I only tried one brainstorming approach among many." He swapped "I don't have contacts that could help me get more bookings or secure an agent" with "I haven't networked with other magicians, bookers, and club owners as much as I could." And he replaced "Most audiences don't care about magic" with "I haven't restructured my tricks around topics audiences care about."

5. Once you've completed step 4, create a new list of action items that are within your control. For each factor, identify how you might go about addressing the issues or making the necessary changes to improve your chances of future success.

    Lenny decided to try three additional brainstorming techniques for his signature trick and to allot himself an additional year within which to do so. He also decided to focus on networking with other magicians, bookers, and club owners and to increase his presence online using social media platforms.

    Eight months later Lenny left me a message letting me know he would be performing his new signature trick—

on television! The trick he came up with was both moving and visually beautiful. But to me, the most magical thing about his television debut was the sheer joy I saw on his face as he performed.

TREATMENT SUMMARY: FOCUS ON FACTORS IN YOUR CONTROL

Dosage: Apply the treatment as soon as possible every time you experience a meaningful failure. Make sure to revisit the goal-planning and execution exercises before making future efforts and whenever you set new goals.

Effective for: Preventing or reducing feelings of helplessness and hopelessness, increasing hope and motivation, and improving chances of future success.

Secondary benefits: Minimizes damage to confidence and self-esteem and reduces performance pressure.

Treatment C: Take Responsibility and Own the Fear

Although it is tempting to make excuses about our failure, doing so prevents us from learning the many useful lessons it can teach us. Worse, the more we deny any responsibility we might have, the more likely we are to feel as though the situation is outside our control. By recognizing that failure usually evokes at least some measure of fear and anxiety, we can begin to get in touch with such feelings, own them, and thereby prevent them from influencing our behavior unconsciously and destructively.

Lydia, the mother who sought to reenter the workplace after raising three children, struggled because her self-esteem and confidence as a professional were extremely low after a long hiatus from the workplace. Her unconscious self-handicapping served to protect her self-esteem by providing ready-made excuses for any failure she might encounter. Unfortunately, it practically guaranteed her failure, a fact to which Lydia was completely blind. Once she finished telling me about her sixth job interview fiasco (arguing with her prospective boss's receptionist), I decided to share my concerns with her.

"I sometimes get a little anxious about coming back to work after a week-long vacation," I began. "I can only imagine how terrifying it must be to jump back into the workplace after an absence of over a decade."

"Well, sure, yeah, it's a little scary," Lydia admitted.

"I'm sure it must be. Do you discuss that aspect of things with anyone?" Lydia shook her head. I continued, "Feeling apprehensive, anxious, and even scared is entirely natural, Lydia, especially given the changes in the marketing industry over the past ten years. In fact, it would be weird if you weren't a little scared. But the way our fears work, if we don't own them and if we don't talk about them, our mind will find other ways of expressing them."

"Like what?" Lydia asked.

"Like getting into fights with the secretary of the person who has to determine whether you'd fit in well with his staff," I responded with a smile.

"But you don't know how irritating she was!" Lydia objected.

"Actually, I assume she was incredibly irritating," I said. "But you have three young kids, Lydia. I'm guessing you must be pretty used to handling irritating and frustrating situations." Lydia nodded. "Again, I think you weren't expressing your fears consciously so your mind decided to express them for you."

"Wait, you mean like the migraine and bad stomach? Those were real!"

"So is your anxiety about failing," I responded. "But unless you own it and figure out how to address it, I see more headaches and stomachaches in your future." I was relieved to see that Lydia didn't argue this time, she just became thoughtful. Difficult as it was, Lydia was eventually able to own her feelings and take responsibility for each one of her failed job interviews (and the self-handicapping that caused them). Once she did, she was able to reengage in her job search in a much more productive manner. It took her several more months of looking and numerous failed interviews but Lydia eventually found a job in her field and reentered the workplace successfully.

We should all assume that where failure goes, anxiety and fear might follow. The best way for us to own both our feelings and our failures is to talk about them with supportive people. Airing our fears and exposing them to trusted friends or family members will minimize our unconscious need to express them self-destructively. Another option is to write about our fears in a journal or blog, as long as we make sure to balance them with more optimistic assessments.

One of the most effective ways to remove the emotional sting of failures is to joke about them when it is possible or appropriate to do so. In studies, seeing the humor in a failure was found to be an extremely effective way to get over the pain as well as any embarrassment or shame a failure caused. Being able to "see the funny" in a situation also helps reduce performance pressure when making future attempts. By verbalizing our fears in joke form we make it less necessary for our minds to express them unconsciously and in self-defeating ways. Of course, not all failures are ones we can or should laugh about, but many are.

One group of people who regularly practice laughing about their failures is stand-up comedians. Many comics turn their painful experiences of failure into jokes, and in doing so drastically reduce the pain the failure evokes. For example, comic Jim Short found a way to deal with his feelings about his financial failures and shortcomings by talking about them in his act. "I'm thirty-four and I make seven thousand dollars a year. I'm a loser! I was sad and depressed. And then I thought, wait a minute, I'm not a loser! I've tried! I'm a *failure!*"

In 2011 Bill Buckner, the Red Sox player whose choking cost his team a ticket to the World Series, played himself on Larry David's *Curb Your Enthusiasm*. In the episode, Buckner is heckled for not catching that crucial ball at first base (yes, even decades later). Later, he passes by a burning building, where a mother on the third floor is instructed by firefighters to toss her baby into their net below. Reluctantly, the mother complies. The baby drops into the net but bounces high into the air. The gathered onlookers gasp and then collectively wince when they recognize Buckner and realize the baby is headed straight in his direction. But Buckner reaches for the baby, makes the perfect catch, and redeems himself, while the crowd breaks into applause. Buckner's appearance represented a real-life example of someone who was able to laugh at his most painful failure and no doubt heal the psychological wounds it inflicted by doing so.

Treatment Summary: Take Responsibility and
Own the Fear

Dosage: Apply the treatment as soon as possible every time
you experience a meaningful failure.

Effective for: Preventing or minimizing damaged confidence
and self-esteem and taking the sting out of painful failures
by finding the humor in them.

Secondary benefits: Reduces performance pressure and fear of
failure.

Treatment D: Distract Yourself from Performance Pressure Distractions

Performance pressure can increase test anxiety, it can make us
choke at crucial moments, and it can drain our attention with worries about conforming to stereotypes. It does so because the stress
or anxiety we feel in the moment steals attention from the task
we're executing, hampers our performance, and makes us more
likely to fail. We then feel even more stressed and anxious going
forward and the cycle deepens.

To treat the psychological wounds of performance pressure we
have to fight fire with fire. When stress and anxiety threaten to
steal our attention we need to steal it right back. Studies have demonstrated a number of ways to distract ourselves from the distraction of performance pressure, and some of them are as simple as
whistling Dixie. In fact, one of them is whistling Dixie, or rather
whistling—whether "Dixie" is your warble of choice is up to you.
Let's examine these countermeasures in more detail.

1. Whistle While You Choke

The Seven Dwarfs (from the Disney film *Snow White*) believe in whistling while they work. I assume they too feared choking under pressure, because studies have demonstrated that whistling can prevent us from overthinking the kinds of automatic tasks we've done many times before and then choking as a result (such as swinging a golf club, throwing a football, carrying a cup of water, and, yes, Bill Buckner, catching an easy dribbler at first base). The reason this works is that once we're focused on the task at hand, whistling requires just enough additional attention to leave none left over for overthinking.

One word of caution: while you might find whistling incredibly useful in certain situations, those around you might not. So keep in mind you don't have to perform a bird-calling aria to combat performance pressure; whistling softly is just as effective.

2. Mumbling to Yourself During an Exam Does Not Mean You're Crazy

The most important thing we can do to avoid or minimize test anxiety is to prepare and study for the test as best we can and avoid procrastinating when doing so. The better prepared we are the less anxious we will feel on exam day. However, test anxiety can strike us even when we're well prepared, hampering our ability to focus during exam time.

We therefore need to do two things: quell our anxiety and regain our focus. The first will require us to sacrifice a tiny bit of exam time to calm ourselves down. Even if we don't realize it, anxiety can cause shallow breathing that limits the oxygen we take in and increases our sense of panic. To restore normal breathing and lower your panic you should put down your pen, look away from the exam, and focus on your breathing for one minute as you inhale and exhale to a count of three (count "in-two-three out-two-three" in your head while doing so). As you count, notice how the air feels filling your lungs and how it feels as you exhale. Roughly a minute should be sufficient to stabilize your breathing and take the edge off your anxiety.

Next, we need to redirect our attention back to the task at hand and we need to prevent our mind from worrying about how well or poorly we're doing and the implications thereof. The best way to keep our focus on the specific steps required to answer the questions is by reasoning through them aloud (but quietly—a whispered mumble will do). By vocalizing the questions and reasoning aloud, we use just enough attentional resources to deprive the part of our brain that wants to focus on worrying.

3. Neutralize the Stereotype

When we're reminded of negative stereotypes about our gender, race, ethnicity, or other group, it can trigger a subconscious worry about conforming to these stereotypes that can prevent us from giving our full attention to the task at hand. The best medicine in such situations is to neutralize such worries by affirming our self-worth.

In a series of recent studies, four hundred seventh graders in a socioeconomically diverse school were asked to choose a personal value (e.g., athletic ability, close friendships, or strong family ties) and write a brief essay about it at the start of the school year. Half the students were instructed to choose a value that mattered to them and write about why it mattered and how they expressed it, and half (as a control group) were told to choose a value that did not matter to them and write about why it might matter to someone else. The results were no less than astonishing. Students who wrote about values that mattered to them narrowed the achievement gap between black and white students by 40 percent and the effects lasted through the eighth grade (two years). A similar experiment was done with college women taking physics (women are chronically underrepresented in the hard sciences). Women who did the self-affirmation exercise did significantly better than their female counterparts who did not.

Of course, stereotype threat does not affect everyone, but the lower our confidence the more likely we are to become distracted by such concerns when reminders of them are present. If you feel you might be susceptible to such worries, take time before the exam to write a brief essay about an aspect of your character you value highly and about which you feel confident and proud. Doing so is a good investment, as it requires little time and it can make you more resilient to any irrelevant worries and anxieties a previous failure might trigger.

TREATMENT SUMMARY: DISTRACT YOURSELF FROM PERFORMANCE PRESSURE DISTRACTIONS

Dosage: Apply the treatment before and during situations in which you might experience performance pressure or anxiety or in which stereotype threat might come into play.

Effective for: Reducing performance pressure, test anxiety, stereotype threat, and risk of choking.

Secondary benefits: Minimizes damaged confidence and self-esteem and eases fear of failure.

When to Consult a Mental
Health Professional

Treating the psychological wounds failure inflicts should bring you emotional relief, foster your future preparation and performance, and allow you to persist in making efforts toward your goals. However, if you've applied the treatments in this chapter and still struggle with feelings of hopelessness, helplessness, shame, or depression, you should seek the help of a mental health professional. You should also seek professional help if these treatments have not helped you lower performance pressure or if you continue to fail at tasks at which you should be succeeding. Finally, if your mood and outlook have become so bleak and despondent that you have thoughts of harming yourself or others, please seek immediate help from a mental health professional or go to your local emergency room.

CHAPTER 7

||||||||||||||||||||

LOW SELF-ESTEEM

Weak Emotional Immune Systems

Everyone desires high self-esteem and if we were to judge by the vast assortment of magazines, books, programs, products, and self-proclaimed gurus that promise to deliver it, everyone can have it as well. That this billion-dollar industry exists at all is remarkable given that decades of research and thousands of scientific studies have demonstrated repeatedly that the overwhelming majority of self-esteem programs simply don't work. It is a shame they don't, because having low self-esteem is akin to having a weak emotional immune system: it renders us more vulnerable to many of the psychological injuries we sustain in daily life, such as failure and rejection. Further, people with low self-esteem are often less happy, more pessimistic, and less motivated than their higher-self-esteem counterparts. They also have much worse moods; they face a greater risk of depression, anxiety, and eating disorders; and they experience their relationships as less fulfilling than people with higher self-esteem do.

The good news is that despite the many failed promises of the self-esteem industry, researchers have found ways to boost our self-esteem and to strengthen our emotional immune systems by doing so. While such approaches cannot catapult someone's low self-esteem into the extremely high self-esteem range, that is probably for the best. Having very high self-esteem has its own set of pitfalls. For example, people with very high self-esteem tend to blame others for their own mistakes, they reject negative feedback as unreliable, and they often struggle to accept the consequences of their own actions. These tendencies render them likely to repeat the same mistakes and have significant problems in the workplace and their relationships and personal lives as a result.

At the very high end of self-esteem, narcissists possess an overly high and grandiose opinion of themselves but are also quick to feel extremely hurt and angry when criticized or devalued even if the criticism is minor (i.e., there are no small insults to a narcissist). Because they feel so crushed by even insignificant slights, they often have the nasty habit of seeking to retaliate against the people who "punctured" their inflated sense of self. Perhaps scientists should be seeking remedies for narcissism instead of for low self-esteem, but then again, life often finds ways to serve humble pie to those who need it most.

While few of us are true narcissists, there has been a general "grade inflation" in our collective self-esteem over the past few decades, spurred in part by the lavish attentions of the self-esteem industry. Consequently, studies indicate that today most of us are of two minds when it comes to our self-esteem: we feel inadequate as individuals on one hand, yet believe we're better than "average" on the other.

Indeed, the word "average" itself has developed strangely negative connotations. I say "strangely" because by definition, two-thirds of the population is "average" at any given thing (with one-sixth of people being above average and one-sixth below).

Yet, these days, telling a student, an employee, or a lover that his or her skills and abilities are "average" would constitute an insult and a blow to the individual's self-esteem. Most of us believe we're better drivers than average, that we're funnier, more logical, more popular, better looking, nicer, more trustworthy, wiser, and more intelligent than average as well.

Ironically, while we've been developing an aversion to being average, self-esteem scientists have been amassing one piece of evidence after another indicating that where our self-esteem is concerned, being average (not too high, not too low) is the best thing for us. Ideally, our self-esteem should lie in a range where our feelings of self-worth are both strong (not too low) and stable (not too high and fragile). Indeed, people with strong and stable self-esteem have more realistic evaluations of their real-world strengths and weaknesses and relatively more accurate assessments of how they're perceived by others, and they are usually the "healthiest," psychologically speaking.

Of course, this raises another question. How realistic are our self-assessments to begin with? In other words, does our self-esteem reflect the real-world value of our skills and attributes compared to others or does it reflect our subjective and often inaccurate assessments of these qualities based on our own psychological biases?

Let's use physical attractiveness as an example. Studies clearly demonstrate that people with higher self-esteem believe they are more attractive than people with lower self-esteem profess themselves to be. But when scientists compared stripped-down photographs of higher- and lower-self-esteem people (no jewelry or makeup, just faces) it quickly became clear that such is not the case. People with lower self-esteem were found to be just as attractive as people with higher self-esteem were. But because low self-esteem can cause us to underestimate our attractiveness we often downplay our strengths and we get less positive feedback about our appearance as a result. On the other hand, people with higher self-esteem might dress more attractively than their low self-esteem counterparts, which brings them more positive feedback and fuels their self-esteem even more.

Is Our Self-Esteem Low if We Don't Think Much of Anyone Else Either?

An athletic young man I once worked with came to therapy to deal with his "terribly low self-esteem." He went on to describe his own body in extremely critical terms and then quickly proceeded to discuss celebrities known for having beautiful bodies while pointing out their "obvious and disgusting flaws" (which were "obvious and disgusting" only to him). "I don't think you have low self-esteem," I said to him as soon as he finished savaging Brad Pitt for having "skinny arms and chicken legs." "True, you hate your body, but you hate everyone else's body as well," I pointed out while sucking in my stomach. "You might have low self-esteem, but the larger problem is your general negativity and unhappiness. Let's discuss whether you might be depressed." Depression can cause us to feel generally negative about everyone and everything (as well as a host of other symptoms) and it can masquerade as low self-esteem.

Of course, not everyone with a negative outlook on life is necessarily depressed, nor does such negativity necessarily indicate low self-esteem. For example, years ago scientists thought people with low self-esteem were also more prejudiced because they rated people of groups different from their own negatively (e.g., people of different race or gender). However, the scientists forgot to account for the fact that people with low self-esteem also rated their own groups negatively, which means their assessments of other groups weren't prejudiced but rather part of their larger negativity. Once they accounted for people's ratings of their own group the researchers found that people with low self-esteem were in fact less prejudiced than people with high self-esteem were.

One last point of clarification is that our self-esteem includes both a general sense of self-worth and how we feel about ourselves in specific domains of our lives (as a spouse, parent, friend, lawyer, nurse, golfer, video game player, etc.). When we think of ourselves as having low or high self-esteem we are usually referring to our global sense of self-worth. That being said, how we feel about ourselves in the specific domains we consider personally meaningful or important has a big impact on our general self-worth. For example, an aspiring chef might be much more bothered at the thought that she was a terrible cook than a professional athlete would be. Therefore, failures and success in meaningful domains of specific self-esteem can lead to changes in our global sense of self-worth as well.

Now that we've covered some of the basic foibles of our self-esteem, let's turn our attention to the psychological injuries we sustain when our self-esteem is low.

The Psychological Wounds Low Self-Esteem Inflicts

Low self-esteem can inflict three types of psychological wounds: It makes us more vulnerable to many of the emotional and psychological injuries we sustain in daily life, it makes us less able to absorb positive feedback and other "emotional nutrients" when they come our way, and it makes us feel insecure, ineffective, unconfident, and disempowered.

Boosting our self-esteem would strengthen our weakened emotional immune system and buffer us against many of these threats to our psychological well-being. Most of us know this from our own experience. When we feel good about ourselves we are often able to shrug off the kinds of setbacks, disappointments, or criticisms that on a "low self-esteem day" would have a much greater impact. In order to apply emotional first aid treatments successfully and boost our self-esteem we need to have a better understanding of how each of these wounds operates. Let's examine them in greater detail.

1. Egos Under Siege: Greater Psychological Vulnerability

Low self-esteem makes us more vulnerable to the psychological slings and arrows of daily life as even minor failures, rejections, or disappointments can sail over our emotional walls, get through our psychological defenses, and smash into our gut. When our self-esteem is low, normal "insults" like our boss frowning at us disapprovingly in a meeting, losing the office football pool, or a friend canceling plans to hang out with us impact our mood and disposition far more than they should. We blame ourselves for such events, we take them too personally, and we bounce back from them more slowly than we might were our self-esteem higher. Indeed, when our self-esteem is low, the barrage of hurts and slights we sustain on a regular basis can make us feel as though our egos are under siege from every angle.

Although there is an ongoing discussion about the extent to

which high self-esteem functions as a general buffer (studies have only recently begun distinguishing high self-esteem from too-high and fragile self-esteem), a substantial body of research demonstrates that having higher self-esteem (i.e., not too low) can make us more psychologically resilient and boost our emotional immune systems on at least several different fronts.

For example, rejection hurts at all levels of self-esteem but brain scans have demonstrated that people with low self-esteem experience rejection as more painful than people with higher self-esteem do. Also, our psychological responses to rejection are far less adaptive when our self-esteem is low, as we typically withdraw and create more distance between ourselves and others to minimize the risk of further rejection and pain. In some cases, our psychological vulnerability and our efforts at self-protection can lead us to push others away so consistently that we become socially or emotionally isolated and place ourselves at risk for acute loneliness. Having low self-esteem also makes us more vulnerable to discrimination and the further loss in self-esteem such experiences cause.

We are also more vulnerable to failure when our self-esteem is low. Failing causes larger emotional blows and sharper declines in motivation in people who have low self-esteem than it does in those with higher self-esteem. In addition, we are likely to be less persistent after failing and to overgeneralize the meaning of the failure such that we perceive it as indicative of a wider and more serious set of shortcomings than it actually is. Failing also sets in motion a vicious cycle of pushing low self-esteem even lower and therefore making it even more vulnerable to future failures.

Having low self esteem can also make us more vulnerable to anxiety. One study examined reactions to emotionally arousing situations. Participants were told they would be receiving "unpleasant electric shocks" (not that an electric shock is ever "pleasant," but these days it always falls short of being outright painful; and most studies never actually shock participants at all, as researchers are more interested in the anxiety generated by the anticipation of a shock than people's actual responses to being "zapped"). One group of waiting participants was given an intervention to raise their self-esteem (they were told they'd scored exceptionally well on a measure of verbal intelligence) and the other group was not. The group that received the self-esteem boost demonstrated significantly less anxiety when waiting to be "shocked" compared to the group that did not.

We also respond to stress much less effectively when our self-esteem is low than we do when our self-esteem is higher, making us more vulnerable to depression and anxiety as well as to a host of stress-related physical ailments and conditions. Straightforward observations of stress hormones such as cortisol have demonstrated that people with low self-esteem generally respond to stress more poorly and maintain higher levels of cortisol in their blood than people with high self-esteem do. High cortisol levels are associated with high blood pressure, poor immune system functioning, suppressed thyroid gland function, reduced muscle and bone density, and poor cognitive performance.

One of the reasons higher self-esteem buffers the effects of stress on both our psychological and physiological systems is that when our self-esteem is low we tend to make negative feedback even more stressful by exaggerating its implications and potential consequences. Further complicating matters, the more stressed we are, the less able we are to exert self-control. We are then likely to encounter slips and failures, judge ourselves too harshly for them, and damage our self-esteem even further.

Self-Esteem, Stress, and Self-Control

Rudy, a commodities broker who had an extremely stressful job, came to therapy to deal with a long-standing gambling problem. As stress built at work, Rudy would have a powerful urge to spend the night gambling in Atlantic City. He was able to resist this urge as long as the pressure at work remained high, but as soon as the stress level subsided, Rudy's willpower gave out and off to gamble he would go. Rudy's gambling binges often cost him thousands and even tens of thousands of dollars, which he could not afford. What made his self-loathing even greater after such episodes was that he was well aware of the role stress played in this cycle and he knew the triggers that preceded it (a reduction in stress after an intense period). Yet despite recognizing the pattern that led to his destructive behavior, Rudy was still powerless to stop it.

By the time Rudy showed up in my office he had gambled away his home, his entire savings, and most of his retirement, and he'd moved in with a friend. Needless to say, his self-esteem was at an all-time low. Determined as Rudy was to change his ways, his company was a breeding ground for cycles of heavy stress. But what made his situation even more urgent was that some years earlier Rudy's aging parents had signed a power of attorney that granted Rudy access to their finances and Rudy worried that his parents' home might be in jeopardy as well. Given his parents' fragile health and their complete lack of awareness about how bad their son's problem had become, Rudy worried that coming clean and nullifying the power of attorney would cause them such significant emotional distress it might even endanger their health.

Rudy's reactions to stress were extreme in their self-destructiveness but not unusual. Stress can substantially weaken our willpower and self-control and make us revert to automatic and old habits without even realizing it. For example, a stressful day might make a dieter leave the supermarket and drive all the way home before snapping out of his daze and realizing that instead of a salad he'd just purchased a large bucket of fried chicken.

When our self-esteem is low, we are far less likely to attribute slips in willpower to mental and emotional fatigue (which are the more likely culprits) and far more likely to assume they reflect fundamental character deficits. Our self-esteem then drops yet another notch and we are even more likely to blame ourselves unnecessarily when our willpower fails us in the future.

The good news is that manipulations to boost self-esteem have been found to help people better manage failure, rejection, anxiety, and (especially) stress. Encouraging as such findings are, they illuminate only the benefits of boosting our self-esteem, not how we might actually go about doing so. Scientists tend to boost research subjects' self-esteem by methods such as giving them bogus feedback about their score on a test of verbal intelligence. Obviously, we can't go around lying to ourselves about how smart we are, or, at least, most of us cannot. But the results of these experiments represent a "proof of concept" that boosting self-esteem can strengthen our emotional immune systems and make us more emotionally resilient.

2. No Dessert for Me! Why We Resist Positive Feedback and Emotional Nourishment

It's bad enough that having low self-esteem makes us more vulnerable to negative psychological experiences but researchers have also demonstrated that low self-esteem limits our ability to benefit from positive ones. In one study, people were exposed to sad music to put them in a bad mood and were then given the option to watch a comedy video to cheer up. Although people with high self-esteem jumped on the chance to have a laugh, people with low self-esteem agreed that watching the video would improve their mood, but they declined to do so nonetheless.

When our self-esteem is low, the resistance we have to positive experiences and information is quite sweeping. Unfortunately it includes exactly the kind of feedback that could play a vital role in rebuilding our self-worth and confidence and strengthening our emotional immune systems. Yet, thirsty as we are for such information, when our self-esteem is low, we are likely to reject it, avoid it, and at times even recoil from it.

Bo was a single man in his late twenties, a Southern gentleman who seemed to have everything going for him. He was tall and handsome with a stable job and in good health. But when it came to his personal life, Bo was miserable. He had no "social circle" to speak of and the few separate friends he did have seemed to walk all over him. His friends often stood him up, leaving Bo waiting on the street or in the movie theater or restaurant. They threw parties they told him about only after the fact. They criticized him relentlessly and they borrowed hundreds and at times thousands of dollars without paying him back. Bo was desperate to meet a woman he could settle down with, but here too his friends were more of a hindrance than a support. On the few occasions Bo tried talking to women at social events, his friends would join the conversation and "jokingly" put him down. At times, they even resorted to flirting with women in whom Bo had already expressed an interest. Although on the surface Bo had everything going for him, he rarely dated, and when he did, the relationships never lasted for more than a few weeks.

Bo knew his biggest problem was his extremely low self-esteem. In fact, one of the first things he told me when he came to therapy was that he was an admitted "self-help junkie" with a penchant for positive affirmation programs. Affirmations are positive statements about our self-worth, goals, and futures, which one reads, listens to, or states aloud. They are widely believed to contribute to healthy self-esteem, greater personal empowerment, and increased motivation and well-being, and Bo had tried all of them. He read *The Secret* and practiced the "law of attraction," he sipped *Chicken Soup for the Soul*, he spent weeks sleeping with expensive headgear via which personalized messages realigned his "neuroprocessing" and "corrected his brainwaves" (alas, the only thing they ended up "correcting" was his bank account), and he listened to countless subliminal messages, such as "I am worthy and able," which he assured me maintained their "subliminal" powers despite the messages being listed in bold print on the packaging in which they arrived.

But after investing many years and thousands of dollars in positive affirmation programs, Bo, like many other positive affirmation devotees, felt as worthless and disempowered as ever. This raises two questions: First, why did Bo keep investing time and money into positive affirmation programs when none of them worked? And second, why did these programs weaken Bo's emotional immune system rather than strengthen it?

One reason Bo stuck with it is that because our self-esteem is so subjective, our ability to assess whether it has changed for the better is rather limited (unless we use more objective measures such as scientifically established self-esteem questionnaires or other tangible criteria). In fact, numerous studies have demonstrated that we are very likely to unconsciously distort our memories of how we felt before starting a self-esteem program such that we believe the program helped us improve when it actually did not.

For example, one study investigated a popular self-esteem product that used audiotaped positive affirmations. Researchers measured participants' self-esteem before and after they completed the program and found that their self-esteem had not improved at all and had even declined in some cases. But despite this stark reality, the participants happily reported feeling significant improvements in their self-esteem because they unconsciously distorted their memory and believed they had felt worse previously. This is why so many bogus self-esteem programs have such glowing testimonials and commercial success despite being entirely ineffective.

This brings us to the second question: why do positive affirmations leave so many of their users feeling worse about themselves rather than better?

The answer requires a brief detour into the science of persuasion. Persuasion studies have long established that messages that fall within the boundaries of our established beliefs are persuasive to us, while those that differ too substantially from our beliefs are usually rejected altogether. If we believe we're unattractive, we're much more likely to accept a compliment like "You look very nice today" than "Why, your beauty is breathtaking!" Since positive affirmations are supposed to change how we feel about ourselves, whether they fall inside or outside the boundaries of our own self-concept is crucial to their effectiveness. When people with low self-esteem, like Bo, are exposed to positive affirmations that differ too widely from their existing self-beliefs, the affirmation is perceived as untrue and rejected in its entirety and it actually strengthens their belief that the *opposite* is true.

Recent research into the usefulness of positive affirmations has investigated these ideas and verified their potential to cause more harm than good. In one experiment, subjects were asked to complete a variety of questionnaires and then identify a trait they would like to possess but believed they lacked. Researchers then told subjects the good (albeit fictitious) news that they actually did possess the trait they desired. But hearing the "good" news made subjects feel worse and register drops in self-esteem. In other words, the very people who most need positive affirmations (like Bo) are those least likely to benefit from them (and most likely to be harmed by them) because they are likely to find such messages too discrepant from their current self-concepts. Rather than strengthening our emotional immune systems, positive affirmation programs are likely to weaken them even further.

When our self-esteem is chronically low, feeling unworthy becomes part of our identity, something with which we feel comfortable, a way of being to which we become accustomed. People with low self-esteem often feel more comfortable with negative feedback, because it verifies their existing feelings about themselves. One study found that poorly performing college students who were given messages to bolster their self-esteem actually declined academically as a result. Another found that when college students with low self-esteem had roommates who thought better of them than they did of themselves, they tended to look for new roommates. Indeed, one of the areas in which low self-esteem and our resistance to positive messages is especially problematic is in our relationships.

Low Self-Esteem and Relationships

People with low self-esteem have greater doubts about their partners' affections for them than people with higher self-esteem do, and they report less satisfaction in their marital and dating relationships as well. When our self-esteem is low, we are quick to perceive any signs of rejection and disapproval from our partners. We not only interpret many such messages too negatively, we also tend to overgeneralize them and read far greater disapproval into them than is intended.

Although our relationships could and should be sources of support, praise, and, hence, increased self-esteem, people with low self-esteem have tremendous difficulty taking in positive messages from their partners and they often bristle against such emotional nutrients. In one study, praising people with low self-esteem for being considerate boyfriends or girlfriends (which is pretty mild as far as compliments go) was enough to make them feel more insecure about their partners and view their entire relationship more negatively.

Regardless of how parched we might be for positive feedback and affirmation, when our self-esteem is low, compliments, reassurances, and praise from our partners makes us feel pressured to live up to their heightened expectations. We worry we will not be able to sustain such efforts, that we will disappoint them (even when their expectations are well within our capabilities), and that their love is conditional on our being able to keep it up. As a result, rather than enjoy the closeness and intimacy that compliments should evoke, people with low self-esteem often respond to praise by shutting down, withdrawing, and becoming more distant. Unfortunately, pulling away and acting defensively often "succeeds," as it lowers our partners' expectations, tarnishes their perceptions of us, and undermines the integrity and longevity of the entire relationship.

Indeed, many of Bo's dating experiences took a turn for the worse when a woman he considered attractive and successful made the mistake of complimenting him for being sweet, kind, or considerate. "Boy, she doesn't know me at all!" Bo would joke self-disparagingly. "She has no idea of how screwed up I am!" Bo would then make all kinds of unconscious efforts to demonstrate exactly how "screwed up" he was, which, unsurprisingly, ended in the woman breaking off their brief courtship. Bo would then take her rejection as further proof that he could only "hide" his true (and unacceptable) self for so long. The fact that the only unacceptable thing about Bo was his terribly low self-esteem was a reality he was tragically unable to acknowledge.

3. Chronic Backbone Pain: How Low Self-Esteem Makes Us Feel Disempowered

Bo's emotional immune system was extremely weak, affording him poor resiliency against the many rejections and betrayals he sustained from his "buddies." Although he did his best to hide it, each backstabbing incident upset him tremendously and left him feeling more defective, more undeserving, and more inadequate than he had previously. Bo recognized he was being taken for granted, taken advantage of, and generally mistreated by his friends, but he felt completely disempowered to do anything about it. Not only was he unable to limit his exposure in such situations (for example, by refusing to lend people money), but he also felt incapable of avoiding the company of people that were bound to hurt his feelings. "I'd rather have bad friends than no friends" was how Bo justified his reluctance to make any changes in his social life.

Studies have repeatedly demonstrated that people with low self-esteem tend to speak up less in groups and social settings and take less initiative to extricate themselves from unhappy relationships and friendships when they find themselves embroiled in them. Having low self-esteem makes us feel fundamentally insecure, unconfident, and undesirable in social situations and our "beggars can't be choosers" mentality leaves us feeling tremendously disempowered and unassertive as a result. We become convinced that setting limits, making demands, or stating expectations, however reasonable, will cause the other person to reject us immediately and drop us like a hot potato. Of course, others quickly recognize our reluctance to speak up, object, or cry foul, which encourages them to take us for granted and be even less considerate of our needs and feelings going forward.

The reality of Bo's predicament was that some of his friends might indeed reject him if he stood up to them or spoke up about their mistreatment of him. However, others would not. I tried to impress upon him that speaking up would constitute an important litmus test as to the quality and potential of the friendship each person offered him. Those who did indeed care about him, even somewhat, would respond to his objections by demonstrating some kind of accommodation or consideration that Bo could build upon. Those who did not were not worthy of his friendship to begin with.

To be clear, Bo's friends were not necessarily terrible people, although they were unlikely to win any humanitarian awards. Most of us only put in as much effort as a situation requires from us. If we can "get away" with being less considerate or less reciprocal, and various other forms of "getting without giving," many of us will, not because we're evil, but simply because we can. If people demanded or expected more of us we would do more, but when they don't, we don't make the effort. This dynamic is true in practically every relationship we have. When our self-esteem is low and we expect very little of others, we are likely to get very little from them as well.

Changing this dynamic once a relationship is already established is difficult because we're in essence "changing the terms of the deal" after the other person has already been operating under a specific set of assumptions and expectations. That is why it is crucial to pay great attention to the expectations we set up when our friendships and romantic relationships first begin. Bo's challenge was to identify which of his friends were worth keeping and to find ways in which he could change the terms of "the deal" so he could enjoy more reciprocity and mutual support from those who did care about him and eliminate the ongoing damage his self-esteem was sustaining from those who did not.

Gladys, a forty-year-old breast cancer survivor, is another example of someone who had low self-esteem, although, unlike in Bo's case, hers was not a lifelong struggle but rather the result of horrific emotional blows she had sustained over recent years. Without any prior warning, Gladys's husband had left her midway through her chemotherapy treatments some years earlier. Demonstrating truly despicable cruelty, he chose to serve her divorce papers by having someone wait for her outside the hospital the day she was released after having a double mastectomy.

Although Gladys's body recovered from the cancer, the chemotherapy, the double mastectomy, and the several reconstructive surgeries that followed, her self-esteem was not as fortunate. She never got over the blow of her husband abandoning her while she was fighting for her life nor the manner in which he did so. When I met Gladys, there was little evidence of the fighter who'd survived a terrible disease, the high school track athlete who had a closet full of medals and trophies, or the successful Web designer who'd built her own business from scratch after her divorce. Instead, Gladys came across as timid, insecure, and extremely unassertive.

Gladys did have a close circle of friends (many of whom were also breast cancer survivors) but she had not gone on a single date since her divorce, especially since she worked from home and had few opportunities to meet eligible men. However, what finally convinced her to start psychotherapy was that her low self-esteem began to have an impact on her business and her income as well.

"I've never been terribly assertive but I became much worse after my husband left. My business suffers because I often don't get paid what I deserve and I get talked into doing too many unpaid extras. I'm just not very good at standing up to demanding people. I try but they bully and pressure and I always end up giving in." Gladys went on to describe how her biggest client was also the worst offender. Despite already extracting huge concessions and discounts for the services she provided, the client kept demanding more. Gladys feared that refusing the requests would incite the company to take its business elsewhere, a loss that would have significant financial implications for her.

Much as Bo felt he had no room to make demands or set limits in his friendships, Gladys felt too insecure, unconfident, and disempowered to do so in her business. They were both convinced that their impoverished self-worth was an accurate reflection of their character and attributes, such that they basically "got what they deserved." Their lack of assertiveness and backbone was a direct result of a weak emotional immune system that led them to believe that any acts of assertion on their part would only bring intolerable hurt, rejection, and disaster.

How to Treat the Psychological Wounds Low Self-Esteem Inflicts

Our self-esteem fluctuates regularly and even people with generally high self-esteem can have days in which they feel poorly about themselves. Such temporary dips in self-worth rarely require emotional first aid as we usually recover from them fairly swiftly. However, when our self-esteem is regularly low, or when we feel unable to stand up for ourselves and to set limits with friends or family members who treat us poorly or with disrespect, we need to treat our psychological wounds and boost our self-esteem.

The treatments in this chapter should help "stop the bleeding" and set us on the path to bolstering our sense of self-worth. However, improving our self-esteem in deep and fundamental ways requires both time and substantial effort. Higher self-esteem is essentially an outcome of doing well in our lives and relationships. Internalizing the lessons of this chapter and applying them cannot change our self-esteem overnight but it can give us the tools to establish a track record of success that, over time, will strengthen our self-esteem and make it more stable. Therefore, in addition to providing initial emotional relief, the treatments that follow should be adopted as daily strategies and life habits. Let's open our psychological medicine cabinet and examine the treatment options available to us.

General Treatment Guidelines

Having low self-esteem weakens our emotional immune systems and inflicts three kinds of psychological wounds: it makes us more vulnerable to psychological injuries, it makes us dismissive of positive feedback and resistant to emotional nutrients, and it makes us feel unassertive and disempowered. The five treatments suggested in this chapter should be administered to correct self-critical habits and negative self-perceptions, especially following blows to self-esteem or if entering periods of increased stress.

Administer the treatments in the order in which they are

presented. Treatment A (adopting self-compassion) helps prevent the self-critical mind-sets that damage our already weakened emotional immune systems. Treatments B (identifying and affirming strengths) and C (increasing tolerance for compliments) are focused on recognizing, acknowledging, and reconnecting to neglected or marginalized strengths, qualities, and abilities. Treatments D (increasing personal empowerment) and E (strengthening self-control) focus on rebuilding self-esteem and feelings of empowerment. At the end of the chapter, I provide guidelines for assessing when one should consult a mental health professional.

Treatment A: Adopt Self-Compassion and Silence the Critical Voices in Your Head

Imagine witnessing an emotionally abusive parent berating her child for getting a poor report card. The parent verbally attacks the child, mocks him, and mercilessly belittles him without displaying a whit of empathy, support, or compassion. Meanwhile, the child's face registers utter devastation as he absorbs one emotional blow after another. Most of us would find such a scene extremely distressing to witness (especially those of us who grew up with such parents) and we would immediately vow never to treat our own children in such an abusive, cruel, and destructive manner.

And yet when our self-esteem is low, that is exactly how we treat ourselves. We blame ourselves for our mistakes, failures, rejections, and frustrations in the most harsh and self-punitive terms. We call ourselves "losers" and "idiots," we give ourselves stern "lectures," and we replay the scenes in our mind while ruminating on our inadequacies and deficiencies. In other words, we treat ourselves even worse than an emotionally abusive parent would. When I catch my patients running such damaging internal sound tracks in their minds and point it out to them, they are usually quick to respond, "I know I shouldn't beat myself up about it but—" and then they go on to justify why they should beat themselves up about it. When I ask if they would ever treat their own children, their spouse, or their friends in a similar manner they look at me horrified, as if doing so would be unthinkable.

When our self-esteem is low, this double standard is a trap we easily fall into. Our reason abandons us and we struggle to implement the premise that if we consider it abusive to speak to others a certain way we should never direct such thoughts toward ourselves either. The first step we need to take on the path toward self-compassion is to embrace the most simple and basic fact that when our emotional immune systems are weak we should do everything in our power to strengthen them, not devastate them even further. Purging the emotionally abusive voices in our heads and adopting kinder, more supportive ones instead is an absolute imperative.

People with low self-esteem often bristle at the notion of adopting self-compassion when I first suggest it. They worry that switching off self-punitive thoughts and replacing them with soothing and compassionate ones will cause them to "slack off" and function more poorly, making their self-esteem even weaker and more vulnerable as a result. But such worries are entirely unfounded, as studies demonstrate that exactly the opposite is true. Practicing self-compassion actually strengthens our emotional immune systems. In one study, self-compassion was found to buffer incoming college students against homesickness, depression, and general dissatisfaction with their choice of school. In others, individuals who practiced self-compassion had quicker emotional recoveries from separation and divorce, and they recovered more quickly from failure and rejection experiences.

Despite the obvious benefits of adopting self-compassion, it remains challenging to do so when our self-esteem is low because the practice is so foreign to our ordinary way of thinking, it can cause discomfort and even an initial uptick in anxiety. Therefore, we must be determined to put an end to the destructive sound tracks that make up the current playlists in our minds. Once we truly accept that we require soothing and compassion far more than we do emotional abuse, we can turn to the following exercise.

EXERCISE FOR ADOPTING SELF-COMPASSION

Complete the following writing exercise three times, each time describing an event from your past (if possible, include at least one from your recent past). Try to write about one event each day so that you complete the exercise over three consecutive days.

1. We've all experienced failures, embarrassments, humiliations, or rejections that made us feel self-critical and badly about ourselves. Choose one such event and detail what actually happened and how you felt about it.

2. Imagine that the event happened to a dear friend or close family member who then felt terrible about herself (or himself) because of it. Describe that person's experience of the event, how she would react and feel in the very same situation.

3. You hate seeing this person in emotional pain and you decide to write her a letter with the explicit purpose of making her feel better about herself. Make sure to express

kindness, understanding, and concern about the experience she went through and how she felt as a result, and remind her of why she is worthy of compassion and support.

4. Now describe your own experience and your feelings about the event again, but this time, try to be as objective and understanding as you can about what happened and about how you felt. Make sure not to sound judgmental or negative. For example, you might note that your date never called you back, as that is factual, but not that your date thought you were a loser, because that is judgmental and nonfactual. Or that you made mistakes during a presentation, but not that your colleagues disrespect you as a result, because, regardless of how you perceived their reactions, when our self-esteem is low we tend to misinterpret people's facial expressions too negatively.

Treatment Summary: Self-Compassion

Dosage: Apply the treatment over three days and repeat regularly until the principles of self-compassion become engrained and automatic.

Effective for: Increasing emotional resilience and decreasing emotional vulnerability and self-criticism.

Secondary benefits: Decreases resistance to positive feedback.

Treatment B: Identify Your Strengths and Affirm Them

Positive affirmation die-hards like Bo, the Southern gentleman with low self-esteem, need not forsake them entirely. Although positive affirmations can be damaging to people with low self-esteem, many positive affirmation routines can be tweaked to make the affirmations easier for us to digest (e.g., by affirming our need to take action when we've been wronged). Bo was hesitant to dispense with positive affirmations altogether but he agreed to adapt them to include action-oriented items such as "When I lend someone money, asking him to pay me back is far less rude than his failing to repay me in a timely manner," and "When a friend upsets me I am entitled to speak up."

That being said, a much more effective way to use affirmations is to use *self*-affirmations that identify and affirm valuable and important aspects of ourselves we already know to be true, such as our trustworthiness, loyalty, or work ethic (in contrast to *positive* affirmations, which affirm qualities we would like to possess but don't believe we do). Reminding ourselves that we have significant worth regardless of any shortcomings we perceive in ourselves provides an immediate boost to our self-esteem and renders us less vulnerable to experiences of rejection or failure.

Another advantage of self-affirmations is they benefit us even when the quality we're affirming has nothing to do with the situation of the moment. For example, if we're hurting because we've been turned down for a promotion we do not have to affirm our value as an employee in order to feel better (which would be a hard sell in that moment anyway). Instead, affirming that we are a good parent or a great wife, a thoughtful friend or a champion quilter, a supportive brother or a great listener is sufficient to make us feel better about ourselves as we walk out of our boss's office without the new title we had hoped to secure.

Ideally, we should employ self-affirmation exercises before we go into situations that might provide a blow to our self-esteem (i.e., before our big date, before the exam, before the job interview). This is also why it is best to use such exercises on a regular basis, as we cannot always predict when blows to our self-esteem might occur. Nonetheless, completing such exercises after the fact still has significant value.

EXERCISE FOR SELF-AFFIRMATION

Complete the following writing exercise as regularly as possible (weekly is good; daily is better). It is especially important to do the exercise when facing situations of heightened stress (e.g., for tax accountants, during tax season; for college students, during finals) or situations that pose potential threats to self-esteem (e.g., when applying to schools or jobs), as that is when our self-esteem might be most vulnerable. You will need two sheets of blank paper.

1. On the first sheet of paper, make a list of your important attributes and qualities, including any achievements you have that are significant or meaningful to you. Aim for at least ten items and preferably many more.

2. If while brainstorming items for your list you think of responses that are negative (e.g., "My boss thinks I'm a terrible employee"), critical (e.g., "I'm a loser"), or sarcastic (e.g., "What am I good at? Let's see, there's napping . . . and I'm a champ at breathing too!"), write them down on the second sheet of paper.

3. Choose one item from the first sheet of paper that is especially meaningful to you and write a brief essay (at least one paragraph) about why this specific attribute, achievement, or experience is meaningful to you and what role you hope it will play in your life.

4. Once you've completed the essay, take the second sheet of paper, crumple it into a ball, and throw it in the garbage where it belongs.

5. On subsequent days, choose other items from your positive attribute list and write about them, preferably each day, until you've completed the list. Feel free to add to your list at any time or to write about specific items several times.

Treatment Summary: Identify Your Strengths and Affirm Them

Dosage: Apply the treatment until you complete your initial list and repeat it whenever you anticipate stress or experience a blow to your self-esteem.

Effective for: Increasing emotional resilience, decreasing emotional vulnerability, and minimizing feelings of disempowerment.

Secondary benefits: Decreases resistance to positive feedback and reduces self-criticism.

Treatment C: Increase Your Tolerance for Compliments

Having low self-esteem makes it difficult for us to absorb compliments and positive feedback from others, especially our loved ones, and to use such communications to rebuild our self-esteem. Instead, we are more comfortable scanning the environment for any hints of negative feedback that might confirm our (mis)perceptions of ourselves as being fundamentally unworthy or inadequate.

Because this resistance to compliments operates on both conscious and unconscious levels, some of us are aware we feel uncomfortable receiving positive feedback from others but many of us are not. Our lack of awareness is especially problematic when it comes to our romantic partners, because when our self-esteem is low, we not only rebuff positive communications from them but we also respond by withdrawing and devaluing the relationship. I should note that the subject pool used in much of this research was composed of college students and young adults. In my experience, long-term couples tend to be more aware when one or both members of the couple are resistant to compliments and they refrain from voicing positive feedback to the resistant person. Of course, that only exacerbates the problem for the person with low self-esteem, as hearing fewer compliments and receiving little positive affirmation from the person who knows us best is itself not conducive to building feelings of self-worth.

On a positive note, several studies that used subjects of all ages have demonstrated that by affirming aspects of our selves that are related to our worth as relationship partners, we can bolster our "relationship self-esteem." Doing so renders any compliments we receive from our partners less discrepant from our current self-views and makes us less likely to reject or rebuff them. Affirming our value as relationship partners not only makes us feel better about ourselves (by boosting our self-esteem), it also makes us feel better about our partners and even about the relationship itself.

EXERCISE TO INCREASE OUR TOLERANCE OF COMPLIMENTS

The following is a writing exercise that can and should be completed on a regular basis (weekly or more when possible).

1. Think back to a time your partner, family member, or friend conveyed that he or she appreciated, liked, or enjoyed something about you, such as a personal quality you have or something you did that the person felt strongly about. Describe the incident and explain what made the person feel positively about you when it occurred.

2. What does displaying this attribute or behavior mean to you?

3. What benefits does having the attribute or behavior bring to your relationships and friendships?

4. What other significant or meaningful functions or roles can the attribute or behavior contribute to your life?

TREATMENT SUMMARY: INCREASE TOLERANCE FOR COMPLIMENTS

Dosage: Apply the treatment regularly until you become more comfortable with receiving compliments. Make sure to repeat whenever you experience a blow to your self-esteem.

Effective for: Decreasing resistance to positive feedback and increasing relational self-esteem.

Secondary benefits: Increases emotional resilience, decreases emotional vulnerability, and minimizes feelings of disempowerment.

Treatment D: Increase Your Personal Empowerment

The vast majority of articles, books, and programs that promise to help us feel more personally empowered fail to recognize a critical flaw in their thinking—personal empowerment is not something one *feels* but rather something one *has*. Sure, we might feel empowered after reading a book about improving marital relationships, but unless we're able to initiate a productive dialogue with our partner and create actual changes, we are no more empowered than we were when we started. To have an impact on our self-esteem, feelings of personal empowerment must be supported by evidence of having actual influence in the various spheres of our lives, whether in our relationships, in our social or professional contexts, as citizens, or even as consumers.

Converting our low self-esteem into assertive feelings of empowerment might sound like a tall order but there is one aspect of personal empowerment we can use to our advantage. Acting assertively and getting results in one area of our lives tends to empower us in other areas of our lives as well. Choosing our battles wisely and starting with smaller and simpler acts of assertiveness can quickly get the ball of empowerment rolling, as even small triumphs provide a significant boost to our self-esteem and make us feel generally more powerful, effective, and assertive.

For example, many of us have had the experience of feeling so "pumped up" by resolving, say, a consumer or customer service complaint (successfully removing charges from our bank statement, perhaps) that we walked straight over to our teenager's bedroom and told her to do something about the mess with such conviction that, for the first time in months, she actually did as we asked without arguing.

Because one successful act of assertion and personal empowerment encourages another, we need to identify areas for potential assertive action that have both a high likelihood of success and manageable consequences in the event of failure. The best way to do so is first to gather as much information as we can about how to attain our goal and to formulate well-thought-out strategies and plans for proceeding. We can then begin a process of practicing assertive actions in lower-stakes situations so we can refine our technique, our approach, and our skills as we go.

EXERCISE FOR IDENTIFYING OPTIONS FOR ASSERTIVE ACTION

1. Think about aspects of your life that tend to make you feel frustrated. Try to include situations in your community life, work life, family and personal life, social life, and life as a consumer. Describe at least three examples for each of these domains. For example, when thinking about your married life you might feel frustrated about a spouse's personal habits, the division of labor between you, your partner's style of communication, or his or her approach to parenting.

2. Rank your items according to which of them have both a high likelihood of success and manageable consequences

in case of failure. For example, Bo decided to speak up about the two thousand dollars he had lent his friend Timothy; Timothy had promised to return it within three months, and a year had passed. Timothy was Bo's "least-close friend" and Bo felt justified enough in the situation to be willing to risk the friendship and discuss the matter with him. And Gladys decided to speak up about a couple of "website tweaks" her client had asked her to "throw in" free of charge; Gladys felt the "tweaks" in question were not crucial enough to prompt her client to fire her if she refused to do them without compensation.

The final list represents your master plan for practicing assertive actions and attaining personal empowerment. Now that you've identified and prioritized your goals, it's time to consider any additional information or specific skill sets that can help you execute them successfully and to plan your strategy accordingly.

Gathering Information and Strategic Planning

To maximize our chances of attaining each goal, we need to consider how the systems or people we plan to challenge operate. In other words, we need to gain a grasp of the priorities and mindsets of any relevant people; the complaint management systems of any relevant businesses, companies, or local municipalities; or the politics, hierarchy, and human resource practices in our workplace.

For example, I asked Bo and Gladys to describe the situation from the other people's perspectives in order to gain some insight about their mind-sets. Bo explained that Timothy had always been slightly resentful and jealous of his income because he earned substantially less than Bo did. Bo assumed he felt entitled to borrow money from him because Bo could afford it, and therefore, Timothy saw no urgency to pay him back. Bo indicated that Timothy spent hundreds of dollars a week going out so that he certainly could afford to pay him back, even if it were at the rate of a few hundred dollars a month. And Gladys told me that her clients were hoping to launch a minor redesign of their website in the near future and that they were unlikely to shop around for an entirely new Web designer unless they absolutely had to.

Examples of other kinds of information gathering we might do include finding out what human resource channels are available if we have a complaint about a work colleague, looking up relevant departments in our municipality so we know who to call about a missing stop sign on our street, finding out who in our cell phone company is authorized to deal with the dollar amount we're disputing (most customer service representatives are only authorized to deal with small amounts), or inquiring whether our teenager has an exam the next day before we demand he spend the rest of the evening completing his chores.

Once we've gathered the necessary information, we need to formulate and think through our plan of action and anticipate any reactions. For example, we might want to figure out how we can ask a friend why she hasn't returned our phone calls without sounding too accusatory or hostile (because even though we might feel hurt by her disappearing, being accusatory simply wouldn't be productive) or how to phrase a complaint to our spouse so he doesn't get too defensive (because even though we might have the right to be annoyed, we also know he doesn't respond well when we approach him in anger). We might think through the best time and place to talk to a colleague about why he never gave us credit for our part in the team presentation and give careful consideration to what we want to achieve by doing so (e.g., rather than just venting frustration we can suggest that we should take the lead on the next presentation as compensation for his omission).

Practice, Patience, and Persistence

Personal empowerment is a process and not something we attain in a single step. We have to be prepared for the reality that not all our efforts will yield immediate results and that we'll need to persist, practice our skill sets, and sharpen our tools before we're able to wield them both effectively and consistently. Bo's first plan to talk to Timothy at a social gathering failed because Timothy promised to chat later in the evening and then claimed he was too tired to do so. Bo learned that he needed to create the space to talk with Timothy without distractions and that he would have to be on the alert for any attempts Timothy made to prevent the conversation from happening.

When Gladys finally called her clients about the extra work they expected her to do, they steamrolled her, barely let her get a word in, and reassured her it wouldn't take her long to make the tweaks they required. Gladys was extremely demoralized at first but once she reflected on the exchange, she realized the best way for her to convey her message was via e-mail, as her clients would not be able to cut her off and she would be able to express her thoughts fully and assertively.

Practice, patience, and persistence are key ingredients in developing personal empowerment. Once we begin speaking up, we will be able to assess our strengths and weaknesses and learn which of our skills and tools still need work. Each setback will also teach us how to devise more effective plans. Bo decided to propose a manageable payment schedule and send it to Timothy in the mail along with self-addressed stamped envelopes. The factual and nonaccusatory tone Bo used in his letter led Timothy to respond with an apology and a check for the first payment. Gladys continued communicating with her clients by e-mail until she extracted additional payment for the work they wanted her to do.

While both Bo and Gladys were elated by their successes and felt quite empowered as a result, their triumphs were only the first step on their respective paths to stronger self-esteem. Over the next year, Bo continued to "clean house" with his old friends, and he made new ones who were more supportive and loyal. Gladys formulated tighter guidelines for compensation that she distributed to all her clients before she agreed to start work. In time, her self-esteem improved to the point where she felt able to start dating. Although she had made no efforts to improve her self-esteem in the dating domain, feeling more empowered as a businesswoman had created a greater sense of self-worth that boosted her feelings of confidence in her personal life as well.

Once we've tackled the first item on our lists and met with success, we should use the boost we get to our self-esteem and turn to the next item as soon as possible so we find success there as well. Although it will take time for our emotional immune systems to strengthen and to function more effectively, our small successes will soon begin to add up. Receiving a raise or promotion at work, resolving conflicts with friends, working out problems with our partners and family members, and getting satisfaction as consumers will each contribute to significantly strengthening our self-esteem and improving our general quality of life.

Treatment Summary: Personal Empowerment

Dosage: Apply the treatment in each of the different spheres of your life when possible (i.e., your home and work life, your friendships, and as a consumer and community member) and repeat until you complete your list. Add new items to your action list when they arise.

Effective for: Increasing feelings of assertiveness and competence, strengthening weak feelings of entitlement, and demonstrating personal empowerment.

Secondary benefits: Increases emotional resilience and general self-esteem and decreases emotional vulnerability.

Treatment E: Improve Your Self-Control

Demonstrating self-control and willpower increases personal empowerment and helps us make progress toward our goals, both of which are extremely beneficial to our self-esteem. Although many of us assume willpower is a stable character trait or ability (i.e., we either have strong willpower or we do not), self-control actually functions more like a muscle. As such, learning how this muscle functions will allow us to use it wisely, strengthen it, and build our self-esteem as a result.

The most important thing to keep in mind about our self-control muscles is that they are subject to fatigue. Some of us might have bigger willpower muscles than others but even the most bulging willpower muscle will tire and become ineffective if we overwork it. Further, using this muscle in one context will tire it and make it weaker when we try to use it in another. For example, if we spend our day squelching the urge to rip off our tyrannical boss's hairpiece and throw it across the conference room like a Frisbee, our willpower will be depleted by the time we get home and we are likely to find it difficult to stick to our diet and eat a healthy dinner.

Complicating matters further, the limited reservoir of emotional energy that fuels our willpower muscles is shared by other complex mental functions such as those responsible for making choices and decisions. Strange as it might sound, using these seemingly unrelated intellectual abilities saps our willpower and weakens our self-control. For example, when we spend the day making decisions about clothing and accessories for an upcoming photo shoot we're styling, we might find it challenging to marshal the willpower to go to the gym when we get home. Indeed, our self-control often fails us at night after the energy reservoir fueling our willpower runs low and causes it to function less effectively.

In order to maximize the effectiveness of our willpower and use it to build our self-esteem we need to do three things: strengthen our basic willpower muscles, manage the energy reservoirs that fuel our self-control so they don't get depleted, and minimize the impact of the many temptations that exist around us.

Pump Up Your Willpower Muscles

The downside of our willpower being a general muscle is that exerting willpower in one area will cause fatigue and make it harder to exert willpower in another. But this "limitation" has an upside. Exercising our willpower by practicing acts of self-control in insignificant areas will increase the strength and endurance of our willpower muscles in more meaningful and important areas as well. Scientists have investigated several such "willpower workouts," including focusing on our posture (great for slouchers); avoiding cursing (more effective for potty mouths than it is for the "gosh darn it!" set); avoiding sweets, cookies, or cakes (great if you have a sweet tooth); squeezing a handgrip twice a day for as long as we can (handgrips are cheap and can be found in sporting goods stores); and the one I think works best—using our nondominant hand.

Practicing any task that requires us to regularly inhibit an automatic impulse (e.g., to slouch, use our dominant hand, curse, eat sweets, or let go of the handgrip when it becomes difficult) can be effective if we "train" for a sufficient period of time (at least four to eight weeks). In a variety of studies, such exercises provided significant benefits for smokers who were trying to quit, people with aggressive impulses who struggled to manage their anger, and compulsive shoppers who were trying to reform.

Exercise for Building Willpower

Use your nondominant hand for as many tasks as possible every day between the hours of 8:00 a.m. and 6:00 p.m. for four to eight weeks (the longer the better). Adjust these hours accordingly if your schedule requires (e.g., if you work the night shift or if you only wake up around noon). Include tasks such as brushing your teeth, opening doors, using a computer mouse or trackball, drinking (other than hot drinks, which can spill and cause burns), carrying things (other than babies and other breakables), stirring, combing your hair, using a fork (when you're not using a knife), moving objects (other than breakable ones), and any other action for which you typically use your dominant hand.

If you are ambidextrous: Use the posture improvement exercise instead. Monitor your posture so that you are sitting as erect as possible at all times. Avoid slouching, lying down, reclining, or leaning on a desk during the hours of 8:00 a.m. to 6:00 p.m. (adjust the hours accordingly if necessary).

Make Sure You Have Fuel in the Tank

One of the most essential fuels our willpower muscles require (as do many of our other muscles, both cognitive and physical) is glucose (sugars). Scientists have known for a while that when our glucose levels are low, effortful mental processes such as asserting willpower and self-control are impaired (automatic and noneffortful processes such as washing the dishes are not). In one study, people were put through effortful mental exercises to deplete their brain of glucose levels and then given a glass of lemonade. Half of them received lemonade sweetened with sugar and half got lemonade with an artificial sweetener (which tastes similar but has no glucose). After fifteen minutes (the time necessary for the drink to get absorbed into their systems) subjects who were given lemonade with real sugar recovered from their mental fatigue and were able to display significantly greater willpower than those who drank lemonade with artificial sweetener.

In short, for our willpower to operate best we require optimal levels of glucose. Previous exertions of self-control or lack of caloric intake will make our blood glucose levels drop below optimal levels and our willpower will be weak as a result. Sleep and rest also have a big impact on our willpower's ability to function at its capacity and being tired or sleep deprived will cause serious impairments in our ability to exhibit self-control.

Avoid Temptations and Manage
Them When You Cannot

The average person spends three to four hours a day exerting some form of willpower. Dieters are surrounded by fattening foods, smokers trying to quit walk by people smoking outside most buildings, problem drinkers are never far from a bar or liquor store, students studying for finals face innumerable distractions from friends and electronic devices, and individuals with anger management issues encounter frustrating and provocative situations daily. The best way to manage temptations is not to overestimate our ability to manage them but to avoid them when possible. But there are also techniques we can use when it is impossible to do so.

1. Play One Side of Your Brain Against the Other

Our brain uses different systems to process rewards and risks. When faced with temptations, the reward system (go for it!) can drown out the system that evaluates risk (don't!). While we can't lower the volume on our cravings and urgings in such situations, we can turn up the volume on our risk assessment. For example, if we're trying to quit drinking and we find ourselves at a dinner where alcohol is served we can remind ourselves that the last time we had a drink we made a royal mess of things because we never stop at just one. We can consider how demoralized we'll feel if we allow alcohol back into our lives and how empowered and thankful we'll feel the next day if we resist. We can replay snapshots of our spouse's face the last time we fell off the wagon and see the disappointment in the eyes of our friends, or we can remind ourselves of our commitment, of why we started our journey in the first place, and the reasons we've been able to resist our urges so far. Beefing up our risk assessments by preparing a list of them in advance, which we can then refer to in the moment, can buy us just enough time to get through the situation.

2. Minimize the Damage

Many of us become extremely demoralized when we slip and succumb to temptation. "I've fallen off the wagon" or "I've blown my
diet" is a thought that serves no useful purpose other than to give
ourselves permission to indulge. After all, if we've blown our diet,
we might as well eat whatever we want because we'll have to start
all over again anyway.

Viewing slips as simple alerts that our willpower is fatigued
and needs to recover (instead of as indications of failure) will allow
us to acknowledge the lapse without getting further off track.

3. Avoid the Triggers

Many of our bad habits are prompted by triggers. For example,
researchers in one study gave moviegoers stale popcorn and sat
them down to watch a movie. They ate just as much of the stale
popcorn as they typically ate fresh popcorn—but only because
they were watching a movie! When the researchers gave the same
participants stale popcorn while watching a music video in a conference room, they barely touched it. Our habits always have triggers, such as lighting up a cigarette when we have a beer, doing
recreational drugs when we hang out with certain friends, or bit-
ing our fingernails when we sit on the couch to watch television.
If we wish to change the habits, we have to avoid the triggers, at
least until the new habit becomes well engrained. Sad as it may be,
we might have to skip the beers, avoid the drug-using friends
(which is not a bad idea in general), or watch TV on a laptop in
the kitchen.

4. Practice Mindfulness to Tolerate Urges, Impulses, and Cravings

Mindfulness involves a form of mediation in which we observe our feelings without judging them, in essence becoming anthropologists in our own minds. We act like outside observers, noting the strength of our emotions and the sensations they create in our bodies but without dwelling on them or their implications. Rudy, the stressed-out gambler who was in danger of gambling away his aging parents' home, had an extremely stressful job that sapped his willpower and made it difficult for him to resist the urge to gamble. I suggested Rudy use a mindfulness technique, not just because it is effective for general stress management but because certain mindfulness exercises can be extremely useful for managing cravings, impulses, and urges (including the urge to gamble).

When learning to manage our cravings and urges we must first accept that such impulses, strong as they are, always pass with time. I suggested Rudy use one of our sessions to practice and instructed him to do the following: "Relax and focus on your breathing. Feel free to close your eyes. Study the urge to gamble as its waves wash over you, as if you were an alien who was interested in the human experience." (Rudy was a sci-fi fan.) "Visualize the amplitude of the urge's intensity like a seismograph readout that measures earthquake activity. As the waves come, follow the rise and fall of the dial on the readout; note when one wave intensifies and weakens and where another begins. Observe how different parts of your body feel when the urge intensifies and how the same parts of your body feel when it subsides. Continue to monitor your physiological responses this way, tracking one wave of urges after another as they rush toward you and over you, until the intensity of the waves eventually subsides as every earthquake does."

Focusing on our breathing, visualizing the seismographic readout, and noting the sensations in our bodies can help us ride out the "quake" and resist acting on our cravings, urges, and impulses until they pass. Practicing this technique when we are not in the grips of our impulses will help us apply it more successfully when we are. Fortunately, Rudy was able to get in several weeks of daily mindfulness practice before the work stress subsided again and the urge to gamble swept in. When it did, Rudy was ready for it and he was able to ride it out. He described the situation as "touch-and-go for a while," but the confidence he gained by resisting the urge to gamble when he had succumbed to it many times in the past provided a huge boost to his self-esteem.

Treatment Summary: Improve Your Self-Control

Dosage: Apply this treatment daily toward goals that require willpower and self-control.

Effective for: Increasing willpower and feelings of empowerment, facilitating progress toward self-improvement goals, and boosting self-esteem.

When to Consult a Mental Health Professional

Self-esteem is a deeply rooted psychological construct and applying the treatments in this chapter such that they yield significant results requires time, effort, and dedication. If you feel unable to apply these techniques or if you've invested the time and effort to do so but have not been able to boost your self-esteem as a result, you should consider seeking the advice of a mental health professional.

If there are ongoing circumstances in your life that are contributing to your low self-esteem (e.g., if you have an emotionally abusive boss or partner or if you're struggling to find work despite making consistent efforts to do so), a mental health professional could help you assess whether you should take steps to change your circumstances (as it is hard to rebuild your self-esteem if it is still actively "bleeding"). Finally, if your self-esteem feels so damaged that you have thoughts of harming yourself or others in any way, seek immediate help from a mental health professional or go to the nearest emergency room.

CONCLUSION

|||||||||||||||||||||

Create Your Personal
Psychological Medicine Cabinet

We sustain frequent psychological wounds as we go through life. Unfortunately, until now, few of us have had the awareness and the know-how to treat them effectively. Instead we tend either to ignore them entirely or to unwittingly react in ways that deepen them and allow them to cause damage to our mental health over time. The treatments in this book (all of which are based on current research by experts in the field) represent a psychological medicine cabinet starter kit, a set of emotional balms, ointments, bandages, and painkillers that we can apply to emotional and psychological injuries when we first sustain them.

However, being a good self-practitioner means developing our own individualized set of mental-health-hygiene guidelines and you should endeavor to personalize your medicine cabinet whenever possible. Although we all sustain psychological injuries when faced with events such as loss, failure, or rejection, the extent of our wounds and the emotional first aid treatments to which they respond best can vary from person to person. The same is true when it comes to the pills and treatments we use to treat our physical ills. For example, there are numerous over-the-counter pain relievers from which we can choose to treat headaches, backaches, and general pain, but we rarely stock all of them in our homes. Trial and error teaches us that one specific brand of pain reliever works better for us than others do and that is the one we are likely to have on hand.

Similarly, you might find that some of the emotional first aid treatments in this book are more effective for your individual psychological makeup than others. Or you might find that a specific treatment works best for you in some situations but that in a different set of circumstances it is more effective to apply another. Taking note of such things will help you refine your choices when applying emotional first aid techniques and make your future efforts more effective.

Psychology is a young science and one in which new approaches and treatments are continually being discovered and updated. That being said, the suggestions in this book are based on sound and fundamental assumptions about psychology and mental health that are unlikely to be radically revised in their entirety. Even if we find a cure for the common cold, neglecting to treat a cold when we first experience symptoms of one will always put us at risk for developing a more severe respiratory illness such as pneumonia. Similarly, even if we discover more effective strategies for dealing with a psychological injury such as failure, neglecting the psychological wounds failure inflicts will always risk damage to our mental health, self-esteem, and emotional well-being. Therefore, although the contents of our psychological medicine cabinet might need to be updated at some point in the future, having one and using it regularly will always be necessary and beneficial.

It is my sincere hope that prioritizing our mental health and taking the steps necessary to enhance and maintain it will become a daily practice, a habit we all integrate into our lives from an early age. Teaching our children to practice mental health hygiene and instructing them on how to apply the principles of emotional first aid can have an extraordinary impact on their lives and on society at large. All it would take is for the practice of mental health hygiene to become as ubiquitous as the practice of dental hygiene is today, and we could witness, in our lifetimes, a new generation of emotionally resilient and psychologically sophisticated people who confront life's hardships with both strength and resolve, who recover from them rapidly and more completely, and who enjoy far greater happiness and life satisfaction than the average person does today.

If such notions seem foolish or romantic, consider that the goal of leading happy and satisfying lives was one few people even considered several generations ago. Most people were too busy struggling to fulfill basic needs such as food, shelter, and survival to worry about whether they were happy. Perhaps several generations from now, our descendants too will look back at us and marvel at how we took better care of our teeth than we did our minds, of how few of us thought to apply emotional first aid techniques when we sustained common psychological injuries.

Of course, until now, we've lacked the resources and the know-how to adopt such general practices and we've been unable to create a revolution in how we think about and care for our mental health and emotional well-being on a large scale. But we are limited no longer. Anyone who wishes to lead an emotionally healthier and happier life need only open his or her psychological medicine cabinet and reach for the treatments within.

Acknowledgments

For years, I lamented how advances in psychological science would go ignored because cutting-edge research is buried in professional journals and has little impact on the day-to-day life of the average person. I bemoaned how we marginalized emotionally damaging experiences when there was so much we could do to treat them. And I expressed repeated exasperation that we took better care of our teeth than we did our minds and our mental health. Not that I have anything against dental hygiene. I love teeth. I simply felt there was something wrong about the fact that we know so much about brushing and flossing and so little about how to take care of our emotions and our psychological well-being.

Fortunately, two people decided to do something about it. And by "it" I mean my incessant whining about this subject. My agent, Michelle Tessler, and my brother and colleague, Dr. Gil Winch, suggested (more like insisted) I follow the very advice I championed in my first book, *The Squeaky Wheel*, and replace my ineffective complaining with constructive action. "Write a book!" they said. "Distill the information and tell people what they need to know!" they said. So I did. Of course, their duties did not end there, as their encouragement and support was invaluable throughout. Michelle Tessler is truly an amazing agent and I am incredibly fortunate to work with her. My brother Gil, who is also my identical twin, loves, supports, encourages, motivates, and inspires me every day. He has always been the first to read and comment on every word I write, and I could not have written this book without him.

My editors at Hudson Street Press, Caroline Sutton and Brittney Ross, have been enthusiastic, responsive, and supportive from the very inception of this project when Caroline pushed me to find the right frame for the book. Every suggestion they made has been spot-on and their editorial comments have been straightforward, useful, and extremely constructive.

My readers invested a great amount of time and effort to make comments and suggestions that significantly improved the manuscript. I am extremely grateful to Maayan Klein, Yael Merkel, and my dear colleague Dr. Jennifer Hofert for their invaluable professional perspectives. Richard Leff, Frank Anderson, James A. Barraclough, and especially Danny Klein had wonderfully useful and well-organized suggestions. Jessica Rackman went above and beyond the call of duty and took time out of her incredibly busy schedule to give page-by-page comments that were insightful, encouraging, and incredibly helpful as always.

I would like to thank my family and close friends for being enthusiastic, supportive, and extremely patient as I worked on the book, and especially for tolerating me responding to their phone calls and texts with "Writing, can't talk," for so many months.

I owe much to my patients who were willing to try new techniques and emotional first aid treatments when I suggested them, who provided useful and insightful feedback about the work we were doing, and whose openness, trust, hard work, and dedication to their own mental health and emotional well-being I deeply appreciate and respect. I disguised the names and identifying information of people I used as case studies but you know who you are and I'm incredibly grateful to you for serving as examples to me and hopefully to many readers for how employing emotional first aid treatments can truly help us heal, grow, and better our lives in every way.

Notes

Chapter 1: Rejection

5   But when psychologists investigated this very situation: K. D. Williams, "Ostracism," *Annual Review of Psychology* 28 (2007): 425–52.

6   when psychologists asked people to compare the pain of rejection: Ibid.; Z. Chen, K. D. Williams, J. Fitness, and N. C. Newton, "When hurt will not heal: Exploring the capacity to relive social and physical pain," *Psychological Science* 19 (2008): 789–95.

6   The answer lies in our evolutionary past: G. MacDonald and M. R. Leary, "Why does social exclusion hurt? The relationship between social and physical pain," *Psychology Bulletin* 131 (2005): 202–23.

6   brains developed an early-warning system: K. D. Williams and L. Zadro, "Ostracism: The indiscriminate early detection system," in *The Social Outcast: Ostracism, Social Exclusion, Rejection, and Bullying*, edited by K. D. Williams and W. Von Hippel (New York: Psychology Press, 2005), 19–34.

6   the very same brain regions get activated when we experience rejection: N. I. Eisenberger, M. D. Lieberman, and K. D. Williams, "Does rejection hurt? An fMRI study of social exclusion," *Science* 302 (2003): 290–92.

6   when scientists give people acetaminophen (Tylenol): N. C. DeWall, G. McDonald, G. D. Webster, C. L. Masten, R. F. Baumeister, C. Powell, D. Combs, D. R. Schurtz, T. F. Stillman, D. M. Tice, and N.

L. Eisenberger, "Acetaminophen reduces social pain," *Psychological Science* 21 (2010): 931–37.

7   finding out the rejection wasn't even "real": L. Zadro, K. D. Williams, and R. Richardson, "How low can you go? Ostracism by a computer lowers belonging, control, self-esteem, and meaningful existence," *Journal of Experimental Social Psychology* 40 (2004): 560–67.

7   people who'd excluded them were members of the Ku Klux Klan: K. Gonsalkorale and K. D. Williams, "The KKK won't let me play: Ostracism even by a despised outgroup hurts," *European Journal of Social Psychology* 37 (2007): 1176–86.

7   replacing the cyber*ball* with an animated cyber*bomb*: I. Van Beest, K. D. Williams, and E. Van Dijk, "Cyberbomb: Effects of being ostracized from a death game," *Group Processes and Intergroup Relations* (2011): 1–16.

8   Rejections impact our ability to use sound logic: R. F. Baumeister, J. M. Twenge, and C. K. Nuss, "Effects of social exclusion on cognitive processes: Anticipated aloneness reduces intelligent thought," *Journal of Personality and Social Psychology* 83 (2002): 817–27; R. F. Baumeister and C. N. DeWall, "Inner disruption following social exclusion: Reduced intelligent thought and self-regulation failure," in *The Social Outcast: Ostracism, Social Exclusion, Rejection, and Bullying*, edited by K. D. Williams and W. Von Hippel (New York: Psychology Press, 2005), 53–73.

8   Rejections often trigger anger and aggressive impulses: M. R. Leary, J. M. Twenge, and E. Quinlivan, "Interpersonal rejection as a determinant of anger and aggression," *Personality and Social Psychology Review* 10 (2006): 111–32.

10   In 2001 the office of the surgeon general of the United States issued a report: Office of the Surgeon General 2001 *Youth Violence: A report of the Surgeon General, U.S. Department of Health and Human Services.* http://www.mentalhealth.org/youthviolence/default.asp.

10   also play a huge role in violence between romantic partners: G. W. Barnard, H. Vera, M. I. Vera, and G. Newman, "Till death do us part: A study of spouse murder," *Bulletin of the American Academy of Psychiatry and the Law* 10 (1982): 271–80.

10   Studies of school shootings: M. R. Leary, R. M. Kowalski, L. Smith, and S. Phillips, "Teasing, rejection, and violence: Case studies of the school shootings," *Aggressive Behavior* 29 (2003): 202–14.

10–11 In fact, the mere act of recalling a previous rejection: L. Vandevelde and M. Miyahara, "Impact of group rejections from a physical activity on physical self-esteem among university students," *Social Psychology of Education* 8 (2005): 65–81.

13 we are wired with a fundamental need to feel accepted by others: R. F. Baumeister and M. R. Leary, "The need to belong: Desire for interpersonal attachments as a fundamental human motivation," *Psychological Bulletin* 117 (1995): 497–529.

21 One aspect receiving increased attention from scientists: N. L. Penhaligon, W. R. Louis, and S. L. D. Restubog, "Emotional anguish at work: The mediating role of perceived rejection on workgroup mistreatment and affective outcomes," *Journal of Occupational Health Psychology* 14 (2009): 34–45.

23 One of the best ways to mitigate the hurt rejection causes: D. K. Sherman and G. L. Cohen, "The psychology of self-defense: Self-affirmation theory," in *Advances in Experimental Social Psychology*, Vol. 38, edited by M. P. Zanna (San Diego, CA: Academic Press, 2006): 183–242.

28 In one study, even a brief exchange with a friendly experimenter: J. M. Twenge, L. Zhang, K. R. Catanese, B. Dolan-Pascoe, L. F. Lyche, and R. F. Baumeister, "Replenishing connectedness: Reminders of social activity reduce aggression after social exclusion," *British Journal of Social Psychology* 46 (2007): 205–24.

28 In another, instant messaging online with an unfamiliar peer: E. F. Gross, "Logging on, bouncing back: An experimental investigation of online communication following social exclusion," *Developmental Psychology* 45 (2009): 1787–93.

28 Estimating visceral and physical pain: N. L. Nordgren, K. Banas, and G. MacDonald, "Empathy gaps for social pain: Why people underestimate the pain of social suffering," *Journal of Personality and Social Psychology* 100 (2011): 120–28.

29 A recent and compelling study found that teachers: Ibid.

29 Seeking support from members of our group after being the target of discrimination: S. Noh and V. Kasper, "Perceived discrimination and depression: Moderating effects of coping, acculturation, and ethnic support," *American Journal of Public Health* 93 (2003): 232–38.

30 Cancer patients and those with other illnesses: S. E. Taylor, R. L. Falke, S. J. Shoptaw, and R. R. Lichtman, "Social support, support groups, and the cancer patient," *Journal of Consulting and Clinical Psychology* 54 (1986): 608–15.

31   Social snacking: W. L. Gardner, C. L. Pickett, and M. Knowles, "So-
     cial snacking and shielding: Using social symbols, selves, and sur-
     rogates in the service of belonging needs," in *The Social Outcast:
     Ostracism, Social Exclusion, Rejection, and Bullying*, edited by K. D.
     Williams and W. Von Hippel (New York: Psychology Press, 2005),
     227–42.

Chapter 2: Loneliness

37   The 2010 U.S. Census: http://www.census.gov/newsroom/releases
     /archives/families_households/cb10-174.html.

38   What determines our loneliness is not the quantity of our relation-
     ships: J. T. Cacioppo and L. C. Hawkley, "People thinking about
     people: The vicious cycle of being a social outcast in one's own
     mind," in *The Social Outcast: Ostracism, Social Exclusion, Rejection,
     and Bullying*, edited by K. D. Williams and W. Von Hippel (New
     York: Psychology Press, 2005), 91–108.

38   it is also associated with clinical depression, suicidal thoughts: C. M.
     Masi, H. Chen, L. C. Hawkley, and J. T. Cacioppo, "A meta-analysis
     of interventions to reduce loneliness," *Personality and Social Psy-
     chology Review* 15(3) (2011): 219–66.

38   More important, loneliness has an alarming effect on our general
     health: Ibid.

38   otherwise healthy college students: S. D. Pressman, S. Cohen, G. E.
     Miller, A. Barkin, and B. Rabin, "Loneliness, social network size,
     and immune response to influenza vaccination in college fresh-
     men," *Health Psychology*, 24(3) (2005): 297–306.

39   just as large a risk factor for our long-term physical health as ciga-
     rette smoking: J. Holt-Lunstad, T. B. Smith, and J. B. Layton, "Social
     relationships and mortality risk: A meta-analytic review," *Public Li-
     brary of Science Medicine* 7 (2010): 1–20.

39   loneliness is contagious: J. T. Cacioppo, J. H. Fowler, and N. A.
     Christakis, "Alone in the crowd: The structure and spread of loneli-
     ness in a large social network," *Journal of Personality and Social Psy-
     chology* 97 (2009): 977–91.

41   Over 40 percent of adults will suffer from loneliness in their life-
     time: L. C. Hawkley and J. T. Cacioppo, "Loneliness matters: A theo-
     retical and empirical review of consequences and mechanisms,"
     Annals of Behavioral Medicine 40 (2010): 218–27.

43–44   simply asking college students to recall a time in their life when they felt lonely: R. F. Baumeister, J. M. Twenge, and C. K. Nuss, "Effects of social exclusion on cognitive processes: Anticipated aloneness reduces intelligent thought," *Journal of Personality and Social Psychology* 83 (2002): 817–27.

44 Another study videotaped students as they interacted with a friend: S. Duck, K. Pond, and G. Leatham, "Loneliness and the evaluation of relational events," *Journal of Social and Personal Relationships* 11 (1994): 253–76.

44 lonely people are easily recognizable to others: K. J. Rotenberg and J. Kmill, "Perception of lonely and non-lonely persons as a function of individual differences in loneliness," *Journal of Social and Personal Relationships* 9 (1992): 325–30.

44 Lonely people are often seen as less attractive: S. Lau and G. E. Gruen, "The social stigma of loneliness: Effect of target person's and perceiver's sex," *Personality and Social Psychology Bulletin* 18 (1992): 182–89.

44 physical attractiveness provides no immunity: J. T. Cacioppo and L. C. Hawkley, "People thinking about people: The vicious cycle of being a social outcast in one's own mind," in *The Social Outcast: Ostracism, Social Exclusion, Rejection, and Bullying*, edited by K. D. Williams and W. Von Hippel (New York: Psychology Press, 2005), 91–108.

46 loneliness also drives us into cycles of self-protection: Ibid.

62 The following three errors are the most important: N. Epley and E. M. Caruso, "Perspective taking: Misstepping into others' shoes," in *Handbook of Imagination and Mental Simulation*, edited by K. D. Markman, W. M. P. Klein, and J. A. Suhr (New York: Psychology Press, 2009) 295–309.

63 we typically give almost exclusive priority to whether *we* find the joke funny: Ibid.

63 sincere versus sarcastic phone messages: N. Eply, C. Morewedge, and B. Keysar, "Perspective taking as egocentric anchoring and adjustment," *Journal of Personality and Social Psychology* 87 (2004): 327–39.

64 Once we consider how this dynamic might play out in gift-giving scenarios: D. Lerouge and L. Warlop, "Why is it so hard to predict our partner's product preferences: The effects of target familiarity on prediction accuracy," *Journal of Consumer Research* 33 (2006): 393–402.

64 Unfortunately, it is the couple's very familiarity: W. B. Swann and M.

J. Gill, "Confidence and accuracy in person perception: Do we know what we think we know about our relationship partners?" *Journal of Personality and Social Psychology* 73 (1997): 747–57.

65   Women should give men the space and leeway to express their thoughts: J. Flora and C. Segrin, "Affect and behavioral involvement in spousal complaints and compliments," *Journal of Family Psychology* 14 (000): 641–57.

67   Surveys of college students: S. H. Konrath, E. H. O'Brien, and C. Hsing, "Changes in dispositional empathy in American college students over time: A meta-analysis," *Personality and Social Psychology Review* 15 (2011): 180–98.

71   The Internet allows us to connect to people: T. Fokkema and K. Knipscheer, "Escape loneliness by going digital: A quantitative and qualitative evaluation of a Dutch experiment in using ECT to overcome loneliness among older adults," *Aging and Mental Health* 11 (2007): 496–504.

72   online dating is now the second most common way couples meet: E. J. Finkel, P. W. Eastwick, B. R. Karney, H. T. Reis, and S. Sprecher, "Online dating: A critical analysis from the perspective of psychological science," *Psychological Science in the Public Interest* 13 (2012): 3–66.

72   Helping others reduces feelings of loneliness: M. Cattan, N. Kime, and M. Bagnall, "The use of telephone befriending in low level support for socially isolated older people–an evaluation," *Health and Social Care in the Community* 19 (2011): 198–206.

73   Those who spent time alone with a dog: M. R. Banks and W. A. Banks, "The effects of group and individual animal-assisted therapy on loneliness in residents of long-term care facilities," *Anthrozoos* 18 (2005): 396–408; interview with the study's author: http://www.slu.edu/readstory/more/6391.

Chapter 3: Loss and Trauma

76   a phenomenon known as *post-traumatic growth*: R. G. Tedeschi and L. G. Calhoun, "Posttraumatic growth: Conceptual foundations and empirical evidence," *Psychological Inquiry* 15 (2004):1–18.

78   We often move past the most acute stages of grief and adjustment after six months: J. M. Holland, J. M. Currier, and R. A. Neimeyer, "Meaning reconstruction in the first two years of bereavement: The role of sense-making and benefit-finding," *Omega* 53 (2006): 175–91.

80   The challenge of redefining ourselves: R. A. Neimeyer, "Restorying loss: Fostering growth in the posttraumatic narrative," in *Handbook of Posttraumatic Growth: Research and Practice*, edited by L. Calhoun and R. Tedeschi (Mahwah, NJ: Lawrence Erlbaum, 2006), 68–80.

81   loss and trauma can challenge our basic assumptions about the world: R. Janoff-Bulman and C. M. Frantz, "The impact of trauma on meaning: From meaningless world to meaningful life," in *The Transformation of Meaning in Psychological Therapies: Integrating Theory and Practice*, edited by M. Power and C. R. Brewin (Sussex, England: Wiley, 1997), 91–106.

82   Yet, the sooner we reconstruct our worldviews: Ibid.

87   Indeed, a wave of recent research has demonstrated that many of our most cherished notions . . . the five stages of grief: J. M. Holland and R. A. Neimeyer, "An examination of stage theory of grief among individuals bereaved by natural and violent causes: A meaning-oriented contribution," *Omega* 61 (2010): 103–20.

87   Specifically, the mere act of recalling an event changes our actual memory: see Jonah Lehrer's article from February 2012 in *Wired*: http://www.wired.com/magazine/2012/02/ff_forgettingpill/all/1.

87   there is no "right" way to cope with the aftermath of loss and trauma: M. D. Seery, R. C. Silver, E. A. Holman, W. A. Ence, and T. Q. Chu, "Expressing thoughts and feelings following a collective trauma: Immediate responses to 9/11 predict negative outcomes in a national sample," *Journal of Consulting and Clinical Psychology* 76 (2008): 657–67.

88   One online study began following over two thousand people in, as it happened, August 2001: Ibid.

94   Finding meaning was a crucial factor in recovery: L. C. Park, "Making sense of the meaning literature: An integrative review of meaning making and its effects on adjustment to stressful life events," *Psychological Bulletin* 136 (2010): 257–301.

95   Scientists who examined how people go about finding meaning: J. M. Holland, J. M. Currier, R. A. Neimeyer, "Meaning reconstruction in the first two years of bereavement: The role of sense-making and benefit-finding," *Omega* 53 (2006): 175–91.

97   Specifically, numerous studies demonstrate that asking ourselves *why* events happened: O. Ayduk and E. Kross, "From a distance: Implications of spontaneous self-distancing for adaptive self-reflection," *Journal of Personality and Social Psychology* 98 (2010): 809–29.

98 Rather than eliciting a sense of randomness: L. J. Kray, L. G. George, K. A. Liljenquist, A. D. Galinsky, P. E. Tetlock, and N. J. Roese, "From what *might* have been to what *must* have been: Counterfactual thinking creates meaning," *Journal of Personality and Social Psychology* 98 (2011): 106–18.

100 it is the real-world application of these benefits: S. E. Hobfoll, B. J. Hall, D. Canetti-Nisim, S. Galea, R. J. Johnson, and P. A. Palmieri, "Refining our understanding of traumatic growth in the face of terrorism: Moving from meaning cognitions to doing what is meaningful," *Applied Psychology: An International Review* 56 (2006): 345–66.

Chapter 4: Guilt

103 Studies estimate that people experience roughly two hours a day of mild guilt: R. F. Baumeister, H. T. Reis, and P. A. E. G. Delespaul, "Subjective and experimental correlates of guilt in daily life," *Personality and Social Psychology Bulletin* 21 (1995): 1256–68.

103 Indeed, guilt's primary function is to signal to us: Ibid.

105 Rather, unhealthy guilt occurs primarily in situations involving our relationships: R. F. Baumeister, A. M. Stillwell, and T. F. Heatherton, "Guilt: An interpersonal approach," *Psychological Bulletin* 115 (1994): 243–67.

105 we're much less skilled at rendering effective apologies: R. Fehr and M. J. Gelfand, "When apologies work: How matching apology components to victims' self-construals facilitates forgiveness," *Organizational Behavior and Human Decision Processes* 113 (2010): 37–50.

110 Guilt makes many of us experience mental and intellectual disruptions: M. J. A. Wohl, T. A. Pychyl, and S. H. Bennett, "I forgive myself, now I can study: How self-forgiveness for procrastinating can reduce future procrastination," *Personality and Individual Differences* 48 (2010): 803–8.

111 In one study involving regular college students: Y. Zemack-Rugar, J. R. Bettman, and G. J. Fitzsimons, "The effects of nonconsciously priming emotion concepts on behavior," *Journal of Personality and Social Psychology* 93 (2007): 927–39.

112 Some of us even resort to punishing ourselves: R. M. A. Nelissen, "Guilt-induced self-punishment as a sign of remorse," *Social Psychological and Personality Science* 3 (2012): 139–44.

112 people who were made to feel guilty by depriving a fellow student of lottery tickets: Ibid.

112 keep their hands submerged in freezing water: B. Bastian, J. Jetten, and F. Fasoli, "Cleansing the soul by hurting the flesh: The guilt-reducing effect of pain," *Psychological Science* 22 (2011): 334–35.

113 known as the *Dobby effect*: R. M. A. Nelissen and M. Zeelenberg, "When guilt evokes self-punishment: Evidence for the existence of a Dobby effect," *Emotion* 9 (2009): 118–22.

115 their most common theme is one of interpersonal neglect: R. F. Baumeister, A. M. Stillwell, and T. F. Heatherton, "Personal narratives about guilt: Role in action control and interpersonal relationships," *Basic and Applied Social Psychology* 17 (1995): 173–98.

116 In one survey, 33 percent of people indicated they felt resentful: Ibid.

120 The most effective way to treat unresolved guilt: C. E. Cryder, S. Springer, and C. K. Morewedge, "Guilty feelings, targeted actions," *Personality and Social Psychology Bulletin* 38 (2012): 607–18.

121 this simple transaction of apology and forgiveness goes awry: R. Fehr and M. J. Gelfand, "When apologies work: How matching apology components to victims' self-construals facilitates forgiveness," *Organizational Behavior and Human Decision Processes* 113 (2010): 37–50.

122 Scientists have discovered three additional components: Ibid.

129 self-forgiveness reduces feelings of guilt: J. H. Hall and F. D. Fincham, "Self-forgiveness: The stepchild of forgiveness research," *Journal of Social and Clinical Psychology* 24 (2005): 621–37.

129 people who forgave themselves for procrastinating: M. J. A. Wohl, T. A. Pychyl, and S. H. Bennett, "I forgive myself, now I can study: How self-forgiveness for procrastinating can reduce future procrastination," *Personality and Individual Differences* 48 (2010): 803–8.

133 Studies have found that both atonement and reparations: H. Xu, L. Beue, and R. Shankland, "Guilt and guiltless: An integrative review," *Social and Personality Psychology Compass* 5 (2011): 440–57; J. J. Exline, B. L. Root, S. Yadavalli, A. M. Martin, and M. L. Fisher, "Reparative behaviors and self-forgiveness: Effects of a laboratory-based exercise," *Self and Identity* 10 (2011): 101–26.

Chapter 5: Rumination

142 linked to a wide range of threats to our psychological and physical health: for a review see S. Nolen-Hoeksema, B. E. Wisco, and S. Lyubomirsky, "Rethinking rumination," *Perspectives on Psychological Science* 3 (2008) 400–424.

144 Scientists asked regular people on a regular day to reflect: Ibid.

146 researchers gave college students at risk for depression: G. J. Haeffel, "When self-help is no help: Traditional cognitive skills training does not prevent depressive symptoms in people who ruminate," *Behaviour Research and Therapy* 28 (2010): 152–57.

148 Angry feelings activate our stress responses and our cardiovascular systems: B. J. Bushman, A. M. Bonacci, W. C. Pederson, E. A. Vasquez, and M. Norman, "Chewing on it can chew you up: Effects of rumination on triggered displaced aggression," *Journal of Personality and Social Psychology* 88 (2005): 969–83.

149 one study put people through a frustrating experience: Ibid.

149 Rumination involves such intense brooding: S. Nolen-Hoeksema, B. E. Wisco, and S. Lyubomirsky, "Rethinking rumination," *Perspectives on Psychological Science* 3 (2008): 400–424.

150 For example, women with strong ruminative tendencies: S. Lyubomirsky, F. Kasri, O. Chang, and I. Chung, "Ruminative response styles and delay of seeking diagnosis for breast cancer symptoms," *Journal of Social and Clinical Psychology* 25 (2006): 276–304.

150 Other studies found that cancer and coronary patients with ruminative tendencies: P. Aymanns, S. H. Filipp, and T. Klauer, "Family support and coping with cancer: Some determinants and adaptive correlates," *British Journal of Social Psychology* 34 (1995): 107–24.

154 the visual perspective we use when going over painful experiences: O. Ayduk and E. Kross, "From a distance: Implications of spontaneous self-distancing for adaptive self-reflection," *Journal of Personality and Social Psychology* 98 (2010): 809–29.

155 In addition, their blood pressure was less reactive: E. Kross and O. Ayduk, "Facilitating adaptive emotional analysis: Distinguishing distanced-analysis of depressive experiences from immersed-analysis and distraction," *Personality and Social Psychology Bulletin* 34 (2008): 924–38.

158 In now-classic experiments: D. M. Wegner, D. J. Schneider, S. R. Carter III, and T. L. White, "Paradoxical effects of thought suppression," *Journal of Personality and Social Psychology* 53 (1987): 5–13.

158 distraction has proven to be a far more effective weapon: S. Nolen-Hoeksema, B. E. Wisco, and S. Lyubomirsky, "Rethinking rumination," *Perspectives on Psychological Science* 3 (2008): 400–424.

159 imagining the layout of our local supermarket: Ibid.

161 the verdict of all such studies has been virtually unanimous: B. J. Bushman, "Does venting anger feed or extinguish the flame? Ca-

tharsis, rumination, distraction, anger, and aggressive responding,"
Personality and Social Psychology Bulletin 28 (2002): 724–31.

162 The most effective strategy for regulating emotions such as anger:
O. P. John and J. J. Gross, "Healthy and unhealthy emotion regula-
tion: Personality processes, individual differences, and lifespan development," *Journal of Personality* 72 (2004): 1301–33.

165 A series of recent studies examined the power of prayer: R. H.
Bremner, S. L. Koole, and B. J. Bushman, "Pray for those who mis-
treat you: Effects of prayer on anger and aggression," *Personality and
Social Psychology Bulletin* 37 (2011): 830–37.

Chapter 6: Failure

174 Participants were asked to kick an American football: J. K. Witt and
T. Dorsch, "Kicking to bigger uprights: Field goal kicking performance influences perceived size," *Perception* 38 (2009): 1328–40.

177 Another common New Year resolution error is goal bingeing: E. J.
Masicampo and R. F. Baumeister, "Consider it done! Plan making
can eliminate the cognitive effects of unfulfilled goals," *Journal of
Personality and Social Psychology* 10 (2011): 667–83.

179 Failures sap our confidence, our motivation, and our hope: L. D.
Young and J. M. Allin, "Persistence of learned helplessness in humans," *Journal of General Psychology* 113 (1986): 81–88.

181 Failure can also be very misleading: Ibid.

183 Test anxiety is especially problematic: R. Hembree, "Correlates,
Causes, Effects, and Treatment of Test Anxiety," *Review of Educational Research* 58 (1988): 47–77.

183 consider what happens when girls take math tests: S. Spencer, C. M.
Steele, and D. M. Quinn, "Stereotype threat and women's math performance," *Journal of Experimental Social Psychology* 35 (1999):
4–28.

186 Fear of failure makes many of us engage in all manner of self-
handicapping behaviors: A. J. Martin, H. W. Marsh, and R. L. Debus,
"Self-handicapping and defensive pessimism: A model of self-
protection from a longitudinal perspective," *Contemporary Educational Psychology* 28 (2003): 1–36.

187 Fear of Failure in Families: A. J. Elliot and T. M. Thrash, "The inter-
generational transmission of fear of failure," *Personality and Social
Psychology Bulletin* 30 (2004): 957–71.

189 Choking is based on a similar dynamic: M. S. DeCaro, R. D. Thomas,

N. B. Albert, and S. L. Beilock, "Choking under pressure: Multiple routes to skill failure," *Journal of Experimental Psychology: General* 140 (2011): 390–406.

191 Further, providing social and emotional support alone: N. Bolger and D. Amarel, "Effects of social support visibility on adjustment to stress: Experimental evidence," *Journal of Personality and Social Psychology* 92 (2007): 458–75.

194 a surprising aspect about failure: K. M. Sheldon, N. Abad, Y. Ferguson, A. Gunz, L. Houser-Marko, C. P. Nichols, and S. Lyubomirsky, "Persistent pursuit of need-satisfying goals leads to increased happiness: A 6-month experimental longitudinal study," *Motivation and Emotion* 34 (2010): 39–48.

196 One study illustrated this point with a group of seniors: C. A. Sarkisian, B. Weiner, C. Davis, and T. R. Prohaska, "Pilot test of attributional retraining intervention to raise walking levels in sedentary older adults," *Journal of the American Geriatric Society* 55 (2007): 1842–46.

196 Since it is best to pursue one goal at a time: R. Koestner, N. Lekes, T. A. Powers, and E. Chicoine, "Attaining personal goals: Self-concordance plus implementation intentions equals success," *Journal of Personality and Social Psychology* 83 (2002): 231–44.

197 defining your goal in ways that are personally meaningful: R. M. Ryan, G. C. Williams, H. Patrick, and E. Deci, "Self-determination theory and physical activity: The dynamics of motivation in development and wellness," *Hellenic Journal of Psychology* 6 (2009): 107–24.

200 For example, asking women intending to get a breast cancer exam: S. Orbell, S. Hodgkins, and P. Sheeran, "Implementation intentions and the theory of planned behavior," *Personality and Social Psychology Bulletin* 23 (1997): 945–54.

206 In studies, seeing the humor: J. Stoeber and D. P. Janssen, "Perfectionism and coping with daily failures: Positive reframing helps achieve satisfaction at the end of the day," *Anxiety, Stress, and Coping* 24 (2011): 477–97.

207 Jim Short: http://www.jokes.com/funny/jim+short/jim-short--not-a-loser.

209 Whistle While You Choke: S. Beilock, *Choke: What the Secrets of the Brain Reveal about Success and Failure at Work and at Play* (New York: Free Press, 2010).

210 In a series of recent studies, four hundred seventh graders: G. L.

Cohen, J. Garcia, V. Purdie-Vaughns, N. Apfel, and P. Brzustoski, "Recursive processes in self-affirmation: Intervening to close the minority achievement gap," *Science* 324 (2009): 400–403.

211 college women taking physics: A. Miyake, L. E. Kost-Smith, N. D. Finkelstein, S. J. Pollock, G. L. Cohen, and T. A. Ito, "Reducing the gender achievement gap in college science: A classroom study of values affirmation," *Science* 330 (2010): 1234–37.

Chapter 7: Low Self-Esteem

213 the overwhelming majority of self-esteem programs simply don't work: W. B. Swann, C. Chang-Schneider, and K. L. McClarty, "Do people's self-views matter? Self-concept and self-esteem in everyday life," *American Psychologist* 62 (2007): 84–94.

213 Further, people with low self-esteem are often less happy: for a brief review see K. D. Neff, "Self-compassion, self-esteem, and well-being," *Social and Personality Psychology Compass* 5 (2011): 1–12.

214 Having very high self-esteem has its own set of pitfalls: Ibid.

214 there has been a general "grade inflation" in our collective self-esteem: N. Maxwell and J. Lopus, "The Lake Wobegon effect in student self-reported data," *American Economic Review Papers and Proceedings* 84 (1994): 201–5.

215 people with higher self-esteem believe they are more attractive: E. Diener, B. Wolsic, and F. Fujita, "Physical attractiveness and subjective well-being," *Journal of Personality and Social Psychology* 69 (1995): 120–29.

217 people with low self-esteem also rated their own groups negatively: J. Crocker, and I. Schwartz, "Prejudice and ingroup favoritism in a minimal intergroup situation: Effects of self-esteem and threat," *Journal of Personality and Social Psychology* 52 (1987): 907–16.

217 how we feel about ourselves in specific domains of our lives: M. Rosenberg, C. Schooler, C. Schoenbach, and F. Rosenberg, "Global self-esteem and specific self-esteem," *American Sociological Review* 60 (1995): 141–56.

219 having higher self-esteem . . . can make us more psychologically resilient: J. Greenberg, S. Solomon, T. Pyszczynski, A. Rosenblatt, J. Burling, D. Lyon, L. Simon, and E. Pinel, "Why do people need self-esteem? Converging evidence that self-esteem serves an anxiety-buffering function," *Journal of Personality and Social Psychology* 63 (1992): 913–22.

219   people with low self-esteem experience rejection as more painful: K.
      Onoda, Y. Okamoto, K. Nakashima, H. Nittono, S. Yoshimura, S.
      Yamawaki, and M. Ura, "Does low self-esteem enhance social pain?
      The relationship between trait self-esteem and anterior cingulate
      cortex activation induced by ostracism," *Social Cognitive and Affec-
      tive Neuroscience* 5 (2010): 385–91.

219   We are also more vulnerable to failure when our self-esteem is low:
      J. D. Brown, "High self-esteem buffers negative feedback: Once
      more with feeling," *Cognition and Emotion* 24 (2010): 1389–1404.

220   We also respond to stress much less effectively: S. C. Lee-Flynn, G.
      Pomaki, A. DeLongis, J. C. Biesanz, and E. Puterman, "Daily cogni-
      tive appraisals, daily affect, and long-term depressive symptoms:
      The role of self-esteem and self-concept clarity in the stress process,"
      Personality and Social Psychology Bulletin 37 (2011): 255–68.

221   Stress can substantially weaken our willpower: L. Schwabe, O.
      Höffken, M. Tegenthoff, and O. T. Wolf, "Preventing the stress-
      induced shift from goal-directed to habit action with a β-adrenergic
      antagonist," *Journal of Neuroscience* 31 (2011): 17317–25.

222   The good news is that manipulations to boost self-esteem: for a re-
      view see S. E. Taylor and A. L. Stanton, "Coping resources, coping
      processes, and mental health," *Annual Review of Clinical Psychology*
      2 (2007): 377–401.

222   low self-esteem limits our ability to benefit from positive ones: R. A.
      Josephs, J. Bosson, and C. G. Jacobs, "Self-esteem maintenance pro-
      cesses: Why low self-esteem may be resistant to change," *Personality
      and Social Psychology Bulletin* 29 (2003): 920–33.

224   we believe the program helped us improve when it actually did not:
      A. R. Pratkanis, J. Eskenazie, and A. G. Greenwald, "What you ex-
      pect is what you believe (but not necessarily what you get): A test of
      the effectiveness of subliminal self-help audiotapes," *Basic and Ap-
      plied Social Psychology* 15 (2010): 251–76.

225   Recent research into the usefulness of positive affirmations: J. V.
      Wood, W. Q. E. Perunovie, and J. W. Lee, "Positive self-statements:
      Power for some, peril for others," *Psychological Science* 20 (2009):
      860–66.

226   One study found that poorly performing college students: D. R. For-
      syth, N. K. Lawrence, J. L. Burnette, and R. F. Baumeister, "Attempt-
      ing to improve academic performance of struggling college students
      by bolstering their self-esteem: The intervention that backfired,"
      Journal of Social and Clinical Psychology 26 (2007): 447–59.

226 Another found that when college students with low self-esteem had roommates: W. B. Swann and B. W. Pelham, "Who wants out when the going gets good?" *Journal of Self and Identity* 1 (2002): 219–33.

227 praising people with low self-esteem for being considerate boyfriends or girlfriends: S. L. Murray, J. G. Holmes, G. MacDonald, and P. C. Ellsworth, "Through the looking glass darkly? When self-doubts turn into relationship insecurities," *Journal of Personality and Social Psychology* 75 (1998): 1459–80.

228 people with low self-esteem tend to speak up less: R. F. Baumeister, J. D. Campbell, J. I. Krueger, and K. D. Vohs, "Does high self-esteem cause better performance, interpersonal success, happiness, or healthier lifestyles? *Psychological Science in the Public Interest* 4 (2003): 1–44.

234 self-compassion was found to buffer incoming college students: M. L. Terry, M. R. Leary, and S. Mehta, "Self-compassion as a buffer against homesickness, depression, and dissatisfaction in the transition to college," *Self and Identity*, in press (2012).

235 quicker emotional recoveries from separation and divorce: D. A. Sbarra, H. L. Smith, and M. R. Mehl, "When leaving your ex, love yourself: Observational ratings of self-compassion predict the course of emotional recovery following marital separation," *Psychological Sciences* 23 (2012): 261–69.

235 recovered more quickly from failure and rejection experiences: K. D. Neff, "Self-compassion, self-esteem, and well-being," *Social and Personality Psychology Compass* 5 (2011): 1–12.

237 Reminding ourselves that we have significant worth: C. R. Critcher, D. Dunning, and D. A. Armor, "When self-affirmations reduce defensiveness: Timing is key," *Personality and Social Psychology Bulletin* 36 (2010): 947–59.

240 we can bolster our "relationship self-esteem": D. A. Stinson, C. Logel, S. Shepherd, and M. P. Zanna, "Rewriting the self-fulfilling prophecy of social rejection: Self-affirmation improves relational security and social behavior up to 2 months later," *Psychological Science* 22 (2011): 1145–49.

242 feelings of personal empowerment must be supported by evidence: L. B. Cattanco and A. R. Chapman, "The process of empowerment: A model for use in research and practice," *American Psychologist* 65 (2010): 646–59.

248 self-control actually functions more like a muscle: R. F. Baumeister, K. D. Vohs, and D. M. Tice, "The strength model of self-control," *Current Directions in Psychological Science* 16 (2007): 351–55.

249 Scientists have investigated several such "willpower workouts": M. Muraven, "Building self-control strength: Practicing self-control leads to improved self-control performance," *Journal of Experimental Social Psychology* 46 (2010): 465–68.

251 Half of them received lemonade sweetened with sugar: M. T. Gailliot, R. F. Baumeister, C. N. DeWall, J. K. Maner, E. A. Plant, D. M. Tice, L. E. Brewer, and B. J. Schmeichel, "Self-control relies on glucose as a limited energy source: Willpower is more than a metaphor," *Journal of Personality and Social Psychology* 92 (2007): 325–36.

251 Sleep and rest also have a big impact on our willpower's ability to function: R. F. Baumeister, "Ego-depletion and self-control failure: An energy model of the self's executive function," *Self and Identity* 1 (2002): 129–36.

251 The average person spends three to four hours a day exerting some form of willpower: W. Hofmann, R. F. Baumeister, G. Förster, and K. D. Vohs, "Everyday temptations: An experience sampling study on desire, conflict, and self-control," *Journal of Personality and Social Psychology* 102 (2012): 1318–35.

252 The best way to manage temptations is not to overestimate our ability to manage them: G. Lowenstein, "Out of control: Visceral influences on behavior," *Organizational Behavior and Human Decision Processes* 65 (1996): 272–92; L. F. Nordgren, F. van Harreveld, and J. van der Pligt, "The restraint bias: How the illusion of self-restraint promotes impulsive behavior," *Psychological Science* 20 (2009): 1523–28.

253 researchers in one study gave moviegoers stale popcorn: D. T. Neal, W. Wood, M. Wu, and D. Kurlander, "The pull of the past: When do habits persist despite conflict with motives?" *Personality and Social Psychology Bulletin* 37 (2011): 1428–37.

Index

Rebecca Goldstein receives rave reviews for
The Mind-Body Problem

"An absorbing and entertaining novel, penetrating and poignant."
—*Sunday New York Times*

"A terrific novel . . . The first 50 pages or so are so clever and funny that I had to put the book down and go to the fridge to cool off. 'I'm often asked what it's like to be married to a genius' is the first line, and the novel proceeds to explore the answer to that question."
—*New York Times Book Review*

"Goldstein is intelligent and perceptive, bawdy and witty—an articulate writer of great talent. Will keep you turning pages to find out how it all turns out."
—*Los Angeles Times Book Review*

"A confectionery of delight, laced with equal parts of wit, humor, and philosophical argument. Goldstein succeeds brilliantly in smuggling into her novel short courses on everything from the history of mathematics to the trouble with Talmudic logic."
—*MS. magazine*

"A remarkably good novel, full of good writing, wry observations and shrewd characterizations."
—*Minnesota Daily*

"Perhaps the best American Jewish novel to be published in years . . . Vibrant humor and sophistication give *The Mind-Body Problem* a unique dimension."
—*Hadassah Magazine*

"One of the most intelligent and funny pieces of fiction to surface this year. Goldstein's ability to translate complex philosophical or mathematical problems to such basics as friendship and sexual desire leaves the reader giddy with inspiration. . . . One of the most original laugh riots to successfully disguise itself as literature."
—*Kansas City Star*

"Brilliantly humorous, slyly witty—shades of Fran Leibowitz."
—*South Bend Tribune*

PENGUIN BOOKS

THE MIND-BODY PROBLEM

Rebecca Goldstein attended Barnard College and Princeton University, where she earned a Ph.D. in philosophy. She returned to Barnard, where she taught for ten years. She is the author of *Strange Attractors*, *The Dark Sister* (both available from Penguin), and *The Late-Summer Passion of a Woman of Mind*. Her latest work of fiction, *Mazel*, is also available from Penguin.

REBECCA GOLDSTEIN

The
MIND-BODY
Problem:
A Novel

PENGUIN BOOKS

PENGUIN BOOKS
Published by the Penguin Group
Penguin Books USA Inc., 375 Hudson Street, New York,
New York 10014, U.S.A.
Penguin Books Ltd, 27 Wrights Lane, London W8 5TZ, England
Penguin Books Australia Ltd, Ringwood, Victoria, Australia
Penguin Books Canada Ltd, 10 Alcorn Avenue, Toronto,
Ontario, Canada M4V 3B2
Penguin Books (N.Z.) Ltd, 182–190 Wairau Road,
Auckland 10, New Zealand

Penguin Books Ltd, Registered Offices: Harmondsworth,
Middlesex, England

First published in the United States of America by
Random House, Inc., 1983
Published in Penguin Books 1993

9 10

Although this novel is set in Princeton, New Jersey, the characters appearing in it are fictional, composites drawn from several individuals and
from imagination. No reference to any living person is intended
or should be inferred.

Grateful acknowledgment is made to Houghton Mifflin Company for
permission to reprint an excerpt from "The Poet of Ignorance," by
Anne Sexton from *The Awful Rowing Towards God*, copyright © 1975
by Loring Conant, Jr., Executor of the Estate of Anne Sexton.
Reprinted by permission of Houghton Mifflin Company.

THE LIBRARY OF CONGRESS HAS CATALOGUED THE HARDCOVER AS FOLLOWS:
Goldstein, Rebecca, 1950–
The mind-body problem.
I. Title.
PS3557.0398M56 1983 813´.54 83-3268
ISBN 0-394-52474-8 (hc.)
ISBN 0 14 01.7245 9 (pbk.)

Printed in the United States of America

In memory of my father
BEZALEL NEWBERGER

CONTENTS

THE MIND-BODY PROBLEM

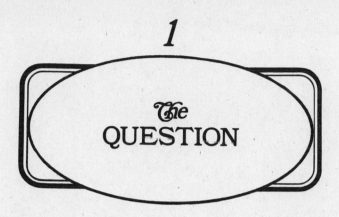

1

The QUESTION

The atmosphere surrounding this problem is terrible. Dense clouds of language lie about the crucial point. It is almost impossible to get through to it.

—LUDWIG WITTGENSTEIN,
NOTES FOR LECTURES ON
PRIVATE EXPERIENCE
FROM *THE PHILOSOPHICAL
REVIEW* (1968)

I'm often asked what it's like to be married to a genius. The question used to please me—as an affirmation of my place, of my counting for something (if only through marriage) in the only world that counted for anything. But even back then, at the beginning of my marriage (three years by the external calendar, more than half my life by my internal one), I was uncertain how to answer. "Wife of the genius" does not in itself define a distinct personality. The description, and my own fluid nature, left me the burden of choice. And I found it hard to choose. I could never even decide how I should arrange my face when I answered. Should I radiate the faintly dazed glow of one who stands within sweating distance of the raging fires of creativity? Or should my features exhibit the sharp practicality capable of managing the mundane affairs of an intellectual demigod? I could never decide, and usually ended up trying to look both dazed and practical, to look a logical contradiction, which is, I suppose, to look a fool. And that, of course, is the very, very last thing I have ever wanted to look.

As you see, the question was never an easy one for me. But these days! These days it's become a test of my strength. (I fear this remark borders on the melodramatic. My present state is perhaps conducive to such excesses. I must take care. The melodramatic pose, especially when directed toward one's own life, is another of the many ways of playing the fool.)

What do they want to hear from the wife of the genius? "Living with Noam is an intellectual adventure, a cerebral challenge . . ."? This morning was a typical challenge. I was drinking my coffee in the kitchen when Noam burst into the room, his face dissolved in anger.

"Renee, where's my pen? My God, I can't find my pen. What did you do with it?"

"Noam, I didn't touch your pen. Wait, I'll get you mine."

"I don't want yours, I want mine." His voice had climbed up into the whining range: "You know I can't stand losing my pen," then slid back down into the register of decision: "Listen, I've got to find it. Would you please help me instead of smugly sitting there?"

"Think back, Noam, when did you have it last?"

"I don't know. You think I can be bothered remembering trivialities like that?" Unstated premise, implied by the focused glare: that's one of the purposes of the wife. "I don't know. I know I was using it last night."

"Do you think that was the last time?"

"I *think* so. God, I don't know. I think so, yes."

"Okay, good. We'll proceed on that hypothesis. Now, where were you using it last night?"

"My study. I was at my desk."

"And you looked all over your desk?"

"Yes."

"Are you sure? Did you look carefully?" My question was informed by experience.

"For Godssakes yes! I wouldn't have said the pen was lost if I hadn't thoroughly searched. That's what it *means* for the pen to be lost! Now would you stop driving me crazy and help me!"

"Noam, I'm trying. Calm down or we won't get anywhere. Now, you must have taken it away from the desk. Did you get up for any reason while you were writing?"

"No. Listen, Renee, you must have taken it. We ought to be cross-examining *you*. You're always taking my things."

"No, Noam, believe me. I'd remember if I had. I know how important your pen is to you. Did the phone ring while you were writing?"

"I don't know. In any case, I didn't answer it."

"Did you get up to get something to eat?"

"Hmmmm, let me think. I can't remember. Renee, how can you ask me to remember a trivial thing like that?"

"What time were you writing?"

"About eleven, twelve, I don't know."

"Well, did you eat late last night?"

"Yes! God yes! I had some ice cream!"

Hearts pounding, we ran to the refrigerator and flung open the freezer door. There, sitting absurdly between a can of orange juice and the rum-raisin Häagen-Dazs, gleamed a very cold black-and-silver Papermate.

Again and again they ask me, the other faculty wives, the worshiping graduate students, the lesser professors: What is it like to live with him, to live with a genius like Noam? If it were only the truth they were after, and not legends of greatness, I think I would know how to answer them. I believe I could describe life with Noam Himmel, that blazing star who first burst upon the mathematical heavens in 1950 at the age of twelve with his brilliant seminal paper, "On the Properties of Supernatural Numbers."

I lay my answer, my life, before you.

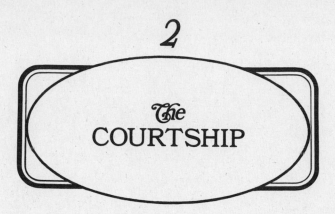

2

The COURTSHIP

Princeton is a wonderful little spot, a quaint and ceremonious village of puny demigods on stilts.... Here the people who compose what is called "society" enjoy even less freedom than their counterparts in Europe. Yet they seem unaware of this restriction, since their way of life tends to inhibit personality development from childhood.

—ALBERT EINSTEIN,
IN A LETTER TO QUEEN
ELISABETH OF BELGIUM

I met Noam Himmel soon after his triumphant arrival in Princeton. The sense of conquest was more on the part of the welcoming community, for once Himmel let it be known that he had tired of Cambridge and wanted to come back to the States, every prestigious mathematics department in the country had courted him. Princeton had had to promise him much. Besides rather a lot of money (in academic terms) and very light teaching duties, he was told that he might pick up and go on leave to another university whenever the spirit moved him. By accepting Princeton he wouldn't have to give up his other suitors entirely.

Noam Himmel was then thirty-eight, and had already been famous for twenty-six years, ever since the first startling publication presenting the supernaturals, the "Himmel numbers"—a new category of mathematical existence, to be counted amongst the naturals and integers, the rationals and irrationals, the reals and imaginaries and surreals and surds, the cardinals and ordinals, transcendentals and transfinites. The supernaturals were well named by their discoverer, for they are numbers so big that they are used for collections too large to form sets. How can there *be* such numbers? And yet there are. Himmel had proved them, these numbers that realize—in their immensity and enigma, their inaccessibility to reason too simplistic—all the suggestions of their name. If the work of the great Georg Cantor in the late nineteenth century had led mathematics up past the finite realm into the sublime heights of the transfinites, then the work of the twelve-year-old from Manhattan had led even beyond—to the transinfinites.

But Harvard had refused to accept the boy until he finished high school. (Some among the faculty had groused about prodigies who often burn themselves out early.) He had entered Harvard at sixteen, and four years later was teaching there. He had never bothered to get a Ph.D., and nobody had bothered to ask him to. And he hadn't burned himself out early. The twenty-six years had produced many mathematically important results, though none perhaps to equal the dazzling supernaturals.

My own position in the world of Princeton was incomparably inferior. I was a graduate student in philosophy, and not a highly successful one at that. My first year there had been disastrous, and my second, just beginning, gave every indication of being worse. In short, I was floundering, and thus quite prepared to follow the venerably old feminine tradition of being saved by marriage. And, given the nature of my distress, no one could better play the part of my rescuing hero than the great Noam Himmel. For the man had an extravagance of what I was so agonizingly feeling the lack of: objective proof of one's own intellectual merit.

My Barnard undergraduate experience had not prepared me for Princeton, not on any level. Even the physical presence of the place confounded my views of How Things Ought To Be. This affluent suburban town, so distressingly similar to the Westchester community in which I had grown up, this was a seat of serious scholarship? And its outrageously suburban-looking inhabitants were serious thinkers?

Princeton is an anomaly among college towns, I suppose because it really is not a college town. What it is is an old-wealth exurb with a pedigree reaching back to colonial times, *further* distinguished by the presence of a prestigious university laid out in the grand English manner: all massive gray stone and ivy-muffled red brick, archways and courtyards, sweeping lawns and ancient trees. There is none of the student-faculty grubbiness of an Ithaca or Cambridge, Mass. The town's tone, rather, is established middle age shading off into contented dotage, with no compromise made in the direction of student youth. The shops lining old Nassau Street, the main drag and the Western border of the campus, are stocked with Waterford and Wedgwood, Lenox and fine linens. Instead of the university's population imposing its character on the town, the school has absorbed the affluent attributes of its setting. Undergraduates are abnormally groomed and tailored here, looking the pampered parts of the children and grandchildren of privilege that they largely are.

My eyes were used to the gloom of Columbia's Broadway campus and were having trouble focusing amidst Princeton's brilliance. And not just my eyes were in need of readjustment. My views on The Life of the Mind had been modeled on the people I had known at

Columbia: urban intellectuals, unkempt, graceless, morose creatures who walked around with eyes downcast, muttering to themselves. Those were the sorts of bodies—neglected, misshapen, decaying—that serious minds belonged in. But here were these first-rate thinkers who worried about their backyards and backhands, who discussed Buber and black holes over barbecues. The genteel goyishness of the place overwhelmed me. There were Jews at Princeton, of course, but nobody *seemed* Jewish. At Columbia even the non-Jews had seemed Jewish.

The need to create this new category of being, the gentile suburban intellectual, threw me into a state of cognitive dissonance. The past few years I had gotten used to thinking of myself as an intellectual. I had assumed that certain properties of mind and body were entailed by this description and had designed myself accordingly. It's hard to discover you've constructed yourself on false premises.

But the dissonance reverberated in far deeper regions of my being. Not just my views of the intellectual were being challenged, but, more personally and painfully, my view of my own intellectual worth. I suffered badly the emergence from the dark womb-warmth of Barnard into the bright, brisk air of the Princeton philosophy department, where vagueness was not tolerated and people conversed fluently in the language of counterexamples. Every time I hazarded a statement someone would hurl a counterexample at it, or else accuse me of meaninglessness or metaphysical tendencies. I couldn't get anything past them.

I am not in the habit of dismissing any criticisms of myself, and am in general always willing seriously to consider any denunciation. Perhaps it was true, I therefore found myself thinking, that all the questions that interested me were really pseudo-questions, mere phantoms of my mental night. I couldn't deny that I suffered from metaphysical tendencies, though I hadn't realized until then that they constituted an affliction. In my pre-Princetonian backwardness I would have said that Reality is the subject matter of philosophy, but the very word, I now learned, was philosophically taboo for its suggestion of metaphysical tendencies.

The field had made the "linguistic turn" and I . . . had not. The questions were now all of language. Instead of wrestling with the large, messy questions that have occupied previous centuries of ethicists, for example, one should examine the rules that govern words like "good" and "ought." My very first seminar, given by a prominent visitor from England whose field, they told me, was metaphysics, was on adverbs. The metaphysics of adverbs? From Reality to . . . adverbs?

It appeared I was to spend the rest of my philosophical life thinking about language. For language is humanly manufactured and thus, presumably, thoroughly intelligible. The questions it posed might be difficult but were not, in principle, unanswerable. No more inexhaustible Reality to contend with and make us feel our human limitations. No more dark, inaccessible regions lying beyond the reach of reason's phallic thrusts. Reality was but a creature formed from one of the intellect's own ribs, from language. *We* could take care of her, fill her up and leave her spent.

The philosophical mind has long craved a limited universe. The pre-Socratic Pythagoreans, in their table of opposites, listed "limited" on the side occupied by "order," "light," "good," and "male." But only the last generation or two of philosophers have managed to show how very limited reality really is, extending no farther than our powers of expression. What a relief. What a blessed relief. No more bogeymen jumping out of dark corners shouting, "It can't be known! You'll never understand it!" These epistemological horrors used to be waiting at every philosophical turn. Now the nursery lamp of linguistic analysis has been turned on, dispelling all those scary shadows. There is the bright, cheery world of the nursery, small and familiar, with no sense of the unknown creeping in.

Einstein found most Princetonians rather green when compared with their ripened counterparts in the European hothouse: "Their way of life tends to inhibit personality development from childhood." Perhaps. It's possible to view the place as a kind of quality day-care center. That's not really my view, but then I'm not so old and wise as Einstein was in Princeton. It has struck me, however, that I know a surprising number of people who have never gotten beyond the "magic years," beyond the child's belief in his own supernatural powers. And a disproportionately large percentage of these are members of the philosophy department. Philosophy used to be thought of as the academic subject requiring the most maturity: it was all old men tripping on their white beards. But that was before they discovered the magic word, "meaningless." A phrase like "the meaning of life" is guaranteed to crack them up, producing the hilarity of preschoolers at bathroom words. They know how to make all such problems disappear. The meaning of life? Sentences have meanings, the conditions and nature of which they can elaborate in the greatest detail. Pondering about "the meaning of it all" is silly baby talk. Abracadabra.

It was confusing that philosophy had become the most antiphilosophical of all academic fields, not only refusing to consider any of the mysteries of existence (which is a position I can understand) but adamantly denying that there *are* any (which is a position I cannot understand). All metaphysical questions are meaningless, and anything that exceeds our comprehension can't *be*. Mystery is as impermissible as the logical contradiction, a sign that something is amiss in the reasoning. There is a kind of *reductio ad arcanum* form of argument employed by philosophers throughout the Analytic Philosophy Belt, from Oxford to Princeton and Harvard to the mispronounced Berkeley (named after the Irish idealist philosopher Bishop Berkeley, whose name is pronounced Barkeley). It's an analogue to the ancient *reductio ad absurdum,* the indisputable method of proving propositions true by showing their negations to lead to absurdities. Only with the *reductio ad arcanum* one proves that certain kinds of things can't exist by showing that their existence would present us with one or more nontrivial questions. Some, for example, have employed this method to argue away consciousness. For *its* existence would present us with the notoriously impenetrable mind-body problem.

"Reality doesn't accommodate itself to the size and shape of the human mind," I protested at one point in a philosophical discussion soon after my arrival, when I still felt entitled to voice philosophical opinions. Everyone stopped talking and stared at me. Finally, mercifully, someone spoke.

"That's a metaphysical statement" came the deadpan reply.

There could not, in that context, have been a worse insult.

Obviously I had little idea of what the philosophical enterprise was about, as I chokingly confessed to my assigned adviser, Professor

Herbert Pfiffel. Professor Pfiffel shook his great mane of yellowing white hair in solemn agreement, an act at once of sympathy and dismissal. For he was a kind man, but one whose philosophical life had been single-mindedly devoted to the opposition of people like me, the incurably metaphysical. He was one of the last living members of the famed Vienna Circle of logical positivists, the group that can be credited above all others with having discovered the powers of the word "meaningless." ("Metaphysicians are musicians without musical talent," said Rudolf Carnap, one of its founders.)

"Vell, my dear Miss Feuer, vat do you propose now to do?" Professor Pfiffel asked.

What indeed? I had come to believe in my philosophical ability and had been planning my life on the assumption of its existence. At college, once I made up my mind to work, nothing but praise and success had come my way. These had entered my bloodstream, never causing much of a high, but I needed them like a drug. Withdrawal was excruciating. My faultily constructed self crumbled. I thought, therefore I was. If I was not a thinker, what was I?

SOMETIME AROUND APRIL of my first year I stopped doing any work and occupied myself instead with seducing various graduate students who lived, like me, at the Graduate College. (This is the great cathedral dorm for unmarried graduate students that was built when Woodrow Wilson, who had wanted to model Princeton after Oxford, the Platonic Form of all universities, had been president of the university.) The world outside the campus gates surrendered itself to the senses, and so did I. If I couldn't find any affirmation of my worth in the mind, I would seek it in the body. There are other faculties of the person besides those of the *res cogitans*. I recalled and cherished once again my feminine powers, which had been lying dormant during the past years of serious intellectual occupation. As it had been in college with my cerebral efforts, which had brought immediate and abundant results, so it was now with my exertions in seduction. (Why am I repeatedly set up for the fall?)

Among my conquests was Peter Hill Devon, an epicene musicologist with exquisite taste and a pallid beauty advantageously displayed against the Princeton background. I had been aware of him ever since my arrival in autumn—the season of decaying beauty, Peter's season, in which he had made a perfect picture, striding across the lushly dying landscape in his genteely crumpled brown tweed jacket and brown cashmere scarf. He was blond and blue-eyed, but not in that banal, open-faced manner common to the Wasp species. His face was shut tight, the intrigue most acute around his eyes, which were large but appeared larger still because of the charcoal smudginess surrounding them. The whole image suggested prep gone slightly seedy, for me an unknown raised to a higher power of mystery. There had certainly been nothing like Peter walking Columbia's Broadway campus. And so, in the spring, when my body reasserted its existence, it immediately turned to Peter.

Student that I was, I had much to learn from this lover, and he assumed the role of pedagogue on the subject of Beautiful Things, his single interest. One couldn't rightly call Beauty his passion, for he had not been put together to be enthusiastic; but the finer things did cause the slight ripples in the general flow of his insouciance. We ate in his room from antique china plates with rims of deep blue and raised gold, and the wines in which he instructed me were sipped from heavy goblets with blood-red stems, while we sat opposite one another on his Dagestan prayer rug. We stared at one another, across that blue expanse of intricate pattern, from backgrounds so estranged as to endow the other with the flattering appearance of exoticism. For my part, the stories he told me of his world—of the upper reaches of Wasp society into which he had been born, and the underside of life to which he had been borne by the variety of his sexual interests —were as remote as fairy tales. He enjoyed, in his perversity, regaling me with anti-Semitic remarks of friends and relatives, which I, in my perversity, mildly enjoyed hearing. (Not that I believed all. The unadorned truth presented no special appeal to Peter's aesthetic sensibility.) Even he once said, with unwonted tenderness, as he lay beside me on the prayer rug in a quiet interlude after making love:

"You really could pass for Christian, you know." He was turned toward me, his golden head propped up on one open palm, while with the other he lightly traced my profile. I remained silent, smiling.

"And your name, too," he continued. "Feuer. It's not tellingly

Jewish. It could simply be German. You really could pass yourself off quite easily as a scion of German Protestant stock."

I laughed. Imagine *wanting* to pass yourself off as a scion of German Protestant stock. "Are you offering me suggestions or compliments?"

He laughed, too, giving my nose—which, like my name, wasn't giving away any secrets of lineage—an affectionate punch.

"Just wondering how to present you to the family."

Jack Gottlieb, another of my lovers at that time, was refreshingly familiar and straightforward, in contrast to Peter. He had gone to Columbia, though we hadn't met there, and when he first took me to his room at the Graduate College, and I saw his Sam Steinberg painting, I was overcome with a nostalgia that surged into desire. (Sam Steinberg has been, since 1931, Columbia's cherished artist, commuting from the Bronx apartment he shares with his sister, selling his pictures and candy bars in front of Ferris Booth Hall. "You don't want that picture. Maybe you want a Milky Way instead?")

Jack too was a first-year graduate student, but in math, with two impossible parents on Long Island mourning the fact that he hadn't gone to medical school. ("They kept hoping I'd outgrow the math.") He was very nervous about treading the sacred Princetonian ground, for the math and philosophy departments were rated the university's best, and tops in the country. Graduate admissions standards were correspondingly high—only eight to twelve were admitted each year by the two departments. Those who made it were exquisitely conscious of their acceptance into the circle of the elect, though some, like Jack and me, worried whether their own particular election was merited. Much anguish resulted from these musings. Everyone arriving had been the best at his or her college, unused to competing with equals. In many minds (mine included) "not the best" was synonymous with "worthless." I'm happy to report, for I actually liked Jack, that he persevered and overcame. His dissertation was an elegant solution to a difficult problem in analysis, and he's now got a peach of a job at Cornell.

Leonard Heiss was the last of that season's amorous crop, a man of letters who *never* removed his pipe. He was a precocious lad, with

18

a young mind already running to pomposity, as his body was running to fat. An interesting fact about Leonard that I gradually discovered was his not much liking women. (I reasoned he must be either homosexual or sadistic—and I always try to think the best of people.) He has me to thank for his eventual enlightenment. He went on to have an affair with Peter Devon, an unpardonable lapse in the latter's fastidiousness. Even I must ask myself, with some distaste, how I could have gone through the movements of love with someone I so little liked. But then I hardly acknowledged the actions as my own. I dissociated myself from them, and from the body so acting. *I* remained untouched and unpenetrated, a bloodless virgin in spirit through all my promiscuity. While I fancied myself a D. H. Lawrence woman, physical pleasure was quite irrelevant to me. What I was after was the feeling that I existed, that I mattered, if only to Peter, who inhabited the world of Protestant privilege in which, despite my profile, I felt my immigrancy; to Leonard, in his world of cocksure scholarship, in which I stood naked and ashamed; or to Jack, who connected me to the familiar and therefore dear world I had left behind. If these men desired me, then surely I counted for something in their worlds. Once again I felt little high, only need.

Things really deteriorated over the summer. The other philosophy graduate students seemed to take no notice of the change of season. Perhaps they weren't even aware of it, down in the climate-controlled depths of Firestone Library, in their minuscule carrels three flights below ground level. They and the mosquitoes thrived through the humidity of June, July, and August. (The university had originally been moved from Elizabeth because of the mosquito problem *there.* If only they had been able to think beyond New Jersey.) That humidity dissolved the last particles of my moral will. All faith grows faint in New Jersey in August. Even making love seemed hardly worth the effort. The embarrassing squashing sound that two damp bodies sometimes emit when they come together; having to peel one's wet body away from the other's: these details alone would have been sufficient to turn me away from the body—which is simply too . . . corporeal in the heat—had there been anything else to turn to. But the pleasures of the mind were gone.

The fall, when it came at last, cheered and revived me. Like all people in academia, I count my years the way the Bible does, from September to September. (Like schoolchildren, too—just one of the many ways in which the life of an academic is continuous with his childhood.) The new year gave me hopes of a fresh start, only slightly diminished when I ran into my adviser, who shook his great yellow-white mane in amazement that I was still around, and proffered no advice.

I went to the first few meetings of almost all the graduate philosophy seminars being given that fall; but my new hopes vaporized in their thin, analytic atmosphere. I'd sit at the large seminar table, trying but unable to keep my mind there. Incorrigible mind. It would drift off and become engaged in vivid fantasies—involving the seminar participants, for example, in arrangements devised by the Marquis de Sade—and then drift back down into the heat of the seminar discussion, in which my peers were devising complicated counterexamples for shooting each other down. A great wave of self-hate would rise up and threaten to knock me over. What was wrong with me? I didn't belong here. I didn't belong anywhere. I'd close my eyes and see myself doing myself some kind of violence, usually shooting a revolver into my head or slashing my wrists and throat. Not a good sign, I decided, and stopped attending seminars. I went back to my seductions in a more deadly earnest.

The teeth dream had returned, almost nightly. The dreamer feels her teeth loosening, tries desperately to hold them in, but tooth after precious tooth drops down into her cupped and trembling palm. The apple into which she has just bitten carries away dozens. I had had the dream so often before that even my dreaming self suspected I might be dreaming, but argued nightly that *this* time (because, for instance, the gums themselves were now loosening) it was no dream. (Do only dreaming philosophers try to determine whether they're dreaming—a habit begun by my namesake, René Descartes?) For those of you who have never dreamt the teeth dream, let me tell you, it's terrifying, much more unnerving than even real dental problems would be. Clearly, *gnädige Damen und Herren,* we are dealing here with the chitter-chatter of the unconscious. But what is it trying to say? Freud's interpretation is that (what else?) this is a castration dream: "The dream-work represents castration by baldness, haircutting, the loss of teeth, and beheading." (And the apple? The apple!) Here as elsewhere, however, the Doktor's thinking seems too narrowly phallic. The loss of a penis is but one of the countless forms of human powerlessness. We thrust not only with our penises. Perhaps the castrated member is itself but a symbol?

ONE MONDAY in October, Jack Gottlieb invited me to a party given in honor of the famous Noam Himmel. I was of course anxious to see the (aging) *Wunderkind*, and grateful to Jack for the invitation. I was familiar with many of the stories about the mathematician; he is rather an important figure in philosophy as well, because of the work in logic he had done some years before, to which there is yet another tale attached. Himmel had once told a colleague that the problem with logic is its traditional connection (due to the accident of Aristotle, the first logician and one of the greatest of philosophers) with departments of philosophy rather than math. A decent mathematician, Himmel claimed, could revolutionize the poky field were he to think about it for a few days. The other mathematician challenged Himmel to do so, and he did—producing a spare and elegant solution to an outstanding problem in modern logic that yielded a cornucopia of consequences.

This was but one of the tales that contributed to the Himmel legend. Like others I possessed a whole stock of Himmel stories, half devoted to his genius, the remainder to his adorable ineptness in dealing with the mundane world: Himmel taking the plane to Budapest while his colleagues were waiting to pick him up in Bucharest; Himmel wandering around Cambridge in his pajamas; Himmel hauled into a Berlin police station after innocently asking for directions. Eccentric personalities like Himmel provide fertile ground for apocrypha (did Einstein really give daily help in sums to a little schoolgirl, and did a local bus driver really snap, as Einstein fumbled around for his fare, "Bad at arithmetic"?). But in Noam's case a rather amazing number of these crazy tales actually turned out to be true. It was a favorite activity at math and philosophy parties to swap these stories—not only about Noam Himmel, of course, but about all our greats (with a preference for those who were still living). And the spirit informing the taletelling was love—hero-love. For when the superiority differential becomes large enough, we stop envying and start adoring.

Everyone loves a hero. What we differ on is the question of who the heroes are, because we differ over what matters. And who matters is a function of what matters. Here in Princeton what matters is intelligence, the people who matter are the intelligent, and the people who matter the most, the heroes, are the geniuses.

We Princetonians live together on the mattering map as well. But now I have lapsed into my private language, constructed around a private image of a vast and floating map composed of untouching territories. Philosophers may prove the nonexistence of mental images; yet I don't think a week goes by that this one doesn't flash momentarily before me, called forth by someone's saying something revelatory of his location in my private picture. A good deal of my thinking happens to go on in images (from which certain people have inferred that I do not think), so that verbalization presents problems of translation. I'm faced right now with a problem of translating all that this particular vision means to me.

People occupy the mattering map, though they don't happen to be present in my mental picture of it. The map in fact is a projection of its inhabitants' perceptions. A person's location on it is determined by what matters to him, matters overwhelmingly, the kind of mattering that produces his perceptions of people, of himself and others: of who are the nobodies and who the somebodies, who the deprived and who the gifted, who the better-never-to-have-been-born and who the heroes. One and the same person can appear differently when viewed from different positions, making interterritorial communication sometimes difficult. And then some of us do an awful lot of moving around from region to region.

At times I picture the separate regions as differently shaded, ranging from the palest of gray to true black, depending on how many and various are the perceptions they contain. Take the territory where what matters above all is music. It's a rather pale gray. Those who live here have heroes, of course, but they lack really general standards by which to judge people. Those who worship Mozart and Bach don't, as a rule, revile the tone-deaf. Gourmets, on the other hand, occupy a slightly deeper gray area, for they know not only whom to look up to—great cooks—but whom to look down on—consumers of frozen dinners, floury sauces, iceberg lettuce. People to whom clothes matter seem to live in a still deeper shade of gray where the heroes are the *couturiers*, or those who are clothed by them, and the *shlumps*, attired in indifference or bad taste, are dismissed out of hand. Since we are just about always presented to one another as dressed, those who see us through our clothes see much.

Then there are those regions (and we're getting into deeper gray now) where what matters is not a person's relationship with some external thing, such as food or clothes or music, but rather some intrinsic quality of his or her own: beauty or physical fitness. Or intelligence. Since we can discard these attributes even less easily than our clothes, we can always be strictly categorized according to the perceptions emanating from these areas: of who matters (the beautiful, the athletic, and the intelligent, respectively) and who doesn't (the ugly, the flabby and the dumb). Contempt for the unfit is stronger, I think, than disdain for the plain. Perhaps because of the passivity of beauty? But no, intelligence is every bit as passive, a gift either granted or denied. And yet the scorn felt for the unintelligent is an almost moral outrage. Never mind that the dull can't help themselves, that they would, granted the sense to do so, have chosen to be otherwise. Their very existence is felt as a moral affront by those of us who dwell where the genius is hero. The color of our zone is only just discernably lighter than the true black of those who perceive people according to their acceptance of some moral or religious or political code.

And so at those parties, when we sat around sharing stories of our heroes, of those now gone, like Einstein, or those still with us, like Himmel, we would get high on love, on love for our idols and love for each other. For in loving our great men and women we unite ourselves not only with human excellence, but also with one another. Those who share my heroes are, in the deepest sense, *of my own kind*.

"I should so much like to do something to hold together our colleagues in the various 'Fatherlands,' " Einstein wrote to the physicist Ehrenfest in the stormy days of 1915. "Is not that small group of scholars and intellectuals the only 'Fatherland' which is worthy of serious concern to people like ourselves?"

And now Noam Himmel had come, like Albert Einstein before him, to Princeton; and those to whom this mattered the most were celebrating. This party was but the first, given by the chairman of the victorious math department, Adam Loft. His house was a large Tudor on a block of large Tudors, all of them owned by the university and rented out to faculty. This particular one had been gutted and redone in very modern style, all white and light and angles, so that its interior was nothing like what one would expect from the outside. Tonight the house was packed with slightly hysterically hilarious mathematicians and their consorts. Himmel himself I picked out immediately, before he was pointed out by the flushed and bright-eyed Jack. (All the graduate students were flushed and bright-eyed that night.) Himmel was surrounded by eight or nine admirers, and everyone else kept glancing his way, like iron chips indicating the position of a magnet. His looks lifted my spirit, for they were of the type I knew best: shaggy and Semitic. His black hair was long and straggly, his beard rabbinically full, his clothes without apparent style or age. His incipiently paunchy body had almost certainly never jogged or chased a tennis ball, unlike the bodies of most of Princeton's population. Nevertheless, he was on the whole remarkably boyish-looking. It was hard to believe that this was the man who had worked out the supernaturals three years before I was born.

I could tell even at a distance that his face was unusually animated as he spoke, which he seemed to be doing constantly. As I came closer, I saw that the basically familiar features had an interesting variation: the eyes were a very clear blue. The voice, when I had worked my way into its range, which was wide, also seemed familiar: loud and unaffected, with lovely subdued hints of New York in the small rise at the end of the sentences. But as I listened more I heard that here too was a variation. The rate of speech was eccentric. For the most part Himmel spoke very quickly, sentences spilling out, as if impatient with the amount of labial effort required for the articulation of thought. Then occasionally his speech slowed down to such a rate as to leave one wondering, in between the drawled clauses, whether he was going to speak again or was rather waiting for a reply. It was the speech pattern of someone who was allowed, by an ever indulgent audience, to speak at the rate at which he thought, the eccentricity of one who could always be assured that his listeners awaited every uttered word.

As I had been majoring in seduction and minoring in parties for the last months, I could, after a little observation, detect the difference in the flavor of this one.

"Having your husband at a party is like adding anchovies to a salad," my friend Ava, who loves to speak in edible metaphors, once told me. "I love anchovies, but you can't taste anything else."

Sometime in the course of the evening I was introduced to him. I was but one in a surrounding circle, yet his eyes rested on me for a flatteringly long few seconds.

It was months before I saw him again. Over the winter I wrote a few papers, so I wasn't kicked out of the department. "But you're marginal, very marginal," the director of graduate studies had warned. I had enjoyed those papers. The old love of philosophy had returned. The process of thinking about philosophy always reminds me of fireworks. One question is shot up and bursts into a splendorous many. Answers? Forget answers. The spectacle is all in the questions.

But the moment I stepped out of the isolation into which I always retreat when I'm really working, and began to talk with other members of my department, all the doubts returned. Doubts not about the objects of thought, but about the thinking subject, me. I was overwhelmed again with the sense that I didn't know what philosophy was all about. One of my fellow graduate students suggested that my problem lay in my religious background; I had transplanted the attitude of Awe Before the Unknown to philosophy, where it definitely didn't belong. This analysis was provoked by my commenting that a certain question seemed very deep to me.

"Nothing is deep," he had drawled back reprovingly.

It was an unusually cold winter that year, with many days of clear blue skies and trees glistening with the frozen moisture. My relationships too became glazed over with ice. None of the men I was sleeping with touched me. Only one human contact, very slow in starting and developing, radiated any warmth. This was with a woman, Sarah Slater, who attended the Plato seminar I had begun but given up along with the others. Sarah's field is history of philosophy, as opposed to philosophy proper. She was almost finished with her dissertation on Locke's theory of identity, but she was still attending as many seminars as she could. At first she infuriated me. She seemed the closest thing to a disembodied spirit this side of the veil. Her face is a Puritan's, quite literally. Her ancestors on both sides go back to colonial New England, where one was burned as a witch. (I can easily imagine a believing age burning my friend on similar grounds.) Physically she's composed of lines and angles and planes: a tall, rigidly held body, long, straight brown hair, long, straight eyebrows stretching perpendicular to the straight outlines of her face. There isn't a compromising curve to be found in Sarah. This external severity made the discovery of the softness and humor within all the sweeter.

But I made the discovery only slowly. I would watch Sarah as I sat in the Plato seminar, her face pale and expressionless, making subtle points about the Greek in her colorless voice. (In college she had written a little Greek grammar book that is still used.) I would watch her and feel rage. "My God, she's a virgin," I would think with fury. I don't know why I was so angered by the thought. I remember the words "She doesn't have the right" going through my mind. The right to what? To purity, I suppose, though it's characteristic of our relationship that after all the years of intimacy I still have no idea whether this initial assumption of mine was or is correct. The physical fact is of no consequence. For what I discovered, as we saw more and more of each other through the late winter and early spring, was that one could tell anything to that puritanical face and have it exposed to intelligence and wit, but never moral disapproval. She shut nothing and no one out.

Sarah and I often shared our meals together in the formal dining hall at the Graduate College, where the university came closest to approximating the Oxford ideal. The immense cathedral-like room has stained-glass windows and wooden gargoyles carved along the beams. (I seem to recall one grinning creature with a toothbrush, being somehow connected with a gift from Procter & Gamble, but the image is so surreal that I suspect it has been gleaned from a dream.) Meals were served promptly, preceded by a Latin grace from the master at high table. I would remind myself that I was separated from Barnard's grubby Barnard-Hewitt-Reid cafeteria not by the Atlantic but by nothing more than most of northeastern New Jersey. We were required to don black robes at meals, yet another Oxford affectation, this one abandoned soon after I left, since the students had taken to shredding the full sleeves into long kinky fringes.

Yet I had loved the sight of Sarah in her robes, in which the rest of us looked so absurd, for her external form had come into its own amidst the severity of those folds. The two of us spent much of our time laughing about philosophy and philosophers, although for Sarah this meant laughing about her life. Always when she left me it was to return to her carrel to work.

IT WAS MARCH when I saw Himmel again. I had just boarded the dinky, the two-car train that shuttles between Princeton and Princeton Junction to meet the trains going north to New York and south to Philadelphia, when I saw a figure loping down the hill toward us. That's what "galumphing" means, I thought, as I watched it approach: hair, tie, jacket, papers all flowing. I was surprised that something could move at once so awkwardly and so quickly. As the localized commotion got nearer, I saw it was Noam Himmel running to catch the train. Wouldn't it be exciting if he were to sit with me, I thought, and then dreaded that he might. How would I ever keep up a conversation with him?

He galumphed onto the train a second before it started. A girl and a boy holding hands glanced up at him, and then the boy whispered something to the girl and they both laughed. I was infuriated on Himmel's behalf. It was outrageous that these nitwits (in comparison, surely) should share a superior laugh at the expense of a genius. Like the prisoners in Plato's cave, I thought, laughing because the sun-dazzled philosopher can't see in their darkness. He spotted me immediately and came toward me. God help me, I thought, feeling stupid and inadequate, dreading the exposure to the bright light of his understanding. Many of the stories about Himmel were devoted to his intolerance of stupidity.

"Renee Feuer, isn't it? Graduate student, philosophy?"

Remarkable memory. But then what else should I have expected? He was looking very pleased as he sat down next to me. And then I remembered, with that small surprise I always feel when I consider myself from the outside, that what *he* was seeing was a delicate-featured young woman with long legs and waist-length honey hair. From that point of view I was acceptable. At least for the moment, I thought, until I start speaking.

"New York?" he asked.

"Yes, of course. You?"

"I'm giving a talk at NYU. You?"

"Oh, I'm just going in for my weekly fix of the city."

He simply smiled at that. I assumed it was a smile of comprehension.

"You're a New Yorker, aren't you?" I asked.

"Well, I grew up in Manhattan, but I've lived there only very occasionally during the past twenty-two years. New York's proximity to Princeton was one of the deciding factors in my coming here."

Common ground. *Terra sancta.* I feel an immediate closeness to anyone who loves New York or hates Los Angeles. Either condition is sufficient, but I've found that satisfaction of the one usually entails satisfaction of the other.

"I would never have lasted out this year in Princeton if I couldn't get into New York and breathe," I said.

"Oh, don't you like Princeton?"

"I find it difficult to breathe in an atmosphere in which one's intelligence is always being assessed. But of course you wouldn't know about that."

"What do you mean?" The blue eyes, which were so unexpected in that face, had a very powerful stare. Noam is a man who insists on eye contact. I was already finding this somewhat disconcerting and kept gazing slightly ahead of him. He, in response, kept moving his head forward to meet my gaze squarely. At this rate he'll be off his seat before the Junction, I thought.

"I don't suppose you ever feel stupid."

"On the contrary, I very often feel stupid. I often have the experience of not being able to understand what everyone else seems to. Somebody will say something and I'll think, Now what the hell does that mean? That doesn't make any sense. And then someone else will answer and his response is as incomprehensible as the first one's statement. And back and forth they go, intelligible to one another, unintelligible to me. Obviously there must be some meaning there if they're understanding one another. And usually the things being discussed aren't even supposed to be deep." He laughed. His laugh was higher pitched than his speaking voice. "It's curious, but the things I find obvious other people find difficult. They're amazed that I can see them so easily, and it sometimes takes me a tremendously long time to get others to see what I saw instantaneously. But then fairly average people will have intuitions on a whole range of topics that I can't get a hold on at all."

"Maybe you're simply not interested in those topics."

"I'm not. However, it's impossible to tell which is a function of which. Am I uninterested because I'm dense or dense because I'm uninterested?" He laughed in a way that showed this question too didn't overwhelmingly concern him.

"Is it lonely to have one's mind work differently from most people's?"

The blue eyes widened: "Lonely? It's damned lucky. A lucky thing for me that it's been decided the things I can see are the important ones, so I turn out smart instead of stupid. Oh, I think maybe when I was very young I was lonely for a while. There weren't too many other kids interested in playing around with numbers all the time. But I discovered early on that I liked ideas much better than people, and that was the end of my loneliness. For one thing, ideas are consistent. And you can control them better than people." He smiled. "Hell, to be honest I've just always found them more interesting. Logical relations are transparent and lovely. Human relations, from what I can tell, always seem pretty muddy."

"I suppose you're right that human relations are rarely very pretty," I said hesitantly. "But there are reasons besides the aesthetic for valuing them, aren't there?"

He leaned toward me as I spoke. He seemed to want to suck all the contents from my comments, as if they mattered that deeply to him. There could be no greater reassurance for me, short of the declaration: "You are brilliant. Speak."

"I'm not talking about valuing them," he answered. "That's a psychological or perhaps an ethical question. I'm talking about thinking about them. One can think they're good things to have even if one doesn't think they're interesting to contemplate. I've just never found anything much to engage the mind there. Of course that might just be my particular brand of stupidity again." He grinned.

"What *about* the ethical questions? Do you think they're interesting?"

"Well, when you talk about ethics you change the subject. It's no longer human relations that are your objects, but rights and obligations. And those are, I would say, important topics. But for myself, I don't derive much pleasure from thinking about them. The properties of rights and obligations are not what I would call theoretically pleasing. They don't form lovely patterns." He smiled. "Of course, perhaps I ought to think about them anyway. That's yet another ethical question, whether we have an ethical obligation to consider ethical questions, including this very one. However, since I haven't considered the question, I don't know that we do have such an obligation and thus feel no obligation to consider this question. If you follow." He grinned.

Self-referring propositions, as I was to learn, are a favorite source of humor for Noam, and he loves constructing them.

I ought to mention that in the course of our conversation we had arrived at the Junction, had crossed the tracks and boarded the New York–bound train. Himmel had never stopped speaking, had paid no attention to the details of descending, crossing, and ascending, of finding new seats. I wondered how he managed when alone.

"I seem to remember a poem by someone, Edna St. Vincent Millay, I think, beginning, 'Euclid alone has looked on Beauty bare.' I can't remember the rest."

"Yes?" He smiled. "Well, surely others beside Euclid have had the privilege. Euclidean geometry isn't even the prettiest of the geometries. But Beauty bare. That's good. I like that. So many people have no sensibility whatsoever for mathematical beauty, are even arrogantly skeptical of its existence. But of course beauty is what math is all about, the most pure and perfect beauty."

"You're really an aesthetician," I said. Or a strange breed of hedo-nist, I thought.

"Yes? Perhaps. Perhaps all mathematicans are. I've never thought about it before. You see," he grinned. "At least I'm consistent. I don't find people in general very interesting to think about, so I don't find myself in particular an arresting object of thought. A lot of people seem to assent to the universal proposition but decline instan-tiation when it comes to themselves."

By now I was feeling quite comfortable holding his high-intensity gaze, and we both laughed into each other's eyes. It was a happy moment.

"Oh dear." I smiled. "We seem, you and I, only to talk about boring things."

"That's true." He smiled back. "I wonder why I'm enjoying it so much. I wonder why I'm wondering when I can discuss these mind-deadening issues with you again."

We made a date to meet for dinner the following evening.

The next evening, as I walked up Witherspoon Street toward La-hiere's, the restaurant I had suggested since Himmel was apparently unaware of the existence of any such establishments, I saw him coming up Nassau Street from the direction of Fine Hall, the mathe-matics building. He was walking very quickly, everything still flowing, including the pile of papers he was carrying under his arm—a figure which, even in a town like Princeton, attracted stares. He of course was oblivious to the attention, lost in his own head. As I watched him cross Nassau Street against the light, I thought surely God must love mathematical geniuses.

His brow was, I saw as he got nearer, deeply furrowed and his lips were moving slightly. He didn't notice me until he was right along-side and I put my hand gently on his shoulder to halt his full pace.

"Oh." He looked at me, blank for a moment, then focused that full beam of his in on me: "How are you? how are you? how are you?" Leaning toward me he searched my face for I knew not what.

"Just fine, just fine, just fine." I laughed.

"You know, it occurred to me that I never asked you what kind of philosophy you do."

"Oh, I guess right now I'm doing philosophy of body."

"Philosophy of body? I've heard of philosophy of mind, but not of body. Tell me about it."

He hadn't understood my comment as the joke I had meant it to be. I was embarrassed at having put forth a joke that didn't even succeed in making its presence felt, and tried to recoup.

"Well, if there's a philosophy of mind, why shouldn't there be a philosophy of body? After all, the main question in philosophy of mind is the mind-body problem. Why assume only the mind makes the relationship between them problematic? Why assume only mind needs analysis? Why prejudge the issue by approaching it only from the point of view of a philosophy of mind?" And I worried that I couldn't think on my feet.

"I see what you're saying. There really isn't any such established area in philosophy. What you're saying is, you're working on the mind-body problem and you believe it's body rather than, or perhaps as well as, mind that is problematic."

"Very problematic. Fraught with difficulties," I drawled in my most pedantic manner.

This conversation took place out on the sidewalk in front of Lahiere's. Himmel had made no move to go in, had become completely absorbed in our conversation out there, leaning toward me, concentrating on my comments. I realized that if we were going to eat at all I'd better take some initiative, so I moved toward the door.

I asked him, as we were being seated inside, whether he was interested in philosophy.

"Oh yes, very, though I've never had the time to read as much as I'd like. I've mostly read in those areas that are contiguous with math, you know, foundations of math, philosophy of logic. I've read a little Quine. I find his views baffling."

Noam then launched into a critical discussion of the views of Quine and Putnam, two Harvard philosophers, that logic is empirical and that it perhaps ought to be revised to overcome the paradoxes posed by quantum mechanics. Noam thought these ideas the height, or depth, of absurdity: "not worth considering, except that they have had, incredibly, some influence, especially among the physicists.

"Some of the most idiotic statements I've been forced to listen to have come from physicists talking about math and logic. It's hard to find one—especially among the younger set, whose minds have all been warped by quantum mechanics—who has sensible views. I have a feeling that they don't even know what they're saying, that they're just mouthing words. That's the most charitable interpretation I can give to their babble. Otherwise I'd just have to conclude that they're imbeciles. Is it anything but imbecile to believe that a truth like the law of noncontradiction is empirical? That the only grounds for its truth lie in the nature of experience? Of course, a lot of these characters don't even know how to make the elementary distinction between the psychological grounds for our *belief* that some fact is true and the actual grounds for its truth. All knowledge turns out to be trivially empirical then, although I wonder if they even realize this. Anyway, it seems this confusion is partly responsible for their imbecile views. Their arrogance seems to be another factor. Everything's empirical, it's all up to them." He was shaking his head and smiling, rather meanly. "They're going to get out their little measuring sticks and meters, and tell us which of the many logics is the empirically true one. As if it really were in the realm of possibility to adopt a new logic, a quantum logic. What's the realm of possibility supposed to *mean* if that's possible? You know, it's rather funny. Previous ages believed that only God is mysterious and powerful enough to transcend logic. God is the only being for whom it's all right to predicate contradiction. Now it's electrons. Irrationality hasn't been wiped out by the physical sciences, it's just been rechanneled."

Noam went on to a less polemical, more detailed analysis of this view he despised, showing how its proponents contradicted themselves, using the very logic they would abandon in the argument for its abandonment.

"Of course"—he laughed—"the charge of self-contradiction may not bother them. They can respond by just giving up the law of noncontradiction."

Noam's "little knowledge" of these philosophers sounded more coherent than anything I'd heard in the countless discussions of them in 1879 Hall, Princeton's philosophy building. And the topic came alive as Noam discussed it. The beauty of his conversation has always been the simplicity with which he discusses the most complex of subjects. Often, as I listened in the early days, there would come into my mind the image of a soggy piece of cloth, crumpled and beginning to mildew, being shaken out with one powerful *thwack*—Noam's intellect—and hung up flat in the sunshine.

His obliviousness to external details was contagious, and when the waiter came to take our orders neither one of us had yet opened the menu.

"I'll have the soft-shelled crabs," I told the waiter, having sampled them on previous occasions. "They're good here," I said to Noam, who was looking pitifully at bay. This transition from extreme intellectual confidence to just as extreme practical helplessness was the sharpest I had ever witnessed. One minute ago this pathetic specimen had been magisterially denouncing the views of the most influential American philosopher as contemptible. It's quite clear where the borders of his turf are drawn, I thought, feelings of protectiveness oozing up in me.

"Good. I'll have them, too." Noam looked as if he had solved a major problem.

"I bet I'll enjoy them more than you." I told him as the waiter left, emboldened to the point of flirtatiousness by the display of Himmel's awkwardness.

"Oh, why is that?"

"Because I was brought up an Orthodox Jew. For me they're seasoned with sin."

"I'm afraid I don't understand."

"They're *trayf*, unkosher."

"Crabs? I thought only pig products were unkosher."

Noam, it turned out, was amazingly ignorant of things Jewish for someone who had grown up in New York (a more relevant fact than his being Jewish). He, in turn, was amazed by my account of my upbringing, particularly the girls' yeshiva I had very hastily been enrolled in when non-Jewish boys from my public school began telephoning for dates. I had gone to public school only because my parents couldn't afford to send both my brother and me to the expensive day school, Hillel Academy, serving Westchester's conservative and (less populous) Orthodox communities. My brother, being male, got priority. And sending me to a yeshiva in the dangerous city had been out of the question. But not quite as out of the question as those boys calling nightly on the phone. So I was soon commuting to the Lower East Side, to one of the more right-wing of the all-girl schools. The teachers here checked our hemlines for modesty every morning, and the principal came into our biology class at the start of our lesson on evolution, informing us that although they were required to teach this for the New York State regents' exam, it was all unproved *apikorsus*, or heresy, and we shouldn't believe any of it. But, as my mother often wails, "It was too late. You were already an *apikoros*."

And so I was. The word is derived from the same source as the noun and adjective "epicurean"—from the Greek philosopher Epicurus, who taught that pleasure is the good and "the root of all good is the pleasure of the stomach; even wisdom and culture must be referred to this." Hence our "epicurean," although in practice the philosopher found that the pain of stomachaches outweighed the pleasures of indulgence and so kept to a diet of bread and water, with a little preserved cheese on feast days. "I am filled with pleasure of the body when I live on bread and water, and I spit on luxurious pleasures, not for their own sake but because of the inconveniences that follow them." Epicurus was really no epicurean. But he was an *apikoros*, even about his own Hellenistic religion. "We, and not the gods, are masters of our fate." Definitely an *apikoros*, this Epicurus. Dante found his followers in hell. *Apikoros* was a much used word in my high school, and it wasn't too difficult to be labeled one.

"We weren't supposed to go to college."

"Why not?" Noam asked. "What were you supposed to do?"

"Get married, of course. And be fruitful and multiply, God's very words to Abraham."

Noam was dumbfounded. "It's a world I never knew existed. I pretty much took it for granted that Jews are generally enlightened. It sounds like a description of the Middle Ages."

"Oh, much older than that. How about the Babylonian captivity?"

"And you didn't swallow any of it. What about your siblings? Do you have any?"

"My brother swallowed what they fed him and hollered for more. My parents had wanted him to go to college, but he wouldn't. He sits and learns."

"He what?"

"Sits and learns. That's the expression for studying Talmud. You have heard of the Talmud?" He nodded. "That's what he does, at a yeshiva in Lakewood, New Jersey. His wife supports him. It's a very accepted, even respected *modus vivendi.*"

"And here you are studying philosophy at Princeton, having been suckled on all this irrationality. It's amazing. You're an amazing woman."

His words kindled my ever ready vanity, but I also felt that pinch of uneasiness I always get when people put rationality on one side and religion on the other. Not that I haven't been known to think in exactly those terms, especially when I'm in the company of my religious relatives. But people remote from religion, whether they were born there or struggled there, tend to simplify the other side. (It goes without saying that the religious do likewise.) I'm amused when people talk of the "religious mentality" or the "religious personality," and always think of my father, my mother, my brother and my sister-in-law, all of whose religious personalities had little in common apart from their being Jewish.

"Oh, I wouldn't say that I don't take any of it seriously, at least on a very primitive level. Sometimes, especially on insomniac nights, I start worrying that there may be a God, and worse, that he may be Jewish."

"So?"

"So, if there is and He is, I'm in a lot of trouble. You too, by the way." I bit down hard on a forkful of crab to give my statement emphasis.

Noam shook his head. "I just can't connect to any of this. It's a world I can't make any sense of."

"Unfortunately, I can. I can make sense out of both worlds: Lakewood, New Jersey, and Princeton, New Jersey. So I can't feel really comfortable in either."

Noam just shook his head and shrugged.

"Is it really so alien to you?" I asked him. "Aren't your parents at all traditional, or your grandparents?"

"My parents are both dead. They both hated religion—opiate of the people and all that. I never knew my grandparents."

"And you hate religion?"

"It doesn't arouse the passion in me it did in my parents, but then I've never had to deal with it. It just seems juvenile, a child's conception of reality. I'm always a little surprised when I find reasonably intelligent people who haven't outgrown it." Again he shrugged.

"Have you ever read *Moses and Monotheism?*" I asked.

"No, what's that?"

"Freud," I answered, again surprised. Noam and I would always amaze one another by what we didn't know. Of course, my shock was always the greater, since I expected so much more; nothing less, in those days especially, than omniscience.

"Oh, him." Noam's smile was nasty. "What's he say? Religion is an incestuous desire for the father?"

"You're not too far off target. It's a neurotic fixation on the repressed tribal memory of the murder of the primeval father."

"Don't bother to explain."

Noam finally gave his food some attention as our first silence fell upon us. I was regretting having brought Freud up. It occurred to me that perhaps this entire subject of religion was utterly boring to Noam and that I hadn't noticed the signs because of my own neurotic religious fixation, tribal or otherwise. But *he* continued the discussion:

"You know, come to think of it, my parents did name me after my paternal grandfather, who was killed in a pogrom in Russia. That's a piece of Jewish tradition, isn't it?"

"Getting killed in pogroms?"

"Cute." Noam laughed. "But what about it?"

"Yes, you're right. In fact, if Jews name after a person at all, it's someone who's dead."

"Why is that?"

"I'm not quite sure. To honor the dead, I guess, to keep their memory alive. It's taken very seriously. I've known people who actually had a child because there was a name they wanted to pass on." (This has always seemed to me an extraordinarily insufficient reason for creating a person. A *person*, for Godsakes. But then the awesomeness of this act of responsibility so impresses me that I don't know if I'll ever come up with a reason I can judge sufficient.) "Wait a minute. I remember once hearing of a superstition that in passing on the names you passed on the souls. That would explain why you shouldn't name after the living, too."

"What?" Noam said very loudly, leaning across the table, his beard grazing my broccoli.

"Well, you know, there was a lot of superstition in the old country."

"But tell me about this, about passing on the souls. I'd never heard that Jews believed anything like that."

"I'm afraid I don't know very much about it. It's not the sort of thing one studies in yeshiva. Jewish thinkers for the most part devote themselves to the interpretation of the law, not to metaphysical questions. It's very different in that regard from Catholicism."

"Is there a belief in transmigration of souls?" he asked impatiently. He was obviously excited, rocking back and forth in his chair. Funny, I thought, he looks like he's *shuckling*, making the rhythmic motions of Orthodox Jews in prayer. Could this too be genetic, another tribal inheritance? Let his *payess* (sideburns) grow, stick a yarmulke on his head, he'd be the perfect picture of a yeshiva *bocher*.

"I don't think so," I answered. "Not officially. Just like heaven and hell aren't official. But there might have been some such belief among the people. And for all I know, that might be the source of the naming tradition."

"Interesting." The self-absorbed *shuckling* was attracting glances and, again, those infuriatingly superior shared smiles. He asked me some more questions, none of which I could answer. It was his turn to be surprised by my ignorance. How could someone of my background have failed to apprise herself of the facts on the subject?

"It's just not the kind of thing one studies in yeshiva," I repeated defensively.

Suddenly Noam (I was now thinking of him as Noam rather than Himmel) looked at his watch, which was fastened at one chink of its band with a paper clip. (Much of Noam's life is held together by paper clips.)

"Oh my God! I'm terribly late! This is really awful. I've got to run." And he pushed back his chair, almost toppling it, and ga-lumphed out. Everybody in the vicinity but me was very pleased by the performance. I hadn't even given him the copy of the Millay poem I had xeroxed in Firestone Library. I paid the check and left.

He called me the next day, having gotten my phone number from the philosophy department. I was touched by these efforts, which I (rightly) suspected were preternatural.

"I'm sorry for rushing off like that yesterday. I had promised to speak at Fitzer's graduate seminar and I was terribly late. I realized after that I had left you with the check." He invited me to a party for the following evening, given by Professor Fitzer.

The party was pretty dreadful. (How much more dread would it have inspired had I realized how many similar parties awaited me.) Fitzer's small brick house was near Lake Carnegie, not far from the Harrison Avenue bridge. It was a modest, strictly Euclidean affair, rectangular from the outside and divided up inside into a few rectangles and squares. The majority of the house seemed to be on the subterranean level, in a paneled den that seemed to enjoy a larger area than the frame of the house would allow, extending out perhaps beneath the small square front garden. The party took place in the den, which was furnished entirely in Lucite, perhaps to minimize the furniture's interfering with the geometry.

After the initial fluttering around Noam, the men, all mathematicians, settled down to talk shop while the women spoke among themselves of children, grandchildren, travel and gardening. It was a party of the senior faculty—in fact, it seemed, the senior of the seniors, the departments' gray eminences. The women were all soft-spoken and sweet, cherishing, quite clearly, the appearance of unflappable exteriors. I tried to modulate my voice accordingly. There was nothing to be done about my obvious raw youth. I was gratified, though, by the women's discreet inquisitiveness about my relationship with Noam. They asked subtle, indirect questions, to which I gave subtle, indirect answers.

There was one amusing little outburst from (of course) the men. Noam and this fellow, Raoul, the only other non-gray mathematician there, had a disagreement over the terms "obvious" and "trivial." Raoul had said that something was obvious.

"No, it's not," said Noam. "It may be trivial, but it's not obvious."

"Obvious, trivial, what's the difference?"

"A great difference. A theorem is obvious if it's easy to see, to grasp. A theorem is trivial if the logical relations leading to it are relatively direct. Generally, theorems that are trivial are obvious. If the logical relations leading to it are straight, it's easy to get to. And conversely. Thus the sloppy conflation of the terms." He glanced darkly at Raoul. "But the meanings are different, as are the extensions. Sometimes the logical relations are direct but not so accessible. You know the old joke about the professor who says that something is trivial and is questioned on this by a student and goes out and works for an hour and comes back and says, 'I was right. It is trivial'?" He paused for the laughter to stop. "Well, he concluded, "you couldn't substitute 'obvious' for 'trivial' in that joke."

"But of course there's another sense of 'trivial,' " someone said. "Insignificant, undeep."

"Yes, of course," Noam said. "That's a secondary sense." This secondary sense is a great favorite of Noam's. Events, ideas, people —oh, definitely people—are classified as trivial or nontrivial. It's his way of distinguishing between what and who matters and what and who doesn't.

"Your explication seems vague to me," the persistent Raoul objected. "A theorem is obvious if it's easy for *whom* to see?"

"For God and Himmel," someone said.

Noam laughed. "Make that Himmel and God."

"I'm sorry, that wasn't really an evening together, was it?" Noam said as we walked back to the Graduate College in soft silk air smelling of spring. Can't he even take my hand? I was thinking. "Unfortunately, I have a dinner party tomorrow night. But why don't we have dinner on Friday? This time I'll pay, I promise. It will have to be quite late, though. I won't be free until after nine."

We had our late dinner that Friday night, and a long lunch on Saturday, lunch on Sunday, and dinner again on Wednesday. Through all this Noam's vivid gaze and conversation were the only things that held me. I hadn't had such a chaste romantic relationship with a man since high school. (I was fairly certain it was romantic.)

I began to realize, as I had on the sidewalk outside Lahiere's, that I would have to take the initiative if we were going to do more than eat and talk.

That Thursday was a glorious, blooming day. When we met for lunch, I suggested that we just buy some strawberries at Davidson's and a bottle of Beaujolais at Nassau Liquors and go have them over on the other side of Lake Carnegie.

"I'll show you where the wild asparagus grow."

And I did.

There's been so much serious discussion devoted to the profound question of the vaginal vs. the clitoral orgasm. Why doesn't anyone speak about the mental orgasm? It's what's going on in your head that can make the difference, not which and how many of your nerve endings are being rubbed. Judged on the quantitative neurological scale, our lovemaking wasn't memorable. It's other details I remember:

Noam downed more than his share of the wine, according to his characteristic style of mechanically finishing off whatever he's given, saving himself from having to deliberate over what and how much to eat. I watched him in pleased (get 'em drunk) astonishment as he gulped the wine down like a bottle of Coca-Cola.

He lay back, positioning his face in the shade of my body, looking up at me. He was quiet for once. Was it the wine or the sight of me with the sun pouring down on my head? I had a very sharp impression —now transformed into an equally vivid memory—of how I must have appeared to him, lit up against the brilliant blue sky.

"Like sunlight made tangible," he said, tentatively touching my hair.

Our first kiss was hebetically clumsy, for I took him by surprise. I took him by surprise a good part of the way. At each early stage of our very linear progress from first kiss to final gasp he searched my face, all his features asking: "You don't mean to . . . ? I couldn't possibly . . . could I?" and then expressing their pleasure at the answer they found in my look. This catechism of facial expressions only once broke out into speech:

"Could we be arrested?" he asked before entering me.

And I remember too the intensity of my pleasure, which wasn't at

41

all physical, as he shuddered within me while inside my head sang the triumphant thought: I am making love to this man . . . to Noam Himmel . . . the genius.

NOAM AND I saw each other nearly every day after that. Often we'd go driving on the country roads that radiate out from Princeton. I always took the wheel. It was my car, for Noam had none—in fact, his license had expired three years after he had gotten it. And anyway I love to drive, and am rather vain about how well I do it: fast and smooth, with consummate skill. (I would really like nothing better than to climax this narrative with a car chase: me at the wheel, burning up the tires on Ivy Lane, Faculty Road, fleeing from or after God knows what. But such, alas, is not the nature of my story.) Some of my moments of deepest self-satisfaction have been brought on by the perfection of my parallel parking. No one can get into tighter spaces with greater ease. (How appealing I find the suggestiveness of language. I don't envy Noam the precision of mathematics in the least.) And there is a metaphysical kick to be gotten out of controlling a car, out of the expansion of one's spatial boundaries that driving involves. One's consciousness almost seems to move beyond the epidermal limits as one maneuvers in space, the body image subtly diffusing itself outward.

Actually, I do recall one occasion when Noam took the wheel. I think it was because I had drunk too much wine at lunch. I discovered then that Noam's rate of thinking set the pace not only for his rates of talking and walking, but for his rate of driving as well. We decelerated from seventy miles an hour to twenty in a matter of sentences, and then, Noam having thought through the point, raced up to eighty. It was my one experience of car sickness, and afterwards I always drove. Noam was quite content to sit back and be chauffeured, as he is content to sit back and let others take care of all of life's practicalities.

And there have always been people only too happy to do so. There was a long chain of surrogate mothers and fathers (but especially mothers) in all the university towns along the way, extending back to the first, the natural mother, who had devoted herself to the cause of his genius almost from his infancy, when it had emerged quite spectacularly. He learned to count early; numbers were among his first words. Before long he was proving some numerical truths algebraically, having discovered this way of thinking on his own. In those early years he recapitulated some of the early history of mathematics, producing, for example, a proof of the Pythagorean theorem.

So Mother Himmel had certainly had a worthwhile cause. The father I picture as having been somewhat alienated by his son's genius and his wife's rapturous devotion to it. But I don't really know. Such details are supplied through the faculty of my imagination. Noam has always had very little to say about the elder Himmels—even back then in the days of our courtship, when, in the first flush of his attraction to me, he found himself a passably interesting object of thought and was willing to talk about himself. Almost all my special acquaintance with his history, knowledge apart from the commonly shared legends, derives from those few months before our marriage. He was willing then to consider almost any of the personal questions I put to him, although he often could not provide the answers. He had noticed so little.

"What was she like, your mother?" We were driving back toward Princeton in the dusk.

"Oh, I don't know. A fairly ordinary kind of woman." He considered several moments. "She was a very good mother."

Both his parents had died when Noam was in his late twenties, within two years of each other, the mother from a brain tumor, the father from a stroke.

"Do you have any pictures?"

"No. I once had a picture of her, when she was in college, I think. It got lost during one of my moves."

I could understand that. I could well imagine the chaos that must have accompanied Noam's change of domicile.

"Was she very smart?" Was she smarter than I, I was thinking. Does Noam long for a woman who can approximate the brilliance of his devoted mother? "Where did she go to college?"

"She was reasonably intelligent." He looked uncomfortable. The question hadn't pleased him. Why? "She went to City College. My father, too. I think they met there. I vaguely remember something about their having met on some campus march. They were both interested in politics."

"Marxist?" I recalled Noam's use of the expression "opiate of the people" in connection with their views on religion.

"Yes, I suppose. I never paid too much attention."

His father had been a pharmacist. I induced Noam, not too long after this conversation, to take me to see the ancestral drugstore, on the corner of Broadway and 89th Street. (The family had lived around the corner on Riverside Drive.) It's still a serious specimen of the kind, given over more to pharmacopoeia than to beauty aids. But a concession to frivolity has been made since the Himmel days, in the form of a long counter stretching along one side wall, cluttered with cosmetics and perfumes. Noam told me that in his family's day a soda fountain had stood there, where he had spent most of his after-school hours playing with numbers. The supernaturals had been pursued and apprehended there. "They ought to have a plaque," I said, staring at the trifling display. "In Europe there would be a plaque. We should tell the owners. Imagine how good it would be for business." But the look of the woman behind the cash register, produced by an abundant application of the goods on the offending counter, didn't encourage the belief that she would be overly moved by the history of the store. We bought some Tums—for old times' sake and for Noam, who suffers from chronic stomach problems— and left.

"Can't you remember anything specific about them?" I asked him once. "They must have been unusual to have had a son like you."

"Why? Why must they have been unusual?" He seemed to be getting angry.

"Because you're so unusual. You must have gotten it from somewhere."

"Not from them." His tone was decidedly short. "I assure you, they were extraordinarily ordinary. No, no, not ordinary, not average. They were certainly a good deal smarter than the deplorable average. But they were well within the range of normal. There certainly was nothing unusual about their mathematical abilities. I could never get either of them to really understand the supernaturals."

44

Had the young Noam felt contempt for his intelligent but unexceptionable parents? To use the terminology of Plato's "one royal lie": the progenitors had been made of silver, the son of gold. Was this anger I was now encountering the guilt the boy had repressed for knowing that he was made of a different stuff? Whatever the reason, the look on Noam's face didn't encourage my pursuing the question of inheritance further.

But when he spoke again, after a brooding silence I hadn't dared to break, it was of his mother.

"You know, it's funny. I've been trying to picture her, my mother. I suppose I haven't in some time. And I can only see her crying."

"Did she cry a lot?" I was intrigued. This was the closest Noam had come to revealing an emotional underside.

"I can't say I recall her crying much. In fact, I remember her as being quite a cheerful sort of person. She used to sing a lot of light opera around the house, when she was vacuuming and cooking." He closed his eyes. "But I keep seeing her sitting at our kitchen table, crying. And it's a much younger version of herself."

"Younger than what?"

"Well, than when I was a man, when she died."

"Perhaps she cried a lot when you were a boy. Perhaps you were a very nasty little boy."

"Oh no, I was quite good, I think. I don't remember her ever having gotten angry at me." From which you infer there was never anything at which to get angry? A very sloppy deduction for one of the world's greatest logicians.

"Maybe it was the miscarriages," he said suddenly.

"What miscarriages? How many?" He was an only child.

"Oh, I don't know. I vaguely remember that she had quite a few. Someone mentioned them to me when I was much older. Perhaps my father. Apparently she took them very hard." He smiled slightly. "She thought probably all the babies would have been mathematically gifted, that either she or my father was carrying something in their genes."

"A genius-gene."

"Yes," he said. "A genius-gene."

I tried but failed to extract more details of this woman, who suddenly emerged real and rather tragic, sitting at her Formica kitchen table, weeping for her dead geniuses.

In general I didn't have to work to get Noam to speak. He usually did most of the talking, and on his chosen subjects. Every time I put forth an idea he'd regard it with his intense concentration, asking me whether I had meant thesis one, two or three by my remark. Very little that I had to say merited such consideration, so I learned to say little. Besides, it was a joy to listen to him, speaking on the most complicated of topics in the simplest of terms. I sometimes pictured his mind as a perfectly tempered knife, moving with awesome speed, paring away the fatty irrelevancies and unimportant gristle, carving up questions at their precise joints. It was exciting for both of us when I'd understand his point, follow the proof. He liked teaching me math, and he is a wonderful teacher. (All my loves have loved teaching me. I'm such a smart little girl.) There was one trivially practical hurdle. Noam finds it almost impossible to talk to someone without that adhesive eye contact, and I find it almost impossible to drive without watching the road. At times Noam, quite unconsciously, would stick his head right over the steering wheel in an effort to catch my gaze. (He's done this when I'm cooking, too, placing his head right over the pot. Once the results were so serious that he had to be brought to the university infirmary.) At this point I'd pull off the road onto the shoulder, where we could talk, or rather Noam could talk and I listen.

The day he spoke to me about the supernatural numbers I had to pull off the road. We were driving along Canal Road in Griggstown, a few miles north of Princeton, a lovely shaded way that runs alongside the old Raritan Canal. I parked right beside the water, which was covered with delicate pale green algae-lace. We left the car and walked to a little white wooden bridge straddling the canal, beside an ancient stone house, still occupied. We sat there on the bridge, and Noam talked to me of his creations.

Actually, Noam regards them not as creations but as discoveries. He holds, as so many great mathematicians have, the Platonist point of view. For him mathematical truths are descriptions of a suprasensible reality, an objective reality that exists independent of our perceptions of it. The moons of Jupiter were circling in their orbits before Galileo put the telescope to his eye, Noam said once, and mathematical truths are there for the mathematicans to see. (*How* see? Through what faculty? Spinoza said the eyes of the mind are proofs, but Noam regards proofs more in the way of spectacles, bringing the visions of intuition into sharper focus.) Anyway, whether they are creations or not, Noam loves the supernaturals.

"I've probably discovered just as important and interesting things since them, but they were my first. When I was very young, before I was two—I know because it was one of my mother's stock stories —I used to count my way up into the millions. I was so excited by there being all those numbers, an unending supply. I can still remember it, it's my earliest memory." (Mine is of getting burned by someone's cigarette.) "I wanted to hit a number no one else ever had, to be the first to get to it." He laughed. "And then, you know, with the supernaturals I really did it. A whole new realm, beyond any of the others." His voice was uncharacteristically soft. "Numbers so big. A beautiful vast infinity of them, waiting there in the great solemn silence, waiting there for me."

We were quiet for a while. I was thinking about the unlikely places in which one can stumble on poetry. I can't report what Noam was thinking, for I haven't the novelist's privileged access to other minds.

Finally I asked him, "Did you name them the supernaturals?"

"Yes, of course. And I worked out most of the important theorems about them."

"There at the soda fountain?"

"There at the soda fountain. They're mine, or at least about as much mine as a piece of mathematical reality can be. They're often called "the Himmel numbers," but I dislike the human presumption of that. It's okay to name theorems after mortals; after all theorems are only our descriptions, they are our creations. But the objects themselves are a different story entirely."

THERE WERE ONLY TWO topics on which I felt I had something enlightening to say to Noam. The first was human behavior. Noam confessed to bewilderment about the motivations of most people most of the time, and he listened in those days with interest to my attempts to characterize individuals and interpret their actions. We tended to like and dislike the same personal qualities, sharing an overriding horror of what we dubbed the "peacocks," a rather common Princeton species (though more plentiful in some disciplines than others), always strutting and posturing and looking around to verify the impression they make on others. Noam hated peacocking when he saw it, but I was better at detecting it.

The other topic on which Noam listened to me as if to a superior was art. Noam has a passion for music, particularly Mozart. He's perfected his whistling to the point, he claims, of obviating any need to learn an instrument. He used to perform quite often for me, whistling entire sonatas and symphonies. Sometimes he would stick to the score, his precise memory of which was truly astounding; other times he would indulge himself in his own variations.

But he has no interest in visual aesthetics, in art or nature itself. Whenever I'd point out some natural scene, he'd glance and nod and continue talking. One afternoon we walked together through the university's McCormick Museum. Noam displayed the same aesthetic apathy, barely glancing at the pictures, while he recounted for me the story of how non-Euclidean geometry had accidentally been discovered through attempts to prove the parallels postulate (that parallel lines never meet) through the indirect method of proof, that is, by taking its negation together with the other Euclidean postulates and deriving a contradiction. But instead of a contradiction several mathematicians had independently derived consistent non-Euclidean geometries. This was a revolutionary event, overturning fundamental conceptions of math and confuting the prevailing Kantian view of space.

"Listen, Noam," I finally said as we stood before a large Pearlstein nude, "this is fascinating, but I can't concentrate on what you're saying and the pictures at the same time."

"Then let's leave." When we were once again outside, he said, "I'm sorry, Renee. I have no appreciation for art, no feel for it at all."

"It's hard for me to understand, Noam. How can you not appreciate art? You love music so much."

"But the two are so different. There's no logical development in art the way there is in music. A picture is just there, static, all given at once. Oh, some things are very pretty, you know, sunsets and flowers—you are extraordinarily pretty—and pictures of pretty things are pretty, too. And I can appreciate the technical facility involved in executing a work of art. I'm really quite awed by people who can do that. I can't draw anything, not a simple face. I have no sense of what to put in and what to leave out. But that's about as far as my critical evaluation extends. I don't know what you're supposed to be looking for in a picture, what's supposed to hold your attention."

"Don't you see, Noam?" I was pretty amazed by his lacking intuitions I considered elementary. "The world isn't simply given to us as it is. It's given to us from within the points of view we each occupy, points of view that condition the way the world looks to us. In certain respects the appearances are probably alike for all of us, just because of the way things objectively are and the way the mind works. But then there are the interpersonal differences. One's special attributes color and shape the world one ends up seeing. The interesting thing about art is you're being presented with another's point of view, looking out at the world from his perspective, seeing the dreaminess of Renoir's world, the clarity of Vermeer's, the solemnity of Rembrandt's, the starkness of Wyeth's."

"That's an interesting way of approaching it, though you're not going to get another's viewpoint as a bare uninterpreted given any more than you get anything else as a bare uninterpreted given. Your perception of his perception is going to be conditioned by your own outlook. But anyway, that's an interesting way of looking at art."

"It's not an interesting way of looking at art. It *is* art." Noam's apathetic ignorance encouraged this outburst of pomposity. It was a rare treat for me to play the authority, even if it did involve a little dishonesty. For I had little confidence in my simplistic pronouncement, am skeptical, in fact, of any statements pretending to say what art is. (How, asked Wittgenstein, can one define "games"? Is there any property all games must share in order to be games? Or are games linked rather in a network of similarities, akin to family resemblance, where some family members have the same nose, some the same walk, some the same temperament?) What I was stating was only my own preoccupation (and not only in matters artistic) with the subtle, pervasive contributions of subjectivity and the different worlds we each occupy as a result.

"Well," Noam answered, smiling at me, "I'll have to take your word for it. If that's art, I can see why it's never interested me at all. I'm just not interested in the qualities of appearances, mine or anybody else's. It's the reality out there, not as it appears from within any point of view, but as it *is* from no point of view at all, that interests me."

But if Noam wasn't particularly interested in the world-as-it-is-for-Himmel, I was. The fact that my account of our courtship is primarily intellectual is no accident. The great attraction for me, of course, was Noam's mind, and the pleasure I had in contemplating the rigor and purity of its executions. And to think that now I was included in the contents of that inestimable consciousness, that the faculties that had apprehended the supernaturals and other *himmlische* marvels should now be preoccupied with thoughts of me. For they were, you know, quite raptly focused on me. Here was a man who had never had to make any effort outside his superhuman exertions in the mathematical sphere. Even the five or six love affairs of his past seemed, from the little he had to tell me (again, he wasn't unwilling to give me details—he simply didn't have them), to have never come about through his own initiative. He was quite content to let himself be seduced (were they all genius-groupies? I wondered), though the idea would probably never have occurred to him on his own.

But that spring he did exert himself in nonmathematical matters, in the matter of me. He wanted me. I would like to make clear what that meant to me, a person of dubious substantiality. Often it had seemed to me that my existence was as ephemeral as the objects in Berkeley's metaphysics; that, like them, my *esse* is *percipi*, my being a function of others' perception. I am thought of, therefore I am. And now I was the object of an adoring attention, not just in *any* mind, but one superior to almost all others. Would I ever again require statements testifying to my existence and worth?

Toward the end of June, Noam had to go to a conference in Vancouver for two weeks. He called me every night, and we held long transcontinental conversations. The evening he returned we ate dinner in my room in the Graduate College. Before he had quite finished his chocolate mousse Noam got up very suddenly, knocking his chair backwards. He stood there in confusion for several seconds, staring down at the chair as if trying to place it. Then he rushed over to me and threw his arms around me, rather awkwardly, as I was still holding a spoonful of mousse.

"I love you, Renee, I love you. Marry me. Please marry me."

Noam Himmel that spring was a thirty-eight-year-old boy drunk on love for the first time. You might say that our relationship soured as he sobered.

3

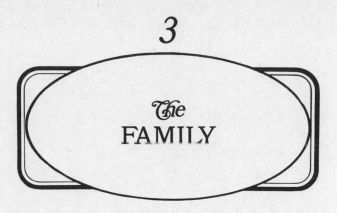

The
FAMILY

Thus suddenly an object has appeared which has stolen the world from me. Everything is in place; everything still exists for me; but everything is traversed by an invisible flight and congealed in the direction of a new object. The appearance of the Other in the world corresponds therefore to a congealed sliding of the whole universe.

—JEAN PAUL SARTRE,
BEING AND NOTHINGNESS

One hour after Noam's proposal and my immediate and euphoric acceptance, I was standing out on the golf course in front of the Graduate College searching the darkened skies for three stars. Let me explain.

The minute Noam proposed to me I wanted to tell my mother. That was about the second or third thought that flashed through my triumphant head. (Can thoughts go faster than the speed of light? I wonder.) Not that my mother and I are that close. Quite the contrary. But I very much wanted to tell someone the news, someone who would consider it momentous. And my mother, who had greeted each announcement of my educational plans with "Nu, Renee, is this going to help you find a husband?" so that the consequence of all my academic honors, Phi Beta Kappa, *summa cum laude*, scholarships, fellowships, prizes, was only a deepening sense of guilty failure; my mother, who had always taught me that a woman is who she marries, that "There's more than one hole a man has to fill in a woman": my mother was such a person. Noam had proposed to me on a Saturday evening. My mother would not answer the phone until three stars were visible, indicating that the skies had truly darkened and Shabbos was over. That night in June, Shabbos wasn't over until after nine.

"*Gute voch,*" she answered the phone. The Yiddish phrase means "good week."

"Hi, Mom, it's me."

"Renee! *Gevalt!* Is something wrong? What's the matter?"

"No, Mom, what makes you say that?"

"Well, here you are calling a minute after *Havdalah,* so anxious." (*Havdalah* is a ceremony that uses wine, a candle and sweet-smelling spices to bid farewell to the Sabbath. The word literally means division—the division of the Sabbath from the rest of the week, of the sanctified from the secular.) "Of course, maybe you didn't know it was a minute after *Havdalah.* Maybe you didn't even know that today was Shabbos?"

"Sure, Mom, I knew. I just came in from counting the stars."

"Renee darling, you're keeping Shabbos?"

"No, Mom, I just knew it would be futile to try and call you too early."

"Nu, so at least you still remember a little something. If you still remember, there's hope."

"Listen, Mom, I have something to tell you."

"I'm listening."

"I'm getting married."

A gasp. Then: *"Oy gevalt!"* Then the question: "Is he Jewish?"

Sadistically, I paused several seconds before answering her. "Yes, Mom. He's Jewish."

Total silence. I couldn't even detect any breathing.

"Mom, are you still there?"

"Yes, of course, Renee, I'm here. When isn't your mother here? I'm just a little speechless with surprise. A daughter calls me up out of the blue, I don't know *how* long it's been, and tells me she's getting married. I don't even know she's going with someone. How *should* I know? So I'm surprised."

"Aren't you happy? Isn't this what you always wanted?"

"Yes, of course I'm happy. Of course this is what I always wanted."

But she didn't sound all that happy. All that anxiety over whether and whom I would marry should, one might have thought, have made this moment one of great jubilation. A giant hosanna ought to be swelling out of the phone. I had pictured my mother—a little woman, barely five feet tall, dark and very thin, for she can't eat when she's worried, which means she averages maybe one good meal a week—bursting out into *Hallel,* the song of praise to God, in which He is called by every good name in the Hebrew vocabulary. How had I failed her this time? What maternal expectations was I once again in the process of thwarting?

And then I understood, saw it as I had never seen it before. My mother's whole life is devoted to worry. In the last few years she had been consumed in despair about two things: Would my brother's wife, Tzippy, who had been trying to have a child for two years, never succeed? And would her prodigal daughter, Renee, remain forever single (I was, after all, an overripe and bruised twenty-two), or worse, marry a *goy?* These were big, satisfying worries, requiring constant attention.

Then a few weeks ago she had learned that Tzippy was pregnant, and now I was calling to tell her that I'm marrying. A Jew yet. No wonder she sounded wounded. We children had callously deprived her life of its substance and meaning. She was holding the telephone receiver and staring down into the existential abyss.

"Of course I'm happy," she repeated weakly. "Overjoyed. Tell me, what is the young man like? What does he do? Don't tell me he's also a philosopher." Do tell me, do tell me, her voice was begging.

"He's a mathematican."

"A mathematician? From numbers he makes a living?" Her voice gathered some strength.

"Yes, Mom. He's famous. He's one of the greatest living mathematicians. He's a genius. He was written up in *Life* magazine." This is true. When Harvard had offered Noam an appointment at age twenty, *Life* had done a story on "the youngest American professor."

"Really? A famous genius? *Life* magazine? This is really something then. This is real *yiches.*" (*Yiches* is prestige.) "You should be very proud, Renee, that such a man should love you. Of course, I know you're not just any girl. Who should know if not me? This is why God gave you such good brains, so that you could make such a man like this love you. I only wish your father were alive today to hear such news."

So did I. God, how I wished it. He would have been genuinely delighted. Everything that he was was genuine. My father. How to describe him in an age whose face is set in a knowing Freudian smirk? Can anyone accept without interpretation a daughter's love for her male parent? But almost everyone, at least everyone who had the slightest bit of good in him at all, had loved my father. Why should I be excluded just because of my incriminating relationship with him? These words, "I loved Reuven Feuer," in anybody's mouth but mine, reflect well on the speaker, revealing a susceptibility to the power of goodness. Why in my mouth alone must they be interpreted in terms of infantile sexuality? A faithful description of my father would contain adjectives like "saintly" and "heroic." How can I protect such a description from analysis?

My father had been a cantor, a *chazzen,* a sweet singer of Israel, as it says in Hebrew on his tombstone. His pure, sweet song was like a picture of his soul. Snatches of *chazzanes* would escape from him

57

all day long, pieces of the internal singing that must have been almost constant with him. He had loved his work in all its aspects: chanting the prayers on behalf of the community, comforting the sick and the sad, instructing the boys in preparation for their bar mitzvahs. His teaching powers were legendary. He was sent all the unteachable boys from around Westchester County—the retarded, the disturbed, the hyperactive. Each yielded to his softness and managed to be bar mitzvahed.

From the external point of view, however, the details of my father's position were pretty dismal. He was scandalously underpaid. In fact, the cantor who was hired after my father's death was given more than twice the salary for doing less. Life in that wealthy community had been hard for us. (I wasn't just the lone Jewish kid in my class. I was also the only poor one.) And there was more, far more, than the mere economic hardships of my father's job. But I won't dwell on the dirty details. My father never did. He soared above it all, leaving my mother and me below to feel the humiliation.

My father's lack of ambition was an acid eating at my mother's life: "I can't understand your father. That such a man, with such a head, such an education, should be content to be a little *chazzen,* to put up with what he puts up with in that community. You should see when we go to the *chazzanes* conventions what kind of people are there. Such plain uneducated *pruste Yiddin.*" (Roughly: vulgar Jews.) "Your father stands out among them like a stallion among the swine, you should excuse the expression. But he's content."

The last line was always delivered in a profoundly accusatory tone. (I think it was while listening to my mother complaining about my father that the image of the mattering map first occurred to me. I know it's been a feature of the internal landscape for a long time.) And there's no denying that the man was supremely content, all in all the happiest person I've known. And he maintained his sweet outlook through his final terrible illness. One of the more illustrious members of his congregation said to me, as we watched my father limping in great pain up to his place on the *bimah* shortly before his death, "There's not a man I envy more."

He was born in Borstav, a little *shtetl* in Galicia, where his father was rabbi and his mother the town beauty. (Around Easter, pogrom time in Poland, she would have to go into hiding. Being the rabbi's wife, and beautiful besides, she was prime rape material.) My father's two brothers loved to tell the story of how the Cossacks would come thundering into town and scoop my father, a little boy with long banana-curl *payess* tucked behind his ears, up onto their horses, and have him sing in his sweet boy's soprano. They roared with laughter at the incomprehensible Yiddish songs—some of which poked fun at the drinking and other habits of the *goyim*. The kid was sweet, but he had a sense of humor.

One of my uncles, Sol, the oldest, left for America and slaved in New York several years until he could bring the rest of the family over. Only one sister remained behind, Raizel, who was also a great beauty, with the delicate-featured blondness of my grandmother. (My father too was fair, with high pronounced cheekbones—very good-looking in his gentle manner, although I suppose you'll find this description also suspect.) A very rich man from a neighboring village had seen Raizel at the marketplace and sent the *shadchen*—the professional matchmaker—over to my grandfather's house. The *shadchen* had laughed when he heard the dowry Raizel's family could offer. "We'll forget the dowry for now." So she was the only one left behind. The family tried to get her out when the Nazis came, but it was impossible. She died at Auschwitz with her rich husband and five children.

My father had been a student of German literature. He had gotten his master's degree from City University and was studying for his doctoral exams. But one of the very minor casualties of the news from Europe was his love of German culture. He didn't even like speaking the language after that. He fell back on his fine tenor to support his family.

Sometimes my father would tell me about his coming to America in that detached, amused way in which he spoke about himself. The older brother, already Americanized, had wanted my father, who was ten, and his brother, who was eight, to go to public school, to learn English faster. The school was primarily Irish and Italian.

"When I walked into the classroom, with my *payess* down to my shoulders, you should have seen how they looked at me. If looks could kill, I wouldn't be here laughing now."

The teacher put him next to the only other Jewish boy, thinking they would understand one another.

"He spoke as much Yiddish as I spoke English. I glanced at him, such a puny little thing. He wasn't going to be any help at protecting me from those hoodlums."

Sure enough, as soon as school was over that day, they all gathered round to take turns punching him.

"When I arrived home, my father took one look at me and said: 'We're putting him into a yeshiva.' "

The following Sunday my father and his younger brother went to a neighborhood park. This brother, Izzy, was as tough as my father wasn't. (He now lives in Houston and is supposed to be quite rich.)

"There were two games going on, baseball and soccer. Since we were from Europe, of course we went to watch the soccer. And who should also be watching but the hoodlums from the public school. They saw me and wanted to repeat the fun. Let's run, I said to Izzy. Let's fight, said Izzy. When they saw he wanted to fight they all fell on him, and he was happily swinging away when I noticed suddenly that one of them had taken out a knife. I was a *chazzen*-to-be, and we *chazzonim* have our own defenses. I hit a high G. Believe me, it was the note of my life. People started running toward us and the bullies ran away."

It was a rare treat when my father spoke about himself. There were so many things I had always wanted to know about him. I wondered if he had struggled to arrive at his moral level or had been born there. I spent a lot of time puzzling over the question of which—the struggle or lack of it—would make him the better man. Many ethicists, following Kant, opt for the struggle: those who are naturally good aren't really good. Yet the striving after moral perfection requires a concern for one's self: one has to want one's self to be good. And it seemed that even this sort of self-interest was incompatible with the nature of my father's pure goodness. This paradox was, and still is, very confusing to me. But on the few occasions when I overcame my shyness and tried to ask him about himself, he didn't get the point of my questions. (Though, natural teacher that he was, he rarely did fail to understand another's perplexity.) It wasn't simply that he didn't think of himself as good. He didn't think of himself at all.

I always worried about my father. When I was a child, I would run upstairs to my bedroom window when he left the house. I would strain to keep him in my sight, trying to watch over him. I knew that goodness suffered in a bad world. Yet he managed to get down the street unharmed. Only at the very end, in the last year and a half of his life, did he suffer terribly, when the cancer spread into the bones of his legs. It was as if they were fractured, the doctor told us, urging us to try and get him to keep off them. But my father was determined to continue working as long as he could, doing what he loved: comforting the sick, teaching his boys, praying for the community. The six-block walk to the synagogue took him forty-five minutes on Shabbos, when it's forbidden to ride. He would go not just for the morning prayers, but for the evening service as well, back and forth, four times, leaning heavily on his cane. Finally the disease invaded his liver, and he had to go into the hospital. He had one more bar mitzvah to prepare, a difficult case. He died immediately after, having assisted his last boy through the token acceptance of manhood.

We heard so many stories the week we sat *shivah*, observing the rituals of mourning. People now felt that they could tell what my father had done for them, the secret acts of charity, the advice that had averted the disaster, saved the marriage, brought the child back home. His was a life built out of quiet words and gentle acts. "The *shtickele chazzen*" I had heard members of my mother's family call him: the little (in a sense implying insignificant) cantor. But the *shtickele chazzen* was a hero, although, like all heroes, you had to be standing in the right place on the mattering map to perceive the dimensions of his greatness.

My father had deserved to have at least one child like him, but all he had was my brother and me. Avram is three years my junior, and, though born in Westchester, he has all the mannerisms of the *shtetl*. Dressed in black suit and hat (the standard uniform of the ultra-Orthodox), the fringed white tassels of his *tzitzith* trailing behind him (all Orthodox males are required to wear these tasseled undergarments beneath their shirts, but people like my brother let it all hang out), he might just have stepped off the boat. He even talks with a Yiddish accent, waving his hands about in the wild gesticulations of Talmudic discourse. Though he used to speak perfect English and play baseball, he now makes the grammatical errors of an Eastern

European immigrant, and is round-shouldered from the hours spent hunched over a Gemara. (The Gemara, written in Babylonia, is the commentary on the Mishnah, which is the compilation of the laws and sayings of the rabbis—part of the oral tradition until written down. The Mishnah and Gemara together compose the Talmud, the primary study material for those who "sit and learn.") Although, like our father, he's passionately religious, the passion—and the religion—are entirely different. His is all anger and hate. Every other word out of his mouth is "pagan." The *goyim* are pagans. The irreligious Jews are pagans. I, of course, am a pagan.

"You're a heretic, a pagan, wallowing in pagan *shmutz.*" *Shmutz* is filth. I noticed that his ears still get red when he gets emotional. "You're a *shiksa,* an idol worshiper."

Of the last charge, at least, I felt innocent. "Avram, I'm not an idol worshiper."

"You are."

"I'm not."

"Are."

"Not." It was nice to see we could still fall easily into the dialogues of our childhood. "I don't worship anything."

"You worship nothing?"

"Yes, I suppose."

"Nothing!" he concluded in triumph. "You worship nothing! That's your god, your idol! Nothingness!"

I urged him to take a course in formal logic so he could see the fallacy of his reasoning, but he just continued to gloat, his ears now red with glee over his sophistical victory. He probably keeps a scorecard: Religion: ———, Philosophy: ———. And he never perceives himself as losing the argument.

Avram, favoring my mother's side of the family, is dark and . . . well, puny. I must admit that my father and his people weren't very big, either. My long legs were among the items in my adolescent catalogue of guilt-provoking personal attributes. I felt like such an overdeveloped Amazon, towering over my mother and brother, involuntarily displaying my physical superiority. Although my interior is unmistakably Jewish, I have an exterior that would have inspired a poster for Hitler Youth. My mother often remarked, throughout my childhood and adolescence, that she couldn't think where I had gotten my looks from. I remember once, when I was about fourteen, she said that, and I was pierced by the terrible thought that perhaps I was a corporeal throwback to some brutally Jew-hating gentile who had long ago raped one of my forebears.

When my brother was eighteen he asked his *rebbe*, who is something like his guru, to find him a wife. The *rebbe* appeared with Tzipporah, a sweet-faced girl of seventeen, who taught first grade at the yeshiva in the Boro Park section of Brooklyn from which she had recently graduated. None of the teachers there had attended college. They were mostly graduates of the school, who taught until they got married and pregnant, returning after the birth to support their husband's "sitting." (The word "yeshiva" comes from the Hebrew for "sitting.")

In my habit of endlessly comparing the various worlds I've occupied, I've given much thought to the variety of forms that women's oppression takes. While liberated specimens among her goyish counterparts struggle against the myth of helplessness and the tradition of dependence, the Orthodox *ayshes chayul* (woman of worth) is traditionally the sole support of her (very large) family. (Contraception is strictly forbidden.) *Her* liberation wouldn't require her being freed from a dollhouse or lifted off a pedestal. As her lucky husband can, if he chooses, sing to her from the prayer book on Friday nights, before he sits down to the Shabbos meal she has prepared for him:

> She is like the merchant ships—
> She brings her food from afar.
> She rises while it is yet night,
> And gives food to her household . . .
> She considers a field and buys it;
> With her earnings she plants a vineyard.
> She girds herself with strength
> And braces her arms for work.
> She finds that her trade is profitable;
> Her lamp goes not out at night . . .
> Her husband is known at the gates,
> As he sits among the elders of the land.

The roles are reversed, but only along one dimension. Hers is still the indisputably inferior position in those matters that matter in this society: the spiritual and intellectual, which are one and the same. (It's no accident that Spinoza, *apikoros* though he was, identified the state of human blessedness with the "intellectual love of God," which is a noetic state, approaching total knowledge, knowing what is truly what.) For Jews learning is the highest spiritual activity, but one from which women are barred. And what, I once asked my mother, does Judaism offer its females in the way of spiritual experiences? At the top of her list was going to *mikvah*, the ritual bath that's a monthly requirement for married Orthodox women. (For the men: Talmud and logic, while the women try to clean up their bloody messes.) In a world where personal merit is measured in the number of pages of the Talmud one has mastered, power doesn't rest in bringing home the kosher beef fry. Ask the *ayshes chayul.*

Avram and Tzippy met once, approved one another, met again, and got married. Tzippy looked terribly pale being led to her wedding canopy, her lips moving in prayer. When she reached my brother's side, they glanced quickly at each other. After the ceremony the women took Tzippy into a little room and cut her long, thick brown hair, replacing it with a *sheitel,* or wig. She had a wonderful time, though, at the dinner celebration afterwards. Men and women sat on separate sides of the *mechitzah,* the physical boundary placed between men and women, in this case a six-foot-high white fence covered with fake greenery. In between the endless courses there was wild Chasidic dancing on both sides. A little band of two clarinets and an accordion played the songs of the Eastern European *shtetl.* The men did the kazatska and cartwheels, making up with exuberance what they lacked in grace. The women danced with more restraint, in complicated circular patterns. There was a bullfight, one of the girls, fingers held up as horns, charging into the napkin flourished by another. Tzippy danced in the center of the women, her partners constantly changing: her mother and mother-in-law, her grandmother and four sisters, the many sweet-faced friends. I too got to dance with the bride. The friends brought out a jump rope, and Tzippy and they played. The men lifted Avram on a chair, the women held up little Tzippy, and they danced around with the two of them. At one point each took hold of a corner of a handkerchief over the *mechitzah* and laughed shyly into each other's face as they were held aloft. I watched them and was filled with disgust at my own life, which, in the glow of their purity, seemed dirty and sordid. I often think of Tzippy as she was that night, a little child-bride with the absurdly mature wig, giggling with her friends, dancing shyly with her new in-laws, jumping rope.

Poor little Tzippy. Six months after her wedding, in her tenth week of pregnancy, she had a miscarriage. Another followed four months later, again in her tenth week. And after that she had been unable to conceive. On one of the rare occasions when I went to visit them in their little two-room Lakewood apartment, right off Yeshiva Plaza, Tzippy brought me into the tiny dark bedroom and closed the door.

"I have to talk to someone. I know why I'm having all this *tsuris*. I got angry at your brother soon after our wedding and I said terrible things to him."

"Oh?" It was not without pleasure that I imagined my righteous brother being called down a bit by little Tzippy. "What was it all about?"

"A great big nothing." She blushed the deep pink of the bedspreads. Sex, I thought. That's why she thinks she's getting this particular punishment. "Stupid, really, my fault completely. But the things I said! They were terrible. I've never spoken to anyone that way, and to my own husband I spoke like that! This must be why I'm being punished, why I'm a barren woman."

"Oh, Tzippy, of course it isn't." I put my arms around her shoulders. I was startled to feel how slight they were, like a child's. But then she was a child, this barren woman. She was crying without noise.

"What else could it be? I've searched my memory over and over. I can't think what else I've done."

"Why think it's because you've done anything? Why think it's a punishment at all?"

"What else?" She pulled back out of my arms to look into my face with surprise. *"Der Aybishder"*—the Everlasting—"wouldn't be doing this for no reason. But one thing I haven't been able to figure out. Your brother suffers because I'm barren. Why should he be made to suffer for my *averah?*" (An *averah* is a sin.) "It must be because I'm his responsibility. He's responsible for my *averah*. That's what's so hard. My poor Avram."

And now sweet Tzippy was pregnant. She had called me the day she found out, laughing and crying. We waited until she was past the critical tenth week, and out of the first trimester altogether, before telling my mother. We wanted to spare my mother the worry. Which brings me back to my mother. And her worry.

All mothers worry. Jewish mothers worry more. But my mother can find something to worry about in anything. No topic is innocent. In some way, direct or Talmudically indirect, some danger to her family might be lurking. "It's her way of loving. Try to understand," my father would tell me when I'd come complaining about something I'd been forbidden to join my friends in doing: going to the beach (the undertow); tennis (sunstroke); hiking in the woods (sex maniacs). Her worrying is, like all the best thinking, vigorous but subtle. Every possibility is followed through and analyzed. And she is knowledge-able, too, admirably informed on current events: local, state, national, international—for all could adversely affect her family. She watches the news on television from four in the afternoon until eight in the evening, and then again from ten until twelve. If the phone rings at eight I know who is calling, to tell me to get rid of my house plants (a four-year-old has died from nibbling on a castor oil plant), not to answer the door (a man-and-son team has raped three women in northern New Jersey), not to make any plans to visit Seattle (a geologist has predicted that Mt. Rainier could go off sometime in the next twenty-five years). She reads the New York *Times,* the New York *Post,* the *Daily News,* the local Westchester paper, and a certain tabloid expression of Jewish paranoia published in Brooklyn (typical headline: COPS SECRETLY ARMING BROOKLYN BLACKS TO RISE AGAINST JEWS). I am always getting clippings in the mail.

My mother has probably worried about my virginity since the moment the doctor announced I was a girl (and after she had prayed for nine months for the blessing of a male firstborn). Our relation-ship, which was never very good, changed drastically for the worse when I hit puberty at around eleven. I looked old for my age, and it was a couple of years before my psyche caught up to my body. My mother, no dualist, held me responsible for the overdevelopment.

"Stop it," she would hiss as we walked down the street to do the shopping.

"Stop what, Mommy?"

"Stop walking like that. Don't you see everyone is staring at you? You're embarrassing me."

She was embarrassed? Was everyone really looking and laughing at me? What was I doing wrong? I tried to concentrate on my gait. It seemed to me that I was walking as I always had . . .

"Stop it," she hissed in our kitchen, having lured me out of our living room where we were entertaining guests.

"Stop what, Mommy?"

"The way you're sitting. It's disgusting. Don't you see the way the Levine's son is gaping at you, the dirty boy? But then you have to expect that from boys. They'll get what they can, a look or more. It's *your* fault. I'm ashamed of you."

She was ashamed? If only I could figure out what I was doing wrong. What had happened to me? There used to be no problems with my walking and sitting . . .

"But, Mommy, I can't help it. I'm not trying to do anything wrong."

We were walking home together from Saturday morning services, my father and Avram ahead, my mother and I behind. She was berating me for the attention she accused me of having attracted in *shul.*

"Bobby Grossman, Frank Nassman, Eli Gherkoff, they all couldn't take their eyes off you. And I saw them laughing together. What am I going to do with you?" Her voice sounded desperate.

Laughing together, about *me?* Those big high school boys? And *she* was desperate? Hot throbbing waves of humiliation swept up from my feet to my head.

"Mommy, tell me what I'm doing wrong. Tell me what I should be like."

"What you should be like? You should be a modest, clean Jewish girl who doesn't attract any dirty thoughts. You should be like Ruth Kornblit and Frances Spitzer, refined and *edel.*"

If you tried to guess the meaning of the word *edel* from the two girls my mother held up as examples, you might arrive at the conclusion that it means pathetically homely. (It doesn't. It means modest and refined.) Ruth had greasy, stringy hair and skin covered by pimples in various stages of development. Frances's face, poor thing, was three-fourths occupied by nose. Both held their shoulders rolled forward, although it was clear neither had anything to hide. But certainly my mother didn't mean I should be ugly or have bad posture. It was their souls she was talking about.

"You don't see any boys staring at Ruth and Frances, do you?" she demanded. I knew she was wishing that I wasn't her daughter, that she was the mother of *edel* Ruth or Frances.

As I got older she worried that the worst was soon to happen, or, God forbid! already had, but she didn't give up. She got more subtle, but persevered, collecting stories of the misfortunes that befell girls who had no morals. Having morals means not having "anything to do" with anyone but one's husband, and not until he is one's husband. I remember mentioning to her once that I was taking a course in moral philosophy at Barnard. She had looked at me queerly. How could there be a whole course on *that?* It was a mistake to mention the class to her; it became her primary obsession for the duration of the semester. Obviously the professor was saying a whole lot more than that a girl should have morals. Whatever he was saying, it couldn't be good.

"I'm only afraid, Renee, that with all your so-called intellectualizing, you're only going to end up rationalizing doing things you shouldn't even think about."

If her normative ethics consists of this one simple proposition, "Girls should have morals," her metaethical theory is somewhat more complex. It's a mixture of intuitionist absolutism ("What do you *mean* what makes it wrong? It's wrong. Anyone can see it's wrong") and utilitarianism ("Men, they squeeze the orange and then they throw it away").

But really the attempt to compress my mother's views into a consistent theory doesn't do justice to her style of thinking. She has a Quinean attitude toward logic: logic is disposable. In fact, she's done Quine one better and has already disposed of it. It's no good demonstrating the logical inconsistency of something she's said. Her response is always to say, irritably or indulgently, depending on her feeling about me at the time, "Oh, there you go with your philosophy again." She seems to think my concern with consistency is like a dressmaker's interest in fabric or a beautician's in hair: a result of my narrow professional concerns.

During my four years at Barnard her life had been full. What wasn't there to worry about with a daughter living alone in New York City? ("Mom, I don't live alone. I live in a dorm with hundreds of other girls." "And how many live in your room?") She could rattle off crime statistics like a police spokeswoman or a politician trying to get elected with a stop-crime campaign. (Subway crime was her specialty.) I thought she'd be overjoyed to learn that I was moving out of the jungle and into the pastureland of Princeton. A few days later I got a clipping in the mail: ANTI-SEMITIC INCIDENTS ON THE RISE: NEW JERSEY LEADS THE NATION.

But the night I stood out there on the golf course counting the stars, I couldn't wait to speak to her. This would be one conversation we would move through together, hearts and minds as one. I was deflated when I finally hung up the phone. I still wanted that exultant conversation I had imagined and decided to call my friend Ava Schwartz in New York.

Ava had been three years ahead of me at Barnard, where she had come from the Bronx High School of Science. She had decided when she was eleven to become a physicist. ("I happened to ask someone what physicists do and was lucky enough to be given a pretty good answer: they study matter and energy, space and time. I decided right then that was for me.") I suppose I owe you a physical description of some sort, although it's hard for me to see that so familiar face objectively. She's fairly regular-featured, with jowls perhaps a bit too full. She's a big woman, large-boned, not fat, very strong. (She has yet to confront a twist-off cap she couldn't handle.) In college she used to wear a kind of round, monkish haircut, the straight bangs ending just above the eyes. It's the eyes—enormously large and warm and expressive, brown with flecks of gold—that lift the face up above plainness. I think they're the most beautiful eyes I've ever seen.

We had met my first month at Barnard, and it was she who helped me make the leap out of Babylonia.

"I don't know if I ought to tamper with you. You're a find, a perfectly preserved specimen of an ancient civilization. I ought to donate you to the archaeology department."

I was surprised. Compared to the other girls at my high school, I had been daringly liberated. Ava laughed for several minutes when I told her that. She worked hard with me, knocking me over the head with her earthiness, and went so far as to devote a large part of one evening to trying to get me to say "fuck."

We had been sitting in the West End Bar drinking beer and I was telling her a story about something I had heard on the subway. The punch line contained the word "fuck." I hadn't known I wouldn't be able to say it. I had never tried before. We were already silly with beer, and my attempts to get out the single syllable had reduced us both to hysterics.

"Look, say 'truck.'

"Truck."

"Muck."

"Muck."

"Suck."

I regarded her with mock reproach.

"My God, Renee, what a mind you have. Suck a lollipop, suck your thumb. There are other things in the world to suck, you know."

"Okay, suck," I managed to gasp between beery giggles.

"Okay, we're almost there. Now, fuck. Come on, ffff."

"Fffff."

"Fffffuck. You can do it, kid, I know you can. Ffffuck."

"Ffffff."

"That's right, ffffuck. Come on, do it for the other daughters of Israel. Fuck."

"Fffff."

"For your mother, Renee, do it for your mother. Fuck."

"Fffff."

"Fuck."

"Ffffffffudge!"

We collapsed into our beers. "Fudge it" became one of our favorite curses.

"Look, Ava," I finally was able to say. "It's the slippery slope of sin. First you'll have me saying it, then you'll have me doing it."

"Let's hope so. But let's take one step at a time."

Ava took maternal pride in any vulgarities I could handle, in word and deed, during my four years at Barnard. Yet she never really did like the men I chose. Noam was the first she warmed to. Hillel, my first, she couldn't stand.

"A yarmulke," she had wailed. "A whole university stocked with beautiful blond gentiles. From the Midwest we've got them, even. And your first choice is a yarmulke from Brooklyn? A Hillel Schoenfeld?"

"I like Jewish men."

"It's just conditioning. You're conditioned to think of non-Jewish men as *trayf.*"

"They're all *trayf.* This isn't a question of keeping kosher. It's a question of taste. I don't even like blonds. I like them dark and Semitic."

"Well, you got it. Hillel Schoenfeld is definitely dark and Semitic. Did he have to be Orthodox, too? He's as screwed up as you. Probably more, since he's a man. You know what's going to happen, don't you?"

"I hope so." I gave what I intended as a lascivious smile.

"Yeah. And then you're both going to wallow in your dark and Semitic guilt. Go running back to your Gemaras to hide. The best thing for Hillel would be a nymphomaniac Irish girl, and the best thing for you would be someone like Paul."

Paul was Ava's current boyfriend—or perhaps "lay" would be the more precise terminology. She didn't take her men very seriously. Whereas *I* have to make heroes out of my lovers, need to be lying under an *Übermensch,* Ava seems to enjoy looking down on her men, which, given the men she prefers, is an almost unavoidable position to assume. I don't know if my friend is specifically attracted to idiocy or whether the qualities she likes just aren't compatible with much intelligence. In any case, her boyfriends were generally a pretty primitive lot, what she used to call "elementary particles." There were the protons with a large positive charge, the positrons with a small positive charge, the neutrons (neutral), electrons (negative), and peons. Ava never expected too much of them out of bed.

Which is why she and I started laughing at the mention of Paul in this context, since the very night before he himself had tried to convince me that the very thing I needed was a Paul. He was one of the freshman mistakes of the admissions office at Columbia College (Ava had a knack for sniffing them out—they could have used her in admissions). Paul was a disciple of Wilhelm Reich, the psychiatrist and madman, charlatan or hounded genius (depending on your point of view) who thought he had discovered "orgone energy"—the life force, which is released during orgasms, can cure cancer, and is yet one more instance of Einstein's $e = mc^2$. In fact, Reich wrote to Einstein in 1940, identifying himself as having been Freud's assistant at the Polytechnic in Vienna, and reporting his discovery of a "specifically biologically effective energy which behaves in many respects differently to all that is known about electromagnetic energy." He added that it could be "used in the fight against the Fascist pestilence," which was a lure that was impossible for Einstein to resist. Probably anyone else would have been warned off by the letter, which also stated that the monumental finding hadn't been reported to the Academy of Physics because of "extremely bad experience." So Reich pilgrimed to Princeton, together with a little accumulator, to demonstrate his phenomenon to Einstein, who found a rather commonplace explanation for it. ("What else do you do?" he asked.) Einstein's explanation was of course rejected by Reich, who continued to nudge poor Albert for years and privately published the exchanges between them in *The Einstein Affair.*

There was a little enclave of Reichians at Columbia who took the hounded-genius point of view, and Ava's Paul was among them. Three sentences into any conversation with him, and he was telling me about, and staring at, my "pelvic armor," which was restricting the flow of my orgone energy. But he hadn't offered to remove the armor himself until the night before this conversation with Ava.

Many such offers were coming my way. I was the object of much male attention and wasn't exactly comfortable with it. I had just come from an all-girl yeshiva. I wasn't even used to the company of males, aside from my rabbi teachers, father and brother. My new circle of friends, Ava's friends, didn't always make me feel comfortable either. I could of course have chosen to associate with Barnard's coterie of Orthodox Jewish women, who pretty much stick together, keeping behind the invisible *mechitzah* that separates them from the alien environment. (And they're not the only ones.) Only that's not what I had come to Barnard for, for more of the same, and I wasn't getting more of the same with Ava and her friends. But it was hard for me sometimes. I envied the other girls their easy, familiar ways, the way they casually touched men, for example. Where I had just come from there were only two intersexual relationships recognized: potential marriage partner and actual marriage partner.

Hillel Schoenfeld was a graduate student in physics over at Columbia, and he was the teaching assistant for the course in classical mechanics I was taking. (I had begun college with the intention of majoring in physics, thinking that was where the most fundamental questions are asked. That's how my friendship with Ava began—she was thrilled to find another Barnard physics major.) And to me, then, Hillel was the most desirable male imaginable. To a certain extent he was what any Orthodox Jewish Barnard woman wants: Jewish, brilliant, kind, handsome. However: his faith was wavering, and that of course is what made him attractive to me. Ava's talk about *trayf* and kosher wasn't really off target. Hillel wasn't *trayf*, not like the Pauls, who were just unthinkable to me. Hillel was certified kosher. He just wasn't *glatt.*

It's true that Hillel had been wearing a yarmulke (knitted by a previous girlfriend; it's something Orthodox girlfriends do.) But a few weeks after we started seeing each other, off it came. If he was going to sleep with me (and we discussed little else), he would have to give up all elements of belief. He just couldn't tolerate inconsistency.

Still, we took a while to take the big step, months of agonizing, delicious, sex-obsessed temporizing and messing around. After some hesitation I described to Hillel the very strange thing that had been happening to me, a gradual buildup of sensation that would end in a towering peak. He had looked at me incredulously.

"That's an orgasm. You've just described an orgasm." I honestly hadn't known. "That's hard to believe. I thought it could only happen to a woman during intercourse."

Our lack of knowledge was no obstacle to pleasure. Quite the contrary, I think. In truth, I wouldn't want anything about that time changed. Rather, I feel sorry for people brought up with no sense of boundaries (all the better for crossing), for whom the sexual terrain appears as unmarked and open as it perhaps really is. Can they ever share such experiences as Hillel and I shared? The sense that what we were doing was momentous, the exhilaration of breaking through miles and miles of fences: a man can't listen to a woman singing; a male above the age of six and a female above the age of three can't be alone together in a room with the door closed. There are a hundred and one such prohibitions, all of them designed to keep one from penetrating to . . . *this very spot.* A group of us were once drinking at the West End when the conversation turned to Alex Comfort's *The Joy of Sex.* Hillel said that he and I were using the *Kitzur Shulchan Aruch (The Code of Jewish Law)* instead: "We're systematically doing everything it says you shouldn't." (Though, truth to tell, this system wouldn't take one very far into kinkiness. It wasn't SM or bondage the author was concerned with, but rather making love by the light of a candle or by daylight, or holding any conversation during or immediately before "except in matters directly needed for the copulation.")

My relationship with Hillel lasted through the end of my sophomore year. I ended it. Of all the men I've known, I wish I had been, could now be, in love with Hillel. For one thing, and this is no small matter I've since learned, we always understood each other's jokes, perhaps because we both knew what it was to make fun of the *Kitzur Shulchan Aruch* by day and to lie in bed in the dead of night in the stomach-churning anguish of repentance. And in human terms Hillel was the best of them all. But it's never been such factors that determine my (or maybe anyone's) desires. The truth is, my attraction to him flagged, despite my desire to desire him.

Perhaps I still idolize him. And of course there's still a haze of guilt: Do I think he's the best because he's the one I hurt the most? I have to remind myself of his failings, his tendency to ignore my wants in typical Orthodox Jewish male fashion. We did what *he* wanted. And I'm not just talking about deciding on which movie to see. When he decided to move back to a modified form of Orthodoxy, he took for granted that I'd make the move with him. I did. I even went to *mikvah* once, at his urging. For he claimed there really isn't any

Talmudic prohibition against premarital sex, but rather the law is against having relations with an "unclean" woman—one who hasn't purified herself in the *mikvah* of her menstrual blood. Of course, there *is* a law against single women, who have no intention of getting married, going to *mikvah*. But that, urged Hillel, was a more minor interdict than the one we would otherwise be violating. He, as you can see, had a solid Talmudic background.

It was also assumed that we'd get married as soon as he got his doctorate. I didn't tell him (so how was he to know?) how little I wanted to get married, how it had seemed to me that I had just begun to live, and that our relationship, which had been part of that beginning, seemed now to have become the end. Not a word. I couldn't bring myself to stand up to the parental authority he had acquired over me. (He was horrified that I smoked; I quit. He told me which courses to take; I took them and brought him my A's. I made him proud, much prouder than my parents had ever been over the school doings of a girl. My mother, in fact, had always hidden my report cards so that poor Avram wouldn't have to see how much better than him his sister had done.) I also felt—this will give you some idea what an anachronism I was—that I had no choice but to marry Hillel, that I had given myself, in the form of my body, to him.

I came very close to marrying him. I can easily picture the life, in some "modern Orthodox" community—Teaneck, New Jersey, or Silver Spring, Maryland. I'd have children by now; the oldest would be starting the local Hebrew day school. Our friends would be other "modern Orthodox" couples whom we would visit and have over on Shabbos, the highlight of our social life. The men would talk to the men, the women to the women. I can see it very clearly. But my counterfactual vision blurs on the matter of whether I'm happier there than here. (I'm fairly confident that my counterpart there thinks she'd be happier here, in Princeton, married to a genius.)

It was a close, possible world that split off from the actual quite incidentally: My professor in symbolic logic began to make some nonsymbolic gestures, coming out finally with a proposition that went beyond the elementary calculus. Hillel's stature in my eyes diminished sufficiently to allow me to take the step away. What was the parental authority of a former teaching assistant compared to that of ·

75

a current full professor? I joke, but it was a painful break. I had assumed that somehow or other Hillel would remain a part of my life. (Had I known otherwise, would I ever have dared to break off? Dear René, most noble and knowing namesake, surely you erred when you claimed that one knows one's own mind immediately and incorrigibly.) But Hillel told me, in the angry scene that continued to play in my head for months, that the only way he could get over me was to have nothing more to do with me. (I've heard echoes of this since and have reconciled myself to being viewed in terms that sound medical, as something to be gotten over, worked out of the system, like a stomach virus. My former loves never remain my friends. I don't know why, but I know it doesn't speak well for me.) A few weeks later I learned that he was making *aliyah*, moving to Israel. Everyone said I had driven him to it. Oh well, we all do whatever we can for the Zionist state. (Hillel, my love, I'm sorry.)

My professor, Isaac Besdin, and I proceeded to deduce the entailed conclusion in his office on a bleak wintry afternoon. I happened to be suffering from a bad head cold that day, and sex in those circumstances proved interestingly suggestive, with subtle associations drifting just beneath the surface of consciousness. As a consequence, nasal congestion has since carried with it the faint whiff of lubricity.

But the affair that followed brought little joy. I was but a part of Isaac's miserable midlife crisis, the symptom known as the infatuation with the younger woman. He was forty-six years old and coming around to the realization that his life had led to this: to the cold, resentful wife; to the son and daughter pursuing their adolescent rebellion with the same uninspired conformity to the norm as their father was demonstrating in his response to his own life change; and, most painfully, to the unbrilliant career. The conclusion was waiting to be drawn, even if he shrank from its final acknowledgment. The promise of his youth would not be fulfilled, the spark had never caught, the moment for it was over. There would be no fire, and now even the feeble glow of hope was giving out.

His was a misery so large and insatiable that it swallowed me whole (and then he complained that he hadn't tasted much of anything). I was paying the price, without knowing it, of having loved a father too well. But if ever a father had been worth the price, it was mine.

This unwholesome relationship (even *I* could see that) ended when the real father, the perfect father, whom none of these father-lovers could ever approximate, passed away. The grief that ensued, together with the misery of this last liaison, sent me hurdling back toward the life of the mind. (You begin to see a pattern? Mind, body. Body, mind. Memoirs of a dangling woman.) Issues of love and death had turned my mind to philosophy. I switched my major and two years of purity followed, two years of intense intellectual introversion, rewarded upon graduation with every kind of academic honor, including a commitment from a leading journal to publish my senior paper and generous fellowships from every prestigious graduate philosophy department in the country. (None of which really convinced me that I wasn't still a dope, briefly enjoying a lucky spell.)

If my father-substitutes have generally left me wanting (their model being so Platonically ideal), I have been abundantly blessed with a mother-replacement. When Ava graduated (the only physics major Barnard had produced in years), she crossed Broadway to Columbia and continued on for her doctorate. I had her with me until my own graduation.

Ava was given a terrible time on the other side of the street. Her adviser, a Big Name, always referred to as "The Shmuck" in our conversations, was milking her for ideas. He was burnt out, a has-been who knew a good thing when he saw it. He had already gotten seven publications out of Ava under his own name and he wasn't about to let her go. He refused to read what she had written of her dissertation until she finished yet another paper for him. When she had, he demanded yet another.

"I'm going to rot away here. I won't be the first. This place reeks from corpses. I can't expose him because I need his recommendation to get a job when I get out. *If* I get out. I'm at his mercy."

At last she decided it was rot or riot. She typed up a letter of resignation to the chairman of the department, telling him her reasons for leaving. She gave a copy to The Shmuck and said that unless he had her dissertation read and back to her with comments within a week, the letter was going out.

"I finally realized I had nothing to lose. He was never going to let me go."

It worked, and now Ava was almost finished.

Ava is wonderful, witty, and wise, but she was the wrong person to call on the night of Noam's proposal. She's suspicious of marriage in general, and her suspicions about mine in particular grew as she listened to me talk about Noam.

"The problem with you, Renee," she finally said, "is that you think the male sexual organ is the brain."

But she did give me wonderful news. She had applied to the Institute for Advanced Study in Princeton for a postdoctoral fellowship.

"It's always been a secret dream of mine," she said. "That place is holy to me, the haunt of gods. Only let's not count on it. I may not be ready yet for the ascent up Mount Olympus."

As it turned out, she was. Two weeks later she called me with the news of her acceptance. Ava and I together again! She would be like a fresh breeze from the Bronx blowing through the stale air of Princeton.

MY MOTHER called me early the next morning, with some of the old fight back in her voice. She was first of all anxious to meet Noam, a meeting I dreaded, but it would have to be. Beyond that, though, she had bigger worries.

"Renee," she began, "do you and your young man plan to get married by a rabbi? Will you have a kosher wedding?"

I am a very spiteful daughter. What did that skinny little Jewish woman ever do to earn such spite? (I could write a book.)

"Okay, Mom. We'll have a Jewish wedding. For you."

"Oh . . . how nice." It came out small and hopeless. I had vinced the invincible.

Noam did not at all like the idea of being married by a rabbi. Religion had never touched his person (he had even been circumcised by a doctor), and in his scheme of things there wasn't that much difference between going to a rabbi to get married and to a voodoo master to have a spell cast. He began to make increasingly vigorous noises of protest, and I don't know where it all would have ended if my mother hadn't put a stop to it.

78

My mother is an extremely ambitious woman. You give her a bean, she wants to make a whole cholent. I was being so amenable about a rabbi that she figured she could slip some other things past me as well. "I'm glad to see love has mellowed you, Renee." First she called to ask if she could make a little party after the ceremony, invite some of the relatives to the house. Fine, I said. This really fueled the fires of her ambition. The next morning she called early.

"Renee darling, I want to speak to you about something very serious, very solemn. I know you're not a religious woman, but I hope you'll give what I'm about to say the consideration it deserves. A good marriage, Renee, is a spiritual marriage. Are you listening?"

"I'm listening," I answered, wondering what she was getting at.

"A spiritual marriage requires preparation. You have to purify the spirit, *cleanse*" (she came down very hard on the word) "the spirit." Suddenly I knew what she was talking about.

"Mother, are you asking me to go to *mikvah?*"

"Well, Renee, I think—"

But I didn't give her a chance to finish her thought. "Mom, I've had it. You're never satisfied. I give you a son-in-law, a Jewish genius son-in-law, you want a rabbi to marry us. I give you your rabbi, you want a party. I give you a party, you want me to go bobbing around naked in holy waters. I've had it. No *mikvah*, no party, no rabbi. Be happy you're getting a son-in-law and an honest daughter."

In the end, we were married by a justice of the peace in Trenton.

4

The
HONEYMOON

What is the soul? We know nothing about it. If this pretended soul was of another essence from that of the body, their union would be impossible.

—BARON D'HOLBACH,
IMMORTALITY: AN ABSURD
SUPPOSITION

I do not want to die—no. I neither want to die nor do I want to want to die; I want to live for ever and ever, I want this "I" to live—this poor "I" that I am and that I feel myself to be here and now, and therefore the problem of the duration of my soul, of my own soul, tortures me.

—UNAMUNO,
THE TRAGIC SENSE OF LIFE

*I*nvitations to Noam are always pouring in from around the world. Any mathematical gathering is distinguished by the Himmel presence. The summer of our marriage Noam accepted invitations to lecture at the University of Rome and to attend a conference at Esztergom, Hungary. We planned to take the train from Italy to Hungary, stopping over for a few days in Vienna. Had we been disposed to use such a word, we might have called the trip our "honeymoon."

A few days before we left I received my mother's bon voyage in the mail, a little pile of news clippings, the dateline of each underlined in red, shadowing our itinerary: *Rome:* "Leftist Terror Heightens: Random Pedestrians Shot in Knees"; *Vienna:* "Neo-Nazis Celebrate Hitler Birthday"; *Moscow:* "Harassment of Jewish Intellectuals Intensifies": (But, Mom, Moscow is in Russia. We're going to Hungary." "It's all the same. It's all controlled by Russia. I beg you, on my knees I beg you, don't venture behind the Iron Curtain. Rome and Vienna are bad enough." "I really can't understand what you're worried about. What exactly do you anticipate?" "I'm afraid to think. You could be kidnaped, made slaves in Siberia, be committed to a mental institution for the rest of your life. Didn't you read what I sent you?" "But, Mom, those are Russian citizens that are being harassed. We're American. Noam's been invited. They want contact with Western scholars." "American, Russian, Hungarian. Anti-Semites don't make such fine distinctions. Jews are Jews.")

Our Alitalia flight left Kennedy at eleven at night. It was my first trip abroad and I was too excited to sleep. Noam worked all night on the lectures he was to give in Rome, pacing the aisles of the 747, muttering to himself. Occasionally, when he passed my seat, he'd lean over and absent-mindedly kiss the top of my head. The stewardesses kept giving me funny looks, but I didn't give a damn. I dismissed them. Since childhood I had been prey to the Look of the Other. Does he like me? Does she approve of me? A look on the face of *anybody* interpreted as a smirk or a sign of dislike would sear me, make me dizzy with pain. But now I was Mrs. Noam Himmel, on a different plane entirely, and I finally had the power to dismiss. "I am flying at last," I thought all night long.

When we arrived at the airport it was three on a steamy afternoon for the Romans, eight in the morning for us. After my night of flying high I felt weak and disoriented, and decided I didn't like foreign travel. But as we straggled out of customs—where the officials listened to Noam's garbled answers with cold stares and glanced at each other with raised eyebrows while Noam frantically went through his pockets, searching for his passport (we found it rolled up in the sweater he had used as a pillow during the last few hours of the trip) —we were met by a smiling delegation of three from the mathematics department of the university. Again I was enveloped in the sweet sense of our importance. I now belonged to an international society. I could travel from country to country with my husband and be swathed in the same interest and regard that surrounded us in Princeton. I had married intellectual royalty.

One of the three, Enrico Trotti, turned out to be the chairman of the math department, and it was his little red Fiat into which we all piled, our luggage tied to the roof. The four men immediately became absorbed in shop talk. Noam was sitting in the back with me (a mistake I never repeated), and Enrico, who was driving, kept turning around to talk with him, gesturing with both hands all the while.

"Perhaps you ought to sit up front," I whispered to Noam, but he ignored me.

So that shabby secret of my inner life is out. But then how could you begin to know what it's like to be me (and that is the end of all this scribbling: to give you myself as I am to myself, the *en soi*, the *être intime* of me) without knowing that at heart I'm a physical coward? I have inherited or learned, I don't know which, my mother's despised habit of imagining the worst. At each risk the mind leaps ahead to visions of possible disaster. And it shivers, it cringes, it longs to stay put. Coward. What chances I have taken in an attempt to erase the inglorious self-characterization. But each leap, each climb, each dive, has always been preceded by a ghastly inner picture of the slip, the plunge, the brain-splattered rocks below. I am my mother's daughter. Beneath the external swagger the phenomenological reality is fear.

I was the only one in that car whose attention was riveted in terror on the road, a horror film of counterfactuals reeling through me: if Enrico had taken two seconds longer turning back his head . . . if the distance between us and that truck had been one centimeter less . . . Noam, oblivious to it all, was far more courageous than I.

But we made it to our destination, a large apartment on the banks of the Tiber, not far from the Vatican. The apartment belonged to Enrico's mother, who summered on the island of Sardinia and made it available to us for our three weeks in Rome. We were whisked by an open elevator, with elaborate grillwork, up the five flights to the apartment—eight or nine rooms filled with large, dusty antiques. Enrico pointed the way to the bedroom, where Noam and I fell into an immense baroque fourposter and a long dreamless sleep. We were awakened several hours later by a festive troop of six mathematicians and their consorts, who arrived to take us out to dinner. We lingered at the restaurant, amidst an air of celebration, well past midnight. "Himmel, *l'enfant terrible*" was repeatedly toasted.

The next morning Enrico arrived about nine in the morning to escort Noam to the university. He gave me a ticket for the bus, good for the week, and a map of Rome. I hadn't realized until then that I would be left to amuse myself.

Noam didn't arrive home that day until after six. I had come back to the apartment at about two, after visiting the Vatican, and had sat waiting. I hadn't been told he'd be gone all day.

"I thought we'd be here together. I thought we'd see things together."

"I'm sorry you thought that. I assumed you understood. I was invited here to work. They *are* paying me, you know. They're all anxious to talk to me. I have only three weeks here." Three weeks, I was thinking, would be a very long time.

"But I don't like going around by myself. It's no fun."

"Well, I'm very sorry. Do I really have to apologize to you? I didn't have to bring you along to Europe at all." Clearly, "honeymoon" was not the right term for our trip. "All you have to do all day long is amuse yourself while I work. And *I* have to apologize? It isn't fun. You sound like a child."

I felt like a child. I had discovered that day that I didn't like knocking about alone in a country where I couldn't understand what the drivers yelled out at me as they passed, couldn't understand the labels on things in the stores, couldn't understand anybody's directions to anywhere. A child is precisely what I felt like, walking with uncertainty through the unintelligible.

Rome is so beautiful, I knew I ought to be rejoicing in its offerings. I thought of Freud, dreaming (quite literally), year after year, of visiting the Eternal City. What kind of soul had I, to walk coldly through such splendor? Why wasn't I charmed by the novelties of a foreign country, as tourists are supposed to be, instead of discomfited by them? It was true: I didn't like foreign travel. And that was like admitting to a dislike of art or music. It indicates a lack in one's soul.

I had walked over to the Vatican that day because it was only a few blocks away and hadn't required my braving a bus. I never did use the passes Enrico brought me each week. If I couldn't walk to it, I didn't see it. The next day I crossed the Tiber and wandered around, inspecting the incredibly beautiful things in the shop windows, never venturing inside. I sat for a while on the Spanish Steps and then made my way dutifully over to the Trevi Fountain, the Pantheon, and Piazza Navona.

At the piazza I finally rested, body and soul. Nobody sitting at the outrageously priced cafés and restaurants was speaking Italian. They were all as foreign as I, and I felt at home. I sat there the rest of the day, sampling drinks and admiring the Fountain of the Four Rivers, the spectacular work by Bernini, representing the four major rivers of the seventeenth-century world: the Danube, the Nile, the Ganges, and the Río de la Plata of the Americas, all of it topped by the papal arms and a dove with an olive branch, indicating the position of the Pope as custodian of the world under God. I became a real connoisseur of this statue.

Every morning I had to force myself to leave the apartment, so dark and protected, its walls lined with books. I stared longingly at the few English titles scattered among them. No, I'd tell myself sternly, you will not sit in an apartment in Rome reading William James' *Varieties of Religious Experience*. Get out there and have some experiences for yourself, religious or otherwise. And I'd push myself out into the relentless noise and glare.

I would have liked, at least, to be able to walk these foreign streets inconspicuously; the Roman men would not allow it. Their demonstrativeness surpassed anything I'd encountered (with the possible exception perhaps of the time I almost caused a riot walking down the Upper West Side's Broadway in a pair of yellow shorts on an airless August afternoon). Here in Rome men would walk beside me for blocks, declaiming. One jumped out of his car and fell before me on his knees. I didn't enjoy any of it. I felt embarrassed and exposed, and was thrown back into the agonizing uncertainty of my early adolescence, when male attention had been undesired and undecipherable. Now here, years of experience later, I once again didn't know what to make of it. In New York I could fit my response to the tone and content of the comments, staring stonily ahead, shrugging my shoulders and smiling, or yelling something back. But here I had no idea what the street protocol is, much less what they were saying. Should I look offended or smile graciously? If only I were with a friend, I wished again and again. If only Ava, brave and wise, were with me now. Ava's purple-stained lips would know how to suck the pleasures from this place. Ava's strenuous tongue would burst Rome's grape. Trying to escape the eyes of the men, aware of (and hating) the involuntary wiggle of my ass, I'd hurry back to the sheltered island of Piazza Navona, where I could order in English, fall into conversations with elderly Irish nuns and wandering tribes of American students, or read.

I had brought two books along from Princeton, Quine's *Word and Object* (I still cherished hopes of a philosophical career) and Eliot's *Middlemarch*. I made slow progress through Quine and rewarded myself generously with rapturous reading from Eliot. Her book is, on one level, about marriage, and in that respect blended well with my own preoccupations. This was particularly true of the central story, setting forth the fortunes of the hapless Dorothea, who had also spent her "honeymoon" in Rome left largely to herself, while her scholarly husband, the fiftyish Mr. Casaubon, toiled away at his research in the Vatican library. Dorothea's Italian sufferings, her "oppression by the weight of unintelligible Rome," were keener than mine. It was here that she got her first whiff of the fetor of marital disillusionment, from which she turned her delicate middle-class English nose. She was altogether too righteous to engage my full sympathy, despite the parallels in our stories, which went further than Rome. For she too had married with the hope of being lifted up above herself by her husband's genius: "Since I can do no good because a woman/Reach constantly at something that is near it," Eliot had quoted from *The Maid's Tragedy*. Only poor Dorothea had made an unfortunate mistake. *Her* husband turned out to be no genius. The appearance of brilliance had slowly faded, bringing into focus the rather pathetic figure beneath. The marriage finally ends in a Pietà of sorts, Dorothea tending the moribund Casaubon, nursing her failed father-figure (instead of a child). It's a good thing, it occurred to me, that such errors as Dorothea's don't happen in math, where a proof is a proof whether of a theorem or of genius. (Casaubon was an historian of religion, his futile research on a *Key to All Mythologies*.) I, at the very least, had the real thing.

Eliot gives us a picture of the inside of a marriage but without divulging any sexual details. Her Victorian readers were meant to infer the hidden reality from such facts as Dorothea's pathetic pallor and the desolate loneliness of that wedding trip. But I am no George Eliot (my misfortune) and you are probably not content to infer (your misfortune). And so I must take you back with me, from the piazza to the apartment, into Signora Trotti's oversize antique bed.

I had had thoughts, early on, of educating Noam in the bedroom, of teaching him the detours and the backways off the main straight road. But he was an unwilling student, when not altogether truant. It was not even possible to speak with him on the subject. He showed such distaste—not for the act itself, but for all reference to it. It was as if one ran the risk of glorifying sex beyond its station by admitting it as a topic of discourse. My few pedagogical attempts left me feeling shamed, and Noam obviously, though silently, furious. Had he responded, it might have been to say that certain things are not spoken of. They are simply done, without words or thought. The body takes over for a while, and when it is finished the mind can resume its activity, giving no indication of having noticed what the other half was up to—like the separated brain hemispheres of a patient with a severed corpus callosum. A sentence begun before desire would plunge him down (no doubt that's the direction) into his body, would be completed when the desire was spent. The prolonged "hmmmm" beginning the second half of the sentence was the only spoken acknowledgment of an interruption. These are perhaps the most interesting and telling details of our early conjugal relations, the sentences that bracketed the unspeakable action—which in itself was swift and to the point.

The young wife was frustrated, you diagnose, using the term as demanded by the context. Not so fast. Don't be misled by the appearance of the obvious. (That is the sum of my wisdom.) Of course I was frustrated, but in attaining precisely *what?* Bodily pleasure had never been the goal that propelled me along. Appearances to the contrary, I was every bit as unsexual as Noam, more so really, since *my* body—in which I was lodged like an ice cube in a furnace —never took over. And always there were dreams of purity, of a body spare and a mind chaste, the waking dreams of sleepless nights.

What tied me to my body was not so much its desires as the desires it aroused in others—the more (both desire and others), the better. Through it (my matter, so to speak) I mattered to others, and thus mattered. Through it I had mattered to Noam, who himself mattered so much, at least from where I stood. But it occurred to me in Rome, where Noam's sexual aloofness seemed to increase, that his interest in me was inconsistent with his general indifference to people, himself included, or so he had claimed. "At least I'm consistent," he had told me on the dinky. "I don't find people in general very interesting to think about, so I don't find myself in particular an arresting object of thought. A lot of people seem to assent to the universal proposition but decline instantiation when it comes to themselves." For how long could Noam—Noam *Himmel*—be expected to suffer a logical inconsistency? This thought terrified me, perhaps as no other ever had. For from it followed, with a certainty almost mathematical, the unrelieved bleakness of my future. Being rational, I therefore dismissed it as best I could. But it lurked in the background of my lonely Roman musings and occasionally would erupt into the words: He has no right. No right to what? I questioned myself nervously. To have married, came the ready answer.

And *I?* Had *I* the right to marry? Other disturbing thoughts pushed themselves forward: One should not marry to save oneself.

Anyone in need of saving has no business marrying. Matrimony is not the cement for a cracked self, but is more like someone leaning on the self's point of least resistance. But these thoughts too were hurriedly pushed away for the frightening consequences they entailed.

The days I spent by myself; at night we were entertained by Noam's colleagues. He would return home between six and seven, and then we and some of the mathematicians and their wives would go to a restaurant or to one of their homes.

"It's almost like we're having *shayva broches*," I said to Noam as we walked back from a restaurant late at night.

"Which you will no doubt proceed to explain," Noam answered, preparing his face to be amused; for I only dredged up my religious past for purposes of entertainment.

"It's a week of festivities following a wedding. The object is to divert the newlyweds from thinking about sex." I paused, trying to goad Noam into asking the obvious question. But attempts to force Noam's thinking are always futile. He ignores the obvious, or perhaps rather has his own ideas of what *is* obvious. He remained silent, his face still set for amusement. "Because after the wedding night's activities, which no doubt caused the heretofore virgin bride to bleed and thus become unclean, the couple aren't allowed to touch each other."

"For how long?"

"She has to count five unclean days and seven clean days, and then she goes to *mikvah* and is purified."

"And the same thing every month, I assume."

"Right."

Noam smiled while raising his eyebrows and shaking his head, a response that had already become part of an established pattern between us.

The Italian mathematicians were a charming, jolly lot. We'd stay out late each night, laughing and drinking, getting up from the table well past midnight, often to go and find an all-night ice cream shop. It was possible to forget in their midst, among their joking and light airy flirtations, that they were mathematicians. Did Enrico, with his black hair shot through with silver and his large, mocking black eyes, with his obvious pleasure in laughter, wine, and women, really spend his daylight hours doing pure mathematics?

"Yes, he's really quite good," Noam told me when I asked. "Very decent, solid intuitions. He'll never do the best, but he'll be one of the first to appreciate it."

And every morning, at a solemnly early hour, Enrico would arrive at our apartment to accompany Noam to the university. No one expects Noam to make his own way on foreign buses, I thought once in anger. But that was ridiculous. Of course no one expects such things of Noam. Noam is Noam—Noam Himmel. Everyone makes allowances. His excuse is his genius. The genius's wife has no such excuse.

I was looking forward to leaving Rome for Vienna, where we would be traveling incognito. Noam hadn't informed any of the Viennese mathematicians that he was passing through. There, at least, he would be a tourist with me.

The train ride from Rome to Vienna is fourteen hours. For the first four hours Noam worked. (Four hours of creative work a day is the limit for a mathematician, Noam always says.) I had thought perhaps we ought to get off at Florence and spend a few hours there. Noam had never been there, either. And disgracefully as I had fulfilled the requirements of tourism in Rome, I hadn't given up completely, which I felt I would be doing if we didn't bother to get off at Florence. But Noam was deep in work when we arrived.

"Get off if you like," he said without looking up from the pad on which he was writing. "I'll meet you in Vienna."

I had little faith in our meeting in Vienna and didn't relish the thought of wandering alone through Florence. So I stayed put, sitting opposite Noam and alternating my observation between the countryside and him.

He was rapidly filling up yellow sheets of blue-lined paper. When the spirit is upon him, the pen flies. If there's no proper paper handy, he'll use napkins, toilet paper, tablecloths, his shirt cuffs. I learned early on in our relationship always to travel with a yellow blue-lined pad, his chosen medium.

Noam in action, in the grip of mathematical intuition, is an awesome sight, like some natural wonder, expending vast amounts of energy. Sometimes the intense outer activity lies in his rapid writing, as was the case now—page after page in his large scribble. If he gets to the end of the pad, he reaches out blindly for whatever is available. His desk blotter at home is an inky mass of symbols, a record of past instances of paper deprivation.

More dramatic even than the writing is the pacing that sometimes accompanies the thinking. I've often watched him at home: hands clasped behind him or gesturing slightly before him, eyes downcast, he moves wonderfully fast across the room. Oblivious as he is at such times to his surroundings, I used to watch for his crashing into walls. But he never does. Just before hitting, he executes a neat little pirouette and continues on his way.

Then sometimes he'll halt quite suddenly and stand there motionless, his REMming eyes now off the floor and on God knows what. I'm entirely free to observe, with little danger of interrupting. Once, for example, I walked into his study at home, this time with the intent of interrupting, for he was wanted on the phone. He was writing at his desk. I stood there within a foot of him, waiting for him to look up. For several minutes I watched and waited, as the symbols appeared on the yellow pages. He never looked up, never knew I was there. Awed, I finally left the room.

These physical manifestations—the pacing, the writing—must themselves consume much energy. But they are nothing but the visible smoke escaping from the great conflagration within, from Noam's intensely concentrated mental activity. Any of you who have ever put in a really good day's worth of mental labor know of what I speak. As there's no suffering like mental suffering, or so they say, so there's no exhaustion like mental exhaustion. And mathematics is probably the most exacting and demanding of all mental activities. No wonder mathematicians are known to burn themselves out relatively young.

There was a rapid turnover for a while in our second-class compartment. An American serviceman and his discontented-looking young wife had gotten on with us in Rome. They were soon going back to the States, the serviceman told me, after having spent two years in Italy. He and I spoke (while the wife stared gloomily out the window) about the wine produced in the Chianti region, which we were riding through. When we reached Florence, they got off to have a last look at the great brass doors of the Battistero S. Giovanni. An enormously fat Italian woman took the serviceman's place on the seat next to Noam, with a fat baby, pacifier stuck in its mouth, under one arm and a big straw basket under the other. She took a huge salami out of the basket, a huger breast out of her blouse, chewed the salami and nursed the baby. Noam, within inches of this agreeably stereotypical sight, never looked up. The greedy consumption of mother and child activated my own enzymes and I went off to the dining car. When I got back, the compartment had cleared out and Noam had put his pad away.

"Hi." He smiled up at me. "How have you been?"

"Just fine. You?"

"Good, good. Come sit down here next to me." He took my hand and beamed into my eyes. "You know, Renee, I wish I could share my work with you. It's been the one sustaining happiness in my life, at least until I met you, and I wish I could share it with you."

These words touched me deeply.

"Yes, I wish you could, too. Try to describe it to me. What's it like, what does it feel like when you're creating?"

"I wish I *could* describe it to you, could capture it in words. But I never could, not even if I had the verbal facility I lack. I wish I were able to describe the beauty and excitement when it's working, when I'm seeing it."

"Like the past few hours?"

"Like the past few hours. It's not always like that, of course. Sometimes I wander round and round in circles, going over the same ground, getting lost, sometimes for hours, or days, or even weeks. It was like that with the H-function theorem"—Noam's latest publication. "But I know that if I immerse myself in it long enough, things will clarify, simplify. I can count on that. When it happens, it happens fast. Boom ba boom ba boom! One thing after the other, taking the breath away. And then, you know, I feel like I'm walking out in some remote corner of space, where no mortal's ever been, all alone with something beautiful."

And I had been peeved about not getting off at Florence while Noam was off in Plato's heaven. I must remember, I told myself fervently, that Noam is not always where his body is.

"All the pleasure's in those moments," Noam continued. "Writing up the results, publishing them, that's all a chore, a bow to the profession."

He sat up and thought a few moments while I watched him and waited, enchanted by these glimpses into the private side of his genius.

"Once," he spoke again, "when I was in Switzerland some friends there took me up in some very high cable cars, climbing up a mountain, that had been built for a James Bond movie. *Diamonds Are Forever*, I think it was called. Anyway, there was a restaurant on top and the view was supposed to be sublime. When we got up there, it was a great disappointment because the clouds were obscuring everything. But then suddenly there was a rent in the clouds and there were the Jungfrau and two other peaks towering right in front of us." He smiled deep into my eyes, in that way he has. "That's what it's like, or the closest approximation to it I can come up with. I've never tried to describe it before. It never was important to describe it."

"It must be a tremendous feeling of power."

"Yes." He sat up very straight. "You understand that. It is a tremendous feeling of power. I suppose any creative act makes one feel powerful, but in math the power seems absolute. It's not art, it's not fiction, one isn't making up stories. It's truth. The scientist discovers truth, too, but his has to conform to physical reality. His creative freedom is severely limited. In the end it's the gross material world that has the last say. Just because a description is the most beautiful, that doesn't mean it's the one nature chooses to realize."

He searched my face, trying to see if I understood. I nodded, wanting him to continue.

"Take geometry, for example. The physicist has to get out his measuring rods to determine which geometry is physical geometry, actually describes physical space, and it's not necessarily the prettiest. But the mathematician's power is absolute. We have an infinity of geometries, each mathematically real, and we can use the standards of beauty in deducing them. The only limits we have to conform to are the limits of logic, and even God can't violate logic."

"Truth and beauty, beauty and truth," I murmured.

"Yes, exactly. The truth of science, the beauty of art. Math exceeds all."

Noam had been speaking very quickly. Now he slowed.

"Physicists like to think they're dealing with reality. Some of them are quite arrogant about it and talk as if they were the only ones with a finger in the belly of the real. They think mathematicians are just playing games, making up our own rules and playing our own games. But with all their physical theories the possibility still exists that space and time are simply Kant's categories of apperception, or that physical objects are nothing but ideas in the mind of God. Who can say for sure? Their physical theories can't rule these possibilities out. But in math things are exactly the way they seem. There's no room, no *logical* room, for deception. I don't have to consider the possibility that maybe seven isn't really a prime, that my mind conditions seven to appear a prime. One doesn't—can't—make the distinction between mathematical appearance and reality, as one can—must—make the distinction between physical appearance and reality. The mathematician can penetrate the essence of his objects in a way the physicist never could, no matter how powerful his theory. We're the ones with our fists deep in the guts of reality."

"You're like a god."

"Some are gods. Archimedes, Newton, Gauss, they were gods."

"A minor deity, then?"

"No, not that either. Euclid, Descartes, Fermat, Euler, Lagrange, Riemann, Cantor, Poincaré, Hilbert, and Gödel—they're the minor deities."

"A demigod, then, the offspring of a god and mortal?"

"Okay." He laughed. "Maybe I'm a demigod in the pantheon of math."

Did I ever love Noam? It's a question I've considered continuously these past months. Did I ever love anything beyond his position in that special world, the only world that's ever mattered to me? Did I ever, even back then, focus on the person who occupied that position? I know I never considered the person behind the genius — if there was such a person. Noam's personal identity was, at least for me, entirely absorbed by his genius. All the properties he had were defined in relation to his genius. But that would be okay, wouldn't it? If one can love someone for the curve of her nose or thigh, the charm of his laugh or his manner of smoking, why can't one love someone for his genius?

Yes, I understood when Noam spoke of the power of his work. I had always thought of intelligence as power, the supreme power. Understanding is not the means of mastery, but the end itself (see Spinoza). This belief, pushed through the dark channels of the libido, emerged as the determinant of my sexual preferences. I am only attracted to men who I believe to be more intelligent than I am. A detected mistake in logic considerably cools my desire. They can be shorter, they can be weaker, they can be poorer, they can be meaner, but they must be smarter. For the smart are the masters in my mattering region. And if you gain power over them, then through the transitivity of power you too are powerful.

And how is it given to a woman to dominate but through sex? Through sex a woman gains control over a man's body that he himself lacks; she can move him in ways he cannot move himself. And she invades and takes over his consciousness, reducing it to a sense of its own embodiment (see Sartre). Sex is essentially the same game for men and for women, but for women, most of whom are otherwise powerless, it assumes a life-filling significance. *La femme fatale, la belle dame sans merci,* is an otherwise impotent person who has perfected her one strength to an unusual degree.

I have always loved in terms of power. Does this mean I've never loved? Does one love only if one loves for the right reasons? Are there right reasons? I don't know. But if I ever loved Noam, I loved him that evening, on a train riding into Vienna, as he talked of his power, and feeling his, I felt my own. *Since I can do no good because a woman/Reach constantly at something that is near it.*

WHEN I WOKE the next morning in our hotel room in the center of Vienna, Noam was gone. I was shocked, for Noam usually sleeps until someone wakes him (and then stays awake until told to go to bed). I went down to breakfast, hoping to find him there, though I was doubtful. Noam rarely seeks food on his own. He'll go hungry until told to eat (and then eat until told to stop). I don't know if he simply ignores, doesn't know how to interpret, or somehow lacks basic somatic sensations. But, as you might expect, his body, in particular his stomach, has suffered the consequences. We never make a move without Maalox.

As I expected, Noam wasn't to be found in the café attached to the hotel. I felt annoyed, and then, as the next few hours passed, increasingly worried. Something must have happened to him. I began to imagine all sorts of unlikely scenarios: Noam hopelessly lost, with no memory of the name of our hotel; Noam once again carted off by German police after innocently asking for directions; Noam hit by a car, his precious brains splattered on the pavement like Pierre Curie's. You're just like your mother, I told myself, but the stream of disastrous possibilities kept flowing on.

Around noon Noam burst into our room, which I had been too nervous to leave after breakfast. He was in a state of high excitement.

"Renee, I've made the most marvelous discovery! Renee, I've been here before!"

"What are you talking about, Noam? I thought you said you'd never been to Vienna."

"Not in this life, Renee, not in this life. Not in the life of Noam Himmel. But *I*"—he pounded his chest with his fist—"I've been here."

"What?" I sat down on the edge of the bed and stared at my husband. "What?"

"Look, Renee, I've been walking all over this city. I *know* this city. This persona, this Noam Himmel, has never been here, but *I*"— again he was pounding his chest—"I've been here. I know the entire layout of the city, the names of the streets—though there have been changes since I was here last—where the parks are, everything. I made my way directly to the Schönbrunn. I didn't make a false turn. I might have done it hundreds of times. I probably *did* do it hundreds of times. I've finally located the space." He sat down on a chair and smiled. "Now all I have to do is find the time."

"You've done what? You have to do what?" If I applied the Cartesian test for whether or not I was dreaming, viz. the *coherence* of my perceptions, I'd have to conclude that I was.

"I know where I lived. I just have to discover when it was."

"Noam, you're saying that you've lived before." A memory-image flashed before me: Noam in Lahiere's, *shuckling* fervently at the suggestion that the Jewish naming tradition is connected with a belief in the transmigration of souls.

"Yes, of course, Renee. And now I know where."

"But, Noam, if you do have knowledge of the city, it's probably because you read about it once or saw it in a movie or something. Something you've forgotten. There has to be some other explanation."

"Don't be an idiot. My knowledge of this city is that of an inhabitant. There's only one explanation. Don't be close-minded. I've always known that I lived before, that this particular persona wasn't my first. All of us probably have. I don't see any reason why I should be special. I've known since I was a child."

This is Noam, I told myself, Noam Himmel, the genius, your husband. He was standing there in front of me, talking as he had so often, loudly and rapidly, intensity streaming from his eyes. This is the way he had spoken to me of his brilliant discoveries—the way he had spoken to his colleagues, who always listened reverentially. I just had to take what he said seriously. Who was I not to? But my *God!*

"Noam, I can't believe what you're saying! I can't believe that you of all people are saying it! You're the one who's always ranting and raving against the lunatic irrationality of religion."

"I don't see what one thing has to do with the other, nor do I rant and rave. This isn't a religious belief. Look, Renee, I'll explain the principles of rationality to you. Rationality consists in accepting what the evidence points to, in figuring out what that is, and then accepting it, the inference to the best—in this case the only—explanation. It's irrational to believe the world is a certain way, when its being so is not supported by the facts, just because you'd like the world to be that way. That means it's also irrational to refuse to believe the world is a certain way, when the evidence supports that it is, just because you don't want it that way. People who pride themselves on their hard-nosed scientific outlooks are terrified of having the world exceed their comprehension. They refuse to recognize any phenomenon that doesn't fit into their simplistic physicalistic framework."

"But what evidence is there for reincarnation?"

"You see! You people don't even bother to examine the evidence! That's really the height of rationality, closing your eyes to the facts if you can't understand them. We can't understand consciousness, either, not in physical terms. Are you people going to deny that you think? Well, maybe *you* people don't." He laughed nastily. "The evidence for reincarnation is overwhelming. Haven't you ever heard of Stevenson, Dr. Ian Stevenson? His *Twenty Cases Suggestive of Reincarnation* is a classic in the field. He's certainly much more cautious and scientific than many of the physicists I know, with their mumble-jumble about giving up logic. He was the chairman of the department of neurology and psychiatry at the University of Virginia School of Medicine. He became interested in reincarnation because he realized that neither heredity nor environmental influences could entirely account for personality; for example, certain phobias some of his patients had. He's traveled all over the world, amassing a wealth of material supporting reincarnation. Children knowing facts about some person who died before their birth, facts they couldn't possibly have access to through natural means. Verifiable facts. And cases of xenoglossy."

"What's that?"

"People, often quite uneducated, knowing some foreign language they've never been taught, sometimes in an archaic form that a scholar must identify. Sometimes these people just recite, as if by rote, and sometimes, in the case of responsive xenoglossy, which is rare, they can actually converse. If you're truly interested in evidence, open-mindedly interested, I can assure you it exists. But you don't want it. You people need your blinders, you members of the so-called scientific community. You couldn't take a step without your blinders. You'd get lost if you had a view of the vast sweeping panorama."

I was mildly taken aback at being cast as a representative of the scientific community. (Professor Pfiffel would have been more surprised.) But this was drowned in the greater shock. The two attitudes were still battling within me, whether to regard Noam seriously or as a lunatic. It was really unthinkable, come to think of it, that I should be debating this question at all. Up until some ten or twenty minutes before, I had regarded my husband as the most reasoning of humans, a very paragon of rationality against which to measure all others. He had always been so cautiously critical, utterly unwilling to accept any claim until it was shown to meet his stringent criteria for justification. He had almost driven me crazy at times with his analyzing, often applied to matters I considered fairly obvious, and his endless questioning: What precisely do you mean by this? Why do you believe that's true? Perhaps Noam is like the anal compulsive who keeps a secret messy drawer in which to indulge in the wicked delights of disorder, I thought. Maybe this is the back drawer of Noam's mind, where he can indulge in the forbidden pleasures of uncritical thinking. Or maybe he's just crazy. For the first time that know-nothing truism of the vulgar crossed my mind: all geniuses are crazy. Good God.

Noam was pacing about the room like a caged tiger, thinking hard.

"How did you know when you were a kid?"

"Wait a minute." The pacing continued for several minutes while I watched him. Finally he came to rest in front of me. "Now, what did you ask me?"

"I asked you how you knew when you were a kid that you had lived before."

"Because I saw things so easily. Mathematical truths, I mean. I just knew things. Before I'd see why, before I'd have any inkling of the proofs, I'd know the results. I knew exactly what to look for."

"You're a genius, Noam, a mathematical genius."

"No, Renee. It's very hard to describe, but I knew these things because I was remembering them. That was very clear to me. The phenomenology of remembering is quite recognizable. You don't in general have any trouble distinguishing when you're remembering from when you're not, do you? And then, of course, there was the question of my parents. It baffled me how they could be so different from me until I figured out the answer." His face briefly assumed the uncomfortable expression it always has when the topic of his parents comes up. "Now, of course, it's different. I've gone beyond the mathematical memories of my former knowledge. I did that long ago, with the supernaturals. I've made progress in this life."

"Plato said that all learning is recollection," I said slowly. "That our souls knew everything before birth." And, I remembered, it was precisely mathematical knowledge he had used in his argument, getting an uneducated slave boy to deduce certain geometrical truths. (The hidden premise of his argument was: all things that we know, we've been taught. If we know something, but weren't taught it in this life, the learning must have taken place in another life.)

"Yes, I know. I read a lot of Plato when I was a kid. I think in this matter, as in so many others, Plato was very nearly on target. Except I don't think we knew everything before." The sentences were spilling out. "We make progress from life to life. That's what gives the entire series meaning. But Plato was very nearly right. He was right about the independent existence of the soul and its survival of the body. And he was right about the obscuring influences of the body. Matter muddles. When we become attached at birth to a corporeal existent, our memories and knowledge are largely canceled. Almost the entire contents of consciousness is emptied. It probably has to be that way. Most people would probably feel that their precious individualities were undermined if they knew they'd existed before. They'd be jealous of that former existence. But the uniqueness of the self is inviolate. It's always the same self, just a different life."

I couldn't resist directing a typical question of Noam's back at him: "How do you *know* all this?"

"It's the only thing that makes sense, given the facts. I figured it all out when I was a kid."

Then maybe it's time to rethink the issue, I thought but didn't say. (I was getting into the marital habit of thinking but not saying.) Instead I asked:

"What do you think the self is? If it's not a body, but can change bodies, and it's not a collection of memories, but disposes of these from life to life, then what is it?"

"That's a very good question, Renee, very penetrating. I've given it some thought, although I'm by no means confident of the answer. I think the identity of the self consists primarily in its moral and intellectual attributes, interpreted as dispositions, potentialities. Not the actual actions and beliefs that are the results partly of these dispositions and partly of external factors, the situation in which the self finds itself. And certainly not any of the properties of the body. Bodies are disposable."

"Our moral and intellectual attributes? That's it? What keeps them together?"

"What keeps material attributes together? I don't see why the one question is more difficult than the other. It's just that you physically see bodies, or at least instantaneous stages of bodies, so you people don't realize there's any problem there." I rather resented that, for it seemed to me I had quite a keen sense of the mystery of bodies. "There is some kind of attractive force. I don't really know. But unlike you people I don't expel things from the universe just because I can't explain them."

You people? Since when was I the thick-skulled positivist? I was supposed to be a misty-minded metaphysician. Noam had quickly assigned me the role of the empiricist enemy, the positivist skeptic. He was, quite obviously, aggressively defensive about his supernatural beliefs. (Had *these* been behind his naming his numbers the "supernaturals"?) And really it was no wonder, for they would have met with little assent, and probably much amusement, in the world in which Noam moved. Come to think of it, I was surprised that this particular Himmel eccentricity hadn't yet been immortalized in legend. Did people know? What an attention-grabber its revelation would be at a party in Princeton—although now, of course, I was barred from such action through the duties of matrimony. One must stand by one's husband, *mishagoss*—craziness—and all.

"But why are you special? Why do you remember your former life?"

"I don't. I don't know who I was. All I had, at least until I arrived in Vienna, was the mathematical memories. I think that the mathematical knowledge was simply too forceful, that the mathematical intuitions really constitute the essence of my person, and so they came bursting through the mortal bounds. Obviously I was a mathematician, a Viennese mathematician. But, as I told you, Stevenson has found plenty of people who have real memories of their former lives, memories that have been independently verified. Look, I don't know, I don't pretend to understand. One possible explanation is that only certain people become reincarnated, that it's a restricted phenomenon. But then why them? It's simpler, and therefore preferable, to assume that reincarnation is the norm and that there is a general amnesiatic effect. My own amnesia about my former life supports this. But there do seem to be exceptions. For some reason the mnemonic block breaks down. Maybe the memories are always there, buried very far down, the way my memories of Vienna were. But, you see, they can be brought up, they can be retrieved!"

He made the motion with his hands—outstretched fingers pushing away air—that means he wants conversation to stop and went back to his rapid pacing. I sat on the bed and considered the question of immortality.

I had never taken the possibility seriously. We are our bodies, we die with our bodies. That had been my metaphysical position. And anyway, the prospect of survival had never much appealed to me on an emotional level. I don't much relish the thought of everlasting consciousness. At very black moments I could always comfort myself with the ever present possibility of self-annihilation. But there's no escape if we're immortal.

And then consider the tedium of eternal life. There's a play by Karel Čapek, made into an opera by Janáček, about a woman named Elina Makropulos, alias Emilia Marty, alias Ellian MacGregor, alias several other names with initials EM, who suffers from immortality. Her father, who had been court physician to a sixteenth-century emperor, tried out his elixir of life on her. EM is frozen at age forty-two, though at the time of the play she's been around three hundred and forty-two years and has had it. No circumstance can tempt her, no creature engage her. The world has become as frozen and static as her own age. "In the end it is the same, singing and silence." She does finally manage to die, having refused to take the elixir again. A young woman, fighting the protests of the old men, destroys the formula.

No, I can't say the prospect of ceaseless survival much appeals to me. Better never to have been born at all. But how many, asks the old Jewish joke, are so lucky? Not one in ten thousand. I do, however, find myself hoping quite often and inconsistently (given my metaphysical position) that my father has managed to survive his death, that he has simply parted company with his body and is still around. Not necessarily around me, though I'd more than welcome his presence (you have an open invitation, Dad), but just *some* where. I don't like to think of a world emptied of him. And, of course, the kind of life-hopping existence that Noam was describing wouldn't suffer from the tedium of EM's indefinitely extended life. But would that reincarnated person really be my father, that same person? Is a bare ganglion of intellectual and moral attributes, stripped of all memories, not to speak of the body, sufficient to ensure personal identity?

I looked over at Noam, who was still pacing madly around the hotel room. Suddenly he stopped and then started toward the door.

"I'm going out again."

"Wait! I'm coming, too."

I spent the next few days trying to keep up with Noam, clinging to his arm, clop, clop, clopping beside him in my Italian high-heeled sandals (my one Roman purchase) as he rushed around the streets of Vienna trying to fix the temporal location of his former life. The Ring encircling the Innere Stadt was quite familiar to him, he said, so he had been around after Franz Joseph mapped it out in the 1860s. But he stared at the Staatsoper in disbelief. What had happened to the opera house? The old one, we learned, had been destroyed in bombardments in 1945. He looked at me in blazing triumph.

"It's as I expected. My other life probably ended around 1938, the year Noam Himmel was born. But I need more architectural evidence."

Actually, I wasn't all that impressed with Noam's knowledge of Vienna. His confident predictions as to what we would find on the next block, around the corner, in the courtyard, were usually wrong. Amazingly, this never dimmed his confidence. He would simply shrug and rush on. The few times he was right he regarded me triumphantly, his expression demanding: How could you ever have doubted? But I remained skeptical. After several hours of circling round and round the Innere Stadt, I too had a kind of blurred knowledge of it and was making (unspoken) predictions at about the same rate of success as Noam.

During the course of our searching Noam managed to relate many tales of the supernatural, complete with names (first, middle, and last), dates, and all the sundry details his capacious memory contained. (It was the first time, I think, that he had allowed himself to talk on the subject to anyone other than his all-accepting mother.) He told me about the "strikingly similar" experiences reported by those who had died and were then resuscitated: their viewing their bodies from outside, their being able to relate what was being done to them, which doctors had wanted to give up, who was crying in the corridor. After some initial confusion most found their separation from their body very pleasurable (especially if their experience included their moving on to another realm, where they were greeted by dead friends and relatives and reviewed their lives with a warm and loving being of light); and they returned to the corporeal state only reluctantly and with no residual fear of death.

But much dearer to Noam's heart were the cases suggestive of reincarnation. He must have told me at least twenty such tales. The eeriest and, I thought, most impressive came from a British psychiatrist, Dr. Arthur Guirdham, who was treating an otherwise normal and intelligent woman for the nightmares she had suffered since a child, one of which was a very vivid experience of being burned at the stake. As a schoolgirl she used to write down her dreams, as well as other things that occurred to her that she couldn't understand, including some verses in what turned out to be medieval French. Dr. Guirdham sent an account to a Professor Père Nellie at the University of Toulouse, who responded that the doctor had sent him an astonishingly accurate description of the Cathars, a group of Puritan-like believers who had lived in Toulouse in the thirteenth century. Some of the details she reported—what color robes the Cathar priests wore, for example—were at variance with accepted scholarly views but were eventually verified when the records of the inquisitors who had persecuted the sect were translated. Many of the names of the historically insignificant people the woman had described were also found in these records.

"Now give me," Noam demanded, his eyes flashing, "an alternative explanation."

Noam is a man of remarkable energy, and his excitement only added to his reserves. He rushed about Vienna, often simultaneously lecturing me on the rationality of the supernatural, and never felt the need to pause for breath. But occasionally, ever the voice of carnal weakness, I would beg for nourishment or rest, and we'd settle down briefly at an outdoor café, where I sampled the inspiring pastries while Noam pondered his identity.

"I can't think of any prominent Viennese mathematicians of the right date. Jacobi, Weierstrass, Kronecker, Kummer, and Dedekind were all Germans. So were Riemann and Cantor, though I'm not in their class anyway. And it's sacrilegious to even mention Gauss—who was German also—in this context. And the university here doesn't have any special feel to me. You'd think it would. Schrödinger was Viennese, but the dates are wrong. He died too late. And anyway, I'm absolutely certain I couldn't have been a mathematical *physicist*" (Noam dislikes physicists as a group; we all have our little prejudices) "or any kind of applied mathematician" (one who seeks mathematical answers with a view toward their application in physics or engineering). "I must have been a *pure* mathematician" (pursuing mathematical matters for their own intrinsic interest).

"How do you know you weren't a butcher?" I asked, risking (and earning) Noam's contemptuous stare. I was feeling cynical. My initial dismay had given way to alternating moods of cynicism, boredom, and, occasionally, receptiveness. The cynicism was acutest when Noam said anything about having thought all this out when he was a kid. He certainly does take himself seriously, I couldn't help thinking. His disinclination to think *about* himself—to think himself as object—shouldn't be mistaken for humility. What he does think, he thinks with the utmost confidence, even if it was thought as a child. I was prepared to take seriously any view arrived at by the mature man; but my reverence didn't extend indefinitely back along his lifeline.

But I was more receptive—approached almost to a suspension of disbelief—when Noam spoke from the viewpoint not of the juvenile, but of (you guessed it) the genius. Of course he sees more, sees higher, wider, and deeper, than we others do. That's what it *means* to be a genius. Do we others have the *right* to cynicism? Perhaps the unorthodoxy of his view redounds to the discredit of the orthodox. That's the attitude Noam took:

"Most people's experience is limited to sensory input, and their capacities for conceiving are limited to the categories appropriate for organizing this input. No wonder so much is inconceivable for them.

They wouldn't even be able to get a grasp on such concepts as the hypercube in fourth-dimensional space, or infinities differing from one another by orders of magnitude, or even the square root of minus one. What are they going to say—that such mathematical facts are inconceivable? For *them* they are. One has to let go of one's sensory imagination, soar way beyond the physically conceivable. The physical limits aren't the conceivable limits."

And another time:

"From where I stand and what I can see from there—and I'm speaking only as a mathematician now—bodies and their space occupy only a rather insignificant stratum of reality. So it doesn't surprise me at all that we—or at any rate our minds—turn out not to be bodies. That's the way it really *ought* to be, that the thinking part of us, the part that can grasp the nonsensible, the purely intelligible, should itself be nonphysical."

From where I stand and what I can see from there . . . These words penetrated through to me. How could I—standing where I did—presume to judge? Remember, I told myself, the prisoners of darkness in Plato's allegory of the cave, judging the truth-seer by their own severely limited view of things: "If such a one," the philosopher, "should go down again and take his old place, would he not get his eyes full of darkness, thus suddenly coming out of the sunlight? Now if he should be required to contend with these perpetual prisoners in evaluating these shadows while his vision was still dim and before his eyes were accustomed to the dark . . . would he not provoke laughter, and would it not be said of him that he had returned from his journey aloft with his eyes ruined and that it was not worthwhile even to attempt the ascent?"

That's Plato I'm quoting, not Noam; but Noam shares Plato's view of the sense-oriented masses and has said similar things of his own.

"You prefer that other world, don't you?" I asked him at one point in Vienna. "You think it's superior."

"Superior? I don't know. It's certainly more beautiful."

"D. H. Lawrence said that all things that are beautiful have to do with the body, that the notion of incorporeal beauty is incoherent."

"That's rot. Arrogant rot. It's like the blind denying the existence and beauty of colors."

My husband sounded so much like Plato at times, I was tempted to suggest that before he was the Viennese mathematician perhaps he had been the Greek philosopher.

It was late in the afternoon on our third day of pounding the cobblestones when we saw a middle-aged man in Chassidic garb. Noam wordlessly followed him down Fleischmarkt, turning left on Judengasse, then right on Hoher Markt. We were in a little medieval square; JUDENPLATZ, the sign said, and in the center was a small chamber orchestra playing "Eine kleine Nachtmusik." Noam moved as in a trance to take a seat. I kept glancing at him throughout the all-Mozart concert. His expression never changed, which is unusual when he listens to music.

Dusk was falling by the time the musicians packed away their instruments. At last Noam spoke to me.

"I think this is it. I think this is where I lived."

"Judenplatz? Do you know what that means? Jews' Place." Noam's knowledge of German, as of French, is exceedingly slight.

"I *know*, Renee," he said coldly.

We walked slowly around the square. It appeared to be a garment district. In one corner was a building that housed some Israeli and Jewish religious organizations. We circled the square again and again, maybe fifteen or twenty times. Finally I said:

"Noam, I'm hungry. Can we eat?"

There was a little restaurant next to the corner building housing the Jewish groups. We sat down at one of the tables outside on the sidewalk.

"Is this restaurant kosher?" I asked the waiter out of curiosity.

"No, I'm sorry," he said apologetically.

"Oh, it's all right. I was just wondering."

"Our proprietess is Jewish," he said hopefully.

The waiter was apparently unwilling to accept my assurance that my question had been motivated by pure curiosity, and when he came back with our fruit soup he told me he had asked the proprietess and had learned we could attain kosher food at the Weihburg restaurant on Seilerstätte. I thanked him for his trouble. Noam asked me what we had been talking about. I was afraid of his reaction at learning that the waiter had mistaken us for observant Jews, but Noam simply nodded at my explanation and went on eating.

In the middle of the schnitzel the proprietess herself came out to talk to us. I explained to her that I had only been curious about the restaurant, about whether there were any kosher restaurants in Vienna.

"Only one now. We have only twelve thousand Jews left in all of Austria, eleven thousand of them in Vienna."

I noticed that the inside of her arm was stamped with the blue numbers of a concentration camp. "Were you born here?" I asked.

"Oh yes, I am Viennese. I was born right here on Judenplatz, that house." She pointed across the street.

"And you still live right here?"

"No, no, but not far. I lived in America for a few years after the war, in New York's Washington Heights." She spoke the name with pride. "But I am Viennese." She smiled and shrugged. "In spite of it all. In spite of the fact that I can look out onto this square and remember when it flowed with blood. I am Viennese," she repeated with her shrug.

"Doesn't he speak any German?" she asked a little later on, tilting her head toward Noam, who, having finished his schnitzel, was staring off into space. I felt the derogatory slight of her tilt and smile with the already familiar explosion of outrage I had first experienced on the dinky. I always had to contain myself, as I contained myself now, from saying irrelevantly that my husband is a genius. "Why don't you pin a little sign onto his clothes?" Ava said to me when I told her this. " 'Please excuse the appearance of stupidity. I am a mathematical genius.' "

"How iz your *Speise?*" the proprietess said to him slowly, smiling proudly at her linguistic fluency. Noam turned and looked at her. He stared at her without saying anything until the grin faded from her plump face and she shrugged and turned back to me. After a few more sentences, she left us and went back inside.

"You know what this means?" Noam asked.

"What what means?"

"I was probably Jewish. In my former life I was most likely Jewish. I find that extraordinary, don't you?"

"I don't know."

"Think of it. Think of the improbability of two consecutive Jewish lives. It can't be coincidental. Do you understand?"

"No.

"It means that my Jewishness is essential to my identity." (So I guess he wasn't Plato. Maybe he was Philo.) "I find that extraordinary." (*This* he finds extraordinary.) "One's membership in a religious or racial class seems so incidental. You see, Renee, these things just are not a priori." (I certainly wouldn't dispute that.) He didn't speak for several more minutes, then:

"Well, all I have to do is find a Jewish Viennese mathematician who died in 1938. The more complete the description, the easier the task. But, you know, maybe I wasn't a professional mathematician, though I've always assumed it. Maybe I was a Jewish tailor or a Talmudic student with innate mathematical ability." Or a kosher butcher. "I really can't take anything for granted. Wait a minute! 1938! I was born in 1938! That's the year the Nazis invaded Austria! It all fits! I was a Viennese Jew killed by the Nazis. Maybe I was very young, a child, killed before the flowering of my mathematical talent. That would explain my anonymity. Renee, I think that's it. Many of the cases of reincarnation concern the death of a child." His eyes shone vividly blue. "It has the ring of truth to it."

The next morning Noam woke in a happy mood, whistling "Ride of the Valkyries" as he dressed.

"I've really been somewhat absurd," he told me over our rolls and coffee in the hotel's café. "I shouldn't be overly concerned with the identity of one particular individual, even if that individual is me. It's the general facts that are important. Before I only had a heuristic grasp of the truth. Now I have proof."

WE WERE expected in Hungary the next day and discussed how to spend our last day in Vienna. We were both anxious to visit the Figarohaus, the museum devoted to Mozart in the house where he had lived the brief good years of his life. After leaving the museum we walked the short distance to the building where Mozart had ended up, working on his *Requiem* and dying a pauper at the age of thirty-five. The block was gloomy, preserving through the years the depth of the fall—a fall at least when viewed from one perspective. In terms of the music there had been no decline. He had died with his powers still raging. I said something of the sort to Noam, and he answered:

"Do you think that's a tragedy?"

"Well yes, of course, for him and for us. Don't you?"

"I suppose. Certainly for us. We have some similar stories in the history of mathematics, particularly the one about Galois. He was killed at the age of twenty in some sort of political duel. The night before, as legend has it, he feverishly wrote down page after page of ideas, mostly just in outline form, jotting down in the margin, 'I have not time,' working until dawn, when he was shot."

"My God. Were they very important ideas?"

"I don't know what he wrote that night. Legend says it was the foundations of group theory, but that's too romantic to be credible. But he really was the founder of group theory. He developed the whole concept of groups. He had started out considering the question that was the fundamental problem in the theory of equations at the time: namely, under what conditions is an equation solvable? And in trying to answer this he developed methods that went way beyond the theory of equations, although I don't know if he himself knew that."

"But think what he would have done."

"Perhaps." Noam stared straight ahead for several moments, then continued: "Perhaps not. Perhaps his greatest work had all been done before the morning of the duel. Then he would have lived out a different kind of tragedy."

I found this so perverse a reaction to the story of Galois that I wondered whether Noam himself was worried about outliving his powers, or that his greatest work had been done when he was a child of twelve. But I would never have dared to ask him such questions. So instead I quipped:

"That's one of the compensations for being mediocre. One doesn't have to worry about *becoming* mediocre," and we both smiled.

Noam also insisted on visiting the Schubert Museum, the Haydn Museum and the Beethoven Museum. I suggested the Sigmund Freud Museum. Noam was livid.

"Absolutely not! I'm not going to waste my last day in Vienna paying homage to that charlatan with scientific pretensions."

I forebore pointing out to Noam that I had wasted three days in Vienna chasing after Noam chasing after himself. He would, I feared, respond that my presence had been neither requested nor desired. Instead I asked him why he thought so little of Freud.

"Freud! Don't tell me you take that stuff seriously."

I mumbled something about Freud's having been the Galileo of the mind.

"The Galileo of the mind!" Noam exploded. "Is that what you people think?" (Among whom was I being classed now? It couldn't be the positivists anymore. Nonmathematicians? Humanists? Idiots?) "The Galileo of the mind," he repeated contemptuously. "What rubbish. You really surprise me." (It was his turn to be surprised.) "I can't tell you how enraged I feel when I read or hear people coupling Freud's name with Einstein's as the geniuses of the century. Coupling Freud with Einstein! How can anyone compare the achievements of the two? Anyone dumb enough to do that wouldn't have the brains to understand what he was comparing Freud to in the first place. It's not that I have such respect for the empirical sciences, but to call psychoanalysis a scientific theory is absurdly high praise. Freud's ideas are completely ridiculous, unverified and unverifiable nonsense. The whole thing's got a built-in mechanism for discounting all counterevidence. I read some of Fraud's—sorry, Freudian slip —so-called case studies when I was in high school. The Rat Man, The Wolf Man, Dora. Hysterical, all right. Not the patients, the doctor. He makes up some story that might be true, but then again probably isn't. If the patient accepts it, it's verified. What a genius. But if the patient rejects it, that's just because he's still repressing the truth.

"I remember at the crucial point he gives poor Dora his analysis, which she vehemently rejects. She's in love with her father, of course." Noam was laughing now. "The very force with which she denies it, shows how true it is. And had she accepted it, that also would have shown how true it is. Everything confirms his theory, so nothing does. In *The Interpretation of Dreams* he comes out with the lawlike statement that all dreams are wish fulfillments. What about dreams that don't seem to be wish fulfillments? *They're* motivated by the wish to falsify Freud's law that all dreams are wish fulfillments. I ask you: is that a scientific theory? It's a pseudo-theory, the fantasy of a sloppy and, I think, rather sick mind. The emphasis on sex is ludicrous. I'm quite confident that sex plays a very trivial role in my psyche." (I was, too.) "It's ridiculous to devote so much thought to it. It's a bodily sensation, very pleasurable to have, but what's there to *think* about? What's there to hold the mind? People give it too much thought anyway, but Freud gave this mindless preoccupation intellectual respectability. Sex is a subject for little minds that can't get a grasp on the truly interesting things."

I felt profoundly rebuked, as Noam, I'm sure, intended me to. For I, as I had made the mistake of revealing in Rome, am one of the little minds that thinks about sex. Noam's silent Roman fury had finally found its words in this attack on Freud. The intellectual disdain was genuine; but the anger with which it was spoken was for me, I felt, for my having revealed myself among the contemptible masses who find sex interesting.

But isn't it? I glanced up at Noam, who was furiously scowling down into his *Schlag,* and decided to keep the discussion of the matter to myself.

Is sex really uninteresting? It *seems* so interesting. If sex isn't provocative, what the hell is? That special dimension of excitement attaches itself even to sexual thinking, to sexual discourse. But then Noam would say that our finding something interesting doesn't show that it actually is. In fact, if ever an evolutionary explanation offered itself, it does so here. A species concerned with the processes of procreation is going to get the edge on survival. And so we evolved sex-obsessed, biologically determined to find intercourse fascinating.

But sex in itself? The noumenal phenomenon? How would it look from the point of view of extraspecies intelligence? The reproductive act, accompanied (at best) with pleasurable sensations associated with certain regions of the body. These sensational accompaniments also have obvious survival value: the better it feels, the more we do it. But just how interesting can sensations—even the Big One—be? There just isn't enough conceptual complexity to allow for much analysis.

And sexual desire is merely the desire for these sensations, and no more exciting to think about then they are. Isn't it?

Of course, there is the other view of sex, the view that elevates sex to the status of ultimate truth, the truth that tells us the truth about ourselves, the fundamental fact about our conduct and existence, the secret dark meaning pervading our thoughts, our actions, and our dreams. What of *that?*

That, I could imagine Noam replying, would be evidence not for the nontriviality of sex, but rather for the triviality of us. If our essential truth is sexual, we're just not very interesting.

But how, I asked my mind's Noam, could a simple appetite such as you've described be categorized in terms of such distinctions as obscenity, perversity, and sin? There must be some complexity involved to admit such qualifications as these.

So what? answered he. So we impose these categories on sex. It's just part of our biologically determined obsession and the delusions thus produced. Think of what the Jews do to the simple appetite for food.

But, Noam, I persisted (it's significant, I suppose, that I should have taken to discussing sex with "Noam" in this fashion), haven't you left a rather important element out of your analysis? Haven't you failed to consider that the object of sexual desire is not a sensation . . . but a person? If you overlook that, then all sex is a kind of masturbation, rather an awkward kind at that, when you do it with someone else. Only that's all wrong. Masturbation isn't even sex, not really. It's the form of sex without the content; even when attaining the sensations (often more successfully than in the real thing), it's still missing the point. Because the point lies, somehow or other, in the other person, in the reciprocal desiring. No, no, Noam, you are wrong. Sex is a personal relation, and that's what makes it so deep and complex and interesting. It's not a logical relation. It's not as transparently lovely as logical relations. But it's still damn interesting.

This was my first real rebellion, unvoiced and unmanifested, but still deep and complete, against the supremacy of Noam's thinking. An image floated briefly before me. I tried to call it back and identify it, and finally succeeded. It's an image that's occurred to me frequently since: of the odd little sketch by Leonardo da Vinci that

Freud discusses in his study of the artist, *Leonardo da Vinci and a Memory of His Childhood*. (I was grateful that Noam hadn't read that one. His outrage, particularly at Freud's theory that genius is sublimated libido, would have been uncontrollable.) It shows a man copulating with a female whose face isn't drawn, *his* face turned away with a slight grimace from the act in which his body is engaged. One would never guess from the man's expression that he was at the moment in intimate union with another person. (Leonardo is also quoted there as having said: "The act of procreation and everything that has any relation to it is so disgusting that human beings would soon die out if it were not a traditional custom and if there were no pretty faces and sensuous dispositions." Freud, deductively leaping with an abandon that would not have excited Noam's admiration, suggests an unresolved Oedipal complex and latent homosexuality.)

Noam and I did not visit the house at Berggasse 19. We compromised instead on the Schönbrunn and Belvedere palaces.

WHEN WE ARRIVED at the chaotic Budapest train station, we were at a loss. We didn't know whether anyone from the conference was coming to meet us, and since, as Noam now bethought himself to mention, he had never met any of the Hungarian organizers, he wouldn't recognize them anyway. Would we ever make our own way to Esztergom, wherever that was?

"Why didn't you think of this before?" As I said this, I turned to Noam and noticed a man parading up and down the side of the tracks with a large sign on his chest printed (in red) with the word HIMMEL. We were not forgotten.

The young man was a mathematician from the Bolyai Institute, which was organizing the international conference. (Bolyai, Noam told me, was one of the five independent discoverers of non-Euclidean geometry.) Our brief ride through Budapest was enchanting. The beautiful city was nothing like the somber gray socialist presence I had anticipated. It's really two cities, Gabor, our driver, told us, divided by the Danube, which approximates more closely to its sung description here than in Vienna. Buda is primarily residential, and Pest, where we had arrived on the train, is more commercial.

We drove past the Parliament on the banks of the Danube (looking like Westminster upon the Thames), then crossed the wide river to Buda and continued out of the city.

Esztergom was a forty-minute drive from Budapest. It's a very pretty, hilly little village on the shores of the Danube, the view of which is dominated by the large bishopric built on a hill in the center of town. But for the few days we were there what dominated the town was the presence of the mathematical luminaries who had gathered from around the world. For the first time I saw Noam with people whom he regarded as on his level. There was one in particular, the Russian Nicolai Maralov, for whom Noam felt a respect bordering on reverence. It was a unique experience to see Noam speaking deferentially to someone.

There was an ordering of mathematical talent at the conference. First were the *Kohanim*, the high priests, descendents of Aaron— about seven or eight mathematicians who conversed directly with God. Then came the tribe of Levis, very special but not allowed entry into the Holy of Holies. And last came the congregation of Israelites, awaiting word from those on high, but still a nation apart, chosen by God.

The mathematical hierarchy was duplicated in the groupings of the spouses. My first morning there, I was invited by the wives of the *Kohanim* to join them at breakfast, thus confirming, had confirmation been needed, Noam's position in the mathematical world. I met Olga Maralov, wife of Nicolai and a linguist; Marta Künig, wife of Hermann Künig and a museum curator in Munich; and Barbara Stern, the wife of Eric Stern of Harvard, who, at twenty-six, was the youngest member of the inner sanctum.

"I'm afraid," Barbara said, "that about completes my humble description. Wife of Eric, mother of Karen, Jonathan, and David, sometime poet, lousy housewife."

She was a large, pleasant-faced woman who gave the overall impression of sloppiness, though all the individual parts appeared presentable enough. Perhaps the impression had its source in her movements. But whereas the other two women's smiles of ostensible welcome left me out in the cold, Barbara's was the kind one couldn't help returning in full.

The rest of the *Kohanim* had either not brought their wives or were wifeless. At breakfast the dining room (outside, under the lindens) was almost completely given over to women, for most of the mathematicians had finished long before and gone off to the first lecture. Nina Trotti, Enrico's dark, chic wife, toward whom I had been heading, was sitting at another table with, I eventually discovered, the women of the Levis.

Olga and Marta were both in their late forties and very good friends, so I naturally turned throughout the conference to Barbara, who is warm, natural, and very talkative. She was visibly delighted to have the select circle enlarged by one. For it could be expected that we would meet at international conference after conference.

"We were terribly surprised when Noam showed up with you," she said as soon as I had sat down. "No, not terribly. Happily. Eric had just seen him in Vancouver in early June, I think it was, and he never said anything about being married."

"That's because we weren't married yet. In fact, Noam proposed to me the night he returned from Vancouver."

"You mean you just got married?"

"Yes, a little over a month ago."

"A month!" Marta, given to exclaiming, exclaimed. "Then this is your honeymoon!"

"Well yes, I suppose." A honeymoon with precious little honey and plenty of stings.

"And I bet you'll be seeing very little of your new husband," Barbara said. "At least in Esztergom. Well, I suppose that's good. Honeymoons shouldn't create any illusions. That's what makes their ending so awful. Noam was very wise to show you immediately what it's like to consort with a mathematician." They all laughed.

"I'm so happy for Noam," Barbara said to me at one point. "He really needs someone to take care of him. I've always wondered how in the world he managed. Every time he's stayed with us I've just wished I could keep him on, adopt him or something. But I guess he's more practical than he appears. Eric could never have survived all those years on his own." (They had married when Eric, also a prodigy, was nineteen and Barbara was twenty-three.) "He would have gone floating off if there hadn't been me and the kids to weigh him down.

Of course, sometimes I worry that the weight may be a little too much. Three kids add up to an awful lot of distractions. Sometimes when they're all yelling for his attention or one of them is having problems, I worry that I've set math back hundreds of years because of my irresistible maternal urge."

I was interested in watching Barbara with her Eric, a boyishly shy man, amazingly (and obliviously) handsome. Barbara revered and babied him. But there were few opportunities to observe them together, for the mathematicians were consumed from morning to night in mathematics. I would catch glimpses now and then of Noam walking the narrow hilly streets between lectures, never alone and quite often with a large group of talking men. But here, unlike in Rome, I had the company of the other nonmathematician wives (and two husbands). The organizers had not forgotten us and had arranged for various trips: around Esztergom; to the neighboring villages to view the remains of the numerous invaders who had passed through; on a boat down the Danube.

At night the mathematicians would rejoin us, and we'd gather in the dining room after dinner to play charades. I only watched (I have a horror of making a spectacle of myself), but Noam, who never gives a thought to such considerations, threw himself into the game with great enthusiasm and was very good. At one point he had to act out *Saturday Night Fever* (the Americans were counting on the Russians never having heard of the movie) and he began by madly wiggling his hips, a sight I'll never forget. But the Russians were the undisputed charade champions, triumphant and unbeatable. They must play a lot. The first night they challenged everyone else, chanting, "The Russians against the world." The next night it was the communists against the capitalists; the night after, the "imperialists" (Russians and Americans) against the Europeans. There was something wonderful, I thought, about their laughter at the differences that loom so large in the other world. As far as they were concerned, they all lived within the same borders, the only borders that mattered. They were all mathematicians.

Barbara and I decided to make a trip together into Budapest. The Künigs had their car with them, having driven from Munich, and Barbara asked Marta if we could borrow it for a day. So Saturday afternoon, the day before the conference ended, we drove the Mercedes along the Danube into Budapest.

"Barbara," I said as I pushed down hard on the accelerator, "I have to get myself one of these little toys."

"Try to get Noam to turn a fraction of his attention to the stock market. You'd probably be rich before the next semester was over." She laughed. "I've been trying with Eric for years."

"Fat chance. Unless there's some mathematical beauty to be found in the fluctuations of Wall Street."

Barbara was very excited on the trip in, for she was going to try to track down some relatives in Budapest.

"I've tried each time we're here." She and Eric had been in Hungary twice before. It seemed there wasn't a European country they hadn't visited in the seven years since they'd been married. "But this time I have what I think is their address. They're the only family left in Europe. My grandmother came to the States alone when she was something like fifteen. She had eight brothers and sisters. She managed to send for one, but they sent the wrong one. Grandmother never forgave Great-aunt Sophie for being the one to survive. The rest were all killed during the second world war, except for one brother and his two sons. This brother and one of his sons were walking back to their home after being liberated from Auschwitz and some Hungarian peasants shot them on the road only a few miles from their village."

"God, how awful! To have survived all that and then be shot."

"Yes. I've been hearing these stories all my life. Anyway, the address, which I have right here"—she patted her pocket—"is, I hope, the address of the other son's son."

The conference organizers had given us a map marked with the address, so we had little trouble finding it. It was in an old building in the center of Pest, the bottom floor taken up with stores.

"It's supposed to be on the fifth floor," Barbara said, looking up doubtfully.

"I'll wait down here for you."

She returned after five minutes, jubilant. "It's them, all right. They're not home. I met a neighbor, who luckily spoke German. She said they'd be home from work around five o'clock. There's my cousin, who's an engineer, his wife, a teacher, and their three-year-old boy, she told me."

We decided to go sightseeing until five. We drove around the beautiful streets of Buda, wondering who lived in its palatial homes now. My imagination rioted with scenes (greatly influenced by *Dr. Zhivago*) of aristocrats fleeing, once haughty women with beautiful children clinging to them. We also visited the old Buda castle, now a museum, and the new Hilton. Finally it was almost five and we drove back to Pest.

"Good luck," I said as Barbara stepped out.

"Thanks. We'll meet here at six-thirty."

I decided to drive around for a while, stopping if anything caught my eye. The traffic in Pest was very bad, and I decided to return to beautiful Buda. But before I reached the bridge crossing the Danube, I noticed out of the corner of my eye a large stone building that I thought was decorated with Stars of David. (Things like that still leap out at me.) I circled back, and sure enough there were Jewish stars worked into the stones.

I parked and got out. It was obviously a very large synagogue. The main doors were locked, but there was a side door open. I went through and climbed two flights of stairs, finding myself at the top in a long, narrow room that housed a Jewish museum. There was a rich profusion of old silver and gold religious articles crowded on long tables: ornate Torah decorations, kiddush cups for blessing the wine on the Sabbath and holidays, menorahs for lighting the candles on Chanukah, and spice-boxes for *Havdalah*, the ceremony bidding farewell to the Sabbath. Another table was heaped with old holy books. A wall was lined with pictures of Hungarian synagogues, the majority now destroyed. This synagogue, I learned, is the second largest in Europe.

At the end of the long room was a smaller one, devoted entirely to the destruction of the Hungarian Jews under the Nazis. There were framed copies of the various edicts issued against the Jews, a map showing exterminated communities, and the most simple and eloquent statement of the horror: a faded pair of the black and white striped inmate's uniform and a pile of tattered boots.

The main part of the synagogue was closed, but I went out back into a large courtyard, now a cemetery for Nazi victims. I wandered around, searching for some information beyond the blankness of the names, yielded by an occasional "Doctor" or "Professor." Against a long wall were small metal plaques with more names, a memorial bulb burning beside each.

I left the courtyard and walked the surrounding streets. Many of the buildings were engraved with Stars of David or Hebrew letters. This had obviously been the center of Budapest Jewry. During our three days of pacing Vienna, Noam had told me something of the history of the Austro-Hungarian empire. His knowledge is quirkily detailed, full of odd stories, names, and dates. He always overwhelms me with his factual knowledge (and sometimes with his ignorance) of the most unexpected topics. If something about a subject attracts his attention, he sucks up every detail and remembers it forever. For some reason, at some point in the past, the Catholic Hapsburg dynasty had attracted his notice.

Maria Theresa, in the eighteenth century, had been warm and motherly, but, alas for the Jews, very pious. The Jews had been expelled. Franz Joseph, on the other hand, the last of the Hapsburg rulers, had been stern and soldierly, but had a Jewish mistress, and the Jews had prospered under him. The Hungarian Jews, in fact, became the wealthiest of the European Jewish communities. Now I was seeing the marks of this former prosperity chiseled into the stones.

On Dub *utca* I came to a very large iron gate and peered inside to a long dark courtyard surrounded by great gray buildings. On a far flight of stairs I saw two girls supporting between them a crippled dwarf. I followed them up and found myself in what appeared to be a restaurant of sorts. The dwarf was leaning near the door (the two girls having deposited him and left).

"*Salut,*" he said to me.

"*Salut.* Is this a restaurant?" I asked him in German.

"A welfare kitchen. Everyone is free to eat." He bowed slightly. "I am Janos Seifert, electrical engineer." He barely came up to my waist. His head, topped with a black beret, seemed freakishly large on his twisted shriveled body, but the face looking up into mine had an expression of almost aristocratic refinement and intelligence. It was jolting.

"Are you German?" he asked.

"No, no, American. I am Renee Himmel."

"An American," he said in beautiful English. "How do you do." He bowed again, then turned to a woman sitting at a table right behind us. The left side of her face was all crumpled up, as if it had collapsed inwards, and the right side slanted toward the left as if partially sucked in by the implosion. "Helena, this young lady is an American. Her name is Renee Himmel." He spoke in German. "Helena does not understand English," he explained to me.

Helena smiled at me with half her face. "Won't you please join us for dinner?"

"I'm very sorry. I would like to, but I have to meet a friend at six-thirty."

"Well, we have a little time," Janos said. "At least share a cup of coffee with us. Would you mind, my dear young lady, helping me over to the table."

When he had succeeded in getting himself seated, and had ordered a cup of the sickly sweet Hungarian coffee for me, he spoke again.

"Now, tell us please how you come to be in Budapest."

I explained to them about the conference at Esztergom, all the while wondering about them. (They were not, it turned out, related.) Both were stamped with blue numbers. I could imagine the blow that had destroyed Helena's face, but what had been done to Janos' body to produce such total deformity? He would have been a boy then.

"And you?" Janos asked. "What is your profession?" The assumption that I too would have a profession was universal in Hungary.

"I study philosophy."

"Ah, philosophy. The queen of the sciences. I am most impressed. But, you know, this is Providence. You are just the one I need. Can you tell me please the name of the French bishop who said that reality exists in the individual sensorium?"

"French bishop? I'm afraid I don't know. You don't mean Bishop Berkeley, do you?"

"No, no, Berkeley was British. This was a French bishop."

"I'm terribly sorry. I don't know."

"Oh no, don't concern yourself." He waved his shrunken, crum-

pled hand with an aristocratic gesture. "It will come to me. I only
wanted to save myself a little time."

"Speaking of time," I said, "I really must go or my friend will be
kept waiting. She's been trying to locate some relatives." I explained
as I stood up. "It's been a pleasure." It had been, though also disori-
enting. We whole-bodied persons make assumptions.

"Ah well, we must be philosophical and graciously permit you to
go. The pleasure was ours, my dear young lady, a short pleasure, but
sweet.

"Auf Wiedersehen," I said.

"Auf Wiedersehen." He looked at me questioningly and then said
with a smile, *"A guten* Shabbos."

A guten Shabbos. It was Shabbos. I had been sitting at a table with
people who had been enclosed in a different space, with people for
whom it was Shabbos. I had, unknowingly, been sharing a Shabbos
meal.

I walked slowly down the stairs and across the darkening courtyard.
There were some elderly men at the other end of the yard, entering
a doorway inscribed with Hebrew letters. They're probably going to
evening prayers, I thought, to *Maarev.* As I passed by, I saw that one
of them looked a little like my father: the delicate face structure,
high, pronounced cheekbones, and gentle expression. I watched him
disappear into the building and felt stabbed through with longing. I
wanted to watch him *davening Maarev,* but I thought of Barbara
waiting for me.

"It's Shabbos." The longing in me—for my father and his world
—had risen to my eyes and was blurring my vision. And then suddenly I was back inside it, inside Shabbos. The world had that
different feel, that closed-off, restful, floating calm. I was back inside
its space, enfolded in its distances, feeling the enforced but real sense
of serenity, bounded round by prohibitions. The appearances of
things were softened, muted, subtly but thoroughly transformed.

I walked slowly out of the courtyard and back to Dohemy *utca,*
where the car was parked. I tried the doors of the great synagogue
again, but they were still locked. As I got into my car, the noise and
hard outlines of the world reasserted themselves. I had broken
through the cobweb borders, had stepped outside of Shabbos, was on

the far side again of *Havdalah,* the separation between the sanctified and secular.

I drove back to meet Barbara. She was waiting outside the building where her relatives lived, and she looked close to tears.

"Barbara, I'm sorry I'm late. What's wrong?"

"Oh, Renee, it was such a disaster. They didn't speak any English or German or French, my only languages. They only spoke Hungarian and Russian. We couldn't communicate at all."

"It's a reflection of the political realities. The older people speak German; the younger ones, Russian."

"Yes, I really should have thought of it. But I just felt that if I could track them down, we'd find some way to communicate. I didn't think about being separated from them by anything so mundane as language."

"So what happened?"

"Nothing. It was awful. We just stared at one another. They seemed to understand I was a relative. I think the neighbor had mentioned it to them before she went out. They pointed to her door. And they acted very friendly. They seemed to know I wasn't just someone off the streets. I kept mentioning the name of my grandmother, but it didn't seem to mean anything to them. We just stood there staring at one another, smiling and shrugging. It was embarrassing. I left after about ten minutes, still smiling and shrugging."

We drove back to Esztergom in near silence, both of us brooding over the worlds out of which we had been shut, the pasts from which we were cut off. There's no going back, I kept thinking. You've made your choice, and now that life is dead to you. It was a world almost as inaccessible to me as that former existence Noam thought he had glimpsed in Vienna was now to him.

5

REALITY

We have no reason to seek for some criterion of personal identity that is distinct from the identity of our bodies as persisting physical objects. We find our intelligence or our will working and expressing themselves in action, at a particular place and a particular time, and just these movements, or this voluntary stillness are unmistakably mine, if they are my actions, animated by my intentions. . . . I can only be said to have lost a sense of my own identity if I have lost all sense of where I am and what I am doing.

—STUART HAMPSHIRE,
THOUGHT AND ACTION

*W*e returned to New Jersey in the middle of a heat wave. As we stepped out of the terminal at the airport, a steamy wave of air hit us smack in the face, knocking the breath out of us. Noam, usually so oblivious to his physical environment, stopped in midsentence:

"Hell, how are we going to breathe in this noxious stuff? This place isn't fit for human habitation."

My car was parked at the airport. I had to use a tissue to get the key into the burning ignition and then to hold the steering wheel. I'm usually paranoid about speeding on the well-patrolled turnpike, but right then I needed the sense of liberation that speeding gives me. Doing eighty blurred without softening the depressing scenery to our right and left, the factories eliminating their poisons into the already sick air.

New Jersey in August.

We left the turnpike at Exit 9. New Brunswick, a dying city, was never a pretty sight, and now it lay gasping in the heavy air. Its black inhabitants were sitting out on stoops and curbs, wordless, hopeless. We followed Route 27 out of the urban decline and into rural despair. Forlorn little houses stared out from behind their tangle of withered weeds, a sad, tired landscape in yellow and brown, parched and panting.

But when we reached the outskirts of Princeton—the northern shore of the large lake built with Carnegie money, where Einstein had done his sailing—everything changed. Stately homes looked serenely out over high, clipped hedges, and lush green lawns sparkled under whirling sprinklers. Even Dutch elm blight had been halted at Princeton's borders. Unperspiring women with tennis tans pedaled their bikes slowly through town, under the deep shade of ancient elms. The fertility of rationality. I had never before been so struck with the isolation of this world, our world. It floats like a glittering island of privilege in the vast dull Jersey sea.

And now it belonged to me. Nobody could question my right now to occupy this space. I was *there,* and not just anywhere. "You're marginal, very marginal," I remembered the graduate director telling me. Not anymore, not Mrs. Noam Himmel. (Gladly, gladly I took the name as my own.) I was at the glorious center, with all my world converging toward me in my new identity. I didn't have to try and hack it with my own questionable intellectual equipment. Any hacking I did (because I did plan to try—I planned on everything as I rode triumphantly into town) would be blissfully supererogatory. By the time we reached Princeton proper I was buoyant, floating high over the oppressive atmosphere.

We stopped off at Davidson's to pick up some provisions. As we walked together down the frozen food aisle, I heard someone calling Noam. It was Mel Bright, a mathematician I had met at several parties. He was with a man I didn't know.

"Hi, Noam, Renee. When did you get back?"

"Just now. We just got into town."

"Well then, welcome back. Welcome back to the heat. Don't think you've picked a particularly bad time to return. It's been like this all summer."

"Yes," the other man said. "We've been simmering in our own juices all season. I'm Ted Berliner, computer sciences." He reached out to shake Noam's hand.

"Oh, I'm sorry," Mel said. "I didn't realize you two hadn't met before. And this is Noam's new wife, Renee. Are you going by Feuer or Himmel?"

"Himmel."

"Ah, an old-fashioned girl." Ted shook my hand and then turned back to Noam. "Yes, I've of course been anxious to meet you ever since I heard you were coming. Say, why don't you two come over to our house for dinner tonight? It's a shame to have to start cooking as soon as you get back, and Liz, my wife, would be thrilled to meet you."

Stocked with a few groceries, we drove back to the house on Faculty Road in which Noam had been living and into which I had moved a few days after we decided to get married. The house belonged to a professor emeritus of economics, who would be returning at the end of September after a year in England.

"You'd better go over to the housing office first thing tomorrow,"

Noam said as we walked into the airless house. "See what they can get for us."

But that evening at the Berliners', when I mentioned our housing problem, Ted said to Noam:

"You really ought to buy a house, you know. It doesn't make sense for you to be paying out rent money when you could be investing it in real estate. And then there are the tax advantages."

"A house," Noam said. "I've never really considered it. It would be a burden, tie me down."

"But even if you sold after a year or two, you'd get your money back —probably even make a few thousand, the way real estate has been going up around here. Unless you have some better way of investing your money."

"Hmmmm. I'll have to think about it."

By the next morning the problem had been analyzed, the solution determined.

"Renee, I want you to find us a house."

"You're kidding." I was floored. I had lived either with my parents or in dorm rooms my whole life. An apartment of my own was somewhat daunting. But a house? I wasn't ready for that. It was too adult, too middle-aged. It belonged to the world of parents, and I wanted no part of it. Noam, however, was really sold on the idea.

"Don't be such a child. It's time to grow up."

"You want me to do it all by myself?"

"Well, I certainly don't have any time for it."

"But how do I do it? I don't know how to go about it." I heard and detested the whine in my voice.

"What do you mean? All you have to do is buy a newspaper, read the ads, and call up if something sounds promising. It shouldn't be beyond you. Everybody else seems to manage."

So after Noam left for Fine Hall I studied a copy of *Town Topics*. All the homes sounded very grand, much too much, with sunken rooms, cathedral ceilings, and swimming pools. And I had forgotten to ask Noam how much we could afford to spend. I tried calling him all through the day but kept missing him.

When he came home that evening, he asked me if I had made any progress:

"You know we don't have all that much time."

"Well, I read the ads in *Town Topics*. But I don't know how much we can afford to spend. Things seem very expensive."

"Give me the paper." Noam studied the ads and then paced around awhile. "Look, why don't you see a few houses and get an idea of what can be gotten for how much. Let's not waste time discussing this thing in a factual vacuum."

So the next morning I called up one of the brokers advertising a house that sounded relatively modest. Adele Nitkin, million-dollar realty agent, drove up to our house to pick me up. She was an elegant figure, tall and slim, and dressed in pale shades of taupe with matching makeup. I was impressed. But the image of elegance was shattered the minute she opened her mouth. Actually the voice came (loudly) out of the nose.

"Mrs. Himmel?" she asked icily, inspecting my jeans and sandals.

"You're from New York, aren't you?" I said as we drove over to the house in her pale yellow Coupe de Ville.

"Why, yes. How did you know?" I thought I detected dislike beneath the ice and wondered what I had done. Was it simply my clothes? I hadn't realized one is supposed to dress for real estate.

"What part of New York?" I asked in innocence, hoping to reach common ground with a fellow New Yorker.

"Oh, uptown."

"Really? I went to school uptown. Barnard. Did you live on the Upper West Side?"

"No."

"East Side?"

"No."

I tried farther uptown: "Washington Heights?"

"The Bronx," she said shortly. There was no mistaking the dislike now. Why am I *here?* I thought. She turned to me with a tight smile.

"You're just going to love this house. I know. It's a dream."

I hated the house. It looked like the kind of house they make television commercials in, a house in which to strive for shinier shines, whiter whites, fewer cavities. I could never live in such a house.

Adele sailed through, opening closets, switching on lights. She was enamored of the word "humongous." The living room was humongous, as were the bathrooms, the closets, and the yard. I asked her the price and was numbed by the answer. Up until then I had purchased in terms of tens, twenties, an occasional fifty. Even my darling Volvo, my biggest purchase, had cost only six hundred used. Now I was being asked to think in terms of hundreds of thousands.

"Is that in your price range?" The nasal icicle pierced through my reflections.

"I'm not exactly sure what our price range is. This is my first day looking. I'm going to have to discuss it with my husband."

"Yes, I can see you're new at the game. You haven't asked any of the right questions." She tittered, a tinkle of little ice cubes. "But at least give me an idea of the kind of house you like. Do you like this one?"

"I don't really think it's for me. I don't know. I guess it's a nice enough house"—I didn't want to insult her taste—"but it doesn't appeal to me at all."

"No? Why not? What do you want in a house?"

It was a question I had never considered, probably placing me, in Adele's scheme of things, at the far limits of eccentricity. "I'm not sure. This one feels alien, I don't know, cold. It's just not my world."

"I understand. You want warmth. You want charm and character. Am I right or am I right?"

Warmth, charm, and character sounded good, at least as properties of people. I wasn't quite sure how it came out translated into architecture, but could warmth, charm, and character be bad?

"Yes, I think you're right."

"You see? I know. I know the kind of house for you. Maybe an older house. That's where you usually find your character. Don't worry, I'm going to take care of you. I didn't actually think you'd like this one. Too sterile and nonindividualistic. You're an individualist."

She had apparently plummeted the depths of my person in the twenty minutes she had known me. I couldn't wait to get away from her. But life was not to be so kind.

During the next weeks Adele called me every few days with a house to show, with a humongous fireplace or family room or yard. Some of them were quite lovely, but I couldn't imagine how we could afford them, although *maybe* we could. I still hadn't been able to pin Noam down on that subject. Anyway I couldn't picture myself living comfortably in the midst of such grandeur. Then there was the other type of house, similar to, in fact indistinguishable from, the first house I had seen—happy-houses that depressed the hell out of me. I certainly couldn't imagine myself and Noam living in *them*.

For two weeks I did nothing but see and think houses. I was getting more and more depressed about the whole thing, and the prominent presence of Adele in my life didn't help. She always intimated that she and I were soulmates, of the same kind; that of all her many clients I was somehow special. I suppose that's how one gets to be a million-dollar agent. Only it was pretty obvious that we were not in the least of the same kind (and I began to fear that perhaps the difference was to her credit.) In fact, it was pretty obvious that she didn't care for me at all. And I'm always very hurt when people don't care for me, even if I can't stand their guts. On my part it wasn't just objective dislike of Adele; it was more self-referential. She made me doubt myself, my view of what—and therefore who—matters. She was coming from a distant mattering zone, and the self-assurance of her judgments made me suspect the validity of my own. She made me feel like a child, inadequate to the serious business of adulthood. Certain things (first and foremost, Property) were supposed to matter to grownups. I had better get *with* it.

I pondered the ethics of calling another agent. It wasn't exactly clear to me (little of all this was, and yet Noam presumed it was my affair), but from what Adele said it seemed she was my exclusive agent. She kept repeating that she could show me houses listed with other agencies, that if I saw anything that interested me I was to tell her about it. It seemed I had bonded myself to this realty tyrant with that first accursed phone call. I wanted to discuss the matter with Noam, but he grew impatient each time I mentioned it. I remembered Barbara Stern's worry about keeping Eric free from distractions, under which she included her three children. I too did not want to set math back hundreds of years.

Adele Nitkin invaded and took over my nightmares, dressed at one moment in coordinated shades of purple, makeup in plum, and the next in icy blue clothes and makeup. I wanted her out—out of my nightmares and out of my life. But how? If I could just find a house, that would be the end of it. My fingers itched to sign a contract.

Finally one morning I went in desperation down to the university housing office and was given a list of available apartments. The first one I looked at, a duplex in a stucco row on Prospect Avenue, owned by the university, was wonderful—a dark and woody place in which it would be possible to sit and daydream at high noon, unvisited by guilt's dark demons. This was the element, I now realized, missing from all of Adele's offerings. I could never have felt equal to those houses.

But this apartment, though classy, was comfortable. It would never challenge my right of occupation. On the first floor was a kitchen, a dining room, and a long, lovely living room. The kitchen had a back door leading out to a small garden (daffodils in the spring, I fantasized, roses through the summer, mums in the fall). The glorious living room had exposed oak beams, a red brick fireplace, and floor-to-ceiling bookcases stained in the same dark tone as the wooden floors laid throughout. (All very Oxford, I imagined. Leave it to Princeton.) A weighty oaken staircase led upstairs. Here there were three straightforward bedrooms (we could convert two into studies) and a big white bathroom with an oversize tub on legs, which would have launched Adele into schemes of modernization but which I adored.

Apartments, unlike houses, were something I could judge, and this was the most wonderful one I had ever seen. In fact, I felt quite confident that it had charm, warmth, and character. It was, I felt, the right kind of home for a gifted man and his devoted wife, for it was just comfortable enough not to distract with either the deprivation or the superfluity of material goods.

When I spoke to Noam about it that night he was surprisingly agreeable, having lost interest in the housing project.

"Fine. If you like it, go ahead. As long as we have someplace to live."

Exit, and not very gracefully, Adele.

Some friends told us about a place that rents furniture to university people, and within two weeks we were all settled in (as I was once again settled into my view of the world). I'd buy furniture slowly, I told myself; to date, I have not purchased a stick. But anyway, Noam was pleased and told me our first night in our own (rented) bed in our own (rented) place that I had done a good job, quite sweeping me away on a crest of self-satisfaction.

It had been a narrow escape. I hadn't realized at the time the dangers with which I was flirting, the precarious nature of the world of property ownership we had almost entered: that world of intimate, complicated, aggravating relationships with painters, plumbers, carpenters, gardeners, and electricians. Much of the conversation at dinner parties was devoted to the intricacies of these relationships, the degree of sensitivity they required. And though they were always amusing tales, told with the lightness and gaiety suitable to the occasion, I could glimpse the soul suffering that lay behind, and always felt correspondingly grateful for a situation that allowed us to go running with any household woe—from a clogged toilet to a mouse in the pantry—to the kind and efficient people at the university housing office. Even *if* the Adele Nitkins are right (a question I could now happily forget), and people like Noam and me *are* inadequate to the business of adulthood, here, in the nourishing womb of the university, we need never feel it.

Thus Noam and I settled down to our housekeeping. Or rather I settled down to keeping, Noam to being kept. It was assumed, of course, that Noam would be under no petty domestic obligations. None of that liberated fifty-fifty stuff for us. My shoulders would bear, and bear gracefully, gratefully, all the sundry and tedious details of the house. Plenty of women before me, *without* the benefits of matrimony, had done no less—or not much less, anyway. There had always been some colleague's wife only too happy to mother Noam, to do his laundry and sew on his buttons, and thereby do her bit for the history of mathematics. But—and this will not be the last of the dirty confessions about my married life—I did not assume these burdens joyfully. I was of two minds. When I thought of Noam as The Genius, then of course I was only too happy to wait on him hand and foot, to pick up the dirty socks he thought nothing of kicking off in the middle of the living room, or jump up from the dinner table when he announced he wanted a glass of water. But then, in the course of our day-to-day living, I would sometimes just think of him as my husband Noam; and then I would feel the resentment curdle.

This resentment had historical associations. It had been suffered throughout my childhood, when, as the girl in the family, I was expected to help wait on The Men—a class which included that little twerp, my brother. "Hurry up, dish it out. You'll keep The *Men* waiting." God forbid! The women—even guests—always got the last and the worst, the dried and the burnt. God forbid The Men shouldn't be satisfied. Any shmuck with a shmuck was a power before us. I couldn't believe it when I first heard that in some segments of society women are actually served first. (This order of dishing out carries over, of course, to bigger goodies than portions of roast chicken. Education, for instance. I could never have gone to Barnard without arguing and a full scholarship. My mother still mourns it as a terrible mistake.) I had been brought up to believe it is God's way for women to wait on men. And yet still I would mutter as my brother ran off after dinner to play baseball, while I scrounged around under the table picking up his filthy crumbs.

So, you see, the assumed division of labor in my marriage smacked too much of an aspect of traditional Judaism I had hated and had hoped to leave behind. (And yet I accepted with delirium the name Mrs. Noam Himmel.) I didn't go to Noam with a list of his and her chores. Mostly I just continued my childhood habit of muttering under the table.

Occasionally, when things got to what I considered a ludicrous point, I'd say something. For example, at dinner soon after our return Noam asked me repeatedly to get him something or other: a sharper knife, another glass of water (he consumes great quantities of the stuff), another napkin (his was all greasy). Finally I allowed myself to show a little annoyance. The man had a great brain, of course. But he also had legs.

"Why can't you get yourself a napkin? I've been fetching for you all night."

"*I* don't know where they are."

"Well, *I* could tell you. Don't you think you should know where things are? This is your house, too."

"I don't see any need for me to know. You know."

I soon gave up on such arguments. They only ended in my feeling petty.

All in all, though, it felt good for us to be back in Princeton, where we were accorded celebrity status. We became, especially in the first months following our return, the most sought-after of guests. For the first time in my life I was faced with decisions as to which invitations to accept. (Noam wanted no more than one party a week.) But the real pleasure of the return lay in the opportunity to view Noam once again in his natural setting. Here his outline, which in Europe had occasionally shifted disconcertingly, firmly readjusted itself. He could be difficult, but he was unquestionably the great man I had married.

September came. The air thinned, the undergraduates returned, and classes began. Noam and his colleagues reluctantly resumed the yoke of teaching and grumbled over the numerous distractions from research that the students presented. It's amusing how outsiders think *teaching* is the job of professors and ignorantly exclaim over how few hours academics have to work. Just last week Noam's gastro-enterologist (we've discovered an ulcer) asked him how many hours a week he has to teach and then laughed smugly.

"Three hours? That's all you guys have to work a week?" (Noam's teaching load is much lighter than the average—one of the lures Princeton had used to attract him.) "And with summers off? Boy, you people are really overworked." And he was the man treating Noam for an ulcer. Noam didn't—never does—bother to correct the man's faulty inference from three hours of teaching to three hours of work. What does he care what such people think?

But grumble though it might over the start of the academic year, the university world became more positive and purposeful. Here was a new year, a fresh morning in which to forget the terrifying nightmare shared by the town's collective unconscious: that the research won't pan out, or worse, that it won't matter a hoot if it does; that one's lifework is just so much mental onanism in the night. September brought the light of day, chased the nightmare away. No, no, it *is* important work, it *does* matter.

MY OLD FRIEND Ava Schwartz drove down from New York in a U-Haul truck the third week in September, with all her belongings. The Institute for Advanced Study provides neat furnished apartments with fireplaces for visiting members, set in motel-like buildings that wind along Einstein and von Neumann drives. (Einstein you of course know; von Neumann, perhaps not. He was one of this century's most important mathematicians, best known, perhaps, for his theory of games, which has so influenced economics. He was appointed to the Institute in 1933 and remained there until his death in 1957. All permanent members of the Institute, I think, choose to stay until they die.) Fuld Hall itself, the main administrative and academic building, looks like a grandish Howard Johnson's: a red brick Georgian building with a white cupola on top. (Had this architectural style motivated the remark of J. Robert Oppenheimer, the physicist who became the Institute's second director, that the place is "an intellectual hotel, dedicated to the preservation of the good things men live by"?)

Ava, who had lived with rats and roaches in her fifth-floor walk-up on Amsterdam, around the corner from Columbia, was thrilled with the ethereality (beats reality) of her new environment. It took the two of us about six hours to unload and sort out her stuff, mainly books. When we finished, we collapsed with a bottle of wine onto the modern blue couch and stared out the large picture window—across Olden Lane to the expansive green lawn, and beyond that to Fuld Hall. If ever a building stared wisely back, Fuld Hall did. In another setting the rather squat edifice would not have been prepossessing. But here, atop a slight incline, with the great lawn before it and the circular drive leading up to it—it dominated. Ava turned to me with a beatific smile:

"Oh, I'm a happy woman, a happy woman. Here I am sitting with my best friend looking out a window at Fuld Hall in my own glorious apartment on Einstein Drive. Einstein Drive," she sighed, "the sheer beauty of it." (Ava worships Einstein: "He wasn't just a genius. He was a *mensh.* ") "I've got two whole years. Two years to work on my own stuff for the first time in my life. There's nobody over me. Free at last, free at last, thank God Almighty I'm free at last."

My friend's euphoria wasn't just a matter of what she was escaping from, the captivity of The Shmuck; it was also what she was escaping to. The Institute for Advanced Study has a special place in our region of the mattering map, whose terrain I am concerned to lay out for you. For how can I give you my life without describing my zone?

If Princeton is one of the sacred spots, then the Institute is Princeton's holy of holies. It was created in 1930, when Abraham Flexner, a reformer in education, persuaded two New Jersey department store heirs, Louis Bamberger and his sister Mrs. Fuld, to charter a new type of institution dedicated to the "usefulness of useless knowledge." (You see why the place means so much to us.) Here the "permanent members," chosen with infinite care, and the promising young "temporary members," would be free to pursue their ideas, unencumbered by teaching responsibilities. The Institute is composed of administration and faculty. The bothersome remainder of almost all other seats of scholarship, the students, has been mercifully eliminated.

In 1932 Flexner announced that the first two appointed members would be Oswald Veblen, the leading mathematician at Princeton, and Albert Einstein, the most famous scientist in the world, on the run from Nazism. Hitler ranks only after Bamberger and Fuld, someone once said, in terms of helping the Institute become what it is, as scholar after scholar fled Göttingen for Princeton.

The Institute was established from its inception as the incomparable gathering place of genius, the Mount Olympus of pure thought. Each of the permanent members must be judged by the faculty at large as godlike. (Gödel, the only contemporary on Noam's roll call of mathematical minor deities, and another legendary figure, was a permanent member until his very recent tragic death. Having convinced himself of an attempt to poison him, he refused to eat and eventually died of starvation. He published papers totaling less than seventy-five pages in his life, but every field he touched was thereby revolutionized. Our world is eagerly awaiting the posthumous publication of his works, which are rumored to contain an a priori proof of God's existence—a situation which has prompted me to flirt with the idea of a symbolism-heavy play entitled *Waiting for Gödel*.) This requirement of divinity has produced problems from the beginning.

At first Flexner thought to restrict the faculty to mathematicians. Mathematics, "the severest of disciplines," he called it, enjoys a great advantage when one demands only the best: mathematicians can unanimously agree on the identity of their leading peers. Just as the results in math are objectively certain, so too are judgments of the significance of the results, the degree of their importance, beauty and depth; and so too, therefore, are the evaluations of just how good the mathematicians themselves are. Arguments over the ordering do not exist, as they so destructively do in other fields. Mathematicians are also quite inexpensive to maintain, Flexner observed, requiring only "a few men, a few rooms, books, blackboards, chalk, paper, and pencils."

But Flexner and his successors eventually decided to expand and diversify the Olympian population. Flexner wanted some humanists, economists, and political theorists; Oppenheimer wanted more physicists. But the existing population, the mathematicians, fought the attempts of the would-be émigrés. They fought not out of the selfish desire to keep it all for themselves (these are *pure* mathematicians, remember) but rather out of their understanding of the nature of their Institute and the requirements it entailed. Were these others indeed gods? Where was the certainty: in the results they produced or the evaluations of them? The people in these other fields couldn't even agree among themselves. Why should they be taken seriously?

The Institute finally succeeded in establishing, in addition to the School of Mathematics, a School of Natural Sciences, composed primarily of physicists with interests sufficiently theoretical to require no labs, and a mongrel School of History (which even includes some historians of philosophy). But bitter controversy broke out anew when the current director, Carl Kaysen, an economist who had, from the point of view of the mathematicians, dubious credentials to begin with, decided to establish a School of Social Sciences. He had gotten his first appointment, a sociologist with credentials about as unchallengeable as a social scientist can hope to attain, past the puritanical mathematicians; but they balked at his second appointment, another sociologist, who, like the first, worked on the sociology of religion. The fight got ugly (although not personal, you understand), spilling over into the pages of the New York *Times* and even into an article in *The Atlantic Monthly* entitled "Shoot-Out on Mt. Olympus." Said one particularly pure mathematician: "Many of us started reading the worthless works of the candidate. I've seen poor candidates before, but I've never had the feeling of so utterly wasting my time." Soon the mathematicians were boycotting the cafeteria, which had been a pet project of Kaysen's. They were joined by some historians (whose motives I rather suspect—were they trying to appropriate some of the appearance of certainty from their allies?). The physicists for the most part sided with Kaysen, arguing that the standards for each discipline are intrinsically different, that the certainty of pure mathematics can't be expected anywhere else.

I tell you all this to give you an idea of how things look from within this region of the map, the sort of issue that intensely matters. A similar antagonism exists within my own field, between the so-called analytic or linguistic philosophers, who aim, at any price, to purify philosophy of all vagueness and uncertainty, and those who will tolerate (and even revel in) obscurity, accepting the uncertainty that comes with grappling with the foamy stuff. (Kant: "For long before men began to inquire into nature methodically, they consulted abstract reason . . . So metaphysics floated to the surface, like foam, which dissolved the moment it was scooped off. But immediately there appeared a new supply on the surface, to be ever eagerly gathered up by some; while others, instead of seeking in the depths the cause of the phenomenon, thought they showed their wisdom by ridiculing the idle labor of their neighbors.")

My husband, by the way, as purest of the pure, was in complete agreement with the mathematicians at the Institute. In fact, he a priori dismisses the work of sociologists, "pseudo-scientists all."

Ava came for dinner the night after moving in. It was the first time she and Noam were to meet, and I was very nervous. They both have such strong personalities, and I was afraid they might explode on contact. And, as I've mentioned before, Noam holds an uncharitable view of physicists as a group.

My worst fears were realized as dinner progressed. Ava had been speaking of Einstein's years at the Institute (which became popularly known as the Einstein Institute), the last twenty-five years of his life.

"It was tragic. His life as a physicist was essentially over. He didn't produce anything worthwhile, just kept toiling away at that unified field theory, a supreme exercise in futility. He was completely alienated from the mainstream of physics because of his refusal to accept quantum mechanics, even though the theory was the consequence of his own earlier work. He just refused to accept that reality didn't conform to his own philosophical presuppositions, that the most basic laws of matter are fundamentally statistical. He couldn't buy the indeterminacy of nature: 'God doesn't play dice with the world.' "

Ava shook her head. "Even the strongest minds have their weaknesses, and in the end he was destroyed by his."

"Einstein was absolutely right," Noam said.

"What?" Ava almost choked on her wine.

"Quantum theory is absurd. It produces paradoxes."

"It works. It gives us predictions that are confirmed."

"Hah." Noam turned to me and said contemptuously, "You see what I mean about physicists? That's a typical physicist's response. It works. They don't give a damn about reality. They're a bunch of tinkering engineers for the most part. Einstein was different, of course, and for that he's criticized."

"The fact that a theory works is pretty good evidence for its being true," Ava said. "That's the test in science."

"A theory with illogical consequences is not true, can't be true. If anything counts against a theory, it's that."

"What makes logic so absolute? Physical facts come first. Logic has to conform to them."

That remark raised the temperature of the atmosphere way beyond Noam's kindling point. He exploded.

"I'll tell you the consequences of quantum mechanics. Physicists' minds have been destroyed by it. They work with an illogical theory and they forget how to think." He turned away at last and addressed Ava. "You people don't know how to think anymore. Throw out logic, will you? How the hell are you fools going to deduce the physical facts, how are you going to deduce *anything,* without logic?"

Ava smiled calmly. "Look, it's just like with Euclidean geometry." "Everybody took it for granted that it was necessarily true until they discovered other geometries. Then they found that not only isn't Euclidean geometry necessarily true, it isn't even empirically true. It isn't the geometry of our space. It's the same thing with logic. We have to discover which is the empirical logic."

"Oh, you're going to lecture me on geometry. You physicists don't understand physics anymore. Don't presume to explain mathematics to a mathematician."

The nastiness of Noam's tone blew me over to Ava's side. Throughout the evening I silently sided with first one and then the other, depending on who I thought was being given the harder time.

"The analogy between logic and geometry is completely far-fetched," Noam said. "There aren't any alternative logics to choose from. What you get in so-called deviant logics are distortions of language. The logical laws aren't changed."

"I think the analogy with geometry isn't at all far-fetched. The lesson there was perfectly general. What determines truth is the brute facts of the physical world. The world is the way it is and it's all we've got. And if we want to know what it's like, we've got to *look* at it. There aren't any a priori necessarily true facts."

"Well, that's very interesting news to me, because I spend my whole life a priori discovering necessary truths."

"Uh huh. You only think they're necessary. Just like everybody used to think about geometry. The appearance of necessity isn't reliable. It ain't necessarily so. Nothing is."

"I'm afraid you don't understand the first thing about it."

"So explain it to me. Where do these necessary truths come from? I understand where physical truths come from, from physical reality. But where the hell do your necessary truths come from? Plato's heaven? *In den schönen Regionen, wo die reinen Formen wohnen?*"

Where had she picked up that one? She laughed snidely, and I swung back to Noam's side.

"You're thinking of it all wrong," Noam answered. "Logic doesn't derive from the way the world is. It determines the way the world has to be."

"And what determines logic?" Ava asked.

"That's a stupid question." Noam's tone was matter-of-fact and calm, but I cringed at the words. "Nothing, of course. Or logic itself."

"So logic is the Absolute, the Unmoved Mover, the First Cause."

"If you like."

"I don't understand such mysticism."

Noam laughed. "Well, if I'm a mystic, you're a farmer."

"A farmer?" Ava wrinkled her brow in perplexity and then grinned. "Oh, I see. You mean I get my hands dirty in the grubby real world."

"In the grubby *physical* world," Noam rejoined. "Which by no means exhausts reality."

With this remark they were off again, Noam accusing Ava of absurdity, Ava accusing Noam of obscurity.

"You Platonists all suffer from Plato's weakness. As soon as you get to the heart of the matter, you lapse into metaphor. Can't you say anything clearly? It's misticism, spelled with an *i.*"

"I prefer a vague but vaguely true view to one that is clear and clearly false."

Ava left at two in the morning.

"Nice girl," Noam said. "Terrible views, but then what can you expect? I like her, though."

And Ava called the next morning to tell me how much she had enjoyed the evening and how much she liked Noam: "He's great. The real goods. A genuine article. I can't tell you how relieved I am."

So was I. It's always the same when they're together. It took me a while to get used to it. The first few times when Noam called some statement of Ava's idiotic, her view nonsense, I suffered on my friend's behalf. Until I noticed that the insults didn't bother her in the least. Both of them have the same impersonal attitude toward ideas, whether their own or others'. It's the validity that matters, not the person incidentally attached. When I tried to apologize once to Ava, after an evening when I thought Noam had been particularly abusive, she laughed.

"It's not a personal insult, Renee. Don't you understand that? It's the view he's calling stupid, not me. And, you know, this time he was right. Sometimes I argue things with a force greater than I believe them with. You know, just to try them out, see how far you can push them. I think Noam understands that. Anyway, you don't have to worry about *my* feelings, sweetie. The only thing I feel toward Noam is grateful that he takes me seriously enough to call me dumb."

I felt, for the billionth time, overwhelmed with admiration for Ava. This was the kind of woman Noam ought to have married. *I* could never shrug it off when Noam called something I said stupid. Blind terror seized me. I had, from the beginning, feared that he'd penetrate to my essential confusion, that he'd make the simple deduction from stupid statements to stupid thinking, and from thinking stupid to being stupid. In short, to my secret: My intelligence, like my beauty, has always been overpraised, misperceived. The conjunction favors both conjuncts. I am beautiful for a brainy woman, brainy for a beautiful woman, but objectively speaking, neither beautiful nor brainy. My very presentation is an illusion, a deception practiced on others even with no help from me. The phenomenal self appears phenomenal, but the uneasy noumenal self knows. Beneath the external swagger, the phenomenological reality is fear.

Why did it matter so much, you wonder, whether I was brilliant or not? You have to remember where I stand, and how things look from in here. (Most of us manage to situate ourselves in that region of the mattering map where one's own self comes out mattering. Sick is the soul that can't quite manage to bring this off.) Here intelligence is the issue that draws the boundaries, provides the distinctions that make the difference: who are the somebodies and who the nobodies; who the cherished and who the despised; who the heroes and who the misfits.

These words of mine recall for me the dirgelike chant repeated throughout the Jewish period of repentance that falls in the autumn, beginning with Rosh Hashanah, the Jewish New Year, proceeding through the Ten Days of Repentance, and closing with Yom Kippur, the Day of Atonement, the holiest day of the Jewish year:

"On Rosh Hashanah their destiny is inscribed, and on Yom Kippur it is sealed, how many shall pass away and how many shall be brought into existence; who shall live and who shall die; who shall come to a timely end, and who to an untimely end; who shall perish by fire and who by water; who by sword and who by beast; who by hunger and who by thirst; who by earthquake and who by plague; who by strangling and who by stoning; who shall be at ease and who shall wander about; who shall have comfort and who shall be tormented; who shall become poor and who shall become rich; who shall be lowered and who shall be raised."

This first part is sung by the cantor. But at this point the whole congregation breaks out into a great rousing shout:

"But repentance, prayer, and charity cancel the stern decree!"

I would like to find some new words to end my own dirgelike chant: a great rousing shout that could inspire the same hope the other once did. For failing that, there is no salvation from the agony of suspecting I can't measure up.

And how long could Noam be hoodwinked? My reticence with him was the product of fear. Each statement potentially exposed me. Just let his infatuation wear off a bit more (it was already showing thin), he'd see me for what I am, or what I feared I might be, awaiting final confirmation from others. I'd managed to fool some, but they were ipso facto fools, just as those who judged me harshly were wise. I had captured the prize: the love of the genius. The trick was to keep it.

Ava has no fears like these. She's terrifically smart, knows it, and hardly gives the fact a thought. It's taken for granted, like the color of her eyes. She has confidence in her views, but I've never seen anyone give them up less painfully on good evidence. (Noam, for example, has persuaded her to change her mind about logic. They had been arguing the issue for months, Ava giving no indication of moving. And then, after one of Noam's little speeches attacking her view, she said: "You know, you're right.")

Unlike most people, Ava's behavior when with Noam isn't unlike her behavior at any other time. My friend Sarah Slater, on the other hand, with whom I became so thick my first year at Princeton, undergoes a radical decomposition when exposed to my husband. The first time he turned his high beam on one of her statements, she squirmed like some pitiful little creature pinned down on a biologist's slide. After that she hardly ever spoke in his presence. Even when he was somewhere in the house, I noticed, her already soft voice would fade still more. It was painful for me to watch that great expanse of intelligence and humor shrink inward to a vanishing point in fear of my husband. I asked Noam a few times if he couldn't try to be particularly friendly and encouraging to her, to try to coax her out of her shell.

"I think I'm friendly to her. I don't know what you mean."

"If she says something, don't pounce."

"I don't think I've ever pounced on her. I don't remember her ever saying anything for me to pounce on. I don't remember her ever saying anything at all."

"That's because she's afraid of you. It's such a shame that you can't see what she's really like, what a great person she is. She just shrivels up when you're around."

"Afraid of me? Well, I certainly haven't done anything to cause her fear. You can't blame me for her irrationality."

"Maybe it is irrational, and I'm not blaming you. I just wish we could do something about it."

"What do you want me to do? Agree with everything she says, should she ever say anything?" (This, you understand, was not a genuine suggestion. To feign agreement with a view not his own would be a violation of his deepest ethical instincts. He was trying to point out the absurdity of my request.)

"It's that way you have of dissecting every comment. Couldn't you be a little less critical with her?"

"Look, Renee, you can't ask me to stop being me. If one of your friends doesn't like me, okay, she doesn't like me."

Sarah had undergone a happy change of status. The previous spring she had come on the job market and had had spectacular success, made all the more impressive considering the current glut of Ph.D.s. In the great boom of the late fifties and early sixties, graduate departments, particularly at state universities, had expanded and conferred degrees in great abundance. But then the funds, from both government and private foundations, had dried up, and departments had shrunk, resulting in diminished need. Suddenly there was a large superfluity of Ph.D.s, compounded by demographic changes. And, of course, the uncooperative tenured faculty has refused to retire or expire at the necessary rate. The result has been a severe depression, in both the economic and psychological senses, in the academic community.

A field like philosophy, considered an impractical and therefore dispensable luxury, is especially hard hit. Some colleges have even eliminated the department altogether, or (sub)merged it into linguistics or comparative literature. At the annual meetings of the American Philosophical Association, the hunting ground for philosophical employment, there have been in recent years about eighty applicants for every one of the jobs coming up. Many of those on the breadlines are there for the second or third time, having come to the terminus of their non-tenure track job, or having been turned down for tenure.

As difficult as it has become to get those first jobs, it's become even more challenging to hold on to them. It's much more practical for a university to refuse tenure, and the salary increase that goes with it, and instead hire a freshly minted Ph.D.

What adds to the bitterness is that so few of the judging older faculty could themselves pass the standards they impose on their juniors. The majority of them were tenured in the good old days, when tenure was more or less automatic, when the whole tenure system was meant to protect faculty from unfair dismissal on political or other grounds. But the economics of university life have changed and tenure has become the exception on most campuses. One state university has been automatically turning down all young faculty who haven't managed to publish a book in their first six years of teaching. Recently they turned down a candidate who had written a book, and a well-received one. Unfortunately, judged they, he had written the book only to get tenure.

It's depressing but also impressive to consider these very bright people struggling after these insecure positions with salaries less than the average blue-collar worker's (the result of the laws of supply and demand and the absence of strong unions), when any one of them could, for example, take a short course in real estate and soon be driving around in a pale yellow Coupe de Ville, should he or she so desire. But then again, should one be impressed? It's not as if they're selfless. They're all reaching for prizes, too, even if not the cruder sort that one can ride around in or display in one's home. They, too, are motivated by the will to matter, which expresses itself in conformity to *their* mattering zone. So why should one be impressed, objectively speaking? Only if this is the zone that truly matters—not just mine, but God's very own.

My friend Sarah had sailed through the academic slump, getting interviews wherever she applied (the interview alone is, when so many are applying, a juicy plum) and receiving in the end five job offers, one from Princeton itself. But nothing could ever make her feel good about herself. There's always some way to interpret the evidence so that it doesn't reflect well on her.

"It's just because I'm a woman. Departments all need their token woman."

"That's ridiculous. There were plenty of other women hunting there. No one did as well as you. And beside, most departments already have their token woman."

"Well, I was the only woman this year from Princeton. And there was only one woman from Harvard. She, by the way, did very well, too. And that's not true about most departments already having their woman. Three of the five that offered me jobs don't have any." Whatever else one might think of affirmative action, its effect on people like Sarah has not been healthy.

Sarah is wonderful so long as she's looking outside herself, but she's dark and brooding Salem when she turns her gaze inward. Instead of rejoicing over her triumphs, she spent the next weeks agonizing over her decision. The thought of joining Princeton's faculty terrified her, but so did the thought of moving to a new and unknown academic setting. In the end inertia, as she put it, won out, and she accepted Princeton's offer. I, of course, was overjoyed. I had tried to be unbiased, but somehow had always managed to be very impressed with the virtues of Princeton when discussing the choices with her.

It was probably the wrong decision, and I've always regretted my part in it. It's difficult enough to come to regard one's former professors as colleagues, but in Sarah's case her shaky ego made it almost impossible to jump the Great Divide. I didn't get to see her all that much once the decision was made, especially after the semester got under way. She was constantly working, feverishly trying to build up a dam against the great sea of her self-perceived inadequacy. Her soft voice acquired a new quiver. She found her graduate seminar particularly terrifying.

"It was kind of fun to catch up the professor when I was a student, but the awfulness of being on the other side! I can't think with all those gun-happy sharpshooters aiming straight at my head, just waiting for a false move."

It was a night in late October, and I was visiting Sarah in the little monk's cell of an apartment, in the attic of a private house a few blocks from campus, that she had moved into when a student. The stairs leading to it were outside, in back of the house, and became treacherous when they iced over in winter. But this separate mode of access gave a fitting sense of isolation to the little set of rooms floating above. One never felt they were attached to a substantial house below. They were a world unto themselves, stark and pure. One walked into a smallish room, meant to be a living room, where Sarah had placed a mattress on the floor where she slept the four hours a night she allotted herself. A long, right-angled hallway led to a small but windowed kitchen on the left and the larger, lighter room where Sarah lived on the right. Here the furniture was a large desk she had built into the wall under the attic-slant of the ceiling, and orange-crate bookcases neatly crammed with books and papers. The desk functioned as a table, when one was required, and was large enough so that a place could always be found for one's plate without disturbing the work. There was a wooden folding chair before the desk, and Sarah could produce three more, if necessary, from a closet. I was sitting on one now across the desk from her.

Watching her as she talked to me of her trials, I thought again how surprising it was that this Puritan's face should belong to a dear friend, should be a face to which I could tell everything. She passed from relating the miseries of her teaching to the agonies of her research. One after another of her interpretations of Locke's notion of substance had collapsed. Her voice was flat with despair. How wrong we all are about her, I thought while I listened. Everyone thinks of her as without passion and blood. But it's all there, all tied up with her work. Or is it? For the hundredth time, at least, I found myself wondering about the inner Sarah, curious about whether all her passion is intellectual. I felt free to tell but not ask her anything. There is a fragility in her that I'm in fear of shattering.

But though Sarah's inner life was, and probably will remain forever, a mystery to all but Sarah, surely the facts of her outer existence were settled. When I thought of my own life in ten years, I really didn't know what to picture. Would I be in academia or out in the real world? A mother? I wasn't even absolutely confident I'd be married. But with Sarah the picture was all completed, the outlines all filled in. Did Sarah see it that way?

"Can you picture yourself in ten years?" I broke into Sarah's narrative suddenly. "I'm sorry for interrupting, but I was wondering if you think you'll be then exactly as you are now."

Sarah thought for a few seconds and then smiled. "Realistically,

I suppose I'll be then exactly as I am now. But very deep down, below the realistic level, I think in Cinderella terms."

"Cinderella terms?"

"You know, Cinderella, wicked step-relatives, fairy godmother, Prince Charming. Deep down I believe—no, it's too deep down to be called belief. It's just reflexive. Deep down I reflex that because I'm such a good, hard-working girl, someday, on the night of the ball, the great transformation will take place."

I tried to recall the details of the Cinderella story: the abused, overworked girl living among cruel step-relatives; the invitation from the castle to the great ball, given by the King and Queen (was it for the express purpose of finding the most beautiful girl in the kingdom for their son? I couldn't remember); the ugly stepsisters primping themselves, ordering poor, unwashed, sooty Cinderella around. And then, after their departure, appears the Fairy Godmother, that incarnation of all our desperate childhood hopes about our parents, who some of us continue to seek in friends and lovers and others throughout our lives. And the perfect mother has perfect power, possessed of a magic wand and the precisely right words. A pumpkin is transformed into a golden carriage, white mice into white horses, lizards into liveried footmen, and Cinderella's sad rags into the most beautiful dress ever seen. On her small (that's important) feet gleam little glass (glass?) slippers. "Be back by midnight," F.G. warns. Did she herself impose this condition or was it dictated from without? In any case, Cinderella departs for the castle and the glory that awaits her there. Everybody stares as she walks in. Even the musicians stop playing a moment to gape at the vision. Who is she, they all wonder, including the step-relatives, who have never seen the beauty beneath the cinders. And then she's whirling around the room in the arms of the smitten Prince, until her fast exit at midnight, the Prince in hot pursuit.

My recollection of the story was accompanied—dimly, at the back of my mind—by the kind of sarcastic annotations so easy to append to such a tale. The story contained all the elements of the feminine mystique, culminating in the final outrage: the girl's passive salvation by means of the handsome male, thanks to her beauty (and small feet). Was any tale more explicit?

And of course I believed in it, too, and, more importantly, believed I was living it. *I* had been forlorn among cruel insensitive step-relatives (the Princeton philosophers), abused and unappreciated; *I* had been saved by the unconquerable superhuman hero, chosen from all the others and swept away. The wonder was that Sarah believed in it. Had none of us escaped?

"It's a lovely story." I smiled across the desk at my friend, who was smiling back at me, the intelligence lighting up the planes and angles of her face.

"The loveliest," she answered.

I discovered that my own status at the Princeton philosophy department had changed as well as Sarah's. When I ran into Professor Pfiffel, my adviser, he greeted me quite cordially.

"Ah, Mrs. Himmel. I was delighted to hear of your marriage. My deepest congratulations."

His great yellow-white mane nodded in satisfaction at the happy conclusion of the case of the advisee with the unfortunate metaphysical bent. He obviously assumed, from the way he went on and spoke, that I had withdrawn from the department. This was the first time he showed any pleasure with me, and I didn't have the heart to tell him I hadn't sensibly withdrawn my sadly unanalytic person but had merely given it a leave of absence. I had told the department chairman, who also addressed me respectfully as Mrs. Himmel, that I wanted to take the year off to work on the problem on which I planned eventually to write my dissertation, the mind-body problem.

I never had told Noam that I was only making a poor joke out there in front of Lahiere's. And I suppose it wasn't only a joke. I've always been obsessed with the mind-body problem. During those periods when I think of myself as a philosopher and those periods when I don't, I never can get away from that problem that Schopenhauer called, quite wonderfully, the *Weltknoten*, the world-knot. That's exactly what it is, bringing together in one inextricable clump strands that weave in and out of the entire fabric of reality, entangling each of us (certainly me).

And I'm in good company here. The mind-body problem was the obsession of most philosophers before this century's crop discovered that it is, like all metaphysical questions, either meaningless or trivial. But I'll never be convinced of that. It's the essential problem of metaphysics, about both the world out there and the world in here. In fact, the dichotomy between the two worlds—the outer public place of bodies and the inner private one of minds—is exactly what it's all about. Are both these realms real, and if so how do they fit together? Can one of them be absorbed into the other? The answer a philosopher gives determines the entire shape of his metaphysics. Idealists reduce in the direction of mind, materialists in the direction of body, and dualists heroically assert the separate and equal reality of both. One after another of the great philosophical systems have attempted to untie the world-knot, pulling out some threads but leaving others impossibly entangled. What is the world? What am I? This is the mind-body problem.

There is reality, or the world, consisting of all the things that are. Scientists are in the business of describing reality, as metaphysicians hope to be. Common sense, too, has its ontological commitments.

To describe reality one must say what things exist and what they are like. What is the common-sense view (one has to begin somewhere, and where else but with common sense)? Certainly that material bodies exist, their most important feature being their objective existence: they exist "out there," independent of our observation of them. This typewriter doesn't pop in and out of existence as I look at and away from it. (If it does, it's not a material body.) It and its properties persist. And it and its properties are public. All of us can, in principle, know about the typewriter, both through observation (as we know its shape) and through science (as we know it is composed of atoms).

But in speaking of observation and knowledge we commit ourselves to beings who observe and know, to things with experiences, to conscious entities. And their inclusion is also a central part of the common-sense ontology. In fact, that there exists at the moment at least one such thing, namely, myself, seems an ontological truth impossible to deny (unlike all others). I can never falsely believe that I exist. The condition of this fact's being believed at all is sufficient to ensure its truth, as Descartes observed in his Second Meditation. (In his *Discourse on Method* he put the insight more crudely: "I think, therefore I am"—a phrase as catchy as it has been misunderstood.)

But the unavoidable inclusion of this category of thing, the conscious, in our ontological tally means we can no longer confine ourselves, in describing reality, to the facts "out there." Now there are also facts about the "in-here" of each of these conscious things, facts about what reality is like, at each moment of their conscious life, *for* them. To describe reality we must describe the things that exist, and a description of conscious entities includes a description of their inner worlds. And the interior decorating of a human being, even when it includes a consciousness of the world out there, will be lush with particulars not to be found out there, some of them determined by such givens of the moment as her sensations, moods, and memories, others by less transient features (such as where she stands on the mattering map).

In fact, if we believe the story science tells about what's out there, if we believe that what's out there is bundles of mathematically describable particles behaving mathematically in mathematical, relativistic space-time, then very few particulars of the in-here are to be found out there. The out-there appears more and more remote, as the in-here gains in prominence.

The ways the world appears to those things for which there are appearances are facts about the appeared-to's. And since a description of reality must include a description of all things that are, these facts too must be included. In this way the description grows by many orders of magnitude. Reality's complete description includes accounts of all the myriad inner worlds.

But more important than this quantitative increase is the qualitative uniqueness of these facts—the interiority, the privacy of them. And the question is: Can such facts as these be about material bodies? Material bodies exist in the objective and public out-there. Are they capable of inner lives? Does a rich and vastly complicated interiority, an *être intime*, gape open in the essential guts of some of them? For Godssakes, am *I*, who carries an entire world within me, a *body?*

I here give you the problem in its pure form. Unlike so many others dredged up out of the deeps in the course of the history of philosophy, this one is, I think, capable of engaging us all, *once* it is understood. For it concerns not only the nature of the world, but also the nature of that object which matters to each of us as no other does: one's self. What *is* it? And if this question seems still too abstract to engage, consider another, its logical bedfellow: Can you survive the death of your body? Not *will* you, but is survival even within the realm of metaphysical possibility? Not if you *are* your body. And if you are not, then what follows? Not the fact of survival. For it may be that even if you are not your body, you are so causally dependent on it—each one of your states preceded, because caused, by a bodily one—that you couldn't exist without it. If this were the case, we would find one-to-one correlations between the mental and the physical. Those who think too hastily and therefore miss seeing this (and every) philosophical problem, might think such linkages between the mental and physical dissolve the mind-body problem by showing that the mind is nothing but the body. But of course nothing of the sort is shown. For such correlations are perfectly compatible with—in fact, entailed by—the dualism between mind and body as Descartes presented it.

Descartes first posed the question: What am I? And he answered that he is most certainly not a body, but rather a separate entity, a mind, the subject of his consciousness. What makes Descartes Descartes, he argued, is the qualities of his consciousness; and what makes his body that particular body is the qualities of its extension. Two distinct sets of qualities, determining two distinct entities, although, quite obviously, intimately connected:

"I am not lodged in my body merely as a pilot in a ship, but so intimately conjoined, and as it were intermingled with it, that with it I form a unitary whole. Were not this the case, I should not sense pain when my body is hurt, being, as I should be then, merely a thinking thing; but should apprehend the wound in a purely cognitive manner, just as a sailor apprehends by sight any damage to his ship."

Descartes happened to have made things needlessly difficult for himself (and consequently too easy for the hasty to dismiss him) by ascribing two quite incompatible properties to the mind that he was: it's not located in space, and yet it interacts, in the region of the pineal gland, no less, with the spatially located body. By "located in space" he means situated in the out-there occupied by bodies. But if bodies are out there, while minds are not, how do they manage to interact, especially in the region of the pineal gland? But then why say that conscious subjects are not out there? Their experiences are not, their teeming inner worlds are not. But can't the subjects whose inner worlds these are be located in the same out-there as material bodies? Clearly, I am. I am right here, within four walls, in front of a typewriter, to the left of the window. In fact, I am precisely where my body is. Sufficient to show that I *am* my body, you point out, since two distinct things can't occupy the same space at the same time. Insufficient, the Cartesian retorts. Two *material bodies* can't occupy the same space at the same time.

Descartes presented the problem; not all philosophers have agreed he gave us the answer. His very own rationalist children, Spinoza and Leibniz, set about trying to mend the Cartesian rupture of reality into the two halves of objectivity and subjectivity. Spinoza absorbed all the world into the objectivity of that substance which can be viewed alternatively as God or nature *(Deus sive Natura)*. Both minds and bodies get sucked in and dissolved in the reality of the one objectively existing substance. Leibniz went in the other direction. Descartes, he said, leads us "into the vestibule of philosophy," and Spinoza "would have been right were it not for the monads." Spinoza's philosophy asks us to deny the reality of that inner world which is for each of us the world we know best, and to negate the existence of that subject of experience which each of us knows he is. Subjectivity is not to be denied. Much easier to deny objectivity, which is what Leibniz did. Reality consists exclusively of monads, an infinity of them, each of which is something like a mind, though not all achieve the full self-consciousness and distinct perceptions of those monads which we are. But all monads are like us in having successive points of view of the world. The world, in consisting of monads, consists of nothing but an infinity of inner worlds. There isn't exactly perception as we normally think of it, since, for reasons too complicated to get into here, the monad's points of view are determined from within, each representation following from the preceding according to the internal laws of the monad. The monad doesn't interact with anything outside itself; the appearance of interaction is but appearance. Monads are, says Leibniz in one of the more whimsical statements of seventeenth-century rationalism, "without windows." Whimsical, but terrifying too. At least, I've been terrified on those occasions when I've suspected that we may indeed fit Leibniz's description: that interaction between us is only apparent, that we are each of us a closed world, without windows.

Spinoza's approach to the problem is so unique that one can only tautologically categorize it as "Spinozistic." Almost all other philosophers can be accommodated by the following categories: the materialists, who assert that everything that exists is a body; the idealists, who claim that nothing that exists is a body, but is rather mind or something like it; and the dualists, who, like Descartes, say that some things are bodies and some things are not.

But there are categories within the categories. Take materialists. Some have inferred from the identity of people with their bodies the fundamental mystery of matter. "I know very much less than you do about matter," wrote Bertrand Russell. "All that I know about matter is what I can infer by means of certain abstract postulates about the purely logical attributes of its space-time distribution. Prima facie, these tell me nothing whatever about its other characteristics." The public view of bodies we get through observation and science can never penetrate into the interiority of which some of them are capable, we know, because we know the interiority of which we are capable. And then there are materialists who make no such inference, who believe there are no secrets from the public view. Any facts there are to be known about those bodies which are people can, at least in principle, be known through observation and science.

The hatred of mystery and worship of science characteristic of Anglo-American philosophers of this century has dictated that this last is the position almost all of them take. And, of course, they arrive at it through linguistic analysis. The world-knot, they maintain, can be unraveled by studying how certain phrases function in the language. Logical behaviorism is a favored answer: all states of the inner world are simply defined to be states of, or dispositions to, behavior. Abracadabra. With this trick one not only dispels the mystery of the mind-body problem; one gets rid of the annoying inaccessibility of the inner Other. One need never wonder. That moaning and thrashing about, for example, just *is* the orgasm.

My pre-Noam intuitions had put me with the materialists who assert the mystery of bodies. The view I grabbed for that day in front of Lahiere's had been ready at hand because I really did believe that it's body, not mind, which is the great unknown. Noam, of course, is a confirmed antimaterialist. Clearly if a person survives his body's death and decay, if he migrates from body to body, he's not identical with his corporeal lodgings. Idealism doesn't seem an unlikely hypothesis: "It wouldn't surprise me greatly to discover that there really are no bodies." But he finds dualism the more natural view.

In addition to his supernatural evidence, Noam believes that the nonidentity of a person with his body can be argued for on purely a priori grounds. In fact, he claims to have a deductive proof. We had rather a lot of discussions of this proof, its logical structure progressively simplifying so that it finally emerged quite spare and elegant. The overall strategy is to show that the assumption of the identity of a person with his body is conceptually absurd, that it leads to a logical contradiction. I here present a reconstruction.

HIMMEL'S PROOF FOR THE NONIDENTITY OF A PERSON WITH HIS BODY

1. If a person is identical with his body, he would not survive his death.
2. If a person is identical with his body, he would survive his death.
3. So if a person is identical with his body, he both would and would not survive his death.

   Since any proposition that entails a contradiction can't be true, we can deduce from 3 that:
4. A person is not identical with his body.

This proof is logically valid; that is, the premises, *if* true, entail the conclusion. But are the premises true? The first seems rather obvious, but hardly the second (although perhaps it's trivial). So here's another proof that has as *its* conclusion the disputed second premise of the first proof:

First some informal remarks on the strategy used here, which is known technically as a *reductio ad absurdum*. One denies the conclusion to be proved, in this case the second premise, and derives a contradiction. In this way one shows that the denial is false (leading as it does to contradiction), and therefore the conclusion is true.

The conclusion in this case is a conditional proposition, of the form: if xxx, then ——. One denies a conditional by asserting the xxx and denying the ——. So *ex hypothesi:*

A. A person is identical with his body.

B. A person doesn't survive his death.

Now we produce two more premises, seemingly quite innocent:

C. A person's body survives the person's death.

D. If a person is his body, then if his body exists, he exists.

From A, C, and D follows:

E. A person does survive his death.

But B and E contradict each other, showing that you can't assert A, B, C, and D. Since C and D are supposed to be obvious, the inference is that you can't assert A and B; that is, if A, then not B: If a person is identical with his body, then he does survive his death: and that is precisely the conclusion to be proved here, the second premise of the first argument.

I was suspicious of this second proof. One cannot challenge A and B, since they're simply assumed for the sake of the argument. D looks unassailable. Of course, if two things are identical, then if the one exists, so does the other. That leaves C.

"Listen, Noam, maybe a person's body doesn't survive his death."

"Then what are they burying?"

"Maybe it's a different body, not identical with the one that was alive. Maybe there are two different bodies, before and after."

"Do you really want to say that? It's a way of avoiding the conclusion, but think of it. It's crazy. You're going to have to say that at the moment of death the old body just vanishes and is instantaneously replaced with a brand-new one. Quite a trick. And all the physical properties of the brand-new one are going to be spatiotemporally continuous with the just vanished one, which is usually, in the case of other material bodies, sufficient for saying they're identical. Human bodies are going to turn out to be very weird things, quite spooky."

"Look who's talking about spooks."

But I saw his point and turned my critical gaze back to the main argument. If the second premise was okay, maybe the first wasn't as obvious as it seemed:

"What makes it so obvious that if a person is his body, then he doesn't survive his death? Maybe so long as you've got the body, even if it's a corpse, you've got the person."

"Because you don't. That corpse is not a person."

"Why not? Maybe it's just a very quiet one."

"Listen, Renee, I think this is really the heart of the matter. The individual identities of a person and his body, what makes that person that person and what makes that body that body, are just different. The identity of a person has to do with his memories perhaps, certainly his intellectual and emotional dispositions. If you've got a corpse, a thing without memories or conscious dispositions, you definitely don't have a person. But you do have a body, and clearly the same body that you had before. Obviously a lot of its properties have changed in changing from a living to a dead thing, but its identity hasn't changed. It's identically the same, though qualitatively much changed body. The identities of people and bodies just rest on different facts."

"I don't know, Noam, I can't help feeling there's something wrong here."

"Where? Look, you have the possibilities before you. If you're that desperate to escape dualism, then you could claim that corpses are very quiet people or that you've got a simultaneous annihilation of one body and re-creation of another at the moment of death. Now, do those alternatives seem more palatable than dualism?"

"But dualism seems crazy, too."

"Why? I think it's the intuitively natural view."

He would. "I don't even know how to conceive of this disembodied subject you've identified me with. What *is* it?"

"I should think you've had a rather intimate acquaintance with it.

When you say you can't conceive of it—that is, of yourself—you're probably conceiving of conceiving in the wrong way. You probably mean you can't picture it, the way you can material objects. If you try to conceive of immaterial subjects in the same way as material things, of course you're going to fail. I have no trouble at all conceiving of the incorporeal, since that's what math deals with. It's the realm I know best."

"There's got to be something wrong," I persisted.

"Why?"

"How can there be an a priori proof for something like dualism?"

"First of all, the proof isn't entirely a priori. It's not a priori that there do, in fact, exist people and their bodies. All that's a priori is that *if* they exist, they're not identical. Secondly, I happen to think that probably most facts about the world are in principle a priori. We're simply not smart enough to deduce them."

Oh.

Noam himself wasn't absolutely confident of his proof. He places much more faith in his supernatural evidence. With Noam proofs are usually an afterthought, even in math. He "sees" things first, then proves them. The brilliant success of his method in math has given him much confidence in its general reliability, even when he extends it beyond matters mathematical. Noam was very confident of his answer to the mind-body problem.

And I must say, I took his answer very seriously. In general I find it extremely difficult, in the presence of Noam's intellectual confidence and established brilliance, to dismiss anything he says. Ava, however, has no trouble rejecting Noam's views, and finds this one —especially resting as it does on his supernatural beliefs—eminently dismissible.

"He's completely nuts on the subject, totally *meshugge*. Just because he's a mathematical genius, that doesn't mean he's a genius in other things as well."

"Are you saying my husband is an idiot savant?" I smiled.

"No, of course not." Ava smiled back. "Of course he's brilliant. He couldn't have his mathematical gift if he weren't. But that doesn't mean his intuitions are always sound. Look at Newton, with his crackpot theology."

"So tell me what's wrong with Noam's argument."

"I don't know what's wrong. I haven't given it much thought and I don't intend to. There's something wrong. Look, it took centuries to find out what was wrong with all those so-called proofs of God's existence, that one that tries to show that God's existence follows from his definition as all-perfect. It took centuries to find out what the fallacy was there. You've got to trust common sense before a priori reason."

Trust common sense. But I don't think common sense has an answer to offer here. What's the common-sense answer to the mind-body problem?

6

MORE
REALITY

Perhaps I am no one.
True, I have a body
and I cannot escape from it.
I would like to fly out of my head,
but that is out of the question.
It is written on the tablet of destiny
that I am stuck here in this human form.
That being the case
I would like to call attention to my problem.

—ANNE SEXTON,
   "THE POET OF IGNORANCE"

My sister-in-law Tzippy gave birth in December to a six-pound, twelve-ounce boy. The baby was named Reuven, after my father. Reuven Feuer.

My mother's chief worry had been Caesarean section, or, as she put it, "the knife." Tzippy is very slight, "not built for childbearing," my mother repeated throughout the five months she knew of Tzippy's pregnancy. Tzippy had been reading about pregnancy, birth, breast-feeding, toilet training, sibling rivalry—the whole megillah—ever since she felt the first kick in the fifth month and began really to trust in this third pregnancy. She had become a firm believer in the Lamaze method of childbirth, but this required a partner and my brother Avram wanted no part of it. It was *weibeszachen,* woman's business. (Not surprisingly, the Yiddish term has a pejorative connotation.) Miriam Teitelbaum, whose husband also "learned" at Lakewood and who was herself still childless, came to the rescue. Miriam and Tzippy had gone through all the grades of *Bais Yaakov* together. (*Bais Yaakov* means "house of Jacob." There is an international chain of very Orthodox *Bais Yaakov* schools for girls. The high school that had so disastrous an effect on my future religiosity was one.) They went together to the Lamaze classes, and then finally to the birth. The closeness that developed between them shone from their faces at the *bris* of little Reuven. Tzippy's delivery had been a difficult one, seventeen hours in hard labor.

"I could never have done it without Miriam. I can't begin to tell you how she helped me. I was ready to give up. I told the doctor, all right already, put me out. But Miriam and he overruled me." Tzippy was radiant.

"I knew she was near the end by then, " Miriam radiated back. "She was in transition, and people always feel pessimistic then. They had warned us at class."

"Just think, if not for Miriam I would have missed seeing Reuven in those first moments of his new life. Oh, Renee, I still can't get over it. Every time I close my eyes I see it. As soon as he came out and the doctor lifted him up, he turned his head very quickly from side to side, three times: 'Nu, so what's this?' I'm going to see that my whole life."

"Tzippy didn't have any drugs at all. That's why Reuven was born so alert. When we brought him to the nursery, all the nurses commented on how alert he was. He was given a nine-point-nine Apgar out of ten. The nurse told me none of them gets a ten," Miriam bragged. "Already he's getting the best grades."

I regarded little Tzippy with awe. The years of worry over her infertility had lightly written over her sweet face. There was a certain pinched expression that hadn't been there before, and three vertical lines between the eyes. But hers was still very much the face of a child. And this child-woman had passed through the vastness of the experience of giving birth, and now looked back at me from across its great distance. For the first time I felt that she was the woman and I the girl.

Little Reuven regarded everything, including me, with immense dark eyes that spoke of infinite wisdom. He protested loudly at the indignities he was made to suffer at the hands of the *mohel,* but was quickly pacified by a Q-tip dunked in sweet red wine. I searched the little face closely for signs of similarity between the two Reuven Feuers, suddenly quite receptive to the superstition that lies perhaps behind the Jewish naming tradition. Let it be, I kept thinking, let this be my father returned.

Noam had come along with me to the *bris,* after some pleading on my part. He seemed very uncomfortable for the first fifteen minutes or so, standing among the *davening* men. But then he simply tuned out, became involved in his own thoughts, swaying slightly back and forth as he does when unable to pace. He looked like a natural, as I had known he would, the yarmulke perched on his head, *shuckling* in the midst of the *shuckling* men. Several people, I learned, assumed he was one of the *rebbayim* from the yeshiva, and when told he was my husband, those who knew the sad history of my profligacy rejoiced over my return to the fold. My mother was very pleased with this misinterpretation and didn't correct it. Noam remained tuned out.

Two of my mother's three sisters had made it to Lakewood from their homes in the Flatbush section of Brooklyn. The third, a xeno-phobic, agoraphobic hypochondriac, never travels past Ocean Ave-nue. They had all been born in Brooklyn. My mother was the only one whom cruel fate had tossed out of that yiddishe paradise into the Westchester wilderness, and from the way she spoke it might have been the Dakotas. She always complained bitterly that of all her sisters she, the most pious, had to live out her life in exile. The funny thing is, after my father died, leaving her free to move where she wanted, she had stayed put in the desert.

My mother was at her peak at the *bris, shepping naches,* presenting to the world at large, and the aunts in particular, her triumphs: her grandson and son-in-law. The expression on her face was pure bliss as she led the aunts over to be introduced to Noam, who greeted them all with his most absent stare and an occasional "hmmmm." To be able to maintain one's inner peace and psychic distance in the midst of that group requires true greatness of mind. They're all thin and under five feet tall, but they take up a lot of space.

Aunt Sophie is a bargain mavin whose life is devoted to the cause of getting shlock for less than half. Almost all her conversation revolves about this one issue, relating the ecstasies of bargaining merchants down below cost, the agonies when she suspects she could have gotten something for less. Hers is a fairly deep gray mattering zone. She feels genuine outrage for those who overpay. And yet I have a warm spot for her; she had been my unexpected ally in the war I waged to go to Barnard.

"How can you not let her accept that scholarship? Do you realize what a school like that costs? Don't you see what a bargain you're getting?" (Can I help it if I come from a family of Jewish-American stereotypes?)

My Aunt Myra was also at the *bris,* and she was really pouring it on for Noam. She's the prettiest of the sisters, managing to look, in her thinness, chic rather than scrawny. She's always smartly dressed, with her hair somewhere or other in the blond-red range. Right now her thin voice was trickling out, in Noam's honor, in her version of an educated accent. Knowing that Noam wasn't Orthodox, she even made some mildly mocking noises about the *bris:*

"What did you think of our little religious ritual?" Little laugh, type consistent with accent.

"Hmmmm," Noam answered, his eyes darting about in that way that told me he hadn't heard a word.

"A little barbaric, perhaps"—tiny laugh—"but it's supposed to be hygienic. Even the gentiles do it now." Smile, faded-blue questioning stare.

"Hmmmmm."

The aunts Sophie and Myra exchanged glances.

Aunt Myra apologized to my mother for her daughter Felicia's absence. There was a very important sale at Bloomingdale's today, and even though Felicia "really argued with me, put up such a fight to come to the *bris,* I knew she had been waiting so long for this sale, I just couldn't let her miss it."

My aunt then turned to me and began, in sweet charity, to fill me in on every detail of Felicia's recent goings-on. My infelicitously named cousin is Myra's only child, and as a kid I had spent a good amount of time fantasizing that I was she. (That was before I learned to tame my fantasizing to the possible.) I had never seen a mother so in love with a daughter. (My mother, too, was in love, but with my brother.) Myra's husband, Harry, had a rather limited role to play. He had been required, of course, to make Felicia's existence a reality. After that I'm sure his services in *that* department were never again called upon. The meaning of the remainder of his life has lain in his fur business, which has kept his daughter in the best of everything money can buy. I still remember Felicia's canopy bed, all creamy eyelet embroidery floating on the thick apricot rug in that apricot room. Is this where my passion for the color stems from—from the green envy of those days? How I used to imagine myself in that bed. (You see that my fantasies have involved a bed from the earliest.) We always used to play the princess and her slave when I came over. Very occasionally, she'd let me be the princess.

My cousin is exactly my age, or actually ten days younger, so naturally we've been compared since infancy. (She walked before me, but I was toilet-trained first.) The sole comfort my mother took from my going to Barnard was Barnard's having rejected Felicia. I had always been the better student. One might expect this superiority to have given me the lead in the race with my cousin. Forget it. There's no way I could ever win. She, you see, is described by her mother, whose faith has never wavered, while I am represented by mine, whose attitude is at best lukewarm.

I see I can't probe the old wound, no matter how gently, without the pain bursting forth in full dazzling vigor. In a moment I shall start sobbing that my mother has never loved me, that she cared only for my brother. What a bore; so banal a solution to the mystery of my personality. And yet there it is. I've done what I can. I've transformed the woman into a parody (perhaps you've noticed) in the attempt to dilute some of her awesome strength. But though that's the picture I present to you, it's not the view I naturally occupy. I can maintain it only with great effort before the pull of subjectivity becomes too strong. In the end it is a feeble attempt, as are they all, the pathetically elaborate battlements we construct against the power absolute: the power of the parent. The effects keep on long after the exertion itself has ceased. For they're woven into the very fabric of one's soul. They are one's self. *Can nothing be done?* Must the self that one is, this poor "I" that I am and that I feel myself to be, remain permanently disfigured—encrusted with the oozing scabs of ancient bruises even as the Others are admiring the self-applied surgical dressing? Must the old pain influence every action, as a dull ache shapes a limp?

As a child I was full of schemes for winning her love. Of course my father loved me, but not in the partial way I craved. He loved everybody. He didn't favor me over Avram, as my mother favored Avram over me. He didn't love me *exclusively.* (Thus is a father-fixation forged.) For some reason (perhaps because I'm Jewish) I hooked onto the idea that I had to be smarter. I had always brought home straight A's, so I asked the teachers for extra work and carried home their praise. My fifth-grade teacher gave me a ninth-grade math book to work on. I wrote poems and stories and won prizes for them. And only watched my mother's anger grow. I really was dopey not to catch on, for she could be pretty explicit:

Some friends of my parents were visiting for Shabbos, and we were all sitting at the dining room table, having Friday night dinner. Avram, as was his way, hadn't said a word all through the meal, and I, as was my way, had been chattering throughout, wisecracking and telling stories. My mother got me into the kitchen on some pretext, where her gracious company face instantaneously transformed itself into wild rage. (These transformations were terrifying.)

"You're embarrassing me and your father with all your showing off. You're just a girl," she hissed, trying to pack all the anger into her voice without raising it, for fear the guests would overhear. "You're pretty enough. Why are you always trying to show off how smart you are? Why must you always outshine your brother? Can't you ever give him a chance?"

Avram and me. Felicia and me. Descriptions have always come in pairs, in contrapuntal duets. The good and the bad, the perfect and the problem, the *naches* and the *tsuris*.

But no matter how biased the maternal descriptions, the objective fact is that I got married before my cousin. And my husband *is* a genius. That's on the plus side. But on the minus side, and this must be weighted very heavily, he is *fifteen* years older than I am. Let's not total up the points until we see whom Felicia finally condescends to marry. She's still roaming the Catskills, seeking her intended (doctor) at singles weekends at Grossinger's and the Concord.

There have always been, since the birth of Felicia, states of the world to provoke Aunt Myra's indignation: girls chosen before Felicia to play Queen Esther in the Purim plays; teachers who marked her compositions in ignorance and apathy. But none of this compares to the present singles situation. These young men (especially the Jewish doctors) were spoiled rotten. None of them wanted to get married anymore because these other stupid girls were all giving it away for nothing.

"And they talk about Jewish *princesses*," my mother had sympathetically quoted my aunt quoting my cousin, who—sorry, coz—will for me always present an ostensive definition for that hated term.

My mother always keeps me informed of the aunts' views on my life. They had all been "overjoyed" to learn I was getting married, "except your Aunt Myra, that jealous witch," my mother had chirped in ecstasy. They had been "very impressed" to learn of my husband's prominence. (My mother had found the old *Life* article at the library and sent them all xeroxed copies.) They were also "a little surprised" when their arithmetical computations revealed the age difference between Noam and myself. My mother had never commented directly on Noam's age. She frequently chooses the medium of "the aunts" to make her points. Then, if I react very badly, she can say sympathetically, "Well, you know your aunts."

The morning after the *bris* my mother called with the reactions of the aunts on meeting Noam in the flesh.

"Well, they thought he seemed a little eccentric, but of course that's a mark of his genius, as I told them. You can't expect geniuses to be normal. They were surprised at how good-looking he still is. They all said he doesn't look his age."

I thought often of my little nephew and spoke to Tzippy at least once a week. At three months Reuven began to sleep through the night, and Tzippy, after happily informing me of this, said:

"Now I can finally invite you and Noam for a Shabbos."

Noam absolutely refused. "No, Renee, I couldn't take it. I couldn't take a whole Shabbos. And I certainly couldn't take your brother for that long. I can tolerate the word 'pagan' just about twenty times in one day. That's my limit and it's surpassed in five minutes with Avram."

So I went to Lakewood by myself, after making sure that Noam had invitations for dinner Friday and Saturday.

Lakewood has two identities. It's a pretty little resort community, and it's also the Princeton of *yiddishkeit*. Life there presents Judaism at its purest: the men learning in the elite *kollel*, which is like a graduate department for Talmud; the women producing children and also teaching or running little businesses in their basements to augment the meagre stipends the *kollel* pays their husbands. Some of the families actually live quite well, supported by the wife's father. This is one of the great blessings of wealth, to be able to buy a scholar for a son-in-law and support him in the way of life one couldn't choose for oneself.

Reuven had changed tremendously in three months, as people his age tend to do, I guess. I was initially disappointed to see that he had lost the look of ineffable knowledge, but I soon became enchanted. He was delicate-featured and pale-skinned, and the hair that was coming in was the blond of my father, my brother, and me. He was a real Feuer. He seemed to me to be remarkably beautiful, although I was somewhat skeptical of my aesthetic judgment. I have heard parents of pathetically homely children marvel at their offspring's beauty and debate the pros and cons of a career in child modeling. For all I knew, such creative perception might extend to doting aunts as well.

Tzippy was completely absorbed in her maternity. She was nursing Reuven, and he was a hungry little soul (my mother worried he wasn't getting enough), feeding for about forty-five minutes every four hours. Tzippy, though much larger on top than before, was thinner every place else; especially her little face, which was more pinched than at the *bris*. But she was ebulliently happy:

"I have to restrain myself when he's sleeping not to wake him. I miss him."

I didn't mind the exclusiveness of her concerns. In fact, I enjoyed this glimpse into the maternal world-view. I was rather glad that Noam hadn't come after all.

Avram was also overjoyed in his role as a parent. When I watched him play with Reuven, throwing him high in the air as Tzippy begged him to be careful, making silly faces and noises, I felt for the first time in fifteen years like hugging my holy brother.

Friday night, after the Shabbos meal, Avram sat at the table swaying over a Gemara, and Tzippy and I went into the tiny bedroom so we wouldn't disturb him with our talk. There was a little night light casting a soft glow on the white walls and pink bedspreads. Reuven fell asleep at the breast, and Tzippy looked down at him.

"Ah, Reuven, you have a *tzaddik's shaym*" (a saint's name). "You should only have his *neshuma*" (his soul).

All at once I was crying, and Tzippy silently joined in. She had only known my father in the last year of his life, but a strong and special closeness had developed almost immediately between them. It was she who had shown my numbed family the way when he lay dying in the final days. We had already distanced ourselves from the man lying there, smelling of death and wearing the face of martyrdom. That wasn't my father suffering; my father had already gone. But little Tzippy had shown us who that person was, had walked into the room and straight over to him, kissing him, holding him, talking to him as she always had. How he had smiled at her with that wasted face. Were it possible to feel envy for Tzippy, I would certainly have envied her that last smile. It was four years since my father had died, and still when I spoke or thought of him my eyes often welled up. When I was with Tzippy, her eyes did the same in response.

We didn't speak for a while. The only sounds were the clock on the night table ticking, Reuven's soft breathing, and out in the living room the rhythmic squeak of Avram's chair under his swaying. Tzippy finally broke the silence:

"Oh, Renee, I almost forgot. I'm so absent-minded these days. You have an old friend here in Lakewood, a school friend. Her husband is learning here. She was so excited when she discovered you're my sister-in-law. Her name now is Fruma Friedbaum, but I can't remember her maiden name."

"Not Fruma Dershky? Thin, red hair, great giggle?"

"That's her, but she's not so thin anymore. She's expecting her fifth child, *kayn aynhoreh.*" (This is a Hebrew phrase automatically uttered when any good news is spoken. It's actually an incantation to ward off the evil eye, although now it's hardly ever spoken with that intent. It's like saying "God bless you" after someone sneezes, the original purpose of which, according to Bertrand Russell, was to keep the devil from jumping in as the soul momentarily leaves the body.)

"You're kidding," I said. Again I felt my childishness, felt that I'd been left behind. And left behind by Fruma! We had been best friends in high school, and she had accompanied me, always a step in back, in that heady first flush of doubting. In our schools, as in most yeshivas, the morning classes were devoted to religious studies, taught by rabbis with beards and *rebbetsens* (rabbis' wives) with *sheitels.* In the afternoon we were taught secular subjects by moonlighting public school teachers. Fruma and I called the morning the dark ages, and the afternoon the enlightenment:

"It's like experiencing the renaissance every day of our lives."

We often cut the morning classes and hid down in the lunchroom, where I'd propound the narrowness of Judaism, the naïveté of theism. We read Spinoza and Nietzsche, Freud and Bertrand Russell; and, most glorious of all, David Hume. Oh, what David Hume and his

Dialogues Concerning Natural Religion did for my life.

Imagine the exhilaration of a chronic invalid suddenly transformed into an Olympic athlete and you glimpse my mood of those days. Judged by religious standards my want of belief was a weakness, an ailment requiring therapy. I was always being told to go and speak to this rabbi or that *rebbetsen*. And so I went, like a barren woman wandering from one fertility doctor to another. But barren I remained. They offered me reasons, which I criticized. They told me the criticisms were beside the point because the reasons were really beside the point. They're a crutch for those who need them. The good and the strong get there without them. But I couldn't get there, with or without them.

Can you imagine, then, what it was like to turn from the spirit of religion to the spirit of philosophy, or, as I liked to call it in those days, the spirit of rationality? For here, reasons for beliefs are never beside the point but are the entire substance of the matter. The distinction between the mere belief and the reasoned belief is the distinction that grounds all philosophy. If truth is our end (and what else should be?) we must reason our way there. The leap of faith is not heroic but cowardly, has all the virtues, Russell said, of theft over hard labor. (And we can take his word for it. After all, he was described, in the squabble over whether he should be allowed a professorship at City College of New York because of his book *Marriage and Morals*, as "lecherous, libidinous, lustful, venerous, erotomaniac, aphrodisiac, irreverent" and more; which is recommendation enough for me. Einstein, a habitual scribbler of doggerel verse, wrote him: *Es wiederholt sich immer wieder/In dieser Welt so fein und bieder/Der Pfaff den Pöbel alarmiert/Der Genius wird exekutiert.* [It keeps repeating itself/In this world so fine and honest/The parson alerts the mob/ The genius is executed.] The controversy brought Russell an invitation to Princeton, where he spent the next four years at the Institute. Anyone who is anyone in our world has done time here.)

For me, in those days, the turn from religion to philosophy was like stepping from one ethical system into another, which was the inversion of the first. My moral weakness became my moral strength, the barrenness of my belief was in truth the fertility of my rationality, and I was saved at last.

I had been in the habit since childhood of sending up urgent little prayers: God make me know the answer; make my mother love me; let me not strike out with the bases loaded. The original intent was religious, but over the years the words had simply become a formula for expressing these surges of desire. Now, in high school, the little plea became: God make me rational—even though part of what I meant by being rational was ceasing to believe in the divine presence.

My goal was Barnard, for me the beacon of reason, shining forth on the shores of the Hudson, beckoning to me like a liberation. Smart girls went to Barnard, and I wanted like hell to be one of them. The college's acceptance was not sufficient. I also had to overcome the undertow of religion, in the persons of my mother and the rabbis and *rebbetsens* she enlisted, trying to sweep me out to sea where I would drown. No high has ever quite equaled that first time I took the Seventh Avenue subway uptown and got off in the general exodus at 116th Street, *my* promised land.

And Fruma, whose name derives from the Yiddish-German *frum*, for pious, was there with me at the time of my conversion, sometimes arguing the other side but usually ending up agreeing with me. Finally we were ready to act. We walked into a McDonald's and ordered a cheeseburger each. Not just a plain *trayf* hamburger, you understand, but a *trayf* hamburger with cheese, meat and milk together. We discovered, however, that it's one thing to reach a conclusion and another to act on it. After an hour of sitting and staring shamefaced, we walked out, leaving behind two untouched cheeseburgers.

My friend and I had sporadically kept in touch our first year out of high school, when I was at Barnard and she was going to Brooklyn College at night and the *Bas Yaakov* seminary during the day. ("I have to. My parents expect it.") But we soon drifted apart. The last time I had seen her was at her wedding, when we were both eighteen. We spoke on the phone a few times after, but our increasing estrangement was both annoying and painful. So far as I was concerned, her brief experiment in thinking was over; she had returned to the proper role of the *Bas Yaakov*, the little girl who never questions or challenges, but patters through life collecting little gold stars for good behavior. She had also been, I now learned, accumulating children, one a year since her marriage, not at all unusual in her world.

My first reaction upon seeing Fruma again was shock. I would never have recognized her. She was in the advanced stages of pregnancy and was absolutely enormous, probably because this was her fifth child and she hadn't many stomach muscles left. There had been an all-round thickening of the thin body I remembered: the arms, the neck, the calves and ankles. The gorgeous red hair had been cut off and replaced by a brown *sheitel* with demure red highlights. Only the clear blue eyes were as I remembered them.

But the minute she began to talk in her fast bubbly way, I knew it was the old Fruma.

"Renee, Renee, look at you! You're exactly the same, only better. Tzippy told me you just got married. *Mazel tov!* Look at you. I can't believe it, what a beauty. But why shouldn't I believe it? You were always beautiful. So how are you, what's new?"

We exchanged summaries of our lives.

"I wish your husband was here. I'd love to meet him, he sounds so fascinating. Is he *frum?*" she asked, trying to sound casual.

"No, not at all. I'm his first brush with Orthodoxy. Not that I'm at all observant anymore," I added hastily.

"So you finally tasted the cheeseburger." Fruma grinned. I nodded and grinned back. "Was it good?"

"I don't know. I really don't. Not half so delicious as we imagined."

"None of it?"

"None of it that I can think of. So you're still wondering. You look as if you had put all doubts aside long ago."

"Yeah, I do look it, don't I? I look in the mirror and I can't believe what I see. I look just like our teachers." She grinned. "Our dark-age teachers. In fact, I do teach in the local *Bas Yaakov*. But I'm really a fake. I only look the part. I live a *frum* life, but I don't live it out of my own convictions."

"You don't believe in it?"

"I don't know if I do or I don't. The choice wasn't mine to decide what I believe in. Maybe I would have discovered that I actually do believe in it. I don't know. I went right from my parents' home to my husband's," she said very slowly. "Do you see? Tzvi would be so horrified if he heard me talking like this. I never talk like this."

"I always was your *yaytzah harah.*" That's the evil inclination, dear reader, the snake in the Garden of Eden.

"Yeah." She grinned and then immediately became serious. "Once I said something mildly skeptical to Tzvi and he told me he wondered if I was fit to be the mother of our children. You can't believe what that did to me. More than anything else I want to be a good mother to them, just as I wanted to be a good daughter.

"You know, it's funny my talking to you like this after all these years," Fruma mused. "Don't think that I'm unhappy, that I go around in a blue funk all the time. I'm very happy. It's just that deep down I feel like I'm not really an adult yet, that I haven't reached maturity, because I've never decided for myself how I want to live my life. Someone just handed me the script and I started reading. I don't think I'd even know how to make up my own words, the way you have. I wouldn't know how to decide for myself, to go against everybody else. But you know," she giggled, the same little-girl giggle I remembered, "sometimes I cheat on Tzvi."

"What?" I stared at her, dumbfounded. I thought myself not easily shocked anymore, but I was having trouble assimilating Fruma's words. Was there wife-swapping going on in Lakewood? Was the *sheitel* crowd swinging? Impossible! Fruma looked at me, as if a little puzzled at the effect of her statement. Then she suddenly burst out laughing.

"Oh, Renee! Oh, is this beautiful! Too bad I can't tell Tzvi. Renee, you nut, I didn't mean *that* kind of cheating!" Her laughter was always infectious, and I was laughing, too. The great low belly was bobbing up and down so violently that I feared for the child inside. "What I *meant*—oh boy, is this going to sound ridiculous after what you thought—what I *meant* was that sometimes I don't wait the full six hours between *flayshig* and *milchik,* and once—boy, I thought I was going to shock you with this." She was laughing so hard that she had trouble speaking and the tears were streaming down her face, "Once, Renee, they were offering free samples of a *trayf* cheese spread on *trayf* crackers in the supermarket and I ate one. In fact, it was so good I ate two."

I had planned to leave Saturday night right after *Havdalah,* but

I hung around talking with Tzippy and playing with Reuven until it was quite late. And when Tzippy suggested I spend another night on their lumpy little couch, I happily agreed.

Sunday morning, as I made the trip back to Princeton, I considered for the first time whether I wanted to have a baby. It wasn't a question of whether to have one at all. I'd always taken it for granted that I would someday become a mother. The question was whether this was, metaphorically speaking, the day. Why not? I was a married woman. Noam was already forty. I wouldn't want my child to be embarrassed by a father whom other children mistook for a grandfather. (Would he come with me to Lamaze or, like my brother, decline any involvement in *weibeszachen?*)

I had always pictured myself with a daughter—a golden child, loving the world and herself. And now there was the possibility that she would inherit her father's genius. (I remembered, but briefly, the sorry hopes of Mother Himmel, weeping at her Formica kitchen table.) I could be the mother of a Marie Curie. How's that for compensation for not being a genius oneself? Wife *and* mother of. And if she were brilliant—not that she need be; my love would be unconditional—but if she were, I'd make sure the flames of her creativity were never smothered by self-doubt. It was an exciting thought: Daddy's mind, Mommy's body. And what, Shaw's unbidden ghost whispered in my mind's ear, what if she inherited Mommy's mind and Daddy's body? No matter! She would be loved.

Now, I'm not saying that I was really at the point of taking the step and discarding the remainder of my birth-control pills. I had discovered a new identity to fantasize about, and this was exciting. I don't know if the excitement would have been sufficient to carry me into action. It is, after all, quite a choice: whether to create a person, to take responsibility for another's existence and, to some extent, essence. "Mother" is not an identity one can just try on for size, as I have others. How do all these people do it, I've always wondered, cavalierly *do* it?

But then I have noticed that others don't seem to have quite the problem with freedom that I have, to suffer the burden of choice as I do. Most seem to have their fixed solid natures, cast in one form or another, not this liquefied matter flowing first one way and then another. Fruma wondered whether she had it in her to make up her own words. My problem is, I can think up too many words. Freedom for me is a pain in the Buridan's ass.

And now having a child has been taken out of the sphere of biological determinism and placed instead in the domain of intentional action. Another option to consider and decide upon. And this one qualifies, in the terminology that William James formulated to characterize religious choices, as a momentous decision: not to choose is to choose. I really needed this. Wouldn't I have been better off without so many options before me requiring my attention? I haven't been *bred* to make choices.

Consider my forebears. Consider my maternal great-grandmother, who was married at twelve and lived to have sixteen children and sixty grandchildren before she was carted off, at ninety-four, to Auschwitz. I'm named after her: she was Reine, which means pure. (Fruma and I used to joke about our names: "Pious and Pure, what choice did our parents give us?" But that was the idea, wasn't it?) Since I was her namesake, my grandmother used to feel it was only right for me to hear stories about her. Most of them emphasized her saintliness, but my favorite was this:

It was shortly after her marriage, one Shabbos morning when all the men were in *shul,* and she and her friends were out playing in some mud they made by peeing in the dirt lane that ran through the town. My great-grandmother was using her *sheitel* to mix the mud in. Suddenly the men were spotted returning from *shul,* my great-grandfather among them. And here was his wife with her head uncovered. So she dumped the *sheitel* (after all, what choice did she have?), mudpie and all, on her head and ran.

You know, I think I would have functioned tolerably well in such a world. My energies are considerable, quite equal to sixteen children, I think, if only they weren't being constantly dissipated in making fundamental decisions as to my essential nature.

In any case, this new fantasy of mothering—of mothering a genius —was so exciting that I actually mentioned something to Noam that night at dinner.

"Noam, how would you feel about having a child?"

"A child?"

"You know, Noam, children. You've seen them around. Very young people, tend to be rather short."

"Don't attempt sarcasm, Renee, you haven't the wit. A child is out of the question. A wife is distraction enough." He stared at me coldly for several seconds. "You know, hardly any of the great mathematicians in history were married, and I've come to know why."

That was March; so Noam's hostility had already started by then, that deep numbing anger. When had it first begun? I find it hard to pinpoint, since the change was gradual. There were the walks, I remember.

Noam and I both enjoy walking. We used to love to tramp through the extensive Institute woods where so many great minds have wandered, pursuing so many great thoughts. In the good days, certainly before our marriage and after our return to Princeton as well, we had walked there together often, talking the whole time. Even in the course of our mad Viennese ambulations, when Noam was so preoccupied with his search for personal identity, the conversation had hardly ever let up. I had always loved listening to Noam, talking on a wide range of topics, always interesting and original. But gradually, over the course of that first year of marriage, the nature of the walks changed until they had become almost silent. The conversation had always been dominated by Noam, but now he seldom wanted to speak. On occasions when I'd break the silence with a comment, it would be followed by more silence, during which I'd consider the now apparent absurdity of my remark, whose existence, however brief, I regretted and he ignored. He wouldn't even acknowledge it with his usual absent-minded "hmmmm." And to think that in Rome I had been annoyed by the abundance of Noam's conversation, at least in bed.

Okay, so he was preoccupied with his thoughts. The world inside his head is more interesting than anything outside, I told myself. That's what makes Noam Noam. Perhaps he's working out something very important. Perhaps he's on the trail of something surpassing even the supernaturals. Don't distract him with your petty childish needs.

Think of the two Mrs. Einsteins, I told myself (I had just finished Ronald Clark's biography of the great man): the bad, complex Mileva and the good, simple Elsa. Mileva had been a (failed) physicist herself, bitter and brooding, whereas Elsa is described by Clark as "placid and housewifely, of no intellectual pretensions, but with a practiced mothering ability which made her the ideal organizer of genius." There! That was the description for me to assume. My instructions were clear. And just in case I didn't yet understand, Elsa, good, stolid, contented Elsa, told me again: "When the Americans come to my house they carry away details about Einstein and his life, and about me they say incidentally, he has a good wife, who is very hospitable, and offers a good table." I would have to work on myself until that is what the Americans would say of *me*.

The most persuasive statement of all came from Einstein himself: "I'm glad my wife doesn't know any science. My first wife did." Succinct and clear. Mileva's insistence on her own intellectual identity had doomed her to divorce, while Elsa had ridden out her marriage in relative peace and contentment, sharing in the glory of her husband. Elsa Einstein had not gone mooning around because her husband didn't take her mind seriously. She had mothered him and understood: "You cannot analyze him, otherwise you will misjudge him," she wrote a friend. "Such a genius should be irreproachable in every respect. But no, nature doesn't behave like this. Where she gives extravagantly, she takes away extravagantly." So even Einstein, most noble of men, had had his faults.

Couldn't I be satisfied? I was the wife of a genius, for Godssakes. *I* was a malevolent Mileva with intellectual pretensions and, if not careful, would end up as Noam's first wife. Grow up, grow up, grow up, I chanted to myself as we trampled through the snow. I didn't know what Noam was working on. He didn't discuss his work with me anymore. When I asked him once he said I wouldn't be able to understand it, and I never asked again.

Why didn't I simply stop tagging along on those ever more painful walks? Because I kept hoping, I suppose, remembering and hoping. Noam's natural gait is much faster than mine, really very brisk, and even though I had compromised my vanity and bought some very sensible boots, I had difficulty keeping up with him for long periods. After a while he'd be twenty paces ahead of me, and I'd bleat out: "Noam." Sometimes he'd mumble "Sorry"; usually he didn't say a word, but would just pause a few seconds while I ran to catch up. Then the whole painful process would begin again. It was obvious that he had forgotten my existence, and, dependent as I am on others' assurances that I do indeed exist, this made me wretched. Still I struggled for objectivity: Can't you stop worrying about yourself? Can't you ever get beyond yourself, you petty-spirited woman? Don't blame him because he's different from other people. That's why you married him.

But there was actually very little danger of my blaming him. It was clear whose fault it was. The explanation was ready at hand, because it was the thing I had feared from the first, even before Noam had sat down with me on the dinky. If Noam wasn't interested in talking to me anymore, it was because he had discovered what an idiot I am. How could I have hoped that he would fail to do so? Had I, in my heart of hearts, even wished him to? Fear that p is not always incompatible with fear that not-p. One by one the sacred symbols of intelligence had lost their meaning for me, as I managed, with little effort, to collect them. How many of one's idols can one bear to see exposed?

I believed in genius. Genius that remained duped would try my faith. Noam's infatuation had provided the explanation for his mistaken regard for me. His besotted perception had wrapped me in an intellectual grace and loveliness. His interpretation of my remarks had been generous, often creatively so, making of them something far more brilliant than I had intended, than I ever could intend. I had enjoyed an intelligence of his own making, a little runoff from the great gushing well of his mind. He had finally located the leak.

It's hard to remember the exact timetable of the breakdown between us. I can remember lovely times that first year, when Noam spoke to me as in the old days, the golden spring days when we had first come together, excitement and intensity lighting up his vivid eyes. Sometimes he would come home from Fine Hall full of something to discuss, rushing into the kitchen where I was preparing supper. There was the famous incident I have mentioned of his getting burned when he stuck his head over the pot of soup I was stirring, in an effort to catch my gaze, just as he so often used to place his head over the steering wheel.

But now so many times the face he turned to me was frozen over in anger. That seemed to be the heart of the matter. He was furious with me. It became increasingly obvious that he harbored a very deep and constant rage that would come bursting through with great violence at unexpected moments. When I said something vague, unclear, half-baked, he'd pounce, tearing away with a ferocity that seemed no longer impersonal but vengeful. He wouldn't stop until I was completely broken. Now he's getting back at me, I'd think, for having hidden my membership in the class of dopes he despises.

The attacks paralyzed my mental processes so that I couldn't think, would blather out idiocies, contradict myself left and right; in short, produce ample evidence for his opinion that I didn't know what I was talking about. Once he said to me, it was shortly after our first anniversary: "Now I see why you're having so much trouble hacking it in philosophy."

Noam knew what such a statement would do to me, particularly coming from him. He knew the damage inflicted on my sense of self by my failure to be appreciated by the Princeton philosophers. I had poured out all to him, in the glowing days before our marriage, and he had listened sympathetically, and encouraged me:

"Don't be overwhelmed by this technical turn in philosophy. They're trying to turn philosophy into math, which can't be done. Not that I'm an expert on philosophy, but I know enough about math to know it can't be done. There's a great story about a debate between Euler and Diderot on the existence of God." (Euler, you'll remember, was on Noam's roll call of mathematical minor deities.) "Euler was supposed to take the pro side and Diderot the con. Diderot didn't know much mathematics and Euler decided to trick him. He got up and said that he could prove the existence of God mathematically, that God's being is a mathematical theorem." Noam was laughing. "Then he wrote down some equations, concluding on the last line: therefore God exists, Q.E.D. There's some uncertainty as to how the debate ended. Actually, there are two endings. One says that Diderot walked out in great embarrassment, unable to follow the so-called proof; the other, which I hope is the true one, maintains that Diderot called Euler's bluff.

"Anyway, Renee, I suspect that a lot of contemporary philosophers are playing Euler's trick, probably on themselves, too. Don't let them fool you. Call their bluff."

Noam had made me feel that perhaps the problem lay outside me, in the situation in which I found myself, in the philosophical step-relatives who mocked me. The hero could see through the cinders to the Ella underneath. But now he was spurning me: "Now I see why you're having so much trouble hacking it."

Why this anger that would pour over me at the slightest provocation? Why? I never doubted the answer. Noam despised me. I'd always known he had a low tolerance for stupidity, and had married in full awareness of the risks. Who was there to blame but myself?

Noam and I didn't go abroad that summer. He had deliberated for a while over accepting two of the more tempting invitations, one from the Institute Hautes Études Scientifiques, outside Paris, the other from the Hebrew University in Jerusalem. But in the end he declined, and adventuress that I had proven myself to be, I was relieved. I spent the summer days by myself, tending my little garden and reading about existential despair.

In the evenings there were of course plenty of invitations, but the joy had gone out of them. They were usually flat occasions, and sometimes worse. Noam doesn't have private and public personalities. He is what he is, intensely and always. If contempt was what he showed me at home, it was what he showed me with others. I now welcomed those parties with the invisible *mechitzahs,* the boundaries separating men and women, for I breathed easier away from Noam. The small intimate dinner parties were trying. I could either remain silent throughout or speak and risk Noam's attacks. More and more I chose the first alternative. Much better to be suspected of having nothing to say, than to have repeated the scenes of public humiliation:

The gathering was once again at the home of Adam Loft, the chairman of the math department, where I had met Noam. The invitation was the first in a long time to spark my interest, for a couple I had wanted to meet would be there, Saul and Margaret Kripke. Both are philosophers. He had just recently joined the Princeton department, and his reputation in the field is analagous to Noam's in math (Princeton having once again scored a triumph). The conversation around the dinner table developed, not surprisingly, into a discussion of whether math and philosophy required different kinds of intelligence. Kripke, who himself has done much math, including important work in logic, nonetheless argued that the kind of thinking required by the two fields wasn't exactly alike, although both required much clarity and precision.

"Many very competent mathematicians," he said, "are unbelievably naïve and unsubtle when it comes to philosophy."

"But then, so are many philosophers, wouldn't you say?" Noam smiled.

"I'm afraid I would." Kripke smiled back.

Another mathematician, Herbert Freiburg, argued that intelligence is intelligence:

"The person who can think can think about anything. He may not choose to, he may not be interested in everything. But the potential is there. Intelligence is potential."

"I don't think it's only a matter of differences in interests," Noam had said, agreeing with Kripke. "Even the neurological facts, the differences between the functions of the right and left hemispheres, argue against the monolithic interpretation of intelligence."

"Oh, I'm willing to grant that difference," Freiburg answered. "I was talking only about the functions of the left hemisphere. That's what I mean by thinking."

"But even within the left hemisphere," I said, feeling confident since I was on the side of the gods (or at any rate demigods), "there are differences, aren't there?"

Noam turned and stared at me, the anger already rising in his eyes. I felt the muscles of my stomach begin to tighten. "What did you" —slightly emphasized—"have in mind?"

"Well, the difference between mathematical and philosophical intelligences, for example." I smiled shakily.

"*Are* they different?"

"I thought you said they were."

"No, I didn't. Saul did. And I'm sure he has good reasons. I'd like to know what *your* reasons are."

"You often say how many mathematicians turn to philosophy

when they're unable to do math anymore. Doesn't that show they're different?"

"Not to me."

"Oh," I whispered.

"Oh," he mocked. "Don't you think you owe us an account of your reasoning?"

I was aware of the embarrassed glances around the table. I saw the Kripkes exchange a look of concern. But mostly I was aware of the pounding in my head.

"I don't know, it just seemed self-evident." My voice was pleading. "We always disagree over what's obvious."

"Why is it self-evident?" His voice was a monotone.

"If a person can't do one but can do the other, doesn't that show the intelligence required is different?" I whispered.

"A non sequitur. The topics toward which the intelligence is applied are different. It's possible that the one merely requires more intelligence, not a special sort. A slight decline in powers might incapacitate one mathematically, but not philosophically. Do you understand?"

I shook my head dumbly.

"I think," he said, finally looking around at the others, "that whatever is required for doing math or philosophy has not been very brilliantly displayed just now by my wife."

Noam smiled. I would have welcomed a responding smile or laugh, since silence would only indicate pity for me. And I didn't—have never—wanted that. But unfortunately everyone was quiet for a long moment, until Margaret Kripke, in an obvious, although nonetheless kind attempt to divert attention, began to compliment the hostess on the food.

Our first anniversary passed unnoticed. Noam gave no indication of remembering it, and I thought it better not to remind him of the mistake he had made. I could even sympathize with him, for he must have been terribly disillusioned. I had been, for however brief a time, the one romance of his life, excluding the supernaturals. In some ways he was naïvely romantic, for he had given such matters so little thought (as was consistent with his view of how much thought they deserved). What opinions he did have were simply those most commonly held, those he had unconsciously absorbed from the prevailing attitude. (He was, for instance, always taken aback if I showed any sign of enjoying sex too much. A woman shouldn't be cold, but she shouldn't be a whore.) He had, in those spring days of our courtship, perceived me in impossibly ideal terms. I could sympathize with his disillusionment.

I spent the day of our anniversary alone, crying a great deal, remembering how things had been a year before. Things certainly happened fast with Noam. He had fallen in love virtually immediately and fallen out of love almost as quickly. The "falling" idiom was exactly right. I had little faith the marriage would last. Still, we had made it past the year mark, and now simple annulment was impossible.

Noam seemed to have become much harsher in general. His assessments of others, whether talking with them or about them, were less charitable. I blamed myself for this, too. His disgust with me had poisoned his attitude toward everyone. One incident in particular stands out. It was November, our second. We were discussing which of the several invitations for Thanksgiving dinner to accept. A graduate student who had called earlier in the evening came by to talk to Noam about some ideas he hoped might be developed into his dissertation. Noam acted ferociously, hammering the student over the head again and again with the triviality and emptiness of his ideas. I watched in horror as the student cringed there, stuttering out his answers to the questions Noam kept shooting at him. When he finally slouched out the door, I went up to Noam and screamed into his face:

"*Why? Why* did you do that to him?"

"What are you so hysterical about? I was helping him. He came here to find out if the ideas were worthwhile, and I told him. I did him a favor. I saved him weeks, probably months of wasted effort."

"But the *way* you did it, Noam! Did you have to be so cruel, so relentless? Did you have to mortify him?"

"I assure you, Steve was not mortified. You don't understand these things. Steve was interested in the objective value of his ideas. He's not going to be bothered by the trivialities that concern you so much."

"Trivialities like human feelings?"

"Yes. Trivialities like human feelings." He looked at me for several seconds, considering me. "You know, Renee," he finally said, "you are an essentially trivial woman. You have a lovely face and body, but in essence you are very trivial."

I felt as if I had flunked my final exam, my very final exam.

I HAD BECOME quite frigid by this time. It was my first experience of sex without desire. What a cold, cold thing it is, the bare, dry facts, scraped clean of the film of desire.

On one of my trips into New York at about this time, I overheard a group of pubescent girls, maybe thirteen or fourteen years old, chattering and giggling, and I caught the phrase "making out." It startled me. I hadn't heard the phrase in so many years. In fact, now that I heard it again I was surprised it still had a place in adolescent vocabulary. For the phrase is used by those who are teetering on the brink, approaching without yet plunging in to the inestimable depths; the plunge known in that same vocabulary, at least as it was employed in my adolescence, as "going all the way." I hadn't thought teenagers now hesitated on the other side long enough to have use for a phrase like "making out."

I sat there on that subway remembering the time of my own delicious teetering with Hillel, when each step closer convinced us of the overwhelming power and mystery of what lay beyond. And now I had passed through to that great knowledge, and this was the reality. It was horrible. (How many other mysteries would end this way, were one finally to see through them? How desirable *is* the parting of the mists?)

I was incapable of arousal with Noam. My flesh under his touch was dead, only stirred now and then by a ripple of revulsion. For a while I pretended orgasms, but then I saw that I needn't make the effort. Noam wasn't watching.

He was staring away, and not only in bed. When he wasn't raging, he was absent, at least in spirit. That day he first sat down next to me on the dinky, we had been strangers to one another; and yet he had held my eyes with such direct intensity that I was made uncomfortable by the implied intimacy. And now we were man and wife, and that vivid gaze, which had first settled on me with admiration as I stood in the surrounding circle at Loft's party, that gaze which had directed all its brilliance and enthusiasm at me in the course of the accompanying conversations, that gaze, and all its intensity, had turned away.

Frigidity we call it in women, impotence in men. The terms reflect, I think, the male point of view. But there's coldness and want of power on both sides. I certainly felt impotent, a thing of naught.

I briefly considered masturbation, as (and in much the same spirit) I considered jogging: as something that, no matter how unpleasant, might be good for me. For I thought it possible that my body would go quite dead, become incapable of ever feeling pleasure again; and that, at least according to the collective opinion of the day, couldn't be healthy. But then again perhaps a sexual death, if possible, would be the most reasonable solution. I had once read a former inmate's account of prison life, and he had written that after several months of celibacy all desire had mercifully vanished. Prison had been much easier after that.

But could it all be made to disappear? Despite my respect for Noam's views, and Noam's contempt for Freud's, I couldn't rid my thinking of such concepts as repression. I had an image of molten libidinous matter, seething in the psychical depths, which could be buried but never destroyed. And eventually the volcanic eruptions in personality would come, the lava of the libido spewing forth in geyser-like behavioral aberrations. The best one could hope for would be sublimation (which might, if Freud was right, even make a genius of me). Is it possible to die a merciful sexual death? And where would that leave one?

Sartre says the object of sexual desire is a "double reciprocal incarnation," most typically expressed by the caress: "I make myself flesh in order to impel the Other to realize *for herself* and *for me* her own flesh. My caress causes my flesh to be born for me insofar as it is for the Other *flesh causing her to be born as flesh.*"

But it seems to me that even deeper than Sartre's object lies another: a double reciprocal mattering, the most typical expression of which is the gaze. In gazing with desire on the Other I reveal how he, in my desire, takes me over, permeates my sense of self; and in his gaze I see how I similarly matter to him, who himself matters at that moment so much. It's *this* double reciprocal process that accounts, I think, for the *psychological* intensity of sexual experience. It answers to one of our deepest needs, a fundamental fact of human existence: the will to matter.

Noam had sadly missed the point in thinking the object of sexuality is no more, and no more interesting, than a sensation. His is the solipsistic view of sex, and it leaves out the complexity, the depth, and the reason this part of life matters so much to us. Without the Other and his gaze, the act is little more than clumsy masturbation. And so it was for me with Noam, who now was always turned away, psychically if not physically, like the man in the da Vinci sketch. Making love under such circumstances is hardly the powerful affirmation of mutual mattering it's meant to be.

To matter. Not to be as naught. Is there any will deeper than that? It's not just unqualified will, as Schopenhauer would have it, that makes us what we are; nor is it the will to power, Nietzsche, but something deeper, of which the will to power is a manifestation. (And who am *I*, daughter of a *shtickele chazzen* from Galicia, to argue with the likes of Schopenhauer and Nietzsche?) We want power *because* we want to matter. Neither sex nor power lies at the level of fundamental facts. Beneath are the heaving thrusts of the will to matter. And the will to create? to procreate? These too are expressions of the fundamental will. Deeper even than the will to survive. We don't *want* to live when we become convinced that we don't, can't, will never matter. That is the state which most often precedes suicide—always, I think, when the cause of suicide lies within.

To matter, to mind. Curious to compare the verbs we have formed from the nouns. What we mind is in our power, but whether we matter may not be—and there's the tragedy. Spinoza tried to help us out of it: We can make ourselves matter because of what we mind. No, no, rather: We shouldn't mind that we don't matter. *It*—of which we're a part—matters. Dissolve the individual will to matter in the objective picture of the whole. It's rather a drastic solution, but then perhaps nothing less will do. And does one thereby dissolve the individual? Is this the solution to the problem of personal identity? Is this will our very essence, with which we are and without which we are not? Perhaps. In any case, it's very close to the realization of the self. We no sooner discover that we are, than we want that which we are to matter. In spite of Spinoza.

Can anyone truthfully say, I don't matter and I don't mind? Not I. Of all my many mind-body problems, the most personally and painfully felt has been this: Do I matter as a mind or do I matter as a body? This is the problem that produces the pattern, the pendulum swings of my dangling life. But somehow or other I *must* come out mattering.

And where was I now? I had hoped, like the good fairy tale taught, to save myself by marrying Noam. My mattering to him, who himself mattered so much, was going to do the trick. It had always been a battle against self-hate, and that's a bloody battle. I certainly didn't have the stuff to stand up to Noam's attacks, his palpable contempt. If I have quaked before every idiot's judgment, if the shrug of the shoulders has always been a movement I'm incapable of executing, imagine how it was to be standing before the Highest Judge, the Genius, before whom no invalid inference could be hidden, and to hear the verdict delivered: You are damned, you are dumb.

The sex was the least of it, if that can be comprehended. I am concerned to distinguish my voice from that great chorus of sexual lamentation being sung by women throughout the land, in first novel (the autobiographical one, right?) after first novel. The voices are different. Some sing raucously, some delicately, some with a constant whine. But all are singing the Marital Blues:

> My husband don't please me
> Takes all but don't give me
> In-out and he's done
> And I never come.
>
> I don't say that he beats me
> But the way that he treats me
> Makes me feel old and done
> And I never come.

Then the Love Affair, and the music changes . . . to Rachmaninoff, climax after climax.

> Then he came
> And I came . . . and I came . . . and I came . . .

Till back we go to the blues:

> That bum went off humming
> And there's no second coming.

Women being done wrong, with all the action below the belt. Pelvic drama. I'm not denying the pleasure and pain involved. (Who was it who said bad sex is better than no sex at all? What a blessed sexual existence he must have enjoyed.) Sex that's gone dry and tasteless, that one can swallow only with effort, is one of the more unpalatable experiences life offers. Especially when one is remembering or imagining the cognac-soaked flambé possibilities. But orgasms —weak few or nonexistent—are not the stuff of tragedy.

Nor is my story, although Noam was certainly killing off something more than sexual desire in me. But between my father's tales of Jewish martyrdom and my mother's predictions of catastrophe, I had been brought up with the tragic possibilities of life always before me and I never saw myself as a bowed victim of persecution. If there was one element of the Jewish consciousness my parents had managed to instill in me, it was the true meaning of persecution.

I continued to see much of Sarah and Ava, but I never spoke to either about what was happening to me. Sarah was sunk deep in her own miseries and Ava . . . Well, Ava was exactly the same as always. I could have spoken to her, but I didn't. It was all too painful, and the duplication of the hurting facts inside her head would only have increased the pain. I didn't want anyone inside my head. When I spoke to Sarah and Ava it was usually about their lives, which at this point meant their work.

Sarah and Ava never became friends, as I had hoped they would, for I am always hoping that the people I love will love one another. They thought well of each other but never became close. Each was amused by the other; their respective peculiarities were strengthened to a point just short of burlesque in one another's company. Sarah became purer and starker, and Ava blunt to the point of brutality.

Ava nicknamed Sarah "Reine Vernunft," that is, Kant's Pure Reason. Sarah knew and was amused. Once, when the three of us were having lunch together in the faculty dining room in Prospect, Sarah said something that caused Ava to hoot, to which Sarah replied: "Is that your *Kritik der reinen Vernunft?*"

I saw more of Ava than of Sarah, whose gloomy ancestors would set up a great chorus of whispering accusations if she left her work for more than an hour. Consequently, I often spent my evenings with Ava. (Noam went back to his office after dinner almost every night.)

One night I came very close to telling Ava about my problems, prodded by her own self-revelations. It had started off by her complimenting me:

"You know, Renee, you really look great. You're a damn good-looking woman."

I probably did look particularly good at this time. I had lost all interest in food, something I would never have imagined could happen to me. (But then I would never have thought I'd become frigid, either.) I had lost a few pounds and always look best when underweight and Camille-like. In the past I had only been able to maintain my matter in this form for short periods before my love of food brought me back to my healthy-looking self. (This love, finally acquired sometime in later childhood, is one of my mother's minor triumphs. "If only I live to see my children someday dieting.") But now it was hard to eat, for I always had the feel of cinders in my mouth.

"Look at me, on the other hand," Ava was saying. "I've really deteriorated since college."

Unfortunately, this was true. Ava was about fifteen pounds heavier than she'd been at Barnard and seemed on the whole to take no trouble with her appearance. Her thin hair, shaped like a monk's in college, now drooped unbecomingly down the sides of her too full face. She never wore a trace of makeup (as she had at Barnard) and her wardrobe was confined to jeans, which did not sit particularly well on her zaftig bottom.

"And you know this uglification is intentional, in the sense that compulsive hand-washing is intentional. There's a need behind it. I don't really want to look pretty. I don't want to look feminine. You know why? Because feminine is dumb. Or at least that's how I feel. Look around at the women in academia, the women who make their living from their brains—especially those in the so-called masculine disciplines like math and physics, to take two random examples. They all feel it too. They're telling you with the way they look and dress, the way they hold themselves and speak: feminine is dumb. You've got to stamp out all traces of girlishness if you want to be taken seriously by the others, but more importantly by yourself. I know. I can see it in myself and can't do anything about it. It was okay to be a girl when I was only a student, but not anymore. When I'm attracted to a man and start playing the part of a woman, there's a voice sneering inside me: Dumb. You dumb cunt. You just can't be a cunt with intelligence. You can have a brain and a prick, there's no incompatibility there. 'Brainy prick' sounds all right, but 'intelligent cunt' is ridiculous, a contradiction in terms. We've all swallowed it. I tell you, I think it would be an act of feminist heroism, an assertion of true liberation from the chauvinist myth, to wear eyeliner and mascara. If I ever saw a female physicist dressed to kill and wearing makeup, I'd be impressed.

"But it won't be me," she continued. "I don't care what the others will think; I care what I'll think, what I'll feel like. I can't manage to regard myself as a woman and a physicist, so one of them's got to go. And I suppose being a physicist is more important to me, so goodbye, sex. Men don't have to make the choice, but we do. For us it's either-or."

"Either mind or body," I said.

"Right. Your old mind-body problem again, or a different aspect of it. Ah, well."

I felt close to telling Ava about my own farewell to sexuality and battled with the decision for several minutes. Finally she suggested we get high.

Our dope-smoking was largely a thing of our college past, but occasionally we still smoked if only for old times' sake. While we passed the joint back and forth Ava described some people she had just met at the Institute, using her favored gustatory imagery:

"That guy working with Dyson reminds me of a piece of strudel. Layers and layers, but all of them flaky. And remember that logician

I told you about, the one with the pregnant wife who propositioned me? The husband, not the wife. I finally figured out exactly what he's like. An overcooked Brussels sprout." She added in explanation: "He's English."

"God, Ava, what an awful image that conjures up. A guy with a Brussels sprout for a head. I *hate* Brussels sprouts."

"Me, too. Can't tolerate them. Nor people who remind me of them."

"I've always thought that after the mind-body problem, or perhaps side by side with it, the most important question in philosophy of mind is whether people who like Brussels sprouts taste them the way I do and actually like that awful taste, or do they taste something different?"

"Baffling. Here's another: Do people who don't like chocolate taste it the way I do and not like it, or do they taste something else? Maybe something like my taste of Brussels sprouts?"

"Who can say? The mystery of consciousness and the inaccessibility of the Other."

My memory of the conversation ends here, for the stuff we were smoking proved to be very strong. I have no recollection of what we spoke about. I couldn't even remember then. By the time I reached the end of a sentence, I couldn't recall its beginning. I'd start a new sentence not knowing what I'd just said before, just plunge in blindly. At first such freedom was terrifying, but I gradually adjusted to it . . . and then *exulted* in it. (Why was there the faint suggestion of sexuality, like a softly breathed whisper against my ear? Was it because sex is another analogue for freedom?) I didn't have to be hampered by the requirements of coherence, I didn't have to make sense. I was beyond the bounds of sense.

I had made a monumental discovery, and I struggled to put it into words. It was too big but I tried, for I had to capture it in words if I were to share it with Ava. Finally I had it. I got up on the chair and shouted, "Logic sucks!" and sat down again, very pleased with my statement, my attempt to squeeze the immensity of my intuition into linguistic constraints.

Ava got up on her chair and declaimed:

"Logic is the ladder of pure reason, but alas;

"The ladder's a mere cobweb, and we fall down on our ass."

Oh, Ava! Oh, wonderful, brilliant, incomparable Ava! I was dazzled, overcome. It was too perfect, said it all. She understood. She understood everything. I loved her. Always had. How could I tell her? How could I put all this soaring feeling into words? It was spilling all over, sweeping me away. I fought to get back in. It was important. I had to tell her.

I was dimly aware of various eruptions at the periphery of my visual field, but I was completely absorbed in the problem before me. Suddenly Ava's face loomed up right in front of mine. She was waving a plate of spaghetti under my nose.

"Renee? Are you here? Are you there? Have you penetrated into the womb of the universe?"

"Huh?"

"Renee? Everything okay? You've been sitting there in a trance for almost an hour. You're not hallucinating or anything, are you? That stuff was stronger than I realized. Here, eat some spaghetti."

"Huh?"

"You're repeating yourself, child. Here. Eat."

I ate. Slowly the pieces of my mind began to drift down. I began to remember from one moment to the next. I wasn't sure whether I was gaining or losing something.

Ava had made an enormous quantity of spaghetti, sprinkled with raw garlic, red pepper flakes, and fresh Parmesan. She was busy eating, and so was I. She glanced up.

"You okay?"

"Yeah, sure. I was just trying to figure out how to say something."

"What?"

"I didn't figure out how to say it, so I can't tell you. I'm not even sure now what it was, if it was anything at all."

My friend laughed. "Yeah, it's like that. Only Coleridge could write a work of genius doped out."

But I felt dissatisfied. I still had something to tell her. But the inhibitions and shyness of my unhigh self were imposing themselves on me, together with the bonds of memory and logic. The words "I love you" had seemed too puny to carry my meaning when I was high, but now they seemed too strong. I was afraid. I was afraid of what they might open up before us or close behind us.

I did love Ava, loved her less selfishly, more trustingly, with less hostility than I'd loved any man. As I loved Sarah and Tzippy. But above all, and for the longest time, Ava. And she loved me, I knew, loved me deeply and acceptingly. She would, I think, have taken me that night had I thrown out my arms and embraced her as I longed to do—attracted by her warm receptivity, repelled by Noam's cold anger. There had been times in the past. Always I had been the one to pull away. And if that night I had not? I wonder, dear Ava, I wonder.

You knew I was afraid, as you knew everything else. That was the whole point, the very source of my fear. I was afraid of that knowledge which would be too knowing, that intimacy which would be too intimate, soft skin against soft skin. With men there's never the danger of getting too close. They're too essentially different. They don't know what we feel, we don't know what they feel, and nobody's mental privacy is seriously threatened.

I left a half-hour later, still dissatisfied, and filled with unvoiced longing.

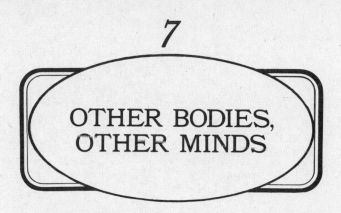

7

OTHER BODIES, OTHER MINDS

Thus the final state of sexual desire can be swooning as the final state of consent to the body. It is in this sense that desire can be called the desire of one body for another body. It is in fact an appetite directed toward the Other's body, and it is lived as the vertigo of the for-itself before its own body. The being which desires is consciousness *making itself body.*

—JEAN PAUL SARTRE,
BEING AND NOTHINGNESS

*T*he fauna of academe are various. Among the most interesting are the members of the mathematical species. The characteristics found here are very distinctive, facilitating identification. A few times I've described to Noam some unknown creature spotted in town, concluding with: "It's a mathematician, isn't it?" Four times out of five I've been right. (The fifth is usually a mathematical physicist.) The trick is this: If you see someone walking about in the vicinity of a campus who looks as if he's either very backward or very brilliant, then if he's not backward he's a mathematician. There is not another group of people, I'll wager, with eccentricities so pronounced and pure, with personalities so undiluted by the attempt to conform. Why is this so? I have a theory.

(The Other) Himmel's Theory of Academic Types

Observers of the academic scene may be aware that there are distinct personality types associated with distinct disciplines. The types can be ordered along the line of a single parameter: the degree of concern demonstrated over the presentation of self, or "outward focus."

One of the more interesting facts about academic types is that very few fall within the middle range of outward focus (with engineers, geologists, and other very applied scientists perhaps being the exceptions). The majority of academic types are clustered at the two extremes.

At the low end, with outward focus asymptotically approaching zero, we find the pure mathematicians, closely followed by the theoretical physicists (the more theoretical the physicist, the more closely he follows). At the other end, with the degree of outward focus asymptotically approaching infinity, we find sociologists and professors of literature.

The author's special interests demand that she consider the location of the philosophers, which turns out to be complicated.

Philosophy's own ambivalent position between the humanities and the sciences has resulted in a corresponding schizophrenia in the personality type. There are, in fact, two distinct philosophy types, both extreme. Some philosophers approach the pure mathematician's end of the spectrum, while others (probably the majority) rival the members of English departments in their obsessive concern over the impression they make on others.

That philosophy's ambivalent position can result in a split in the philosophy type suggests that the variation in outward focus is itself a function of the nature of the given discipline; and closer examination shows this to be the case. The degree of outward focus is in inverse proportion to the degree of certainty attainable within the given methodology. The greater the certainty of one's results, the less the concern with others' opinions of oneself.

Thus at the end of the spectrum occupied by sociologists and professors of literature, where there is uncertainty as to how to discover the facts, the nature of the facts to be discovered, and whether indeed there are any facts at all, all attention is focused on one's peers, whose regard is the sole criterion for professional success. Great pains are taken in the development of the impressive persona, with excessive attention given to distinguished appearance and faultless sentence structure.

At the other end, where, as the mathematicians themselves are fond of pointing out, "a proof is a proof," no concern need be given to making oneself acceptable to others; and as a rule none whatsoever is given.

Within the walls of Fine Hall, Noam doesn't appear eccentric. There are plenty stranger—some who appear to be straddling the line between sanity and insanity, others who seem to have already taken the step beyond. There is, for example, the much celebrated Phantom of Fine Hall. The corridors of the math building are hung with huge blackboards every few yards, just in case someone is smitten by an intuition on the way to the bathroom. Many of these blackboards bear the legends of the Phantom, complicated equations between political and mathematical terms. At first I used to study them, believing they were sophisticated jokes I wasn't getting. Then I learned they were the work of a former member of the department who had done foundational work in topology before his mental breakdown.

There's a certain degree of danger involved in the life of the pure mathematician, in his intimacy with the inhumanly perfect and the consequent liberation from mortal concerns. Insanity is an occupational hazard, a sacrifice the mathematician risks in his solipsistic splendor.

I suppose the last thing I needed was a mathematician for a lover. But the last thing one needs is often the very thing one chooses, and so it was with me.

SO FAR as I could tell, my buried libidinal lava hadn't produced any publicly observable distortions in the topography of my personality. But there was covert activity, in the form of an igneous fantasy life. Suddenly everybody (with an emphasis on the body) was desirable, with the exception, of course, of my lawfully wedded. I imagined myself with men once known: with Hillel Schoenfeld, my first love, now a physicist at the Weizmann Institute in Israel; with Peter Hill Devon, the epicene musicologist and Wasp *extraordinaire;* with Jack Gottlieb, the sweet mathematician who took me to the party where I met Noam; and even with Leonard Heiss, the cocksure man of letters with unsure sexual tastes, and Isaac Besdin, the menopausal logician.

I didn't only live in the past. I daydreamed about current acquaintances, and sometimes about men I didn't even know: the cheerful blond kid of about seventeen who loaded my grocery bags at Davidson's and always offered to take them right to my home for me, or anywhere else; the muscular man in the tight T-shirts who serviced my Volvo and was also lavish with friendly extra-auto suggestions. (How many men, one wonders, could resist, were attractive women always bombarding *them* with propositions?) I was somewhat surprised by the crudity of my reactions. How could I, with my refined sensibility and overdeveloped mind, respond so violently to those bulging, overdeveloped biceps?

Erotic daydreaming became my favorite pastime. Now it wasn't only Noam who was living inside his own head. Whom would it hurt if I allowed myself absolute freedom of imagination? I could achieve an abandon here—in this disembodied sex, mental and solitary—impossible when it came to the real thing. But gradually my fantasizing began to take on the feel of preparation for action.

I reminded myself often over the course of this winter of my discontent, and the spring and summer that brought no relief, that in Judaism adultery belongs in the same category with murder and idolatry. If faced with the choice of committing any of these three sins or death, one should, and only in these cases, choose death. I tried to feel the awfulness of adultery, but didn't. What a long way I had traveled (backwards or forwards?) from my days with Hillel, when we two had quakingly, achingly perceived the enormity of our actions: tears and trembling, fear and defiance, and the *basso ostinato* of guilt. And then, unlike now, there had been no question of an injured party.

Would Noam be injured? What if he never knew? What if my actions made no difference to his life as he lived it? But no, people can suffer harm even if their experience as such isn't affected. What about a person who is maligned or deceived, even if he never finds out and suffers no ill consequences? Isn't he damaged simply in *being* maligned or deceived? And of course what I had in mind was deceiving Noam. There could be no question of honesty. Noam's views on marriage and morals, as on more romantic matters, are strictly conventional, thus saving him the bother of having to think about these things himself—one of the benefits of conventions in general. He would tolerate no deviations.

So duped he would have to be. Would that constitute the sum of the injury I would inflict? Somehow one feels that more is involved here, a profound betrayal. But that's only if sexual relations have some sort of special significance, if there is a difference that matters between sharing a meal and sharing a bed. "Make love to a pretty woman when you want her, just as you drink a glass of cold water when you are thirsty," goes the French saying. My puritanical husband would never say such a thing, but wasn't some such statement the logical consequence of his trivializing treatment of sex? How could he consistently maintain a difference between sexual desire and other appetites? (Somehow it seemed to matter whether Noam himself could consistently claim damage.) He was the one who thought sex of no consequence. Let bodies do what bodies are given to doing. But what's there to think about? What's there to hold the *mind?* How, I had asked in Vienna, could such a simple appetite be categorized in terms of such distinctions as obscenity, perversity, and sin? So what? had come the answer. So we impose these categories on sex. It's just part of our biologically determined obsession and the delusions thus produced. Think of what the Jews do to the simple appetite for food.

Of course, this was only my mind's own Noam I was quoting, not the paradigm himself. But the words were in character. Noam's opinion was something like this; *exactly* what it was couldn't be known, for it was in the nature of the opinion that it wasn't worth mentioning.

Thus did I work out my rationalization.

LEONARD SCHMERZ WAS an assistant professor in Noam's department, and more and more my fantasies wove themselves around him. By the time I spoke my first word to him, I had already involved him in many of my private adventures. It was the look of the man that intrigued me.

He was tall and thin, with shoulders slightly hunched forward in his worn brown sweater. Crowning the humble posture was a magnificent head, with long black hair, dark complexion, and an uncompromisingly Semitic profile. It was a face, unlike mine, undiluted by the thin bloods of the Diaspora. One could picture it suffering for forty years in the desert sands of the Sinai. It suggested a Hebrew prophet mourning the destruction of his people. Suffering and mourning. Now we get to the heart of it. That was the real attraction: the melancholy depths one read within the liquid brown eyes and downcast full lips. The voice was quiet, low, very somber, with a slightly strained sound to it, as if forced out from beneath a crushing weight on the chest. What was this weight? What was the nature of this sad soul's secret?

It took me three months to unravel the mystery, to diagnose the sickness of his soul, its fear and trembling. Len was an utter bore and knew it. This was what he was mourning. His soul was sickened by its own emptiness; the fear and trembling was that others too might discover its condition.

We would go together to a movie on Nassau Street or a play at Princeton's McCarter Theater, and as the lights came on he would turn to me a face of such unspeakable sorrow that I was pierced through and through. What had he seen that I had missed?

I had experienced such a developed sensibility to sorrow before, in my father. He had been a personally happy man but with great understanding of sadness, seeing it where others didn't. I remember when I was around eight or nine, I was playing by myself in the basement of our *shul* one Shabbos while my father was conducting the evening prayers, and I made an exciting discovery. One of the corridors, which was windowless and led to some classrooms, was unlit on Shabbos, resulting in the thickest, most absolute darkness imaginable. It was thrilling to grope one's way sightlessly, the blackness filling one's eyes, tingling with the delicious fear that somehow one would never reach the end; until finally one glimpsed the pale light seeping under the doors of the windowed classrooms. I couldn't wait for services to end so that I could show my father. Afterwards the two of us walked silently hand in hand down the black passage and back. When we emerged into the light, I saw that my father's face was stricken.

"What is it, Daddy?"

"Perhaps," he said softly, "that's what it's like to be blind."

I had ached with love for my father at that moment, and I ached with love when I saw Len's sad face emerge from the darkness of the movie into the light. What had he understood that I had missed? What had he seen to have caused him such anguish?

He refused to talk, and finally, finally I understood why. Len had seen and understood nothing. Once again he had gone to a movie and didn't know what to think about it, didn't know whether it was good or bad, whether he liked it or not, had no reaction whatever. He would be expected to say something, to offer an opinion, and he had nothing. Once again he stood in danger of having his total absence of taste and personality exposed to the harsh judging eyes of the blessedly opinionated.

If only his physical self didn't promise so much. Wittgenstein said the human body is the best picture of the human soul: *Der menschliche Körper ist das beste Bild der menschlichen Seele.* But here, through some sort of ontological mishap, was a mismatched pair. Len was doomed always to disappoint, never to be able to deliver the depth of which his body spoke. Every relationship was a torment of anticipating that final inevitable moment when understanding would gleam in the Other's eyes, lighting up the vast vacancy yawning within poor Len. His hope was to push that moment off as long as possible, to maintain a suffering silence which the face promised was deep and awful.

This promise is what attracted me to Len, and the attraction ended the moment I penetrated the sad little secret. But the very fact that this had happened made it impossible for me to extricate myself. For this, of course, was the very essence of his tragedy, his knowledge that when others came to understand him they would lose all interest. So I tried to keep the terrible knowledge out of my eyes.

How had it all begun? I had been intrigued by Len for a long time, always aware of his silent presence at parties, *Il Penseroso* lugubriously gazing out at the frivolities of the lighthearted. Whenever I was in Fine Hall I made it my business to pass by his office door, which was usually open. I'd glance in and we'd exchange smiles. The smile on Len's face only deepened the gloom in his eyes. Then one day, it was right after midsemester break, I passed by the office and looked in to see crazy Phil Whiter with his feet up on the desk, his long red hair pushed back behind his shoulders, puffing on his pipe.

"Hi, Phil. What are you doing here?"

"Oh, hi, Renee, how you doing? What I'm doing here is working."

"What happened to Leonard?"

"Leonard? Oh, Len Schmerz. He and I switched offices."

At the next math party I walked over to Len's corner. It was the first time I had ever spoken to him directly.

"Hi," I said momentously. His answering look made me regret the fatuity of my greeting. "I noticed that you changed offices."

"Oh, that." He smiled sadly. "Phil Whiter decided he wanted my office. It has a better view. I never quite understood how I'd gotten such a nice office in the first place. Anyway, when I came back from midsemester break I found all my stuff moved out and his moved in. He had even transferred the contents of my desk, crammed everything in. It was a mess."

"Did he at least ask you first if it was all right with you?"

"No." The sad smile lengthened slightly, increasing its tragic suggestions.

"That's really quite a lot of nerve. Did you say anything to him about it?"

"No." He was made to suffer; I loved him. His face was the history of the Jews: the constant expulsions and wanderings, the forced conversions and blood libels, the pogroms and final solution. My heart went out to him, as it went out to that history.

"It's outrageous! He decides and moves in. It's feudal!"

"Well, I don't know." He glanced nervously at Noam, who was standing a few feet away. It was obvious that he was afraid Noam might overhear this seditious conversation. Len's future lay in the hands of people like Noam and Whiter. If he wanted ever to be in a position of kicking some untenured slob out of a nicer office, he would be wise not to alienate the Himmels and Whiters. "Whiter's a full professor and I'm untenured. He's probably got more right to it."

"He's the mighty lord, you're the grateful vassal." Len's weakness made me feel strong and assertive. His was a pure negativity against which I emerged vividly positive. It had been a long time since I felt this way. "The lord decides he likes the vassal's house or wife, so in he moves." Or the *goyim* decide the yids should go, I thought. But I knew better than to speak analogies like this one, especially to a Jew, no matter how Semitic his profile. "There's no need to talk it over, no need for courtesy. What a hypocrite Whiter is! He passes himself off as such a leftist, but he's sure a friend of the class system when it's to his advantage. Lord, vassal; propertied, unpropertied; tenured, untenured. It's all the same crap. Some people matter and have rights, and some people don't."

"Well, that's the way it is." Len shrugged philosophically, visibly relieved when Noam moved off toward the bar, having never glanced our way.

I had enjoyed my conversation with Len, especially the way I felt about myself when talking to him. Not that it really was myself. It was a role, and I always played it with Len. I stopped by his office the next day and casually asked him if he'd had lunch yet, and we went off to the Faculty Club at Prospect. There I continued to work out the part I would play.

I was the invulnerable adventuress, the remorseless *femme fatale*. I implied that I'd already had many extramarital affairs. Len never found out that it was he who initiated me into the rites of adultery. During our months together each of us worked hard to keep the other away, to shield our respective identities. I finally saw through him, but he never saw through me. When I finally left him it was for another man, the right ending to a polished performance of *La Belle Dame Sans Merci*. I had offered him a pack of lies, a fabricated identity, and unperceptive soul that he was, he bought it all and loved it. Because, of course, I was playing exactly the kind of woman who would fascinate and ensnare a Leonard Schmerz. But that's not why I was playing it. I took on the part because it felt so good. After all the months of being alone with self-loathing and failure, it felt wonderful to step out of myself. And it felt very good indeed to bask in Len's fascination and adoration.

I'm writing about the affair after the fact, with the cynical attitude with which I ended it. But that wasn't the attitude with which it began. It began with wonderful excitement, with born-again ecstasy. My body was alive once again, could give and feel pleasure. Len's melting gaze searched out every swell and hollow. He was worshipful, offering me again and again the highest praise of which the Jewish male is capable: You don't look at all Jewish. Our brothers always expect us to thrill at the words, because of course in their scheme of things there's nothing so desirable as a *shiksa*. I've never understood it. Jewish women seem to me so much juicier and more *betampte* (tasty). It's like the difference between a Saltine cracker and a piece of Sacher cake. The latter may be a bit much at times; but it's moist, it's rich, and it's layered. My symbolic logic professor in college, who regarded himself as a great connoisseur of women, once told me that I was his first Jewish lover and that, judging from me, he had made a great mistake in never sampling from his own kind before. I recognized the compliment, although I was pricked by its suggestion that my qualities could be duplicated in any other daughter of Jacob. And I certainly didn't respect my professor any the more for it. It was as if someone who professed a great love and knowledge of wines told me he had just sampled a Bordeaux for the first time and thought these wines merited further investigation.

Ava and Sarah both knew of my affair with Len. Sarah of the Puritan blood was accepting and sympathetic. I told her a bit about my problems with Noam and she seemed to guess much more. But liberated and earthy Ava was bothered by my infidelity. She likes Noam (one difference between her and Sarah), and she hates deception of any sort. She didn't want to appear judgmental, and never openly voiced the distaste I knew she felt. Her statements artfully sideswiped the issue. She'd come out in her usual forceful manner, only always pointed slightly off target.

"Hell, a person gets married, more often than not he cheats. It's almost become part of the institution of marriage. Courtship, honeymoon, reality, breakdown, affairs, divorce: they could be the chapters of almost any book about the typical modern marriage."

"Thanks, Ava. You're telling me my life is a pulp novel."

"Don't worry, kid. You may follow the general format, but I'm sure you'll do it with panache."

"So you think Noam and I will end up getting divorced."

"No, I didn't mean to imply that. You and Noam could never be accused of being typical."

"But you don't approve of this chapter."

"I don't go around approving and disapproving. I leave that to your religious relatives."

"Call it what you will." Anyone who occupies a mattering zone (and Ava did) approves and disapproves, even if one of the things disapproved of is disapproval. "You don't like it. You're not happy about it."

"I don't like the whole crummy institution. I wasn't particularly happy, if you'll remember, about your getting married in the first place. What I don't like is an obsolete set of conventions that forces people to lie and cheat on each other in order to preserve some empty state of union."

"Oh, come on, Ava. As if lovers don't lie and cheat on each other outside of marriage. It's not marriage that causes the problems, it's human psychology."

"Of course there's dishonesty outside, but not to the same extent. It's just much easier to walk out of an unhappy relationship if you're not legally bonded."

"Is that so good? Maybe if you stick around things can change."

"For the worse. How realistic is it to expect two people to live happily ever after?" Here was one girl who hadn't bought the fairy tale. "Happily ever after isn't human psychology. And also, Renee, you hardly even knew Noam when you married him. You should have expected some surprises." It was the only time she allowed herself to show anything but the most abstract kind of disapproval.

"Hardly knew him? My great-grandmother met my great-grandfather under the marriage canopy."

"Cut it out, Renee, your shmaltzy Jewish shtick. If you want to go back to Babylonia, go already. Just get off that trans-world shuttle."

Now I was an adulteress, in a class with the idolaters and murderers, not nice company at all. (What's a nice girl like you . . . ?) But I breezed along, hardly bothered by guilt. There was no sense of soul-crushing enormity, as there had been with Hillel. The only time I felt like a sinner was when I was forced to make up some story about where I had been or how I had spent my time. I despised the petty deception of those little lies. But about the great lie I was living I was hardly bothered. Just so long as I wouldn't have to make up tales. (Just like the analytic philosophers: the reality didn't matter, just the language.) I tried always to be home before Noam so he wouldn't be there to ask where I'd been.

One night, Len having persistently begged me not to leave, I came home rather late. I walked into a dark house with much relief and switched on the light. Noam was sitting on the couch, his arms folded. I was terribly startled and screamed. He turned to me, his face frozen in his hard, hating anger.

"Where have you been?" His voice was barely audible.

"Oh," I stammered, a lump of fear rising in my throat, "I was with Sarah." I'd call her the minute I got the chance and tell her to cover for me (as friends once had helped me deceive my mother).

"Where the *hell* have you been?" Noam repeated, and the fear spread throughout my body, washing away my strength. I thought I might collapse. All was over, I was finished. He knew. Someone must have told him, or maybe he somehow saw us himself. I was lost.

"What a wife you are! What a wife you've turned out to be!" He was screaming now, standing right in front of me, enraged. I was afraid he might hit me. "Do you know what time it is? Do you ever think about anybody but yourself? Do you ever think about me? I've been sitting here starving for the last hour and a half. You have nothing to do all day. No job, no children, no dissertation. Would it be too much to ask you to have some dinner ready for me when I get home?"

Dinner? That was what he was enraged about? It took a moment to penetrate. I wasn't lost. He didn't know about me and Len. He was angry because I didn't have his stupid dinner ready. The great fear brimming over in me was instantaneously converted into fury:

"Fuck your dinner! So I'm an hour late. Fuck it, Noam! Do you have to make me feel like a murderer for that? You're the selfish one! You're the one who never gives a thought to anybody but yourself! Look!" I picked up one of the lamb chops that had been defrosting on the side of the sink. "Would it have killed you to broil it yourself?"

I threw the lamb chop at him (missing), all the while feeling the absurdity of the situation. This was adultery, a serious business, the stuff of great literature, *Madame Bovary*, *Anna Karenina*. And here I was throwing lamb chops.

Noam didn't answer. He looked at the meat lying between us, and then walked past me and out the door. Late that night he returned, while I pretended to be asleep.

We didn't talk for a while after that. It's difficult to say for how long; we so rarely spoke these days anyway—just the minimum required to sort out our household and social obligations. We had both taken to reading during meals, Noam his math journals and I the New York *Times* and *The New Yorker*. (Occasionally I'd show him a cartoon I liked or couldn't understand.)

I think we ended up speaking more to one another at parties. For sometimes, when we were with others, Noam invariably at the center,

I saw him once again as I first had, and I would feel a pleasurable stir of warmth.

There are many beautiful and charming and accomplished women circulating through Princeton society. Only last night we were at a party, and I was chatting with two other mathematicians' wives, one a clinical psychologist, the other a linguist, both of them stunning. We were discussing adolescence, which the psychologist's daughter would soon be entering. It happened that we all, but especially our husbands, had been lonely outsiders then.

"And where are they now, one wonders, those popular girls we had envied so much," said the psychologist smiling, while my vision of my mattering map made its appearance.

"And our husbands, so spurned by those girls, now married to such fantastic women," said the linguist, opening her arms to include us.

I always watched Noam to see how, or rather if, he reacted to desirable women like these. It may or may not be hard to comprehend, but I would have been happy to see that he noticed and appreciated their charms. I would have welcomed gladly his eyes resting on them a few moments longer than necessary, as they had at that first party lingered on me. Such attentions would have indicated that this part of him was still alive and kicking, and I would have liked to have known that. But his face never reflected the desirability of the women around him.

As long as I'm on the subject, I might mention that at a party the chances were about one in five that I would be asked The Question:

"What's it like to live with a genius like your husband?" The legend-seeker this time was the quivery, faded blond wife of an assistant professor in Noam's department. By now this question depressed me, with the shiver of the cold wind of truth that only I could perceive.

"Hellishly lonely, if you really want to know," I said savagely.

"Oh, I'm sorry," she mumbled, looking down quickly. Her thin white skin reddened unevenly and unbecomingly (I also happened to know her husband wouldn't be getting tenure), and so I relented and didn't ask her what she was sorry for: her indiscretion or my life.

At home all was silent and cold between Noam and me. I hardly even thought of him as a person in those days; he was just a series of annoyances and complications. And in that gappy form he intruded less and less on my consciousness (which anyway was occupied elsewhere), so that now I can barely even remember him then. Where was he? What was he doing and saying? I have no recollection. I can't even remember any other episodes of anger between us. The great rage within him appeared to have boiled off, leaving behind a dry residue of indifference. He was quiet and resigned, and increasingly absent, in spirit when not in body. (This of course suited me fine. I could be his wife in name and yet be spared having much to do with the man.) The evenings he was home, he stayed either in his study or else in the living room, listening to music. He was spending more and more time with his much beloved Mozart, and had recently taken to listening in the dark, long into the night. A disappointed, but now resigned man. I could just make him out as I climbed the stairs to our bedroom, sitting erect in the center of the couch, his arms folded on his chest, staring into the black. Almost every night I fell asleep with the faint music coming from below.

Sexual relations ceased between us after one attempt when Noam, for the first time, was impotent. I was surprised by the reactions of each of us, for I was hurt and he upset—as if it mattered to either of us. On my part I felt pain that he no longer desired me even sexually. It was a further diminution of the linkage between us—even if this particular link had not in itself ever been very satisfactory.

But what was more baffling was Noam's reaction to his impotence. Why should it matter to him? Yet it seemed to.

"What do you think it means, Renee?"

"I don't know, Noam. Don't worry, you're probably just tired. You work so hard." I couldn't help myself, I felt sympathy. Imagine Noam's being bothered by mere physical impotence. It still touched me deeply when he exhibited any of the lesser mortal emotions.

"Do you think that's all it is?" he asked, for the first time in a long time gazing searchingly into my eyes.

EVERYONE IN PRINCETON, it seemed, certainly everyone in the math department—except, of course, Noam—knew of my affair with Len. And my lover, it was painfully plain to see, was proud of this.

Poor Len. Poor Noam. To be cuckolded by a Leonard Schmerz. Noam Himmel deserved better, At least if his wife's lover were a mathematician of international stature . . .

Len made no secret of his infatuation, not that he told anyone in words. But then nobody expected silent Len ever to use that medium for communication. He made it all obvious enough, always regarding me with a look of hopeless, slavish devotion. (You can imagine how well he did it.) We got into the habit of meeting for lunch, and then we would go to his apartment on Spring Street. (He always trotted a half-step behind me as we walked, like a little puppy.) It was there for all of Princeton to see, and see they did. The only one who didn't was Noam, and that's because he wasn't looking. His wife was of so little interest to him that he didn't even notice her flagrant infidelity. I pitied Noam for his ignorance; but I hated him for it, too.

My affair wilted and withered during the steamy Princeton summer, as I gradually penetrated my lover's interior. The mystery of his personality melted, revealing the core of vapidity. For *this* I had entered the class of idolaters and murderers. (I first began to suspect the nature of his secret when he described to me, in tones of deepest tragedy, how he had walked a block with one of the high and mighty mathematicians at Princeton and all they had spoken of was the weather.) My attitude toward Len became a highly noxious mix of interacting emotions: contempt, pity, and, stronger than either, the annoyance over feeling contempt and pity. The more I scorned, the more I pitied him for being the source. Then, overcome by the urge to comfort, I would lick his secret wound, his (all too justified) sense of inner emptiness. I would invent tales for him, describing how fascinating he was and in which respects. It required the inventive skill of a Scheherazade.

"Len, I really think you're one of the most interesting people I've known." We were in the drab bedroom of his depressing little apartment.

"Do you?" Happiness seemed wrong on that solemn face, but there it was. "How? Tell me how I'm interesting."

Dear God, as if a truly interesting person would ever ask. And now what was I going to say?

"Well, there's your face." I traced it lightly with my fingertips: the high noble forehead and weighty black brows; the soulful eyes and mournful lips and substantial, bravely arched nose. "It's got Jewish history written all over it."

No, he didn't like that. He was frowning. First of all, he identified with that history even less than Noam (whose interest in the subject had increased slightly after his Viennese discovery. Upon returning to Princeton, he had even read Lucy Dawidowicz's *The War Against the Jews*). Len too had been circumcised by a doctor and never bar mitzvahed, although he once offered, in the flow of powerful emotion, to have a bar mitzvah now, for me. Unfortunately, this magnificent avowal of sacrificing love caused me to burst out laughing.

And anyway, Len already knew he had an interesting face. It was his soul he wanted me to describe.

"You have such unusual ways of looking at the world, especially at people. I think you can really see through them, into their secret sorrows, and you suffer on their behalf. You have that capacity to imagine what it's like to be someone else, to see the world as he sees it and to empathize with his reactions, and I think that's probably the most important element in the moral makeup."

There, that ought to make him happy. (It takes more than a good body to be a *femme fatale*.) The poor fellow was all puffed up with satisfaction. Was he so pleased because he thought I believed this tale or had I actually convinced him of its truth? I was once again fighting down contempt, which brought on an attack of pity, and the whole sickening cycle began again.

Now I wasn't only a prisoner of a dead marriage; I was trapped into a dull love affair. Neither identity could save me, neither wife of the genius nor *femme fatale*. Was there perhaps a lesson to be learned? Is there something fundamentally wrong and intrinsically unsatisfying about a woman's attempt to define herself through her relationships with men? Impossible. A woman is who she marries, or—to update my mother's almost timeless wisdom—who she sleeps with. Her essential properties are relational. Besides, what else was there to me? Noam thinks the essence of the individual lies in his intellectual and moral attributes, but I didn't have any of these, not anymore.

THERE WAS MORE than my intellectual and moral decline to depress me that summer. For the first time I heard whispers of the decay of the flesh. I was twenty-five, and it happened like this:

I was in the bathroom, putting on my makeup before the medicine cabinet mirror, and the radio was on in the bedroom. Some item on the news had made me laugh as I stroked on my mascara. And there they were: laugh lines. Or, not to mince words: wrinkles, lightly but undeniably radiating downward from my horrified eyes. It was inconceivable. What truck had I with wrinkles? Oh, I knew the general facts, of course, having to do with aging. But I had never made the deduction to the particular: me. I stood there staring into the bathroom mirror, my mouth creased into a joyless approximation of a smile, taking it in. Time's gifts had ceased. From now on, time would be bringing me nothing but *tsuris*.

How long had those lines been there, this intimate fact about me immediately accessible to others and only mediately known to me? And what other symptoms of aging had already arrived, awaiting my discovery? I hadn't inspected my body for changes in a long time. I had viewed it as having reached a fairly stable condition, except for the fluctuations of five pounds more or less, and I knew exactly where to find them (face and waist). I had regarded my body, for the past few dumbly complacent years, as a finished object, its potentiality realized, its matter formed. Better to have been thinking in terms less Aristotelian and more Bergsonian:

"This reality is mobility. There do not exist *things* made, but only things in the making, not *states* that remain fixed, but only states in the process of change. Rest is never anything but apparent, or rather, relative. The consciousness we have of our own person in its continual flowing, introduces us to the interior of a reality on whose model we must imagine all things. All reality is, therefore, tendency, if we agree to call tendency a nascent change of direction."

My body was no more a fixed thing than my mind. Its very form was a process of change, a becoming. I was mortally afraid of *what* it was becoming.

I hadn't really thought about aging before, at least not in the negative sense. Why should I have? Until now getting older had been a joyfully beneficial process; time was an ally, leading me ever upward. Any afflictions along the way—baby fat, overactive glands—had only to be waited out. Time would heal. But abruptly, quite abruptly, I perceived that the direction of incline along which time was leading me had changed. (Reality is a nascent change of direction. You hit it right on the perpetually moving target, Henri.) The ally had become the enemy, leading me downward to . . . Good God. And these afflictions were here to stay and worsen. Is this, Herr Leibniz, the very best arrangement an omnipotent beneficient God could come up with in the best of all possible worlds? A bare seven or eight years from last pimple to first wrinkle?

I stripped out of my clothes and went to stand before the full-length bedroom mirror. It had been years since I'd made a general canvass, an expedition of discovery. The findings of the past had been satisfying: the gentle undulations of flesh, the delicate swells and tapers. Now the undulations would come in the form of wrinkles and sags.

I first tried to determine whether there had been any sagging of my breasts, viewing them in profile. Had their roundness flattened slightly? Oh, I was vain about those breasts: full, firm, smooth, the nipples golden pale and delicately shaped. But, it suddenly occurred to me, the very generosity of their bulk would hasten their decline. Newton's law of gravity. The force is proportional to the mass. No more running free and braless. I would never again allow nothing to come between my breasts and gravity.

And it wouldn't be only my breasts that were subjected to Newton's gravitational law. Thighs, ass, chin, all would be pulled, would droop and deflate. But the real devastation would take place in the face. Was there no way to fight it? I was dimly aware, in the blithe manner of youth, of a thriving business devoted to opposing these forces of nature. I remembered just that past winter having seen a magazine ad that sent a slight sickening chill of presentiment coursing through me: "If you're over twenty-five, you know that beauty is something you work on." I had just turned twenty-five, and the thought had never occurred to me. I exercised fairly regularly, tennis or squash with Ava about twice a week. (What Princeton matron, even if not so self-respecting, doesn't play tennis?) I played these sports only because I enjoyed them and felt so good afterwards. But *work* on beauty? My attitude toward being pretty had been Calvinist. Some are born blessed, arbitrarily chosen to receive God's love. Beauty is passive, unlike the active powers of the intellect, which is why I would prefer being brilliant to beautiful. But that doesn't mean I was prepared to become an ugly hag. It gave me a fright, this ad, with its suggestion that this aspect of God's universe isn't quite so unfair as I had assumed; but the fright quickly gave way to skepticism. They were just trying to sell products. And what was so special about twenty-five, anyway? They pick some arbitrary age. I was young, young. It was impossible to imagine myself being anything but young.

And so I stood there, naked before the mirror, assimilating such elementary truths as: Youth is not an essential, but rather an accidental property. Nobody is in *essence* young. One either ceases to be or ceases to be young.

Where to go? Instinctively I knew that the people with the facts would be not doctors but women, beautiful and vain women intent on finding ways of circumscribing the relentless laws of nature ruling their bodies, if not their minds.

At the next party I asked an acquaintance, an attractive pale blond woman of no determinate age (but that's the object, isn't it?), wife of a mighty figure in the political science department (my husband and I move with the Princeton powers), whether she knew of a good place for skin. She immediately grasped that it wasn't medical help I was seeking.

"There are quite a few good places in New York," she answered. "The best known is probably Georgette Klinger."

And so to Georgette Klinger I went, a bright honeycomb of little white cubicles buzzing with well-tended women, young and old. The queen bee herself I never saw, although I was told that her complexion, fine-pored and flawless, is a testament to woman's conquest over nature. The cubicle I was ushered into held a chair like a dentist's, a hook for hanging up my dress, a white smock to don, and a very serious, white-uniformed girl with a Hungarian accent who began my treatment with questions, writing down my answers.

"How old are you?"

I told her and she leaned over to probe my skin more closely, gently prodding and stroking it.

"You look very good, Mrs. Himmel, especially considering your age."

That hurt. I just couldn't get used to thinking of my age as a liability. I had always been so *young*.

"Very good elasticity. But it's dry. What do you use to cleanse it?"

"Soap."

"What?" She looked at me in genuine horror, her eyes dilated. Her stare was almost exactly duplicated by the young man—velvet skin, velvet eyes, velvet pants—who later made me up and also asked me what I cleaned with. Their expression was that of a missionary who has just been told by the blithe native that his wife is his sister.

"Ivory soap," I half said, half asked. "I thought it was very gentle." She continued to stare. "Well, what *does* one wash with if not soap?"

"*Cream.* You don't use soap, you use *cream.*" I know moral outrage when I see it. I had stumbled on one more floating region of the mattering map, enclosing a system of perceptions and judgments, values and rules. And I know the spirit of religion when I see it. This young woman ministering to my face was very religious.

The treatment was continued. My face was creamed, steamed over camomile tea, creamed, massaged, creamed, and then creamed. The session ended with a fire-and-brimstone sermon against the pleasures of sunbathing, after I admitted to an occasional indulgence.

"Avoid it. Avoid the sun the way you would a blade across your face. It's your enemy, you especially. You're very fair. Your skin has no protection against the rays. The radiation goes down and breaks capillaries, destroying elasticity. And that means terrible damage, wrinkles. Irreversible."

Irreversible. The word froze my heart.

THIS YEAR not even the coming of autumn raised my spirits. There weren't going to be any fresh starts. Noam and I were sharing the same house but little else. Len had begun to beg me to get a divorce and marry him. But I wasn't going to give up being the wife of one of the world's great mathematicians to become the wife of one of the world's great mathematical bores. Len's absurd chatter about my divorce was unbearable to me. But its very absurdity provoked my pity, making it impossible to get away.

The fall brought as always a great rush of parties. New people are always arriving in September, and parties are given for the more important. Ava was very excited about the arrival at the Institute of the physicist Daniel Korper, on leave for the year from Cornell. She had long admired his work, but found him even more impressive in person.

"I suppose he's not really a *great* physicist. He hasn't done anything revolutionary, he isn't ever going to make the headlines, I don't think. But he's got such a subtle mind, a way of seeing new dimensions to old problems. I don't think anyone appreciates the *problems* more. It's not the kind of mind that ever does shake up the world, but it's fascinating. I'm going to learn a lot having him around this year."

The physicists at the Institute are a very chummy lot, having lunch together every day around a large table, discussing the work each is pursuing. Noam likes to claim that mathematicians are much purer than scientists in their pursuit of knowledge, less prompted by the demands of the petty ego. He claims that this is partly because there's no Nobel prize awarded for mathematics (Nobel specifically excluded mathematicians because his wife was having an affair with one), making the whole profession that much freer from the competitive spirit. But it's never been so apparent to me that mathematicians are particularly successful at keeping clean of the stains of ego. They're a markedly paranoid bunch, reluctant, unlike the physicists, to discuss their work before it's safely in print. One indiscreet word and a result could be known down through the ages as "Linsky's theorem," not Himmel's. Noam keeps both his desks, the one in Fine Hall and the one at home, locked. (What does he fear? A masked mathematical bandit? *My* treachery?)

Daniel Korper's name popped up so often in my conversations with Ava that I began to wonder whether he had succeeded in rousing her from her voluntary sexual torpor. I hoped so, though it seemed unlikely. First of all, she's so frank that I couldn't imagine her not telling me. And anyway, Korper didn't sound like the kind of man my friend finds sexually attractive. He certainly wasn't an elementary particle. Ava likes subtlety in physics but not in bed.

Finally I met him. Noam and I were invited to a party for the new arrival, given by one of the permanent members at the Institute who lived in one of the lovely homes built right on the Institute grounds.

I confess to being distinctly disappointed by the guest of honor. He was good-looking in a cute, boyish sort of way, which isn't my sort. I like a face that's been worked over by life, that shows something of what it's seen and suffered. (I couldn't trust anyone who hasn't suffered.) The imperfections are usually what I end up being touched by, especially if they speak of the soul's activity. But Korper's was a face in which one could still easily make out the boy once there. During the years that ought to have squinted the eyes, sagged the jowls, thickened the lips with desire or thinned them with frustration, the features of this face had preserved themselves, maintaining their small, rounded cuteness. Even his body was rather small and boyish. It was easy to see what a fetching child this had been. The only features that saved the face from succumbing to total juvenility were the very thick black eyebrows ending over the well-formed nose in two closed parenthetical furrows of the skin, testifying to the fact that the man thought for his living. The very thick waves of black hair were sparsely streaked with gray, as another concession to age. But these feeble marks of maturity on the otherwise boyish face produced an overall absurd effect. If Wittgenstein was right and the human body is the best picture of the human soul, then this was not a soul that intrigued me. The voice I found somewhat more provocative: very throaty and somewhat drawled. But on considering it again I thought it most resembled the voice a boy might affect in order to sound older.

Noam knew Korper slightly and seemed to have rather a high opinion of his intelligence and intellectual integrity, which was re-markable considering the man's profession. The two chatted together and I stood with them listening, trying to form an opinion of this physicist who impressed Ava so and whom even Noam grudgingly respected.

I took out a cigarette and Korper, glancing at me as he answered Noam, took out a thin silver lighter and lit it for me. It was then that

I noticed his hands. I suppose that what startled me so was the contrast between the pleasant, wholesome, mute features of the face and the painfully articulate hands:

The nails were savagely bitten down. I couldn't imagine that small restrained mouth performing such acts of self-mutilation. The fingers were very long, perversely so for a man of his size. They seemed at once delicate and decadent. The middle finger of the right hand was particularly arresting, twisted as if it had been separated at the knuckle and then carelessly stuck back on. The obviousness of its ugliness was phallic. These might be the hands of an unusually subtle mind, but these were not subtle hands. There hands would go anywhere, probe any darkness.

I glanced at the pleasant, closed face and then down at the hands, then quickly back at the face. It was extraordinary. I couldn't combine the face and the hands into one conception of the man. Which feature gave the true picture of the soul here?

He had meanwhile taken out a cigarette of his own, and Noam was making outraged noises.

"If you two are going to foul up my air, I think I'll move on."

Korper immediately apologized, his words contrite, his eyes amused: "Oh, I'm terribly sorry. I'll put it out."

"No, it's all right, don't let me interfere with your prolonged suicide. I certainly wouldn't expect Renee ever to put out a cigarette on my account," and he was off.

Korper turned to me. Now the amusement was obvious. "It must be difficult for your husband to live with a smoker."

"It's difficult for me to live with a nonsmoker, a righteously non-smoking nonsmoker. We've divided the house into smoking and nonsmoking areas, like an airplane."

He smiled. "Marriage is compromise."

"Are you married?"

"Divorced."

"Did your wife smoke?"

"Yes." He was still smiling.

"I take it, then, that's not what broke up the marriage."

"No." The cigarette commuting back and forth between the hands and face created more continuity between them. The face took on more of the look of the hands. "Did you ever try to give up smoking, if not for your own sake, at least for your husband's?"

"That wouldn't be compromise, that would be sacrifice. And besides, I'm philosophically committed to smoking. It's an act of existential freedom."

"Is it? I always thought it was simply an indication of weakness of will."

"For some it is. You see, there are two kinds of smokers, heroic and unheroic."

"I have a feeling I'm the unheroic kind, but go on."

"Unheroic smokers are worried about the health hazards of smoking, which is weakness one, and would like to quit but can't, which is weakness two."

"Yes, I'm definitely cast in the unheroic mold. You, of course, are not."

I smiled my acknowledgment. A couch became vacant nearby and we sat down side by side.

"Heroic smokers don't worry," I continued. "Worry is for little minds. That goes double for worrying about mere physical danger. Fear for the body should never govern one's actions." You, who know my interior too well, are perhaps snickering; however, I was speaking my *beliefs* if not my feelings. "Heroic smokers disdain death. They laugh at death with every inhaling breath."

"So you disdain death?"

"I disdain death."

"What else do you do besides smoke to thumb your nose at the way of all flesh?"

"I drive."

"That doesn't sound extraordinarily dangerous."

"You've never driven with me."

His laugh was deep and throaty, with a far more natural sound to it than the voice. "But you know there really is a serious ethical problem here." His mouth was serious, but his eyes were playful. Now I could see that his was an intriguing face, despite its cuteness. The separate features spoke separate messages. The mouth fit its expression to the situation, while the eyes watched on in amusement. And then in the background there were always the hands, which I kept glancing at. "I feel, against my wishes, the greater sympathy for your husband. How can you balance your desire for the pleasures of smoking against his desire to breathe healthy air? Both are mere bodily desires, and his seems the more valid."

"Validity is a property of proofs, not desires. Desires simply occur, and are acted on or not acted on. To be free is to act on your own desires." Did he think he could throw philosophy at me? I'd give him philosophy.

He smiled. "Spinoza"

"Himmel," I answered, cringing in wait for the inevitable response: I didn't know Noam does philosophy as well. But it didn't come. Instead:

"Yes, Ava Schwartz told me you're a student of philosophy. The mind-body problem, isn't it?"

Why had they spoken about me? Of course I loved it, as I love any suggestion of my mattering.

His eyes had never left my own. I hate to speak to people who keep peering about all the time, as if always keeping an eye out for something more interesting than the conversation at hand. For this reason, I often find partying quite painful. People flit from one conversation to another, always convinced that the really interesting talk is going on elsewhere. I've found myself saying *any*thing (I'd really like to forget some of the things) in such a situation in a desperate attempt to keep the Other's attention on me.

But Daniel Korper was looking and listening to me as if he'd be content to look and listen all night. I got the very strong impression that this is a man who likes and understands women, and there is nothing more attractive to women in general and me in particular.

Haven't you ever noticed how some of the homeliest men (not that Korper was one) can have any woman they choose? It's such a basic difference between the sexes, that in one of them you can have a coupling of corporeal insignificance and sexual irresistibility, while in the other this combination is unthinkable. This assymetry makes me wonder whether *one* account of sexual desire will do for *both* sexes. A unified theory, being simpler, is preferable. The simpler account is, *caeteris paribus,* the better one. But perhaps reality doesn't always accommodate itself to our theoretical tastes. ("Who knows, perhaps

He is a little malicious," Einstein conceded toward the end of his life, after the years of fruitless searching for the unified field theory.) Perhaps my explanation of sexual desire in terms of the will to matter is biased from the female point of view. (Or perhaps its applicability extends no further than myself. This is a problem with introspective psychology: How far can one generalize? To all consciousness? To the human species? One's "own kind" of person? One's self . . . sometimes?)

You'll have noticed that the focus in my account of desire is not directed at bodies but looks past them. What's affirmed in the reciprocal gaze is reciprocal mattering. Bodies are only the means to the end. This is a crucial point, and one that may, I suspect, divide women and men.

One sex's sexiness has to do with the other sex's desires, and what men seem to lust after is a beautiful hunk of flesh, while women crave to feel understood, liked, and interesting. Take heed, all hopeful Don Juans. A handsome exterior is neither necessary nor sufficient. The most physically underprivileged males can be absolutely irresistible. (I speak from experience.) I can't represent the other side, of course. I don't know what it feels like to be a man, to desire as a man. (The inaccessibility of the Other.) But judging from what's desired, it must be pretty different. A woman's sexiness seems to be a matter of her properties as a material object, which is perhaps why she devotes so much attention to this aspect of herself. The men are the ones who have turned her gaze to her integument, for her interiority seems pretty irrelevant to her desirability. But what makes a man sexy or not is his point of view, the way he regards *us*. A man who has that particular manner that shows you he's noticing it all and appreciating it all can pretty much have it all. A woman can burn with desire, but if her matter isn't molded in the right way, she's the only thing that's going to burn up. But a man who really loves women, who genuinely loves them—not with a slobbering, slavish desire, but with a desire that remains in control of itself—such a man will always light our fires. It sounds so easy, but such men are rare. (Again, I speak from experience.) The way Daniel Korper's eyes played over me as we spoke, the way he smiled, made me feel that I'd found one of those rarities, and I began to smolder.

I turned back to his hands, with that secret dark life of their own, and I began to imagine them in various immodest acts. I kept my face down, staring at them, the images vivid, the throbbing warmth spreading and intensifying. We sat for perhaps a full minute without speaking, a violation of the rules of party small-talk I would normally never permit. (Always keep their attention. Don't let them start imagining the fascinating conversations they'll have when they get away from you.)

I made a conscious decision. I lifted up my face to him without rearranging the expression, without blotting out the desire I knew must be there. I had never done anything like that before, offering my desire first, without having received any indication that I was desired. The risk was of the most dangerous sort: the risk of rejection. He met my gaze straight on, his smile gone, the eyes beneath the weighty eyebrows very kind and, mercifully, showing no surprise. His expression told me: I'm at your service. We arranged to meet for lunch the following day.

The next morning I woke up feeling depressed about the previous night and my impending date. Why had I let my face speak my momentary desire, given that man access into my head? All of his ridiculous aspects presented themselves once again to me. I had compromised my precious mental privacy for *him?* His absurdity rendered me absurd.

I lay there in bed, long after Noam left for Fine Hall, remembering the night before with mental groans. I was tempted, even more than what had become the usual these past few months of wading ankle-deep in depression (with its oceanic possibilities), to bury myself under the blankets and go back to sleep, and thus escape the day in unconsciousness.

But I didn't. I got up and dressed, in fact dressed and made up very carefully, all the while feeling ashamed because of the care I was taking. Why should it matter how I appeared for this man? But I changed my clothes several times, unable to make up my mind as to the look I wanted. Should I wear a skirt and sweater in one of the pale beiges or apricots that suit my coloring so well? An image of Daniel Korper's hands floated before me, and I changed into my tightest pair of jeans, stuck them into a pair of high-heeled black suede boots, and wrapped a filmy violet silk blouse against my chest. My beige-apricot appetite I had already indulged in the choice of my panties, lovely wisps of silk apricot and beige lace. Now why, I thought as I put them on, do you give a damn which panties you wear? That man is never going to see them.

I had to call Len and break our standing lunch date. I hadn't thought about it until then. He was incredulous.

"What do you mean you're having lunch with Daniel Korper? He asked you out?"

"Yes. We met last night at a party at Fine's house." I added, feeling gratuitously cruel: "A party given for Daniel." Did Len make, as I did, the obvious comparison: how very unlikely it was that *his* existence would ever precipitate a party, especially up on Mount Olympus?

"Are you going to sleep with him?"

"For Godssakes, Len!"

"I'm asking you if you're going to sleep with him." The voice was choking on its own despair.

"Len, you have no right to ask me that. I'll do what I like." Pity, annoyance, and, like a faint taste of blood, a smidgen of pleasure, of the sadistic variety.

"What do you mean I have no right? I'm your lover."

"You're my illicit, adulterous lover. If anybody has any right to question me, it's my husband." Who of course had no questions because he had no interest.

"I can't believe you're doing this to me." The voice came out with great difficulty, gasping for air. Only a person without a heart could listen unmoved to its pain. But I was hardened by the apathy born of having hung around much, much longer than I had wanted; and I wasn't moved.

Moribund Len had finally passed on to the afterworld, the world after desire. It is a kind of death of the person, a disappearance of the one who once had been. The presence and then absence of desire transforms the perception of him so radically that it's almost like those gestalt-shifts in visual perception, when the duck is instantaneously replaced by a rabbit. Nothing about him means the same. The lines that used to form one picture now group themselves into another, so that one is presented with a quite new object—making claims on one's affections!

I hung up the phone, feeling as if I had managed at last to shake myself free of a tangle of clinging seaweed and grateful to Daniel Korper for, albeit unknowingly, helping me come clean.

But by the time I was driving out to Fuld Hall, where I was supposed to meet Korper, I was feeling only a sickeningly uneasy mixture of excitement and dread. What are you so stirred up about? I asked myself.

I was supposed to meet him at twelve-thirty. At *precisely* twelve-thirty he walked out the door. He must have timed his walk earlier with a stopwatch. Again I was overwhelmed by a sense of the man's absurdity, and felt correspondingly absurd myself. I reminded myself to ask him his ancestry. I'd have bet anything he was a German Jew, a punctilious, tight-assed *Yekky*. (The name Körper is German. They'd probably lost the umlaut in flight.)

I watched him walk over to my car with ridiculously bouncy strides. This man, I thought, is harboring an irrepressible boy inside his body, one who keeps trying to get out. He has consciously devised all sorts of means to restrain the boy: furrows in the brow, drawls in the voice. But the boy keeps popping out. Absurd—not that there was the boy, but that the man was fighting him.

I watched him bob his way over to the car and had the impulse to switch into drive and press the gas pedal down to the floor. I could just picture the ridiculous look on his ridiculous face as he watched me speed away. Dear God, I moaned, as I fought my impulse, what am I *doing* here?

He smiled at me. "Do you want to drive or shall I?"

"I will, of course," I answered shortly. Out of what dark chauvinist cave had he just stumbled?

"Then at least let me pick the restaurant."

"Be my guest."

"No, you will be mine. On that at least I insist. Let's drive over to Bucks County. I know a nice inn there overlooking the river. The foliage should be wonderful now."

I love that drive over to the Pennsylvania side of the Delaware River, especially in the fall and spring. So even though the long drive there meant extending the date, I agreed.

"What's your ancestry?" I asked as we made our way out of town.

"German Jewish," he said, surprised at the question.

"Both sides?"

"Yes. My parents came over in 1937. I was born in transit."

Bull's-eye! I can spot them anywhere, even the assimilated ones. The German Jews and the Hungarian Jews have the most extreme of the nationally defined Jewish personalities, and the ones that have survived the homogenization of America most intact. Hungarian Jews are materialists, in the economic, not metaphysical sense. They have a deep devotion to *things*, especially wall-to-wall plush carpeting and crystal chandeliers. (The Orthodox sometimes even have carpeting and chandeliers in *succahs*, the little temporary huts, built for the harvest holiday of Succoth.) The women are very devoted to themselves as women. (Georgette Klinger and many of her employees are Hungarian Jews.) It's they who have won the characterization Princesses for the whole class of us. None of them has ever been known to wear eyeglasses. Any who are cursed with bad eyesight get used to contact lenses or to not seeing.

And the German Jews? They're very devoted to themselves as German Jews, at least the first few generations of them. It's a holdover from Europe, where there was complete agreement, at least among the German Jews, on their superiority. They suffered from a (as it turned out) tragic sense of pride in the German *Kultur*, in which they played some part, once they were finally released from the ghettos in the nineteenth century. In the relatively short period from emancipation to destruction, there was a great flowering among them —producing, at the end, the finest bloom of our species, the man who demonstrates the human possibilities. I mean, of course, the hero of my heroes (true in both senses): Albert Einstein. He, however, was one German-born Jew (he renounced his citizenship early on) who detested all things Prussian. His was a repugnance that germinated in the ruthlessly, but typically disciplined atmosphere of Luitpold Gymnasium, where he was educated in his youth, and intensified at the end of his life, with the experience of what the Prussian spirit could produce.

Einstein had absorbed little or nothing of this spirit into his own. In fact, his personality formed in large part in reaction against the detested *Geist*. It was his active suspicion and even contempt for authority that allowed him to challenge the fundamental premises of classical physics. In later life he replied to a young girl who had sent him a manuscript: "Keep your manuscript for your sons and daughters, in order that they might derive consolation from it—and not give a damn for what their teachers tell them or think of them."

But many other German Jews bear the traces of some of the more innocent aspects of Prussianism. I remember one summer my parents and Avram and I spent the week of my father's summer vacation (needless to say, he wasn't given very generous vacations) at a hotel in the Catskills whose clientele was almost exclusively *Yekky*. My father spoke a perfect German, and at first they assumed he was of their own kind. When he mentioned he was from Poland, and his wife's family from Czechoslovakia, a distinct chill was perceived, softened by a little pity. That hotel was the only Jewish establishment we ever visited where everything started precisely on time. Dinner was at seven. At six fifty-eight, the dining room was empty. At seven, everyone was seated. Talk about anal compulsive. Which brings me back to Daniel Korper.

As we got past the Princeton traffic, I accelerated sharply. The road became a narrow, hilly, curving country road, the kind of surface I like best. Let's see if this anal little *Yekky* has any balls, I said to myself. I kept a peripheral eye on him and the speedometer, watching to see if he stiffened or gripped his seat as we approached eighty. (Noam was always my most relaxed passenger. No matter how crazy I got, he never noticed.) But Korper's body remained relaxed, his expression slightly smiling. There was a sharp turn in the road and I accelerated madly around it, wheels screeching. He turned to me with a little laugh.

"You really do drive like a philosopher."

I didn't like the sound of that. "What do you mean?"

"Didn't Plato say that to philosophize is to prepare to die?"

"Are you nervous? Do you want me to slow down?"

"No, I'm rather enjoying it. Perhaps you'll make a heroic smoker of me yet. Although I would hate to lose my life precisely at this moment, just when it's looking somewhat interesting."

"Meaning me?" I usually shrink from being so direct, but the speed was making me reckless.

"Meaning you."

I felt that he too was being unusually to the point. "I take it that's supposed to be a compliment. But 'somewhat interesting' isn't my idea of high flattery."

"But it *is* high flattery. To affect the interest with which a middle-aged man regards his life is a remarkable achievement. But you understand that."

"Do I?"

"Yes. I have an unreasoned belief that you understand it all. We're parallel lines, you and I." His voice was light and playful. So was his face when I glanced at it, an act of daring at the speed at which I was driving. (I see I'm showing off to you.) He was only flirting.

"Parallel lines never meet."

"Who wants to meet? One infinitesimal point of convergence, followed by ever widening distances. Parallel lines can travel along side by side forever."

The perfect metaphor for Noam and me, I thought. Two straight lines that converged briefly one spring, and now could only continue to separate. But I didn't say it. I knew the script: revelations of marital disappointments and disillusionments, listened to with inexhaustible sympathy and understanding. *Prolegomena to Any Future Adultery,* by Emmanuelle Cunt. I could hear the whole scene unfold in my head. Not that I was such a seasoned adulteress; I'd only played that particular role once. But the scenario had a familiar feel to it. My Columbia College professor-lover, Isaac Besdin, had begun by complaining to me of his wife—a real *shiksa* Saltine cracker, from what I could discern from his description and the photo of her on his desk.

Yes, I could hear the scene play itself out in my head, and so I said instead: "But who says our lives have to be straight lines? Who says we can't change direction?"

"Oh no, straight lines we are. We can never change direction, never turn back."

"A strict determinist."

"Of course."

"Why of course? I thought you physicists had decided we live in an indeterminist universe."

"I'm one of the last holdouts, sympathetic to Einstein's view that quantum mechanics can't be the last word." So that's why Noam could tolerate him. "Anyway, indeterminacy, if it's a fact, exists only on the level of elementary particles. On the human level the appearance of indeterminacy is only a function of our ignorance of the true causes."

"Spinoza."

"Truth," he intoned solemnly, and then we laughed.

"I won't reply to that one. I like discussions that end in one-word proclamations, like 'Truth,' 'God,' 'Existence.' "

"Then this discussion is ended. Shall we begin another or simply hold our peace?"

"Let's hold our peace. I love this stretch of road."

We had crossed the Delaware River into Pennsylvania and driven through the tourist quaintness of New Hope, and now we were following the old Delaware Canal, which runs side by side with the river here. It's a very beautiful road. We didn't speak except for Dan's directions to his inn, which was in a woodsy area about a quarter-mile back from the river, up on a hill. The river could be seen, framed by the peaking autumn leaves, aglow in the sunlight. We sat at a table beside a windowed wall, admiring the scene.

"Tell me," Dan suddenly asked, "what's it like to live with Noam Himmel?"

Dear God, The Question. It shattered my feeling of easy contentment like a rock sent through the glass beside us.

"Do you really expect an answer to that? Shall I give it to you while standing on one foot?"

He, of course, would not understand the allusion: to the mocker who asked the great and gentle rabbi Hillel to summarize the Torah while standing on one foot, to which Hillel replied: "That's easy. What you wouldn't have done to you, don't do to others. As for the rest, go and study." And the mocker became a disciple.

Korper's expression was immediately transformed, all the features, even the observing eyes, pulled into an expression uniformly solicitous.

"I'm sorry, it was a very stupid question." He paused, looked at me and then toward the window. "It's just that I imagined it must be rather lonely."

I pretended to read the menu. Instead of feeling happy about his intuitive plunge into the essence of my life, I felt put off. I didn't want anyone inside my head. He was invading my most private privacy in a way that Leonard never had done in all our months together. I did what I often do when I feel my interiority threatened by invasion. I lied.

He asked me about my background.

"Oh, I come from a family of academics, very enlightened and rational people. My father was a chemist and my mother a psychologist."

"Clinical?"

"Yes, she has a practice and also teaches. Her specialty is neurotic housewives. She discovered an interesting syndrome, and published several papers on it. Many women, she found, fill the emptiness of their lives by creating all sorts of things to worry about. It's a substitute for confronting their own inner void. She's been able to explain a lot of behavior by positing this as cause."

He didn't say anything, just nodded slightly. Then:

"Where did you grow up?"

"Manhattan. East Seventy-second Street." Always give as much detail as possible, to encourage the illusion of veracity.

I continued to lie my way through the meal, dwelling lovingly on the closeness between my older sister and me, and the great care my parents took in encouraging our intellectual self-fulfillment. There. Let him try to get into me now!

We finished the meal and returned to the car. I told him he could drive if he wanted. (I was feeling dispirited. The soul pays for defending its secrets in this way.)

When we were almost back in Princeton, I turned to him and said: "You know, Dan, I've been lying. Hardly anything I've told you is true."

"I know."

I couldn't believe my ears. God, I prayed, let this be a nightmare from which I'll be awoken.

"How?"

"Ava told me about your background."

It was a moment I wish never to have repeated. ("My original fall is the existence of the Other," says Sartre in the chapter "Shame" in *Being and Nothingness*.) The lack of accusation in his voice and face made it all the worse. He had listened so quietly, all the time knowing I was lying. I hadn't put a thing over. If anything, I had made myself only more transparent, exposing how thoroughly pathetic the scene from inside is. How could I ever return to the role of *femme fatale*? I certainly never wanted to see Korper again.

But this was Princeton, and I couldn't avoid him for long. And by the time I finally did see him, I was anxious to. It was about three weeks later, at a very noisy party with too many people in too small a house. If Dan had tried to get in touch with me in the interim, I would have been annoyed and uninterested. But since he hadn't, I found myself, in accordance with the deviant logic of the emotions, wanting him to.

When I saw him walk into the party, I felt my heart give a vigorous push against my rib cage. He walked over to the bar and fell into a conversation with Ned Solo—or an approximation of a conversation. Poor Dan, I thought. Talking with Ned is like falling down the rabbit hole into a Leibnizian universe. The man is a closed system, a self-determining entelechy. His conversation is governed by the internal laws of his own nature, each comment following from a previous one and not subject to external influence. He sometimes gives the *appearance* of responding to something someone else has said. But that appearance is just illusion, the result of the principle of preestablished harmony. Ned is a monad, and monads have no windows.

The first time I spoke to Ned, I of course didn't know he was a refugee from Leibniz's ontology. He asked me what I was working on (remember, the preestablished harmony), to which I responded, "The mind-body problem," to which he responded: "Oh, do you know any gauge theory?" I did not, and I listened carefully to Ned's ensuing soliloquy, trying to make out the connection between the mathematical theory he was lecturing me about and the mind-body problem. Though I believe that my pet philosophical obsession weaves its way in and out of far-flung topics, I was surprised—and disturbed—that I might have to learn gauge theory. I hazarded a few more remarks and observed that they made no difference at all in the flow of Solo's conversation. It was impossible to have any effect on the man.

I saw that Ned was now rambling on, Dan watching and sipping his drink. I wasn't particularly blessed by my partner-in-conversation, either. Nora O'Shea is one of the few female members of the Princeton math department and she's so awfully pleased with herself, but not in any honest, straightforward manner. She's an example of the more obnoxious sort of peacock: a closet peacock. Once you get the dictionary to her private language, you understand that everything she says translates into self-praise. But it takes a little insight and lots of experience in the varieties of peacocking to acquire the dictionary. And of course once you do, the annoyance is sharpened by the fact that few other share it. On occasions when I exploded over Nora's obsessive egotism my listeners, including Noam, always expressed wonder.

Outwardly she's a drab little figure, with a bony Irish face crying out for makeup. (I'm only a bitch when provoked.) But Nora would never dream of putting a frivolous blusher to her aggressively intelligent features. Femininity is beneath her. She disapproves of all its manifestations. At parties where I knew she would be, I always tried to remember to wear particularly low-cut clothes for the sheer pleasure of watching Nora—whose chest is concave—stare in thin-lipped severity at my cleavage.

Right now she was complaining to me about the *enormous* size of her classes and her need to procure a second graduate student to help with the grading. Translation: "I'm such a *popular* teacher." It would be at once an act of self-help and altruism to free myself and Dan of Nora and Ned, neither of whose self-involved sicknesses was contagious, but one didn't want to get too close.

I interrupted Nora's gloating lament. "Oh, look, there's Daniel Korper. I have a message to give him. I hope you find another preceptor."

As I left her for Dan, I felt suddenly magnanimous. After all, would large classes ever satisfy her longing for large breasts, or a second preceptor approach attracting a lover?

"It's your own fault, Nora," I called back. "If you weren't such a terrific teacher, you wouldn't have such big classes."

As I moved off in Dan's direction, I could see Nora pinking with pleasure, the chest, which would never be in any danger of revealing cleavage, rising up in exultation.

Dan smiled warmly when I reached his side, extracting himself skillfully from Solo's monologue.

"I was hoping you'd be here," he said after Solo had moved on.

"Why don't we escape outside?" I answered. "The noise is so awful."

The silence and slight chill of the night fell on us like an old friend. I was slightly drunk, my body feeling as if it enclosed an inner warmth that no cold could penetrate. We walked down the quiet streets toward the lake.

"I'm sorry about lunch the other day."

"Why?"

"I'm sorry I kept lying. I'm even sorrier that you knew I was lying."

"Why did you? It doesn't fit the heroic mold."

"I was afraid you saw through me."

"Is that so bad? Are you such an awful person?"

"I think so," I said softly, for only the night to hear.

But he heard. "I don't," he said just as softly.

We had reached Carnegie Lake and walked along it for a while. I discovered we were holding hands. When had he taken mine, or had I taken his? The night had such an old-friend kindly feel to it.

"Noam and I made love for the first time right here, this very spot. It was spring. We'd been picking wild asparagus."

"It sounds very romantic."

"It was."

Dan kissed me. "How sad your voice just was," he said. "So wistful and sad. I'm sorry."

I wasn't sorry. I only wanted him to kiss me again. He did.

"Come." He took my hand and we began to walk again. "This spot already has enough memories for you."

We walked farther upriver to a soft, grassy hillside almost under the Harrison Avenue bridge. We moved slowly. I was right about him, I remember thinking, he does love women. Someone was moaning softly in the night. For a moment I thought it was the night herself, and then realized it was me. He was playing with me, bringing me to the edge and then away. But then he couldn't hold me back any longer. How long did it last? I don't know. The internal observer, with her play-by-play descriptions, her stopwatch and her scorekeeping, was silenced.

When I opened my eyes, Dan was looking down at me. He stroked my cheek and said, so softly, so deeply, like the voice of the tender night hugging us:

"Are you back yet?"

"From where?"

"From where we both were just now."

"Were we in the same place? How do you know?" Ever the skeptic.

"Knowing that is part of being there."

We lay together for a while, neither of us wanting to move, kept warm by each other's body.

"Come to me tomorrow morning," he said. "Come to me early. Can you? I want to see your body in the daylight."

I went to him early the next morning. He answered the door in his bathrobe.

"I was afraid you wouldn't come."

"Why?"

"Because I wanted you to. And you want people to want you desperately and then can't stand it when they do."

"Did Ava tell you that too?"

"No, you did. I must tell myself never to want you too much." He kissed my hair. "Come, let me see what you look like in the harsh glare of an October morning. I've been lying here thinking the moonlight must have been flattering."

He led me into the bedroom, lay me on his bed, and undressed me. Then he stood back and smiled.

"You're a lovely woman. That curve from the waist out to the hips." He sat down and traced my outline with his open hand. "It's the most moving curve in a woman's body. And yours is so particularly lovely."

"Are you going to sit there and admire me like a piece in a museum?"

He shook his head slightly and turned me over. "Such a lovely ass." He ran his hands over it. "What fine food must have gone into the perfect marbling of this flesh. It was all the finest food, wasn't it?"

"I'm afraid not all. I have a weakness for pizzas and all kinds of chocolate."

"Ah, I'm going to forget the pizzas altogether. As far as I'm concerned, this firm flesh was built of galantine of duck and pâtés de foie gras with fresh white truffles."

"I very much doubt if truffles build marbled flesh."

"No? Then rich, runny Bries and deep, dark, lascivious Swiss chocolates. If I didn't want you for your subtle philosopher's mind and gentle Madonna's face, I'd want you for your ass alone."

And I'd want you for your hands, I thought, but I didn't say it. I was afraid of saying anything that might interrupt the wonderful things those hands were doing. I could not believe their genius, their knowledge of what it's like to be a woman. How did they know to move in just that way in just that place for just that long? His hands worked their way back under me, never pausing in their certainty, as he entered deep inside me. How could a man know a woman's body so well?

We lay in bed afterwards, smoking his cigarettes. I was pursuing my preorgasmic thoughts, marveling at the knowledge of Dan. Did he really know what it's like to be a woman? How could he? I don't know what it's like to be a man, what it's like to have a penis and enter a woman. It must be very different for them, for Dan. I longed to know. If an angel of God were to appear at that moment and grant me any knowledge I desired, that's what I would have asked. What does it feel like to have a man's body, to have Daniel Korper's body? What does it feel like to be he? It was the question that most mattered that moment.

There it was once again: the ineradicable separateness of consciousness. The world he inhabits is his alone—with precious few of its details expressible in language and thus accessible to us Others. How I would have loved to slip into his world and see things as he does, to merge our two worlds like two drops of water. That would be to become one with him—for we *are* our worlds, just as Leibniz said. (But *windowless?*) Of course, one bumps into the metaphysical facts. How close can we get? One penetrates, the other is penetrated, but we never break through. Sex is a battle against metaphysics.

"What are you thinking about?" Dan turned to me.

"Oh," I answered, "an aspect of the mind-body problem."

"I am as well, a very practical aspect. Come, let's get dressed, have some coffee, and we'll discuss it."

We sat at his kitchen table, sipping his Melita-dripped coffee from Institute mugs (they provide everything).

"Now," said Dan, "here's the problem. You make a very strong argument for the body, so strong that I'm afraid my purpose here will be forgotten. This year in Princeton is very important to my work, and I'm afraid of getting hypnotized under your power. Oh, but I'm assuming that you feel as I do, that you want to continue our relationship. Am I assuming too much?"

"No."

"No, of course not. It's too good, we both know that. Look, here's my proposal. I hope it won't sound too brutally practical. I propose that we arrange a kind of schedule as to when to meet. Since you're married, you have more restrictions, so I'll fit my hours around you. What times are good for you?"

"A schedule? A schedule for fucking?" The tight-assed little *Yekky* with his stopwatches and schedules. My first impression of him had been the right one. "Are you going to write it down in your appointments book: Monday, Wednesday, and Friday, nine to ten, fuck Noam Himmel's wife?"

"You're very angry." My God, the man had powers of penetration. "I'm sorry. But I really don't know any other way. Affairs will fill up all available time if you don't draw rather rigid boundaries around them. You're angry. I'm sorry."

I damn well *was* angry. I got my jacket and left. Damn brainy prick. The trouble with you, Renee, is that you think the male sexual organ is the brain. Why do you keep fucking around with these great minds? Go be an intelligent cunt, paradoxical as it may sound, and find yourself a nice blue-collar lover. Stop trying to be a combination of Jean Paul Sartre and That Cosmopolitan Woman, and find yourself a nice simple mind with an ever ready erection. Yeah, fat chance in this town, this princedom by the turnpike, with its puny demigods on stilts. Effete, effeminate, impotent, prickless pricks. Fuck you, Daniel Korper. Fuck your fucking schedule for fucking.

I cooled down after a while. Why was I really so angry? I wanted Daniel to fill up my life, and he didn't want me to fill up his. For me, there was nothing else. My former loves—philosophy and Noam —now both reproached me with my failure and inadequacy. But there was more than me in Daniel's life, things that were important and that he didn't want displaced. And he was right, of course. I would have wanted to make his life as empty as my own, so that I could fill his void as he would fill mine. But that would be wrong. It would be unforgivable to take out what was already there. Len Schmerz, of course, had begged me to do that, but such was his weakness and I had despised him for it. You can't have it both ways, kid. I called Dan at his office.

"I'm free any day, all day. Nights are harder. Sometimes Noam works at his office, sometimes at home. And we have a lot of social engagements."

"Why don't we spend every morning together? And I'll work afternoons and nights. And come as early as you possibly can. It will never be too early. That way it's almost like waking up to you in my bed."

I was nervous about telling Ava. I knew how she felt about cheating in general, and now it was with Daniel Korper, about whom I wasn't sure how she felt. I went over that evening. We sat on her couch and listened to the Zuckerman recording of the Tchaikovsky violin concerto.

"Ava, Daniel Korper and I are lovers."

"When?" Her head was back, her eyes closed, as they had been while listening to the music.

"Last night. We wandered away from the party at the Searles'."

She nodded. "You don't seem surprised."

"I'm not. The morning after Fine's party Dan talked to me about you, asked me questions. He wasn't prying or anything. He didn't ask me anything I couldn't tell him. But it was obvious you had captured his fancy. He told me you two were having lunch—a few weeks ago, wasn't it? Actually I expected it would happen sooner."

"And you're not angry? Or unhappy or whatever?"

"No. It's your business, yours and his." And Noam's, I knew she was thinking. "And anyway, if you're determined to have affairs, which it seems you are, let it at least be with a Daniel Korper. That kind of temptation I can understand."

So it was as I had suspected. "Ava, did you want him yourself?"

She didn't answer right away. Then: "Yeah, I wanted him. But that was all it was ever going to be: wanting. If I'm going to draw a line around sex in general, I'm going to draw a double line around Dan. He's a professional colleague. And not just any colleague. He's important to my work, and I can't afford to have any other kind of involvement with him." She leaned her head back against the couch again and closed her eyes. "I guess I even feel a little vicariously happy about you and him." She grinned. "It's the next best thing." I grinned back. Her eyes were open again, and she was viewing me sideways. "I'm not going to go panting and drooling over the details, but just tell me. Is he good?"

"He's good." We were both still grinning.

"Good. Good for him. I'll take your word for it. But you know what? No matter how good he is, he can't be as good as my fantasies of him." She laughed. "It's just as well. He could never have lived up to those fantasies."

"Well, feel free to go on fantasizing," I said generously.

"Oh no. I couldn't do that. Just like I could never fantasize about Noam."

Fantasize about Noam? What a thought. "You know," I said, "I haven't exactly swept Dan off his feet. He wants us to keep a fucking schedule, mornings only."

I expected to hear her familiar hoot, but instead she nodded seriously. "Good," she said. "I'm glad. He has important things to do here this year. His work is very significant, Renee. Always remember that."

I was terribly shamed by her words, and the concern they revealed. She seemed to sense my shame, and smiled, trying to wipe out the solemnity of her tone.

"In other words, kid, you can have the body. Just leave us poor beggars his mind."

I got both. I went to Dan every morning. I'd never known a man could love as he did. I was at long last in the hands of someone who knew what he was about. The men I had known before, being highly educated, were all adequately informed on the technicalities of female sexuality. They all knew about the clitoris, knew it required some stimulation, etc., etc., and conscientiously gave it and the other memorized anatomical facts their due. That was just it, though. It was all done out of conscientiousness, out of their enlightened commitment to equal rights, prodded by the internalization of their mother's voice of long ago, chanting: Now, don't be selfish.

But Dan was so different. He loved the body. And I loved his. I loved its feels, its smells, its tastes. And always the wicked genius hands.

I got his mind as well—a mind supple, and subtle, and inexhaustibly rich. Its special brand of intellectual enthusiasm, the playful seriousness of its constant questions, made it the only place in him in which I still perceived the boy. Only the boy wasn't ridiculous (impossible to believe I had once thought Dan so), but wonderful. I enjoyed the qualities of his mind all the more because they were in such contrast to the tyrannical purity of Noam's intellect, always intent on the purge of the trivial. Nothing was ever dismissed by Dan as too trivial for consideration, and nothing ever was trivial when he considered it. His mind enlarged and deepened everything: Why can't we tickle ourselves? What is the sexual significance of breasts? He had a way of turning over any topic and revealing its deep side. He too liked to stare at simple facts, but unlike me he didn't get lost in confusion. He pushed ahead, got a grip, made connections, spun out theories. Not that he would drop a theory on your head, like a block of cement. (I've known such theorizers.) His method was delicate, open, questioning: Why is it jolting to consider the naked body beneath the undesired clothed body? How did it happen that we evolved hairless? Human beauty—actually beauty of all kinds, but particularly human—was a passionate interest of his.

His former wife, by the way, was not beautiful. I saw a picture of the two of them of long ago, together in Harvard Yard. The pain of discovering that he still carried the damn picture with him was almost counterbalanced by my relief at seeing that she was no contest as far as looks went: short, dark, stocky, looking much more a daughter of Israel than I, although she's only half Jewish. But still she had been incredibly powerful. I was awed by the strength of a woman who could walk away from Dan.

Curious that she wasn't beautiful, when my looks were so important to him, a continuous topic of conversation and analysis. Which was the better profile? (The right.) Did my breasts fit Arthur Koestler's characterization of the perfect breasts as shaped like the cups of champagne glasses? (No, but Koestler had been wrong.) Dan was interested in my looks, but, unlike most of the others, he wasn't fooled by them. This too was a favored topic, the power-duality of beauty, enslaver and slave of others' desires; beauty, the iridescent carapace with the soft, unprotected belly.

"A beautiful woman is more of a person and less of a person. We don't really believe in her suffering. How can the beautiful suffer? Certainly not in the grimy ways of the unlovely. Can a goddess have hemorrhoids, worry about mortgage payments? How can we presume to reason by analogy from our interior to hers?"

"If you prick us, you pricks, do we not bleed? If you tickle us, do we not laugh? If you poison us, do we not die? And if you wrong us, shall we not seek revenge? If we are like you in the rest, we will resemble you in that." I ran my nails lightly down the length of his thigh.

"You're welcome to more than a pound of the flesh," he had answered, in that deep drawl which had become the sexiest sound in the world to me. That voice was but one of the many entrances he provided into the dark and musty cave, D. H. Lawrence's "blue-smoking darkness, Pluto's dark-blue daze." Let him speak in that drawl, look at me and slowly smile, sip wine with a concentrated look, smoke—any of these and more, countless more actions, and I went immediately under. I must have trusted him, to have allowed him to lead me so far down. How could I not have trusted? He was the father-lover incarnate (because he never expressed any need?).

Then perhaps I wasn't really in love, since my passion was the progeny of my infantile sexuality. But the inner-world-transforming attachment to a person is an abnormal response. Something is going wrong—and not only in the thoroughgoing distortions of perception. One isn't simply reacting to the objective lovability of the Other. The explanation has got to lie partly in the quirks of the inspired. The image I have now when I think of such attachments is the one I also get when I think of the biological mechanism of certain poisons: the key jammed in the lock. And it's true that now, as I write, my life has the feel of a convalescence, although I'm not sure what I'm recuperating from.

Strange doubts these, for one who has believed so religiously in the salvation of romantic love. I've always conceived the solutions to my life in terms of "true love." When it became apparent that my marriage wouldn't yield the right answer, my mind immediately began to play with other possibilities (and my body soon followed), but always of a romantic nature, always developed around the repeated theme: someday I'll really fall in love.

But perhaps romantic passion is a pathological response, as Freud interpreted the love of God. And what future has *this* illusion? It too is soul-wrenching to renounce, for, like the other, it provides a division between the sanctified and secular, colors and differentiates the drab and monolithic space and time of experience, and drenches one's life with significance.

That year was a winter of many dark days, "Ithaca days," Dan called them. The bleakness outside gave sharper contrast to the lambent warmth of the rooms on Einstein Drive, lighted by a fire in the grate. The word "cozy" comes to mind, but it is far too mundane to do justice to the atmosphere of those rooms. "Cozy" is for children tucked in bed, the night light on, and the low murmur of the grown-ups' voices nearby. Perhaps it is the right word, after all.

Dan had been divorced for nine years (at the time that he was divorcing I hadn't yet had my first date). He had met his wife, Eleanor, when he was an undergraduate at Harvard, she a student at Radcliffe. They had gotten married the June of their graduation, Dan continuing at Harvard for his Ph.D. They had tried for two years to have a child. There wasn't anything physically wrong with either of them, it just didn't happen. So Eleanor enrolled in Harvard Law School. She changed tremendously in her three years there, growing in self-confidence and becoming increasingly restless in the marriage.

"She felt she had gotten married too young. She wanted to know more about life, about other men. We decided to continue being married, but we would allow each other the freedom of other relationships. I didn't really want it. I went through agonies of jealousy. I was just trying to hang on to her."

But he couldn't. She finished law school and he got his degree the same year. She went off to a prestigious New York firm and he went to Cornell. Still, they stayed married.

"I kept trying to get a job in New York. Finally there was an opening at Columbia. I didn't tell her about it until they offered it to me. When I called her she told me that she wanted a divorce, that there was someone else with whom she was in love."

"And do you still love her?" I forced myself to ask him.

"I don't know. I think she'll always be the most important woman in my life."

It hurt even more than I had expected.

"She married the other man, by the way. He's a lawyer. They have two daughters."

He *did* sound sad when he said that, I didn't imagine it. But he had laughed when he looked at me.

"Don't waste your sweet pity. I'm quite glad we failed in our procreative efforts. I don't think I would have made a good father."

This time I kept my face under better control. I didn't let him see what his words meant to me, the dreams they were negating. My golden daughter, now with Daniel's fertile theorizing intelligence. Our daughter. So he no longer saw children as a possibility. Why not, for Godssake, why not? A young woman could give him children. I could. Why was it not a possibility? And which of the other propositions I was daily, nightly, hourly fantasizing about were not alive for Dan?

It was always a challenge I could rarely resist (and very rarely succeed at) to get him to stay longer with me, to violate the time limits he had imposed. Did he realize the nature of this game for me? Once, half aroused, he leaped out of bed and started for the shower, then turned back, contemplating me and smiling.

"I saw pale kings and princes too,/Pale warriors, death-pale were they all/They cried—'La belle Dame sans Merci/Hath thee in thrall!' " Keats' poem became a running joke with us.

Always I was straining against the boundaries of our relationship, trying to extend Dan's presence, corrode the self-containment of our mornings, which flew by so quickly.

"What do you think sex is the best metaphor for?"

"Sex."

"No, come on, Dan. Sex is the best metaphor for . . ."

"Freedom. The focused surge of what-the-hell freedom. And you?"

"Transience. The ephemerality of ecstasy."

"Poor dear, you concentrate too much on the orgasms of life."

My longing to spread Dan out in the rest of my life first prompted me to invite him to our house for dinner. I was very nervous—not because of the need to dissemble before Noam, for I was confident of Dan's and my abilities in that sphere, as well as Noam's obliviousness. What I feared, rather, was having to cook for Dan, who is an excellent cook himself. I spent hours planning the menu for that ill-conceived, overambitious first dinner, a disaster from soggy soufflé to unflammable flambé.

But I got over the fiasco and my fear, and often had Dan to our house, usually together with Ava, their professional relationship providing the excuse for our socializing with him. The four of us could be very funny together. Ava and I tended to one-liners, Dan to word play and funny stories—many of which presented brilliant men in their ridiculous aspects. (For instance, the mathematician who's stopped by a colleague and asked whether he's eaten yet. He stares in abstraction for several moments and then finally answers: "I don't know. Which way was I headed when you stopped me?") I wondered about Dan's having so many such stories to share with us. Noam's funniest bits were a kind of soft slapstick. He frequently displays a physical humor, acting out things with a body whose awkwardness makes his movements all the funnier. For example, once the four of us were discussing brain bisection and Noam suddenly jumped up and demonstrated how a person whose corpus callosum is severed, leaving each of his hemispheres with a mind of its own, would walk down the street, each hemisphere opting for a different direction. The three of us howled as Noam shoved his body first to one side and then the other down the length of our living room.

Did Noam never suspect? Only once did it occur to me that he might. Ava and Dan were again over for dinner. I walked into our dining room from the kitchen, carrying the food. Noam was smiling and saying (I have no idea what had led up to the odd remark):

"It's very uncommon to believe something that one thinks untrue." He looked at me, still smiling. "Renee, can you think of anything you believe that's not true?"

I smiled back. "No, but I can think of things that *you* believe that aren't true."

Everyone laughed and then Noam asked: "What are they?" And then immediately the smile vanished and his face took on a look I'd never seen—fright, perhaps—and he said quickly, "No, no, don't tell me."

I felt slightly ill. What was he asking me not to tell him? And I also felt touched, as I always did when Noam appeared vulnerable, when he exhibited a raw emotion, although I wasn't sure how to identify this fleetingly present one.

Was there anything else from then to notice about Noam? If there was, I didn't see it, for I had given up watching. I was living in another world, where the only thing that mattered was Dan. (I had relocated on the mattering map. I lived no longer in a zone, but on a point. No wonder I'm left homeless now, uncertain of what matters. I'm in the market for a new world.) Noam is absent in my memory. He intruded on my consciousness only now and then with his explosions of annoyance over some minor domestic mishap, some chore or other I had forgotten to perform. (My unconscious was rebelling against our domesticity. Food was constantly burned, milk spilled, bills forgotten.) I have no notion of his version of this story I'm telling. I'm only trying to describe how it all seemed to me—then, when it was happening.

But while I tell you that version, several others keep clamoring in my head—the same story, only different, describing the same actions, only different. No, perhaps not even the same actions. One changes one's view of them and they transmute. Is there a right way of looking at them—the *objective* way? The view depends, once again, on what matters. I set down one picture and stand back to look at it, and instantaneously it shifts, turns itself inside out and looks every bit as good. I've no clue as to which is the right view, and growing despair over whether there *is* a right view. Is all this mattering business a feature of our subjectivity—and *nothing more?* Is the fractured mattering map, with its floating isolated regions, all there is? Is *that* God's view? Isn't one of those regions the right one, God's very own? If not, then no thing and—since who matters is a function of what matters —no one really matters. The will to matter burning within reduces us all to ashen absurdity. (I think what I am asking is that philosophically disreputable—in fact, slightly scatological—question about the meaning of life. The Princeton philosophy department totally failed with me.)

One of the dinners we all shared at our house was a Shabbos meal. Or in any case it was a meal of traditional Jewish foods consumed (but not in the spirit of Shabbos) on a Saturday afternoon in December. My idea for it was prompted by my reading Isaac Bashevis Singer's "Short Friday"—the beautiful tale of marital devotion, enclosed within the larger love of the Jewish way of life. In the extreme longing the story inspired I ran out and bought Jenny Grossinger's *The Art of Jewish Cooking.* (Typically, I already owned the cookbooks of almost every other cuisine.) I did all my cooking before sundown on Friday, as the Orthodox do. I even managed to find WEVD on the radio, and listened to the Yiddish program that featured the *chazzanes* my father had so loved, as I prepared my challahs, gefilte fish, potato kugel, and cholent (for which I didn't go so far as to buy kosher meat).

"What are these?" Ava asked when she saw the two twisted bread loaves on the table.

"Challahs."

"I know, dear heart. But what are they doing on your table?"

"For Godssake, Ava. We've had plenty of French and Italian loaves on this table. We've had Arabic pita, Irish soda bread, and Southern spoon bread. Why the hell can't we have challahs?"

"Okay, okay, we'll have challahs. What else are we having? It smells good."

"That's the cholent."

"Oh shit," Ava groaned, sinking her head into her hands.

"Okay, we'll call it a cassoulet. That will make it acceptable to you."

Dan and Noam were sitting at the table, too. Noam was engaged in his fervent atavistic *shuckling,* oblivious to it all. Dan was smiling as he watched Ava and me, and now asked:

"What is this cholent that smells so good and provokes such passions?"

"It's what Orthodox Jews eat on Saturdays, especially in the winter. It's a mixture of beans and potatoes and meat, but mostly beans, that's put up to cook before sundown on Friday, when the Sabbath starts, and cooks slowly in the oven until it's eaten for lunch the next day."

The cholent happens to play a prominent role in Singer's story, being responsible for the death of the loving pair through asphyxiation. It wouldn't have been the first time, I'm sure, that Jews have been killed by a cholent.

"That *is* something like a cassoulet," Dan answered. "Minus the pork butt and sausages. What kind of meat do you use?"

"We Jews call it flanken. I think it's beef short ribs. In any case, that's what I used."

I could have called my mother and asked her. But her powers of deduction being what they are, she would have put an ad in *The Jewish Press* announcing that her daughter was returning to the ways of her foremothers.

"And don't you like cholent, Ava?" Dan asked.

"It's just that I don't fully trust Renee," she said, and then a brief look of panic crossed her face and she glanced quickly at Noam. He, however, was still *shuckling* and oblivious. She turned back to Dan. "Renee can't shake off the hocus-pocus she was raised on. You never know what's going to send her shuttling back again. And I choose my directional deliberately, Renee. It *would* be back, you know."

"Oh, fudge off, Ava. It's just a meal."

That was one of the last things I said at that meal. I listened silently to my companions, my husband, my lover, and my best friend—to Dan's witty comparisons between the gefilte fish and quenelles, between potato kugel and pommes dauphine. I had never felt quite so separate.

I stared out at the winter-stripped elms and remembered Shabbos at home. I could hear my father's singing, the sweet warm tenor rising up in his love. Beside it the secular chatter of the Jewish *goyim* I had surrounded myself with, circumcised by doctors and not knowing what it is to yearn for the coming of the Messiah, sounded insignificant and despicable. But I had despised the religiosity of my past. How could I expect anyone to share my outlook, contradictory as it is? And I'm probably no different from anyone else in this respect. How can *any* of us expect others to share our world, particular as each of ours is? One is alone, alone, alone, alone. Alone in one's own world.

LEONARD SCHMERZ HAD offered to have a bar mitzvah. And Noam—though not for love of me—had begun to identify more with his Jewishness as a result of discovering who he was or once had been. But there were no soft spots to chip through in Dan's cynical armor. Like Ava, he never doubted his doubts. And he was much more successful than Ava in detaching me from the pull of my past:

It was about two months into our affair. The month before, during the two days of menstruation (the artificially light period induced by the pill), I had declined being made love to, concentrating just on satisfying Dan, and I planned to do the same on this day. We were both undressed, Dan lying beside me on his bed.

"Unstop yourself," he said, giving the string of my tampon a gentle tug. "And I mean that in all possible senses."

"My limited intelligence can only determine one," I said quickly, pushing his hand away, and yes, blushing.

"You're all stopped up, my poor child, with Jewish tampons, with the Jewish distaste for the body."

"Distaste for the body? That's Christian, I think. It certainly isn't Jewish. God, don't you know anything at all about your own heritage? Why does your vigorous curiosity pick its way so daintily around that one area? If you were really rational and objective about it, you'd at least know as much about its basic tenets as you do about psychoanalysis and the Upanishad. Jews are not ascetic. They don't believe in celibacy. Distaste for the body is not a Jewish value at all. Quite the contrary. It's actually a *mitzvah* to make it on Shabbos."

"That's probably worse," Dan said. "Koshering sex the way they do meat. Soaking and salting it to get out all the blood. Do they salt and soak their women before throwing them into the *mikvah?*"

I had to smile at the image. "I went there once, you know, to *mikvah*. Hillel wanted me to." (By now I had told Dan all about my previous lovers.) "It was a place on the Upper West Side, not too far from Barnard, with a sweet little *mikvah* lady all dressed in white, with a white babushka on her head. First you took a bath, then showered, and then you had to go before her while she checked to make sure your nails were cut short enough"—it had killed me to cut my long nails—"and there were no tangles in your hair, no loose strands of hair on your body. And then you go into the little *mikvah* room, with a pool about four feet deep and four or five feet square. You go under, legs open to make sure the water penetrates the entire surface of the body. It was absolutely imperative that all my hair go under. The poor little *mikvah* lady was so concerned. So much hair, so much hair, she kept moaning. And then you make a blessing, on the *mitzvah* of dunking, and—you're not going to believe this—she gave me a washcloth to cover my head while I recited it. For modesty's sake. There one is, naked before one's God, with a little washcloth on one's head for modesty's sake. I couldn't help it, I started laughing."

"Good for you. Why don't they all start laughing, I wonder."

"Oh God, why do I encourage you in your cynicism? I ought to be advocating the other side."

"Why?"

"Because there *is* another side, and you're too narrow-minded to see it."

"If it's narrow-minded to exclude some possibilities as too remote for consideration, I suppose I am narrow-minded. Rationality demands it."

"Is it so remote?"

"I've never heard of anything to suggest otherwise."

"The survival of the Jews?"

"If you want to explain their survival by hypothesizing supernatural favoritism rather then the somewhat special sociological conditions prevailing throughout their history." He shrugged his naked shoulders.

"Their history? *Their* history? You would have been gassed along with the rest of them. Their history. You're just like the evil son in the Passover Seder service. There's the evil one, the intelligent one, the stupid one, and the one who's too young to ask any questions. The evil one asks, 'What's all this to you?' dissociating himself from the proceedings."

"Sounds intelligent to me. What's the answer he gets?"

"He's told that all this is because of what the Lord God did for us when he took us out of the Land of Egypt. For us, and not for him, because had he been there he wouldn't have been saved."

"And you, poor dear, are wondering whether you too would have been left unredeemed in the land of the strangers."

"Oh, there's no question. I'm an adulteress, in a class with the murderers and idolaters."

"And me. Don't forget me."

"Some consolation for paradise lost."

"Look, I have a request. If you're going to undertake my Jewish education today, I would prefer our getting back to the *mikvah* lesson. That at least is somewhat titillating. Only let's make the *mikvah* lady young and voluptuous. That's a lovely picture, her checking you over for loose strands of hair. Did she stamp you kosher on your lovely ass?"

"No, I wasn't stamped. But when I finished with my dunking, two more times after the blessing, she pronounced me kosher. She really said it, 'kosher.' It was funny, of course, but it did make me kind of happy, being pronounced kosher."

"But you are, my dear child, even unsoaked and unsalted and dripping with blood, you are kosher. *I* pronounce you kosher."

The hand moved back, gave a harder tug at the string between my legs, and then moved inside me. I was horrified, my muscles tensing.

"It's all kosher, Renee," he whispered, his mouth against my ear. "It's all okay. Bodies and sex and blood. Bloody sex, sexy blood. Relax."

I did relax, losing myself in the world of his hand and my body. But I was brought abruptly out of it when he pulled his hand away, bloody. I looked quickly into his face, searching for signs of his disgust. Here it comes, the male revulsion at the state of being female. How could he not be repelled by this uterine debris, the uncleanliness at the heart, or rather the womb, of womanliness? But his face showed anything but disgust.

"Relax, relax," he whispered as he entered me and we began to move through territory that was totally new to me. How to describe the feeling rising in me? It was very intense, joyful, revelatory. A feeling of acceptance. My eyes were oozing tears, my womb blood, and he was embracing it all. And when we finally parted and I saw my blood on his body, I felt clean.

BUT NOT EVEN DAN was totally devoid of the love of God, the "intellectual love of God" of that pious *apikoros*, Spinoza. Only Dan called it "objective reality," or sometimes the "out yonder," recalling Einstein's remark: "Out yonder," Einstein had said, "there is this huge world which exists independently of us human beings and which stands before us like a great, eternal riddle, at least partially accessible to our inspection and thinking. The contemplation of this world beckoned to me like a liberation."

Dan is, as he himself said, one of the dying breed of physicists. He believes in objective reality and, like Einstein, sees his job as one of description. Not Ava, though, with her nothing-is-but-theories-make-it-so line. Hers was always the cynical voice cutting in when the rest of us got fired up with the romance of objective knowledge (Ava mistrusts enthusiasms on principle), with getting a glimpse of the world-as-it-is, in itself, unconditioned by the forces of subjectivity. We all felt the romance of it—Noam in math, Dan in physics, and me (dear God) in philosophy. (Philosophy has long suffered in comparison to math and science. So too here, in her representation in our little triangle.)

This attitude of Dan's was the basic reason Noam didn't subject him to the dismissing glance he directed at most other currently active physicists. And of course Dan has the highest respect for Noam, for he too resides in that region where the genius is hero. When we four sat around the table, discussing science or math or philosophy, then the lines of force were centered around Noam. It was he who would hold forth most freely, with we others questioning or arguing, but never rivaling his position of supremacy. One could dismiss him at other times, but not when we came together as minds.

But otherwise my husband receded into insignificance so far as I was concerned. Most of the time, as I've said, he hardly even seemed a person anymore. He was just a series of annoying events, and the fewer the better. Not that he presented too many obstacles. He was the most obliging of cuckolded husbands. Even when he was there, he usually wasn't there. I certainly never thought of him when I was with Dan.

And even away from Dan my mental processes were saturated with thoughts of him, my thinking an internal dialogue between us: What would he say to this? How could I answer him? All day long he spoke to me. The vaporous intellectual goals I once held were now condensed into an attainable one: to be of interest to this one man. That was all that mattered. His appreciative laughter at my remarks or excited response to my thoughts sent a shaft of satisfaction penetrating deeper than any that had flickered forth from the scholastic praise and awards of the past.

No one but Dan seemed real. The others, even Ava, enjoyed reality only to the extent that they related to him. People who had before meant so much to me now took on a shadowy existence. My sister-in-law, Tzippy, for example, the mother of the child who carries my father's name. Little Reuven was almost two and a half; in fact, Tzippy was pregnant again. If this was my nephew's "terrible two" stage, he has the makings of a saint, for he is a sweet-natured, loving child, with a precocious appreciation for music. He started carrying tunes in his infancy, and sits entranced listening to classical music on the radio. "More Mozart, please!" he cries out when Tzippy tries to turn the radio off. I would speak to Tzippy, though not as often as I used to. I only saw them twice in the past year. (They have no car and so can't visit us. And anyway, their coming would create an embarrassing situation since they wouldn't eat anything in my *trayf* house.)

My friend Sarah was also pushed aside. She wouldn't presume to intrude herself on others' lives unless called upon; and I wasn't calling. It couldn't be helped. My time with Dan was all-absorbing, crowding all else out. In this respect, as in others, this period had the sustained qualities of orgasm. I had finally achieved it. All the rest was foreplay. But, as my lover himself admonished, one shouldn't place all one's focus on the orgasms of life.

8

SOLUTIONS
and
DISSOLUTIONS

All these considerations, said Socrates, must surely prompt serious philosophers to review the position in some such way as this. It looks as though this were a bypath leading to the right track. So long as we keep to the body and our soul is contaminated with this imperfection, there is no chance of our ever attaining satisfactorily to our object, which we assert to be truth. . . . The body fills us with loves and desires and fears and all sorts of nonsense, with the result that we literally never get an opportunity to think at all about anything. . . . That is why, on all these accounts, we have so little time for philosophy. . . . It seems, to judge from the argument, that the wisdom which we desire and upon which we profess to have set our hearts will be attainable only when we are dead. . . . It seems that so long as we are alive, we shall continue closest to knowledge if we avoid as much as we can all contact and association with the body, except when they are absolutely necessary, and instead of allowing ourselves to become infected with its nature, purify ourselves from it until God himself gives us deliverance.

—PLATO,
THE PHAEDO

Philosophy has succeeded, not without a struggle, in freeing itself from its obsession with the soul, only to find itself landed with something still more mysterious and captivating: the fact of man's bodiliness.

—NIETZSCHE,
THE WILL TO POWER

*I*t was spring, and I was growing more and more desperate. Dan would be going back to Ithaca at the beginning of June, and I had no thought but going with him. But he said nothing and I said nothing. I did talk more and more of leaving Noam. I longed for Dan to encourage me in this at least, but he never did, just quietly listened. Was he acting out of scruples, not wanting to affect my decision? Or was it that he didn't really want me? He had never said he loved me, never, not even at those moments when the phrase just naturally slips out. For my part, I couldn't imagine life without him.

It was a cold spring and this gave me the illusion of having time. When the weather turned hot in May, my desperation mounted. I had to speak. I'd test my power over him first, see if I could get him to break our schedule, to give me a whole day. If I could get a day, perhaps I could get a lifetime.

I got my day. He granted it freely, willingly, with no hesitation. We debated where to spend it, whether at the beach home of a friend in Avalon, New Jersey, that was available to us, or in New York (I fancied the Plaza), or just on Einstein Drive. In the end we decided on New York.

"I'll get us a room at the Plaza, parkside. And I want to spend the night there with you, Renee. Do you think you can manage it?"

I'd manage it. But whom to ask to cover for me? My best friends, Sarah and Ava, were in Princeton. With whom could I be going to stay? Tzippy? I could never ask her to be an accomplice to my adultery. And if my brother Avram ever found out, he'd stone the three of us.

I finally just went to Noam without a story at hand and told him I was going to New York and would spend the night with a friend. He never asked me the name, or how I could be reached. I don't know what I would have said if he had. Maybe I would simply have told him the truth. I was tired of covering up.

.   .   .

We had a parkside room. The first thing I did was take off the bedcover to see if there were satin linens. I was very disappointed to find the plebeian polyester blends.

"The Plaza's not what it used to be."

"Nothing is." I was surprised at how serious he sounded. Then he smiled. "You like this, don't you? This sort of luxury."

"Oh, I don't know. It's fun, but probably only because it's so different. Luxury is not something I've ever really lusted after. It was never my dream."

"Yes, I know. Perhaps you would have been better off if it had been." He stared at me a moment, again serious. Then he smiled again. "Anyway, you look very good in this setting. You look the proper part of a princess."

Then make my story end happily ever after, I felt like crying out. No, not now, not yet. First I had to make him feel my power. I lay back on the bed. There was still so much I didn't know about Dan. A year of exploring and there was still so much to discover. I could never exhaust all there was to him.

I had never even asked him one of my favorite questions. But there would be time, there would be time. Or would there?

"Dan, if an angel of God were to appear to you right now and offer to answer any question, what would you ask?"

"Oh, I don't know. There are so many questions. Right off the top of my head, I'd probably ask why the electron has the particular charge it does. That's a classic unsolved problem in physics. We have no idea of the answer, none at all. What would you ask?"

"For the solution to the mind-body problem," I answered promptly.

"Ah yes, of course."

"You've never really told me. What do you think? Are you a body?"

"No, I certainly am not. But everybody else is."

"That's the most improbable answer I've heard yet."

"Yes, but I think it's what we all unreflectively and inconsistently think. It's unnatural to identify yourself as a mere body, but it's natural to identify anybody else with his."

He sat down beside me. I was wearing a yellow sundress, which he slipped off over my head. I had to admit the man had a novel approach to the problem.

"This is you, Renee Feuer Himmel."

He put his hands on top of my head and then slowly ran them down, tracing the outlines of my body: down the outside of my shoulders and arms, up under my arms, and then down again, down my legs and around my feet, and slowly up the inside of my thighs, where they finally rested. I had never known the mind-body problem handled in such a wonderful way.

"You are flesh," Dan whispered. "That's a presupposition of lust."

"Not very logical," I muttered.

"Lust is more absolute than logic."

"Good God, Dan. What sacrilege. If Noam could hear you."

He laughed. "Somehow I think your husband would be more outraged at the moment if he were to see me."

I wasn't so sure. Which would have infuriated Noam more, a violation of his wife or a violation of logic?

We stayed in the room for several hours and then went out walking —window-shopping and visiting several galleries. (Dan knew more about art; he knew more about everything.) In a boutique window on Madison Avenue we saw a glorious little silk number in my shade of apricot, which Dan insisted that I go and try on, and then insisted on buying.

"You'll wear it tonight at dinner."

The gift made me feel like a kept woman, an expensive courtesan, and this was fun, too, as it is always fun for me to slip into another identity. That evening I wore the dress to Lutèce (my first time there), where we shared a rare rack of lamb, a raspberry soufflé, and two bottles of Taitinger champagne. (What were we celebrating? I was afraid to ask.) I can still remember every taste and texture of that meal.

Dan, of course, is very interested in food, as he is interested in everything. He was always intrigued by my gustatory experiences, conditioned as they are by my Orthodox unbringing.

"I just can't imagine what it's like to regard certain portions of inanimate matter as not only edible but evil. It's really fantastic that food can be perceived to have moral qualities. I'll never be able to experience that, the delicious thrill of ingesting the forbidden."

I described for him the period of my life when I first began to break the laws of *kashrut,* the weeks of frenzied fressing in which I tried to experience all the sapid sensations of which I had been deprived in my previous seventeen years. I wouldn't take a bite of meat without spreading it with butter, just for the perverse pleasure of mixing *milchik* with *flayshig.*

After years of *trayf* living, the sinful pungency has of course faded. But there are certain foods that can still evoke the moral dimension for me. As a child I had been taught to read labels to make certain that the ingredients included only pure vegetable shortening, so I still feel a kind of moral shock at the sight of a pure, unashamedly naked hunk of lard. And after learning at age four to first break an egg into a glass and then search to make certain there are no blood spots before scrambling it (ironic that the Jews should have been accused of *blood* libels), I am drawn with repulsed fascination to blood sausage. I don't know if I'll ever be able to regard even a simple pork chop as morally neutral.

We had had only a salad for lunch, in order to be properly hungry for dinner, and now we felt stuffed.

"You'd think drinking all those stars would make you feel like floating instead of like this," I said.

"Let's walk until the heaviness wears off," Dan said, slipping his arm around me.

We walked and talked. There was a wall of tears rising in my chest, and I kept laughing to force it back down, as I remember doing as a child. There was the pervasive feel of an ending, subtle but unmistakable. The champagne had been to celebrate the end of our affair. I won't let it happen, I thought, I won't let him go. I'll use all my power.

Dan had kept his arm around my waist. In the Plaza elevator he slipped it up under my arm so that his fingertips were just resting on my breast. I was very tired and silently doubted that I would be able to make love. But Dan's power over my body had only grown over the year. It was like hypnosis: the more times you go under, the easier it is each time to fall into a deep state. At the very first touch of Dan's hands or tongue (which was as brilliant as his hands) I would go under. I couldn't let him go.

I reached orgasm in the flood of tears that had threatened all evening. Dan switched on the lamp beside the bed.

"My God, Renee! What is it? What's wrong?"

"I love you, Dan, I love you. I love you. I want to stay with you. I want to leave Noam and stay with you. Don't you want me?" I sobbed.

Dan closed his eyes and leaned back against the headboard. He didn't speak.

"I'm sorry, Renee," he finally said. "I can't do it for you. You would like a passion to sweep you away beyond decision, beyond responsibility. You won't find such a passion, at least not in this bed." He paused, and then went on. "I won't be distilled into the essence of your life. I don't have the taste for such things, not anymore." He got up and pulled on his pants. "If you want to leave your husband, leave him. But don't do it for me. Don't do it for any man."

A voice was screaming in my head· He doesn't want me, he doesn't want me. When I spoke, my voice sounded so strangely quiet along-side that other hysterical one.

"What was I for you? Just a good lay?"

"You were all a woman could be for me at this point in my life."

"Which is a good lay."

"Well, yes, if you like. But you're a good lay because you're very beautiful and very bright and very, very sweet. You're a good lay because you're a wonderful woman. And if I were anything but a very tired and burnt-out middle-aged man, I'd feel differently."

Eleanor, I thought, still the power of Eleanor. He had told me how he felt about her: "I think she'll always be the most important woman in my life." But I was so arrogant in these matters, I couldn't believe any woman could defeat me. And now I was defeated, not even by the woman herself, but by her memory.

There was nothing more to say. (A woman with a father-fixation meets many burnt-out men.) I too got up and dressed, and we sat there waiting for the morning. Dan had already left me.

I can't remember the next week very well. It was the closest I've come yet to suicide. When I couldn't stand the quiet of my home anymore, when the chanting in my head became unbearable, I'd go out walking. Every passing car tempted me. I could see it so vividly, the leap that would place me smack against the hood. Why not? What did it matter now? What did I matter? Death is God's way of dealing with adulterers, death by stoning.

And not only God's. The two greatest heroines of fictional adultery, Anna Karenina and Emma Bovary, with whom I had dared to compare myself, both took their lives, Anna by throwing herself in front of a train and Emma by nibbling on some household poison. (Emma's death, prolonged and excruciating, was a how-not-to lesson for all us would-be suicides.) Perhaps the only thing that held me back was the small doubt Noam had planted as to whether death would end it all. He had told me in Vienna, when speaking of those who had died and been revived, that the only returnees to report bad experiences were the failed suicides. "They had a sense of cosmic disapproval." That's all I needed.

I didn't see or speak to Dan, and he didn't try to get in touch with me. The deepest wounds of the past had come from words—rejecting, dismissing, belittling. But no spoken signs had hurt as their absence now did. *Any* word would have been better, would have left me feeling that I mattered somewhat to the man who alone mattered to me.

I agonized over his silence, in the stillness of my home or walking the streets, trying to torture out its meaning. Did it signify ignorance or indifference? Either he didn't know my state or he knew but didn't care. For knowing and caring he wouldn't have held back all words. Both interpretations implied betrayal. Either his understanding or his kindness had betrayed me. And I had believed in both with the perfect faith of a child.

I went around in a daze, unable to eat or sleep, barely able to breathe. (Poor Len, I thought, suddenly sympathetic.) Noam didn't notice. I had run through the gamut of emotions this past year and the man I was living with had never noticed. One thing at last emerged clear and distinct. I had to get out of this marriage. I had to get away from Noam. Our marriage was dead, dead. It had to be disposed of.

It was about two in the morning. I had gone to bed early, about nine, dizzy with exhaustion. But then, of course, I had been unable to sleep, had lain there hour after hour, the voices chanting, until finally the truth had broken over me. Get out, leave him. There's nothing here.

Noam hadn't come to bed yet. He was in the bedroom we had converted into his study. I got out of bed and walked into his room. He was sitting there at his desk, a pencil in his hand, bent over a yellow pad with blue lines. He looked up in surprise.

"You're still awake."

"Noam, I don't want to live with you anymore. I don't want to be married to you."

He put the pencil down on the pad, carefully, right between the two centermost lines, holding it there for a few seconds to balance it.

"Noam, did you hear me? I'm leaving you."

He didn't look up from the perfectly poised pencil. "Tonight? Are you going tonight?"

"Yes. Tonight."

"I see." He still hadn't moved. "Yes, of course. It all fits. I didn't predict it, but it was predictable. Of course I would lose you, too."

His voice was very quiet. I had to strain to hear it. It was a voice I had never heard before and it disoriented me. Something about it didn't make sense, but I couldn't identify what.

"What are you talking about, Noam? What else have you lost?"

"I've lost everything. I've lost everything. You might as well know now. There's no reason why you shouldn't know."

He finally lifted up his face to me and it too was new. I didn't understand. What was going on here?

"I've lost my mathematical powers." His voice broke. "I don't have it anymore. I never knew what it was when I had it, and now I don't have it anymore."

Tears were streaming down his face. So that was it! Noam was suffering! It was too much to take in. This was sadness, the deepest sadness I was hearing and seeing. I had never seen Noam sad. I had seen him excited and triumphant, disgusted and raging, but never sad. I was completely bewildered.

"But you're working, Noam. You're always working."

He laughed, a dry, hard laugh I'd never heard. "Do you want to see my latest results?" He held up the pad, which had been covered by his arm. There was an intricate geometrical doodle. "I sit at my desk. I just sit. Nothing comes. The only thought in my head is: It's gone, you're old. I never knew what it was when I had it, but it was wonderful. It was power. But mathematics is a young man's game. Here, listen."

He unlocked the top desk drawer, where he kept the results he was so jealous of, and took out a thin little paperback, *A Mathematician's Apology*. There was a photograph of a man on the cover, leaning back in an easy chair, elbows resting outward. He peered out at the camera over his specs, brow furrowed, a very interesting young-old face.

"This was G. H. Hardy. He was a first-rate mathematician. This book was written after he lost his powers." Noam laughed, that same eerily new laugh. "Obviously after. A mathematician *with* his powers doesn't have any interest or time to write a book like this. But it's a very fine little book. A justification of the life of pure mathematics. And the joy," he added softly.

He opened the book and quickly found what he was looking for.

" 'Mathematics is not a contemplative but a creative subject,' " he read. " 'No one can draw much consolation from it when he has lost the power or the desire to create; and that is apt to happen to a mathematician rather soon. It is a pity, but in that case he does not matter a great deal anyhow and it would be silly to bother about him.' "

He closed the book and looked up at me, the intense stare of old.

"Hardy was really quite lucky. He kept going until he was sixty, which is very unusual. Even Newton gave up entirely by fifty, and he had discovered around forty that it was gone." (Noam was forty-one.) "Hardy was very lucky. But you know what he did when it finally deserted him? He tried to kill himself. It didn't work, he botched it. But he didn't have to live much longer anyway. Unfortunately, I'm a much younger man."

The sound and sight of him was so strange, I still was having trouble taking his words in, trying to give them sense.

"How long, Noam? How long has it been like this?"

"I'm not sure when I knew for certain. I had suspected it for a long time. I began really to suspect it soon after you and I were married. But I still had work to do. I was working out some ideas I had had a long time ago, ideas I never had time to develope. Compared to the things I was doing they were insignificant. But then I was grateful for them. I finished with them about a year and a half ago" (when I had started up with Leonard, I thought). "And since then there's been nothing."

I tried to think of something to say. But none of this fit. He looked up at me.

"I was angry at you, I blamed it all on you, at least at first. I kept telling myself you were distracting me, that you were draining my powers. I remember when you suggested our having a child." I recalled the incident. I had returned from Lakewood after meeting Fruma, who was big with her fifth child, and I was big with the fantasy of mothering a child with the genius-gene. "That's the whole trouble, I told myself. She's stifling me in the ordinary. I know I've been terrible to you, Renee. I haven't been able to control it. I'm so angry all the time, at least I was. And not only with you. I've been terrible to the younger people, the students, the ones who still have it. They have it all ahead of them, and it's all behind me."

Stop it, I told myself, don't start seeing him as a person.

"But it wasn't their fault and it wasn't yours," Noam was saying. "It wasn't our marriage, Renee. In fact, the marriage wasn't a cause, it was a symptom. At the height of my powers I wouldn't have married. I couldn't have fallen in love." He smiled and said softly, "Not even with you. You see, I didn't have room in my life for two passions."

This stranger was my husband? My view of him, like everyone's, was dominated by the fact of his genius. What was he, who was he, stripped bare of this fact?

"Why didn't you tell me? Why didn't you ever talk to me?"

"Because I knew you loved the genius. I know that all I've ever been to anyone, including you, including myself, for that matter, has been defined by my mathematical gifts. It was all anyone ever asked of me. It was my justification."

The urge to comfort overwhelmed me, in spite of myself. "You always talk about people's justifications," I said. "People don't need justifications. They're people. That's enough."

I said these words without really thinking, moved by the desire to offer him something. And I've been staring at them ever since.

"No, it's not enough," Noam answered. "Most people are worthless. I wasn't, but now I am."

"You mean you're no better than anyone else. Is that so terrible?"

He turned and looked out the window. The sky was still dark.

"No, Renee, I don't think I have to tell you that I'm less than other people. It's not as if I used to be like others, only with something extra added. So that you could take away that extra and there would be a person like others. That extra was my whole being, my substance. It didn't leave room for anything else. But that was okay. If I was less of a person, it was only because I was more of a person. That's the way everyone thought of it, including me, including you. No. Of course you'll go, of course."

He stood up abruptly.

"This self-analysis is disgusting me. I shouldn't take myself so seriously. If I don't matter, it doesn't matter that I don't matter. Look, you stay here tonight. I'll spend the night at the Nassau Inn. We'll talk tomorrow, figure out how to arrange things. Good night."

He walked quickly out of the room. I heard the front door close a few seconds later. I went downstairs and sat there in the dark until daylight, shifting through the layers and layers of shock, trying to understand and absorb it all. Boom ba boom ba boom, one thing after the other, taking the breath away, as Noam on the train into Vienna had described his heights.

I hadn't understood the nature of the story I was living, had misperceived my role in it and misidentified the victim. My own soul-sickness had absorbed my full attention. All else had come to me filtered through it. I had consistently misinterpreted Noam, from the angers of the first part of our marriage to the air of resignation he had borne the last year and a half. I had taken it for granted that *I* was the focus of his discontent. And I had been so angry at him for never looking at me! He had been living in torment for most of our married life and I had never guessed. It had been so long since I had even thought of him as a person.

I called Dan around eight in the morning. I knew he got up around then, for it was then that I used to go to him. Aside from everything else, he was the person who understood everything better than anyone. He listened quietly as I told him the story.

"Poor Noam," he said softly. "How terribly alone he is."

Dear God, yes. The full extent of his isolation suddenly opened up before me and I cried out at the sight of it. I got off the phone, ran up to the bedroom and pulled on some clothes. I ran out to the car and drove over to the Nassau Inn. But the man at the reception desk said that no Noam Himmel was registered there.

My mind froze over in fear. I fled from the place, dreadful images before me: Noam's bloated body pulled out of Lake Carnegie, Noam leaping from the tower of Fine Hall, the tallest building on campus. Fine Hall! Noam's turf.

I drove my car around Ivy Lane, parking in back of the building. Noam's office is on the twelfth floor. I didn't knock. When I walked in he was sitting near the window, staring out at the Princeton beneath him. I went over to him and put my arms around him and we held each other, crying.

THAT WAS several months ago. It's autumn again, my sixth in Princeton. The undergraduates have returned, the classes have resumed, and the leaf-strewn lawns are trod with a more purposeful step. We had spent the summer here again, Noam once more turning down invitations from around the world. Now I understand. It would be like an arthritic former tennis champion looking on at Wimbledon or Forest Hills. And Noam is still so young. He just turned forty-two. What will he do with his life?

He still has teaching, of course, but that aspect of his profession never mattered much to him. It was all in the discovery, all the joy and meaning. Teaching was a nuisance. How little of it would be demanded of him was always a bargaining point in the days when schools were competing to get him. (And they'd still fight.) Besides, I suspect he still harbors bitter feelings of envy toward the mathematically young and vigorous. There's still a very deep anger in him, but now I understand its nature. I know it's not directed at me and I can deal with it.

Once Noam suggested, half in jest, that now it was time for him to turn his attention to philosophy. He had always called my field the pastureland for old mathematicians and scientists. I remember his making some rather brutal remarks about a Princeton physicist who had just published a book on philosophy and the natural sciences. It was the first year of our marriage, so Noam must have been suspecting the failure of his powers. We were at a party, and a physicist named Vince Fonti, a rather lovely man, asked Noam if he had read Price's book. Noam had laughed.

"Poor Frank. I guess this means he's over the hill. When physicists start writing about the philosophical consequences of their former work, you know they've had it. That's the form their senility takes, they start spouting philosophy. It's a real problem with philosophy of science, philosophy of math, too, for that matter. Either you have philosophers doing it, and they don't really understand math and science, they don't have that intimate knowledge that comes only from working in the fields themselves. Or else you've got the has-beens, the nearly senile. And if they don't have the mental energy to do their real work, what makes them think they can solve the problems in philosophy? No wonder no progress is ever made there. A scientist or mathematician in full command of his powers has no interest in or time for philosophy."

"I don't think Price is in his dotage," Vince had answered. "I enjoyed his book immensely. He may not be an active physicist anymore, but he's written a very interesting and maybe even important book." Noam shrugged. "You know, Noam," Vince smiled. "Perhaps you ought to be more sympathetic to men like Frank."

"Why?"

"Getting older is not some sort of disease that only certain unfortunate people catch."

"What's your point?"

"My point is this: Even you will find yourself getting older someday. That is, if you're one of the lucky ones."

I cringed, waiting for the avalanche of fury. But Noam had simply stared at Vince for a few seconds, and then turned and walked away. Vince looked down at the drink in his hand and then at me.

"I'm terribly sorry, Renee. I didn't mean to upset him."

The memory of this conversation and others like it made us both smile when Noam first said, "Maybe I should take up philosophy of math." But Noam has been talking of it more and more of late, and I think he's even written up some of his thoughts. The problem is, he's so terribly young—not young for a mathematician, but for a man whose life is over, or who believes it is. This time Noam really has survived his own death.

It was like living with a stranger, especially in the beginning. Often I'd look at him, thinking, He's not a genius. Is he even the same man? By his own criterion of personal identity it's dubious that he is. He always said his mathematical creativity was his essence. The old Noam would have sooner identified himself with some unknown Viennese schoolboy than with a man without the power to create.

But the power is gone, and sometimes I still feel that the person is, too, that this is a stranger. But unfortunately for him, the stranger has the other man's memories, and those memories torment him. It's funny, especially considering my reasons for marrying in the first place, but it's of course the stranger I've known for the longer time, the stranger with the genius's memories. I don't know if I ever even met the genius.

MY OWN FEELING of mourning has passed by now. At first it was intense, at times approaching what I felt after my father died: a cried-out numbness, occasionally breaking out into something so much worse that one welcomes back the numbness. At its peak I sometimes forgot what I was mourning, believed myself to be grieving the loss of my father. But no, it wasn't my father this time, I'd remind myself. It was Noam's genius that had gone, and Dan, and Ava—I lost her, too—and something else as well. Perhaps the illusion that we need not be alone.

Just in case we in Princeton forget the inescapably transitory nature of life, there is the Institute for Advanced Study, with its stream of temporary visitors flowing in and flowing out like the river of Heraclitus. Nothing remains the same. Dan left in June—I never saw or spoke to him again. There is a very serious-looking economist occupying Dan's former rooms. I've seen the man quite often, for somehow or other all my walks seem to take me down Einstein Drive. The economist is fortunately not a very observing man; he never seems to recognize me, even though he must have seen me staring up at his windows.

Ava left Princeton soon after Dan did, for California of all places, to accept a position at Caltech. Not only did my best friend abandon me to go off to that despised land of alien values; she went off happily, exclaiming about Caltech and the people she would work with there. Her happy chatter about the virtues of California—the *weather,* for Godssake—pelted me like stones. Her eager acceptance of the yoke of banishment betrayed me and the New York existence we had shared. My closest and dearest friend, is there anything we share anymore? I don't even know how to picture you. Has your unwholesome pallor been burned away by those banal sunny skies? Are you still bitingly honest, or is that prohibited there? Oh, Ava, have you lost your Bronx accent?

Our last conversations were painful. She saw my misery, she even sympathized with it, but she would not share it. Our situations were so completely at odds, how could our viewpoints fail to be? Ava had chosen her goals and depended on no one but herself to carry her to them. She felt sorry for me about Dan, but she wouldn't immerse herself in my sorrow. It wasn't just her own happiness. It was her view of me and my misery, how I must have seemed to her in her strength of her own making. "Sometimes, Renee, I regret having ever taught you to say 'fuck,' " she told me.

Ava is gone, Dan is gone. Now it's Noam and I alone with each other. But if I've come to regard him as something of a stranger, I've also come to view him with something new and comforting, with human sympathy. He's on the mortal sphere now, the sphere of suffering. Beneath the iridescent carapace—in his case the mathematical genius—lies the soft exposed underside. And he looks at me differently, too. He regards me as his friend. I think I'm his first.

I haven't gotten him to accept the words of comfort I offered on the night of his revelation: that people don't need justifications, that they're people and that's enough. Noam has always occupied a single region of the mattering map, where the people who matter the most are the geniuses. That this is so was taken for granted, as was his own privileged position. I don't know if it's possible to get him to change his perspective, not to relocate on the mattering map but to turn from it altogether. I've been trying hard to do so myself, to see the map for what it is: a description of our subjectivity and nothing more. From which region does God look out on us? From none, of course. Not because people don't matter objectively, but because they do. They simply do. Any view that confers degrees of mattering, that distinguishes between those who matter and those who don't, has no objective validity. We all count in precisely the same way. That's the view from nowhere inside, the view from out yonder. And its contemplation beckons to me like a liberation.

There's nothing philosophically new in all this. I'd even written it out on exams: "In Kant's ethics the term "person" is not merely descriptive but normative. Persons are ends in themselves and sources of value in their own right." So the words were there, ready to offer that night, even if not backed by belief. (One of the advantages of an education.) But I've been staring at them ever since, and I've watched them as they began to stir and then to leap up and dance. There is that difference when the knowledge is formed from the matter of experience and written in the soul's own blood.

The view beckons like a liberation, and I try to keep my gaze steadily on it. But the pull of subjectivity is so strong—the tug backwards into the muddle, where some people matter more than others and we must constantly be figuring out who they are, sick with the worry of whether we are among them.

People don't need justifications. They're people and that's enough. I wonder if someday these words will be able to do for me all that the old words once did, shouted out in unison by the congregation of Israel. They are shouting them now, for it's the Ten Days of Repentance. My father always prayed beautifully, but his voice took on a new dimension during the holy days of autumn, especially at the *Kol Nidre* service that begins Yom Kippur, when the very gates of heaven are said to open. "Is he singing or crying?" some little friend would always ask me as my father implored on behalf of his people. He felt the enormous responsibility of his position. Wrapped in the purity of his special white robes, he was the messenger of his community, their lives hanging in the balance:

"On Rosh Hashanah their destiny is inscribed, and on Yom Kippur it is sealed, how many shall pass away and how many shall be brought into existence; who shall live and who shall die; who shall come to a timely end, and who to an untimely end." His eyes were shut and he was raised on his toes, his soul straining ever upwards as the chant continued.

And then had the congregation responded, in one great thundering voice:

"But repentance, prayer, and charity cancel the stern decree!"

Long after I ceased believing in these words, the sound of them had caused my spine to tingle and eyes to tear, as there is often a lag between one's rationality and emotive responses. I'm not even confident that today the words would entirely fail in their effect were I to put them to the test.

People and their suffering matter. Noam suffers, and his suffering matters no more nor less than anyone else's. The only difference for me is that I might be able to make a difference for him. I would like to. Dear Noam, I would like to.

But so far I haven't succeeded in getting him to accept my new words.

"Why do people matter particularly, just because they're people? What makes them and their suffering of any more consequence than that of any other living creature? We just can empathize with them more, because they're more like us."

"You think the suffering and death of a person is on the same level of significance as the slaughter of a chicken?"

"No." We both smile. "But only because we're capable of excellence, of scaling the heights. Only because our kind can occasionally produce the Mozarts and Einsteins."

"Okay, that may be. But then we all do matter, we're none of us nobodies. We don't have to justify our existences. The Mozarts and the Einsteins do it for us, by demonstrating our possibilities."

"Perhaps. But even so, Renee, it's a difficult thing to go from being one of the sources of significance to being a mere receiver."

"But you're *not*, Noam. You'll never be merely that. It was you who scaled the heights, up beyond all the others, to the transinfinite realm, to the numbers bigger than all others."

"Yes," he answers softly, smiling at me, his eyes, their most brilliant blue, gazing into mine. "I did do something. The supernaturals."

THE OTHER INHABITANTS of our little world don't seem to have caught on yet to the fact that the spirit of genius has taken leave of Noam. And perhaps it won't matter too much to them. The fruits of its former presence, the supernaturals and all the rest, will always be with us, and perhaps a grateful world will feel that this is enough for one man. Perhaps they'll continue to respect and cherish Noam, not for what he is doing but for what he once did.

But so far, at least, I can tell that even among Noam's closest colleagues the truth isn't known. They are waiting to see what he will produce next, what he will take out of his locked desk drawer. The attitude is still worshipful here in Princeton, where Noam Himmel is a living legend. And often I still see that question hovering on someone's lips, as he debates with himself whether it would be too personal a demand, too much of an intrusion, to ask the wife of the great man: "What is it like to live with him, to live with a genius like Himmel?"

FOR THE BEST IN PAPERBACKS, LOOK FOR THE

In every corner of the world, on every subject under the sun, Penguin represents quality and variety—the very best in publishing today.

For complete information about books available from Penguin—including Puffins, Penguin Classics, and Arkana—and how to order them, write to us at the appropriate address below. Please note that for copyright reasons the selection of books varies from country to country.

In the United Kingdom: Please write to *Dept. JC, Penguin Books Ltd, FREEPOST, West Drayton, Middlesex UB7 0BR.*

If you have any difficulty in obtaining a title, please send your order with the correct money, plus ten percent for postage and packaging, to *P.O. Box No. 11, West Drayton, Middlesex UB7 0BR*

In the United States: Please write to *Consumer Sales, Penguin USA, P.O. Box 999, Dept. 17109, Bergenfield, New Jersey 07621-0120.* VISA and MasterCard holders call 1-800-253-6476 to order all Penguin titles

In Canada: Please write to *Penguin Books Canada Ltd, 10 Alcorn Avenue, Suite 300, Toronto, Ontario M4V 3B2*

In Australia: Please write to *Penguin Books Australia Ltd, P.O. Box 257, Ringwood, Victoria 3134*

In New Zealand: Please write to *Penguin Books (NZ) Ltd, Private Bag 102902, North Shore Mail Centre, Auckland 10*

In India: Please write to *Penguin Books India Pvt Ltd, 706 Eros Apartments, 56 Nehru Place, New Delhi 110 019*

In the Netherlands: Please write to *Penguin Books Netherlands bv, Postbus 3507, NL-1001 AH Amsterdam*

In Germany: Please write to *Penguin Books Deutschland GmbH, Metzlerstrasse 26, 60594 Frankfurt am Main*

In Spain: Please write to *Penguin Books S. A., Bravo Murillo 19, 1° B, 28015 Madrid*

In Italy: Please write to *Penguin Italia s.r.l., Via Felice Casati 20, I-20124 Milano*

In France: Please write to *Penguin France S. A., 17 rue Lejeune, F–31000 Toulouse*

In Japan: Please write to *Penguin Books Japan, Ishikiribashi Building, 2–5–4, Suido, Bunkyo-ku, Tokyo 112*

In Greece: Please write to *Penguin Hellas Ltd, Dimocritou 3, GR–106 71 Athens*

In South Africa: Please write to *Longman Penguin Southern Africa (Pty) Ltd, Private Bag X08, Bertsham 2013*

84, different plane